Studies in
Prose Writing

Studies in
Prose Writing

ALTERNATE EDITION
REVISED

JAMES R. KREUZER
LEE COGAN
Queens College of The
City University of New York

HOLT, RINEHART AND WINSTON, INC.
New York Chicago San Francisco Toronto

Library of Congress Catalog Card Number: 67–14349

2636058

2636108

Printed in the United States of America
1   2   3   4   5   6   7   8   9

To

N.D. and J.K.

and

H.N.R.

In Memoriam

A Note on the Revised Edition

In this edition we have replaced two types of selections: those which seemed to have lost some of their immediacy for students and those for which we have found substitutes promising increased effectiveness in the teaching of one or another rhetorical principle. In keeping with the rationale of the first edition, the new selections are all related to the arts as we described them in the Preface to the first edition.

Each new selection has been supplied with a new teaching apparatus and writing assignment or assignments. New writing assignments have also been added to some of the original apparatuses.

For their assistance in the preparation of the manuscript, Marilyn Ackerman and Judith Anne Kreuzer have our thanks. In the past we have accepted—reluctantly—a Holt, Rinehart and Winston policy that precluded our making acknowledgment of assistance given by members of the company's College Department. Now we rebel against the policy and take genuine pleasure in acknowledging with gratitude and affection all that has been done for us over the years by Kenney Withers, Marie Lonning, and Jane Ross; each, in one way or another, has made our association with Holt, Rinehart and Winston rewarding and deeply satisfying. We look forward to our continued association.

J.R.K.
L.C.

January 1967

Preface to the First Edition

The welcome given the original edition of *Studies in Prose Writing* has encouraged us to compile this alternate edition. In the original edition, we sought to supply essays with a wide range of content—from psychology to nuclear physics, from sociology and history to biography and natural history. For the instructor who prefers to deal with essays which may be related more specifically to his major interests, the present book limits its selections to the arts: for example, to literature, music, and painting; to communication by radio, television, and periodicals; to architecture, sculpture, and the movies. As in the original edition, there is wide representation of the formal types of writing—exposition, description, narration, and argumentation.

Since the organization and rationale of the present book are identical with those of the original edition, we repeat what we said there:

It has long been our conviction that the best class hours in English Composition are those in which a single worthwhile point about writing is made—made once and for all. This book has been designed to provide the instructor with the classroom tools for such hours. It is organized not in terms of the "types" or subject matter of the reading selections but in terms of the fundamental principles of good expository writing. The supporting text—analyses, questions, and assignments—has been designed to focus attention on that principle of writing illustrated by the individual selection (or, occasionally, group of selections). Thus the student is led from reading and analysis to application, with one rhetorical principle under consideration at a time.

The order of the major divisions of content—from whole theme to paragraph, sentence, and word—is a matter of our own preference. We are aware, however, that many instructors prefer some other ordering of parts, and hence we have kept the major divisions sufficiently autonomous to allow for reordering.

One criterion has guided us in our treatment of each selection, namely, how can we most efficiently use the selection to teach a particular rhetorical principle. As a result, some treatments are longer and more intensive than others; some begin with a brief discussion of the principle under consideration; others consist only of questions aimed at directing the student's thinking about the rhetorical principle. The writing assignments grow out of the treatment of selections. Rather than merely listing a number of possible topics for student themes, the assignments guide the student in his thinking preparatory to writing and present in some detail various possibilities for handling the themes.

For the instructor who may find them useful, alternate selections for the teaching of each principle are suggested. It is our belief that the apparatus for a given selection can be readily adapted to the alternate selections.

Our warmest thanks go to a number of people who helped to make this book possible—especially to Judith Anne Kreuzer for efficient but always engaging preparation of the typescript, and to Professor James Edward Tobin of Queens College and Professor Richard Beal of Boston University for exacting and consistently helpful criticism. Publication of this book gives us both an opportune moment to thank the staff of the Paul Klapper Library of Queens College for assistance not only in the preparation of this book but also in solving the many day-to-day problems encountered by college instructors in English.

J.R.K.
L.C.

January 23, 1961

Contents

THE PARAGRAPH

THE SENTENCE

DICTION

ORGANIZATION
OF
THE
WHOLE

Concept of Organization

✍From *Reveries over Childhood and Youth* WILLIAM BUTLER YEATS

[1] My first memories are fragmentary and isolated and contemporaneous, as though one remembered some first moments of the Seven Days. It seems as if time had not yet been created, for all thoughts connected with emotion and place are without sequence.

[2] I remember sitting upon somebody's knee, looking out of an Irish window at a wall covered with cracked and falling plaster, but what wall I do not remember, and being told that some relation once lived there. I am looking out of a window in London. It is at Fitzroy Road. Some boys are playing in the road and among them a boy in uniform, a telegraph boy perhaps. When I asked who the boy is, a servant tells me that he is going to blow the town up, and I go to sleep in terror.

[3] After that come memories of Sligo, where I live with my grandparents. I am sitting on the ground looking at a mastless toy boat with the paint rubbed and scratched, and I say to myself in

great melancholy, "It is further away than it used to be," and while
I am saying it I am looking at a long scratch in the stern, for it is
especially the scratch which is further away. Then one day at dinner
my great-uncle William Middleton says, "We should not make light
20 of the troubles of children. They are worse than ours, because we can
see the end of our trouble and they can never see any end," and I
feel grateful for I know that I am very unhappy and have often said
to myself, "When you grow up, never talk as grown-up people do of
the happiness of childhood." I may have already had the night of
25 misery when, having prayed for several days that I might die, I began
to be afraid that I was dying and prayed that I might live. There was
no reason for my unhappiness. Nobody was unkind, and my grandmother has still after so many years my gratitude and my reverence.
The house was so big that there was always a room to hide in, and
30 I had a red pony and a garden where I could wander, and there
were two dogs to follow at my heels, one white with some black spots
on his head and the other with long black hair all over him. I used to
think about God and fancy that I was very wicked, and one day when
I threw a stone and hit a duck in the yard by mischance and broke
35 its wing, I was full of wonder when I was told that the duck would be
cooked for dinner and that I should not be punished.

[4] Some of my misery was loneliness and some of it fear of old
William Pollexfen my grandfather. He was never unkind, and I cannot remember that he ever spoke harshly to me, but it was the
40 custom to fear and admire him. He had won the freedom of some
Spanish city, for saving life perhaps, but was so silent that his wife
never knew it till he was near eighty, and then from the chance visit
of some old sailor. She asked him if it was true and he said it was
true, but she knew him too well to question and his old shipmate had
45 left the town. She too had the habit of fear. We knew that he had
been in many parts of the world, for there was a great scar on his
hand made by a whalinghook, and in the dining-room was a cabinet
with bits of coral in it and a jar of water from the Jordan for the
baptizing of his children and Chinese pictures upon rice-paper and an
50 ivory walking-stick from India that came to me after his death. He
had great physical strength and had the reputation of never ordering
a man to do anything he would not do himself. He owned many sailing ships and once, when a captain just come to anchor at Rosses
Point reported something wrong with the rudder, had sent a mes-
55 senger to say "Send a man down to find out what's wrong." "The

crew all refuse" was the answer, and to that my grandfather answered, "Go down yourself," and not being obeyed, he dived from the main deck, all the neighbourhood lined along the pebbles of the shore. He came up with his skin torn but well informed about the rudder. He had a violent temper and kept a hatchet at his bedside 60 for burglars and would knock a man down instead of going to law, and I once saw him hunt a party of men with a horsewhip. He had no relation for he was an only child and, being solitary and silent, he had few friends. He corresponded with Campbell of Islay who had befriended him and his crew after a shipwreck, and Captain Webb, 65 the first man who had swum the Channel and who was drowned swimming the Niagara Rapids, had been a mate in his employ and a close friend. That is all the friends I can remember and yet he was so looked up to and admired that when he returned from taking the waters at Bath his men would light bonfires along the railway line 70 for miles; while his partner William Middleton whose father after the great famine had attended the sick for weeks, and taken cholera from a man he carried in his arms into his own house and died of it, and was himself civil to everybody and a cleverer man than my grandfather, came and went without notice. I think I confused my 75 grandfather with God, for I remember in one of my attacks of melancholy praying that he might punish me for my sins, and I was shocked and astonished when a daring little girl—a cousin I think—having waited under a group of trees in the avenue, where she knew he would pass near four o'clock on the way to his dinner, said to 80 him, "If I were you and you were a little girl, I would give you a doll."

[5] Yet for all my admiration and alarm, neither I nor any one else thought it wrong to outwit his violence or his rigour; and his lack of suspicion and something helpless about him made that easy 85 while it stirred our affection. When I must have been still a very little boy, seven or eight years old perhaps, an uncle called me out of bed one night, to ride the five or six miles to Rosses Point to borrow a railway-pass from a cousin. My grandfather had one, but thought it dishonest to let another use it, but the cousin was not so particular. I 90 was let out through a gate that opened upon a little lane beside the garden away from earshot of the house, and rode delighted through the moonlight, and awoke my cousin in the small hours by tapping on his window with a whip. I was home again by two or three in the morning and found the coachman waiting in the little lane. My grand- 95 father would not have thought such an adventure possible, for every

night at eight he believed that the stable-yard was locked, and he
knew that he was brought the key. Some servant had once got into
trouble at night and so he had arranged that they should all be
100 locked in. He never knew, what everybody else in the house knew,
that for all the ceremonious bringing of the key the gate was never
locked.

[6] Even to-day when I read *King Lear* his image is always before
me and I often wonder if the delight in passionate men in my plays
105 and in my poetry is more than his memory. He must have been ignorant, though I could not judge him in my childhood, for he had
run away to sea when a boy, "gone to sea through the hawsehole" as
he phrased it, and I can but remember him with two books—his Bible and Falconer's *Shipwreck,* a little green-covered book that lay
110 always upon his table; he belonged to some younger branch of an
old Cornish family. His father had been in the Army, had retired to
become an owner of sailing ships, and an engraving of some old
family place my grandfather thought should have been his hung next
a painted coat of arms in the little back parlour. His mother had
115 been a Wexford woman, and there was a tradition that his family
had been linked with Ireland for generations and once had their share
in the old Spanish trade with Galway. He had a good deal of pride
and disliked his neighbours, whereas his wife, a Middleton, was
gentle and patient and did many charities in the little back parlour
120 among frieze coats and shawled heads, and every night when she saw
him asleep went the round of the house alone with a candle to make
certain there was no burglar in danger of the hatchet. She was a true
lover of her garden, and before the care of her house had grown upon
her, would choose some favourite among her flowers and copy it upon
125 rice-paper. I saw some of her handiwork the other day and I wondered at the delicacy of form and colour and at a handling that may
have needed a magnifying glass it was so minute. I can remember
no other pictures but the Chinese paintings, and some coloured
prints of battles in the Crimea upon the wall of a passage, and the
130 painting of a ship at the passage end darkened by time.

[7] My grown-up uncles and aunts, my grandfather's many sons
and daughters, came and went, and almost all they said or did has
faded from my memory, except a few harsh words that convince me
by a vividness out of proportion to their harshness that all were ha-
135 bitually kind and considerate. The youngest of my uncles was stout
and humorous and had a tongue of leather over the keyhole of his
door to keep the draught out, and another whose bedroom was at

the end of a long stone passage had a model turret ship in a glass case. He was a clever man and had designed the Sligo quays, but was now going mad and inventing a vessel of war that could not be sunk, his pamphlet explained, because of a hull of solid wood. Only six months ago my sister awoke dreaming that she held a wingless sea bird in her arms and presently she heard that he had died in his madhouse, for a sea bird is the omen that announces the death or danger of a Pollexfen. An uncle, George Pollexfen, afterwards astrologer and mystic, and my dear friend, came but seldom from Ballina, once to a race meeting with two postillions dressed in green; and there was that younger uncle who had sent me for the railway-pass. He was my grandmother's favourite, and had, the servants told me, been sent away from school for taking a crowbar to a bully.

[8] I can only remember my grandmother punishing me once. I was playing in the kitchen and a servant in horseplay pulled my shirt out of my trousers in front just as my grandmother came in and I, accused of I knew not what childish indecency, was given my dinner in a room by myself. But I was always afraid of my uncles and aunts, and once the uncle who had taken the crowbar to the bully found me eating lunch which my grandmother had given me and reproved me for it and made me ashamed. We breakfasted at nine and dined at four and it was considered self-indulgent to eat anything between meals; and once an aunt told me that I had reined in my pony and struck it at the same moment that I might show it off as I rode through the town, and I, because I had been accused of what I thought a very dark crime, had a night of misery. Indeed I remember little of childhood but its pain. I have grown happier with every year of life as though gradually conquering something in myself, for certainly my miseries were not made by others but were a part of my own mind.

The concept of organization can perhaps most easily be grasped by thinking of it in terms of shooting a motion-picture scene. The cameraman stands behind a camera and looks through the view finder at a panoramic scene. He has to focus upon details which best represent the whole. He must, however reluctantly, turn his camera away from some lovely spot, because it has nothing to do with the action. He must determine the order in which he will present the characters and the setting. He must adjust the angle of the camera so that some figures appear larger than others, since this is "their" scene. But most important of all, every move his camera makes—and does not make—must be determined by the ultimate meaning and purpose of the scene.

So the writer must determine his guiding purpose and then be "guided" by it, limit his topic to the expression only of ideas which can be adequately handled in the space available to him, express a consistent point of view, order his ideas most meaningfully, decide what to emphasize and what to de-emphasize, work out a beginning and an ending which will reflect his purpose and tone, find methods of being specific and exact, and rule out material which is not consistent with or relevant to his purpose. In short, he must organize.

In the selection from the autobiography of William Butler Yeats, the author has explicitly stated his meaning or purpose: ". . . I remember little of childhood but its pain. I have grown happier with every year of life as though gradually conquering something in myself, for certainly my miseries were not made by others but were a part of my own mind."

1. Restate this guiding purpose in your own words.

2. What is the "something in myself" which Yeats felt that he gradually conquered during his life?

3. The first paragraph prepares the reader for certain qualities of the reveries that follow. What, specifically, are the qualities? These qualities suggest that the selection may be loosely organized or even disjointed; actually, however, the selection is anything but loose and disjointed. Several of the questions that follow are designed to call attention to the means by which Yeats has achieved significant organization.

4. What is the tone established by the first paragraph? How is that tone related to the guiding purpose? What does the tone contribute to the organization of the whole?

5. Is the incident about outwitting Yeats' grandfather (paragraph 5) out of place in, or inappropriate to, the selection? Why or why not?

6. Make a list of each of the incidents and personalities in the selection. Show how each is related to the "pain" or the "miseries" of Yeats' childhood.

7. Justify the space and detail devoted to Yeats' grandparents. Why does Yeats include a comparison of his grandmother with his grandfather?

8. On the basis of as much evidence as you can find in the selection, indicate what you think is Yeats' attitude toward God. How is that attitude in keeping with the picture he presents of himself?

9. How does the knowledge that Yeats became a great poet—thought by many the greatest of this century—affect your understanding and enjoyment of the selection?

Alternate selections for the study of Concept of Organization: Gilbert Highet, "The Gettysburg Address"; Walter J. Ong, "Is Literacy Passé?"; Meg Greenfield, "Editorial Disorder and Early Sorrow."

Theme Assignment: You may agree or disagree with the underlying assumption of this selection—that the "troubles of children" are worse than those of adults or that childhood is a time predominantly of pain and terror. Write a theme based on your own childhood in which you demonstrate your attitude toward that assumption. Your position should be clearly stated and your recollections should reinforce or corroborate your position.

or

As a child, you may have had one impression of one of your parents, relatives, or friends and now have quite a different impression of that person. Write a theme of about 500 words in which you contrast your childhood impressions with your more adult impressions.

Guiding Purpose

☙From *The Last Days of H. L. Mencken*

ROBERT ALLEN DURR

[1] August Mencken explained that his brother would be down in a few minutes and that I should not be disconcerted if he went up early, because he often tired quickly since his illness. As he and I and William Manchester, who had introduced us, stood talking in
5 the living room just off the hall, I heard the stairs leading from the second floor begin to creak under a slow step, and the realization that this was "H. L. Mencken" struck me with a force near to astonishment. I saw his hand on the banister, and then he reached the bottom and turned toward us, rather briskly. Knowing, of course,
10 about his stroke, I had expected him to appear invalided or odd or distant or incoherent. But as he walked with quick short steps toward us, the name I had known familiarly as an item in my mind and conversation and the man I had come to meet this evening coincided with a jar. He was older than the pictures I had seen, and his hair

was grey; but the same antique center part surmounted the same 15
large face and intense eyes. His oval torso and thin, slightly bowed
legs and arms still wore the neat close-fitting clothes of the 'twenties.
When we shook hands his look was direct and interested. I addressed
him as "sir," and thereafter it did not occur to me to use any other
form but that and "Mr. Mencken." The instant's impression of the 20
man himself overcame the years' idea of "H. L. Mencken"—the beer-
swigging blasphemer of bouboise beatitudes, the liberated man for
whom anything goes. For this clearly was a man of dignity and
principle.

[2] The evening was unusually cool, and our big chairs were 25
formed in a semicircle around the fire with Mr. Mencken's nearest it
and the woodpile. Now and then he carefully chose a piece of wood
and with great deliberation put it on. As they talked with Mr. Manchester I took in the room more fully. It was old, Victorian, with a
high ceiling. The furniture was dark, rosewood, with fine tapestry 30
upholstery on the armchairs. A wood-framed, straight-lined settee
stood against a glass-doored bookcase on one wall, and next to the
fireplace in the nook for which it was built was August Mencken
Sr.'s tall, plain secretary, now filled with old vellum and new blue
morocco books. The room was solid and rich; it was established and 35
quiet. Especially it was unself-conscious. Things had come to be
what and where they were as a consequence of a family's having
lived with them for so long. One sensed no striving after effect. The
conventional, though fine and masculine, Victorian contents of the
room and, as I learned, of the whole house, had come to express, in 40
no definable way and as a result of no conscious endeavor, the
character of the Mencken family.

[3] The way to entertain company, both brothers later assured me,
was to greet them with a drink—a strong drink—in your hand. We
had not been seated long after introductions before August Mencken 45
supposed it might in fact be a good idea if we had something to
drink. Mr. Manchester preferred a special beer the Menckens had on
hand, but the rest of us shared a decanter of very dry Martinis. When
we were settled Mr. Mencken got up for a cigar and asked me if I
would join him. He and his brother were vigilantly yet unobtrusively 50
solicitous of our ease and comfort. My glass was never allowed to
remain empty of Martini nor my fist of a Havana cigar.

[4] After a little while, Mr. Mencken asked me what I was studying at Hopkins, and when I told him Beowulf, Elizabethan drama,
and the romantic poets he said that was very fine and immensely 55

interesting. One felt, talking to him, that he was genuinely interested in what was said; and this assurance made conversation easy. His attention was not, however, deliberate or formal. If the talk appeared nonsense to him, he might say what he thought to be the truth of the matter (though not what he thought about you personally—that would be uncalled for), or he might keep silent. But whatever his response, it was thoroughly honest, and this, perhaps paradoxically, was relaxing.

[5] H. L. Mencken was a renowned talker. He was not only witty in himself, but he provoked wit in others. When I knew him his speech was impaired. He forgot the names of people and places long familiar to him; he might call birds bugs or have to ask for an object he wanted by describing its use, as "the thing to cut with" for scissors; words generally no longer came to him so readily and precisely. But August Mencken could usually supply the exact name or word his brother wanted, and the talk went on. (At times during the months that followed as we sat in the yard, when Mr. Mencken could not recall a name he became disgusted with himself, or rather with it, the fact of his situation. "I've known him over forty years, and now I can't remember his name!" he would say, looking off at something, his mouth set. "How can anyone so stupid live?" But then abruptly he would relax, knowing the uselessness of protest, and the force of his agitation would leave him in a long sigh. "I wish this would stop.") Nevertheless the man expressed himself fully and eloquently even while I knew him. For he had in high degree what most of us never achieve at all—selfhood, being; he was always unequivocally himself, one of the great originals of our time. Such a man manifests himself in all particulars, not only in his talk. Each part of him expresses the whole, and one cherishes him for everything—build, posture, walk, shape of head, grimace, sudden broad smile, gesture, intonation, clothes—not just for his powers of articulation, though these may impress us most and serve to signal the rest.

[6] About ten-thirty or so Mr. Mencken took his leave. He came across the room to where I stood by my chair, looking at me brightly, and asked if he would see me again. (A while before, as he showed me the yard, August Mencken and I had concluded arrangements for me to spend a couple of hours a morning reading and talking with his brother.) I said yes, that I would be free from then on except for the Beowulf class on Thursdays which would continue only two

weeks longer. He shook my hand and said, "Fine, fine, very fine. Then I'll see you on Wednesday?"

[7] "Yes, sir, I'll see you on Wednesday." With just that he was able to communicate the sense that he was truly pleased I would be with him. And now suddenly, after knowing him only a few hours, I 100 felt oddly jubilant to perceive it.

In any writing, organization is a major problem which must be solved if the writing is to be successful. The first step in the solution is to determine and to state precisely the purpose guiding the writer. The guiding purpose is what the writer uses to determine the length of his piece, the tone (apologetic? angry? ironic? facetious? bitter? mocking? calmly reasoned?), the content to be included and excluded, the order of materials, the richness or paucity of illustrative material, the diction—everything, then, that makes the piece of writing what it is.

1. Durr's guiding purpose was not solely to give the reader certain insights into H. L. Mencken's personality; what, precisely, is Durr's total guiding purpose?

2. The first paragraph gives the reader some notion of H. L. Mencken's appearance and manner. What else does it do? Show how the paragraph as a whole is relevant to the guiding purpose as you have stated it.

3. We might have expected the second paragraph to continue the description of H. L. Mencken. Instead, it is devoted to the room and its furnishings. What does this paragraph contribute to carrying out the guiding purpose? Why does Durr limit his description to this one room instead of telling us about the whole house?

4. Several hours spent in conversation with so highly literate and articulate a man as Mencken must have given Durr a welter of impressions of Mencken's ideas, feelings, mannerisms, character traits, attitudes, likes, and dislikes. It is clear that Durr found Mencken a most admirable person. Where do you find Durr's response to Mencken explicitly stated? From his "welter of impressions" Durr has chosen only certain items of information about Mencken, his brother, and their home with which to make convincing to the reader his total impression of Mencken. Make a list of the most important of these items of information and show what each contributes to Durr's purpose. Then make a list, of approximately the same length, of items of information which Durr might have included but did not. Show why you think each of the items on your second list should or should not have been included.

5. In the light of Durr's guiding purpose, evaluate the beginning and ending of his sketch. Why does he begin where he does rather than with, say, the circumstances under which he was brought to Mencken's home or with his feelings as he approached the home or with a description of the exterior of the home? What does the last sentence of the sketch contribute to our awareness of Durr's guiding purpose? Should the sentence—or, at least, the information it contains—be placed earlier? Why or why not?

Most writing assignments—in college and out—come in the form of rather vague topics which in themselves do not supply the writer with much guidance. You may be asked to write a paper on the United Nations or on your home town or on the uses of the atom; you may have to write a letter explaining your absence from a final examination or breaking a date. One of the difficulties in writing on any of these "topics" is that even those that at first glance look most specific and most limited lend themselves to almost numberless treatments. For example, a theme on your home town might have the guiding purpose of proving that the local government is utterly corrupt; an entirely different theme would stem from a guiding purpose of showing that your home town is an ideal place in which to grow up because of its educational, health, and recreational facilities. Clearly, the details you would use to illustrate one of these points of view would be most inappropriate to demonstrate the other.

6. Formulate at least five guiding purposes for the "topics" suggested above. Then, by listing various items that might be included under several guiding purposes for one "topic," see how a guiding purpose governs the inclusion and exclusion of content.

Alternate selections for the study of Guiding Purpose: Joseph Conrad, "The Censor of Plays"; Charles Norman, from *The Magic Maker: E. E. Cummings;* Virgil Barker, "Pieter Bruegel the Elder."

Exercise: Look up H. L. Mencken in an encyclopedia or any other reference source (for example, *The Oxford Companion to American Literature*); write a paragraph of up to 250 words in which you compare the Mencken who emerges in Durr's essay with the Mencken of your source.

Theme Assignment: Write a theme in which you describe a place in order to show a character or personality trait of the person who occupies it. For example, you might describe a dormitory room to show that its occupant is a scrupulously—even obsessively—neat, orderly person; you might describe a professor's office to show that the professor's habitual state of confusion is mirrored in his office;

you might describe the living room or kitchen of your home as a reflection of one of your mother's strongest personality traits. Remember that your guiding purpose is to reveal a character or personality trait through your description; you must limit the description to those characteristics of the room relevant to the trait of the occupant with which you are dealing, and you must make the trait convincing to the reader.

Limiting
a Topic

✍ Last of the Great
Fairy-Talers   RUMER GODDEN

[1] On Hans Andersen's statue in the King's Garden of Copenhagen are the words "H. C. Andersen. Digter," meaning poet, or
writer; that word often comes as a surprise; we are all so accustomed
to think of him as a storyteller for the nursery that we forget that
5 the Tales were conceived, worked over, polished by a hard-working
writer. They seem so natural and easy that few of us realize that
Andersen, by scholars and thinking people, is ranked among the
great writers of the world.

[2] Does that reputation rest only on the Tales? Yes, only on the
10 Tales. Andersen wrote many other things, among them a novel that
was immensely popular in its own day, *The Improvvisatore;* there are
three other novels, as well as travel books, plays—some of them produced at the Theater Royal in Copenhagen—and books of poems
but, except for a few of the poems, none of these is read now by

From *The Saturday Review,* December 25, 1954. © 1954 by Saturday Review, Inc. Reprinted by permission of Curtis Brown, Ltd.

anyone but students of Andersen; it is for the Tales that he has his place. On the surface it seems unlikely that such world fame should come from fairy tales, little stories for children, but if we go deeper it is easy to see how and why it came.

[3] The word *fairy* has become associated in our minds so much with children that we have forgotten its real meaning; it is from the old French word *faerie* that meant "enchantment," which, in its turn, came from the Latin *fata* or *fate,* something inexorable and strong.

[4] Andersen himself once explained what a fairy tale could mean. "In the whole realm of poetry no domain is so boundless as that of the fairy tale," he said. "It reaches from the blood-drenched graves of antiquity to the pious legends of a child's picture book; it takes in the poetry of the people and the poetry of the artist. To me it represents all poetry, and he who masters it must be able to put into it tragedy, comedy, naïve simplicity, irony, and humor"—all qualities of Andersen. "At his service are the lyrical note, the childlike narrative, and the language of nature description." Andersen used them all. He also said, "In a small country a poet must of necessity be poor so that he must try and catch the golden bird of honor." He added, half disbelieving it, "It remains to be seen if I can catch it by telling fairy tales."

[5] In the 120 years since the first of Hans Andersen's Tales were published they have sold, taking the length of time into consideration, more copies than any other book in the world except the Bible, Shakespeare, and *Pilgrim's Progress*—there have been over 2,000 editions—and this is not only as an author for children; grownup people from artisans to kings read him and and keep his books on their shelves; scholars have given their lives to study him—one Japanese professor was so dissatisfied with the translations that he learned Danish only to read Andersen in the original; his Tales are in Japanese, Chinese, Hindustani, Arabic, Swahili, Hebrew, Yiddish, Russian, as well as all the European languages and Esperanto; they have been made into ballets, plays, films. He kept an album as a record of his friendships and the names in it read like an inventory of the most brilliant and famous people of the Europe of his time. Thorvaldsen the sculptor, Frederika Bremer the Swedish novelist, Grieg, Bøgh, Schiller, Heine, Chamisso, Tieck, Schumann, Mendelssohn, Weber, Cherubini, Victor Hugo, Dumas the Elder, Lamartine, De Vigny, George Sand, Rachel, Brandes, Liszt, Lord Palmerston, Dickens, Wilkie Collins, Lady Blessington, Jenny Lind,

55 the Grand Duke of Saxe Weimar, the King of Prussia, the kings and queens of his own Denmark, were his personal friends.

[6] Hans Andersen wrote in his autobiography, "Life itself is the most wonderful fairy tale." For him it certainly was. He started with every possible disadvantage: his father and mother were very 60 humble and poor, a cobbler and a washerwoman. He came to Copenhagen from the country when he was only fourteen years old, and wandered a destitute waif about the city; he had no real schooling until he was seventeen, when the directors of the Royal Theater attracted by his strangeness and his queer persistence in attaching 65 himself to the theater and writing extraordinary and unactable plays, applied for a state grant to educate him. Added to all this he was so tall and thin and ugly that he might almost have been a freak, and so thin-skinned and nervous that he wept at criticism, burst out into violent rages, and was a torment to his friends, while his 70 naïveté would have been laughable if it had not been disarming. Yet he ended as a quiet, dignified, learned, and gentle man, his ugliness mellowed into a nobility that struck everyone who saw him; he was given the title of State Counsellor, with a state pension; he had orders and decorations. He became an accomplished courtier; 75 it is told that once, at table, King Frederik VII raised his glass to Andersen; the drinking of healths in Denmark is a serious business and Andersen had only water in his glass; he thought the green color of the goblet would hide this and raised it in return but the King said, "When you drink to your King you drink wine."

80 [7] "When I drink to my King water is made wine," said Andersen.

[8] He was equally honored abroad; when he visited Portugal the ships in Lisbon harbor ran up their flags for him, and while he was in Scotland he lost his walking stick and it traveled safely back to 85 him all over the Highlands, labeled simply "Hans Andersen, the Danish poet."

[9] What was there in these fairy tales to merit all this? Was it simply popularity? No, because it has lasted; Hans Andersen is as much read now as when he was alive, or even more. Kings and 90 queens, artists and statesmen still read him as children do. But why? What is it that makes him so different from Perrault, for instance, or from Grimm?

[10] Andersen's countryman Kai Munk, the poet and playwright, has remarked that there are two kinds of writing: writing of enter- 95 tainment, which is ephemeral, and writing of existence, which can be

very entertaining as well. It would seem that a fairy tale must of necessity belong to the first group, but the tales of Hans Andersen are writing of existence—they have their roots in eternal truths.

[11] In the Bible we are told that God formed Man out of the dust of earth and breathed into his nostrils . . . and Man became a living soul. Without irreverence it might be said that Hans Andersen did something like that, too; he formed his stories of the dust of earth: a daisy, an old street lamp, a darning needle, a beetle, and made them alive. His breath was unique; it was an alchemy of wisdom, poetry, humor, and innocence.

[12] He was adult, a philosopher, and a lovable man; his stories are parables and have meanings that sound on and on—sometimes over our heads—after their last word is read. He was a poet and knew the whole gamut of feeling from ecstasy to black melancholy and horror. People call him sentimental; in a way he was, but in the first meaning of the word, which is not "excess of feeling" but an "abounding in feeling and reflection." He was a child; children have this godlike power of giving personality to things that have none, not only toys, but sticks and stones, bannister knobs and footstools, cabbages; it dies in them as they grow up, but Andersen never lost this power. "It often seems to me," he wrote, "as if every fence, every little flower is saying to me, 'Look at me, just for a moment, and then my story will go right into you.'" "Right into you," that is the clue. The daisy, the street lamp, the beetle—they are suddenly breathing and alive.

Once upon a time there was a bundle of matches; they were tremendously proud of their high birth. Their family tree—that's to say, the tall fir tree that each little match stick came from—had been a huge old tree in the wood. And now the matches lay on the shelf between a tinderbox and an old iron cookpot, and they told the other two about the time they were young. "Ah, yes," they said, "in those days, with the velvet moss at our feet, we really were on velvet. Every morning and evening we had diamond tea; that was the dew. And all day we had sunshine. . . . But then the woodcutters arrived; that was the great upheaval, and our family was all split up. Our founder and head was given a place as mainmast on board a splendid ship that could sail round the world if she liked; the other branches went to other places and, as for us, we've got the task of lighting up for the common herd; that's how we gentlefolk come to be in the kitchen."

"Well, things have gone differently with me," said the cookpot which stood alongside the matches. "Right from the time I first came into the world, I've been scrubbed and boiled again and again. I've got an eye for the practical and, strictly speaking, I'm Number One in this house. My great delight, at a time like after dinner, is to sit clean and tidy on the shelf and have a nice little chat with my friends. But except for the waterbucket, who now and then goes down into the yard, we spend all our time indoors. Our one news-bringer is the market basket, but that goes in for a lot of wild talk about the Government and the people. Why, the other day there was an elderly jug so flabbergasted by what the basket said that it fell down and broke in pieces. It's a red Radical, that basket, mark my words!"

"How you do chatter!" said the tinderbox; and the steel let fly at the flint, so that it gave out sparks. "Come on, let's have a cheerful evening!"

"Yes, let's discuss who belongs to the best family," said the matches.

"No, I don't like talking about myself," said the earthenware jug. "Let's have a social evening. I'll begin. . . . On the shores of the Baltic, where the Danish beech trees . . ."

"It does sound interesting the way you tell it," said the broom. "One can hear at once that it's a lady telling running through it all."

"That's just how I feel," said the basket, and it gave a little hop of sheer delight, and that meant "splash!" on the floor. Then the cookpot went on with its story, and the end was every bit as good as the beginning.

The plates all rattled with joy, and the broom took some green parsley out of the bin and crowned the cookpot with it, knowing this would annoy the others and "if I crown her today," she thought, "then she'll crown me tomorrow."

"Now I'm going to dance," said the tongs, and dance she did—my word, what a high kick! The old chintz on the chair in the corner fairly split himself looking at it. "Now may I be crowned?" asked the tongs, and crowned she was.

"After all, they're the merest riffraff," thought the matches.

[13] That is a whole live kitchen world. After reading it a kitchen never seems the same place again; one is almost afraid to take a shopping basket out for fear of what it might think; it is almost as if the dustpan might speak; and notice in how few words it is told.

[14] All the stories have this economy, this startlingly quick effect. Andersen is verbose and boring in his novels and autobiography, but the Tales are his poems. Each story has the essence of a poem and a poem is not prose broken into short lines, but a distilling of

125

thought and meaning into a distinct form, so disciplined and finely 130
made, so knit in rhythm, that one word out of place, one word too
much, jars the whole. With Andersen we are never jarred and it is
this close knitting and shaping that give the Tales their extraordinary swiftness—too often lost in translation—so that they are over
almost before we have had time to take them in and we have had 135
the magical feeling of flying. The children, he remarked, always
had their mouths a little open when he had finished; that is the
feeling we have too.

[15] But they were not written swiftly, were not the happy accidents that some people think them; anyone who has studied one of 140
the original manuscripts from the first short draft of a story, through
all its stages, the crossings out, rewritings, and alterations in Andersen's small spiky handwriting, the cuttings and pastings together,
until it was ready for the printer, can see how each word was
weighed and what careful pruning was done, what discipline was 145
there. Even the discipline was skillful: Andersen never let it kill
the life in his style.

[16] That life is his hallmark. A sentence from one of Hans
Andersen's Tales is utterly different from a sentence by anyone else.
"The children got into the coach and drove off," Perrault or Grimm 150
would have written but Hans Andersen wrote: "Up they got on the
coach. Goodbye, Mum. Goodbye, Dad. Crack went the whip, whick,
whack, and away they dashed. Gee up! Gee up!"

[17] "It's not writing, it's talking," the irritated critics had said but,
one after another, serious writers have found in it a source of in- 155
spiration: "From that moment," said Jacobsen, "a new prose was
born in Danish literature; the language acquired grace and color,
the freshness of simplicity."

[18] It is this freshness and simplicity that are lost in most English
translations, but the newest, by R. P. Keigwin, Danish scholars say, 160
catch the essence of Hans Andersen as never before; American and
English people brought up on the sentimental verbose Andersens
we have all known may find these a surprise. "But he makes the
kitchenmaid in 'The Nightingale' say 'Gosh!'" said one American
critic. Precisely, because *Gosh* or *Lawks* is nearest to the Danish of 165
what she did say. "Where's your spunk?" the witch asks the Little
Mermaid. That critic would no doubt have preferred "Where is your
courage?" but *spunk,* its one syllable snapped out so quickly, is
nearer to Andersen. The difference in translations can be shown by

170 studying the story of "The Tin Soldier." He has been called "The
Dauntless Tin Soldier," "The Constant," "The Steadfast"; Mr.
Keigwin uses "The Staunch." That small taut firm word *staunch* is
exactly right for a little tin soldier and it has the quickness and
economy of the Danish; and with all their slang the stories keep
175 their beauty; Andersen is one of the few writers who uses slang
beautifully.

[19] He always had a turn for phrases. "She is like a little black
coffee pot boiling over," he once said of a plump, small, dark and
talkative woman.

180 [20] Not everyone liked the Tales. There were some bad reviews:
"Although the reviewer has nothing against good fairy tales for the
grownups," said one, "he can only find this form of literature entirely unsuitable for children. . . . Ought their reading, even out of
school, to be merely for amusement? . . . Far from improving their
185 minds," he said severely, "Andersen's Tales might be positively
harmful. Would anyone claim that a child's sense of what is proper
would be improved when it reads about a sleeping princess riding
on the back of a horse to a soldier who kisses her? . . . or that its
sense of modesty be improved by reading about a woman who dined
190 alone with a sexton in her husband's absence? Or its sense of value of
human life after reading 'Little and Big Claus'? As for 'The Princess
and the Pea,' it is not only indelicate but indefensible as the child
might get the false idea that great ladies must be terribly thin-
skinned. . . ." The critic ended by saying, " 'Little Ida's Flowers' is
195 innocent but it has no moral either."

[21] We smile at such criticism, but there are others that threaten
Andersen just as seriously; for instance, there is an idea now that
children should be given books without shadows, books of brightness
and lightness, and laughter, nothing else; perhaps the reason why
200 such books are so lifeless is that living things have shadows.

[22] This has led to what can only be called a desecration of
Andersen's work; judicious editors have cut it, changed the endings,
in some cases simply taken the plot away from the story and told it
again, until, as Professor Elias Bredsdorff says, what we have is
205 Andersen murdered.

[23] No one can deny that Andersen has his dark side; he could
hardly escape it; he was writing in the first half of the nineteenth
century and had been brought up among crude and ignorant people.
As a child he was told macabre stories and superstitions; he had been

terrified of his grandfather, who was mad, and, when he went to the asylum with his grandmother, he had seen dangerous lunatics kept in cells. In his day Denmark had capital punishment and as a boy he was taken to see an execution, supposed then to be an edifying sight for children; in Copenhagen, in his early days, he lived among the dregs of the city; besides all this, as a true poet, once he began to write a Tale he became possessed by it.

[24] Stories as vividly horrid as "The Girl Who Trod on a Loaf," as sad as "The Shadow," should perhaps be kept away from children altogether but to expunge parts of them, to tell them in another way, is to destroy them, not too strong a word; and almost always it is safe to trust the children to Andersen. "The Little Mermaid," for instance, has terrible parts, but the ultimate feeling is of joy and tenderness, the story is one of the saddest on earth but it is also one of the very best loved.

[25] In pictures and statues of Andersen tiny children are shown listening to the stories; this is sentimentally false. The stories were not meant for them. In the 1840s, 1850s, and 1860s very little children were kept in the nursery when visitors came to the house; it was not until they were seven or eight years old that they were allowed to go down to the drawing room or in to dessert to meet Mr. Hans Andersen and perhaps hear his Tales. Even then they did not understand the whole; they were not meant to; all Andersen wanted was that they should love them.

[26] In "The Apple Bough" the apple branch realizes the difference in people. "Some are for ornament, some for nourishment, and some we could do very well without," it thinks. A poet, if he is a good poet, is for both ornament and nourishment and the world would be a poor place without him.

[27] Andersen charms and pleases us and he feeds our hearts and minds and souls; he has few conventional happy endings. Terrible things happen, but no matter what happens the ultimate pattern comes clear and a wholeness is reached that is better than happiness because it satisfies.

[28] When Denmark was at war with Prussia, a friend wrote to Andersen and told him how in a house that had been ruined with cannon and grapeshot a storks' nest on the broken roof held a new stork family. It seemed to Andersen a symbol of the great pattern in which he believed. He had glimpsed it before. When King Christian VIII had died and all Denmark mourned, a swan had flown against

250 the spire of Roskilde Cathedral, where all the kings and queens have their sarcophagi; it brushed its breast and fell but soon it was able to fly again. When Oehlenschlager the poet died a songbird built its nest in one of the wreaths, and once Andersen, in a black mood, wrote with his cane in the snow, "Snow is like immortality. In a little 255 while there is no trace." He went away, there was a thaw, and when he came to the place again he found all the snow had melted, except for one spot, where remained the word *Immortality*.

[29] It was Spinoza who said, "The more we understand individual things, the more we understand God." For Hans Andersen 260 every fence, every small flower, seemed to say, "Look at me and my story will go right into you"; a thistle, a tin soldier, a snail, opens a breadth of vision and understanding; he knew that the little is part of the big and it is this sense of largeness, of infinity, that comes to us; the stories do not need a moral for they are each a parable.

Student writers are usually acutely—even painfully—aware of the need for answering the question, "What shall I say about this topic?" It is just as important, however, to answer another question: "What shall I *not* say about this topic?" We have already pointed out that a well-formulated guiding purpose is the key to determining what should be included in, and excluded from, a piece of writing. It is also the key to limiting the topic, to focusing the topic so sharply that not only is extraneous material excluded but adequate, satisfying treatment is given to relevant material in the wordage available.

A five-hundred-word theme on college life obviously cannot adequately and satisfyingly treat all facets of the topic. A good guiding purpose might limit the topic in time: to describe college life at lunchtime, showing that serious intellectual conversation is more important than the quality of the food. Or it might limit the topic in place as well as time: to describe college life in a typical dormitory from 7:00 A.M. to 8:30 A.M., showing particularly the annoyances of institutional living. Or it might limit the topic by focusing sharply on a single idea growing out of it: to show that college life with all of its complexities presents serious emotional problems even to well-adjusted students. However the guiding purpose limits the topic, it is essential for the writer that his topic be limited in proportion to the wordage he has available.

1. Had she wanted to, Rumer Godden could have written a book-length study of Hans Christian Andersen. She might have dealt with his life in detail, with the times and places in which he lived, with his

entire literary output other than the Tales, with the Tales one by one, with his travels, with his literary progenitors, with his reception by the public in his own country and in others, with his finances, loves, friendships, enmities, with the philosophic background of his writings, and with his own philosophic convictions. And, indeed, with much more. Indicate at least three additional large topics which might have been part of a book-length study. To what specific matters does Miss Godden limit her treatment of Andersen? Formulate the guiding purpose of the essay to reflect the limitation Miss Godden chose. In what sentence of the essay does Miss Godden most explicitly indicate her guiding purpose? In light of the guiding purpose, show why your three additional topics should or should not have been included in the essay.

2. Show why the material in paragraphs 3 and 5 does or does not violate the limitations imposed on the topic by the guiding purpose.

3. Which of the people listed in paragraph 5 can you not identify? What printed source or sources would you consult to get biographical information on each?

4. How is the material in paragraphs 6, 7, and 8 relevant to the guiding purpose?

5. What is the function of paragraph 9?

6. In some detail, supply the answers to the questions raised in paragraph 9.

7. What literary qualities other than those mentioned by Miss Godden characterize the Tale quoted after paragraph 12? Did the limits Miss Godden placed on her topic prohibit her from mentioning these qualities? Explain.

8. Explain how the material in paragraph 18 falls legitimately within the limits of Miss Godden's topic.

9. Explain why you agree or disagree with Miss Godden's statement (paragraph 24) that "Stories as vividly horrid as 'The Girl Who Trod on a Loaf,' as sad as 'The Shadow,' should perhaps be kept away from children altogether . . ."

Alternate selections for the study of Limiting a Topic: Max Shulman, "Love Is a Fallacy"; Archibald MacLeish, "Of the Librarian's Profession"; Carl Sandburg, "How to Read a Newspaper."

Theme Assignment: Write a theme of no more than 500 words consisting of your answer to question 9. To do the assignment justice, you may have to read (or reread) some of Andersen's Tales. You will also have to do some thinking about child rearing, perhaps using your own childhood as a source of information and reactions. And you will certainly have to formulate a guiding purpose that will limit your topic so sharply that you can deal with it adequately in your relatively short theme. Submit with your theme a statement of your guiding purpose.

or

From your own knowledge and experience, select one group of people whom you know well. For example, you may select parents, high school students, young adults. Limit this group further: parents of teen-agers, high school students taking examinations that will affect their admission to college, young adults who are in love for the first time.

Decide upon the one outstanding characteristic of this group which you wish to comment upon, and the advice you would like to give about that characteristic to the members of the group you select. For example, you may feel that one outstanding characteristic about young adults in love for the first time is their belief that no one could possibly understand what they are experiencing. You may want to tell them that other people can and do understand. Or you may feel that the outstanding characteristic of parents of teen-agers is their resistance to change, their inability to think of their children as anything but "children," and you may want to advise them that many of the conflicts could be avoided if parents could see their teen-agers as people.

Write a well-organized theme expressing your guiding purpose. Remember that it is necessary for you to determine in advance your own attitude toward your subject and toward your reader. Submit with your theme a statement of your guiding purpose.

Point
of View

✐ Letter from the Editor

MAXWELL E. PERKINS

Aug. 28, 1928

DEAR ————:

[1] We have read with interest your letter in criticism of *The Great Gatsby* by F. Scott Fitzgerald, and we thank you for it. Probably if you had read the book through, you would not have felt any the less repugnance to it, but you would no doubt have grasped its underlying motive, which is by no means opposed to your own point 5 of view.

[2] The author was prompted to write this book by surveying the tragic situation of many people because of the utter confusion of ideals into which they have fallen, with the result that they cannot distinguish the good from the bad. The author did not look upon 10 these people with anger or contempt so much as with pity. He saw that good was in them, but that it was altogether distorted. He therefore pictured, in the Great Gatsby, a man who showed extraordinary nobility and many fine qualities, and yet who was following an evil

15 course without being aware of it, and indeed was altogether a wor-
shipper of wholly false gods. He showed him in the midst of a society
such as certainly exists, of a people who were all worshipping false
gods. He wished to present such a society to the American public so
that they would realize what a grotesque situation existed, that a man
20 could be a deliberate law-breaker, who thought that the accumulation
of vast wealth by any means at all was an admirable thing, and yet
could have many fine qualities of character. The author intended the
story to be repugnant and he intended to present it so forcefully and
realistically that it would impress itself upon people. He wanted to
25 show that this was a horrible, grotesque, and tragic fact of life today.
He could not possibly present these people effectively if he refused
to face their abhorrent characteristics. One of these was profanity—
the total disregard for, or ignorance of, any sense of reverence for a
Power outside the physical world. If the author had not presented
30 these abhorrent characteristics, he would not have drawn a true picture of these people, and by drawing a true picture of them he has
done something to make them different, for he has made the public
aware of them, and its opinion generally prevails in the end.

[3] There are, of course, many people who would say that such
35 people as those in the book should not be written about, because of
their repulsive characteristics. Such people maintain that it would be
better not to inform the public about evil or unpleasantness. Certainly
this position has a strong case. There is, however, the other opinion:
vice is attractive when gilded by the imagination, as it is when it is
40 concealed and only vaguely known of; but in reality it is horrible
and repulsive, and therefore it is well it should be presented as it is
so that it may be so recognized. Then people would hate it, and
avoid it, but otherwise they may well be drawn to it on account of
its false charm.

Very truly yours,

[For treatment of this selection, see pp. 35–36.]

✒ Cloister Culture

SAUL BELLOW

[1] We can't master change. It is too vast, too swift. We'd kill ourselves trying. It is essential, however, to try to understand transformations directly affecting us. That may not be possible either, but we have no choice.

[2] The changes on which I would like to comment are those in the relations between the writer and the public in the English-speaking countries. I shall begin with the sort of description of these relations an avant-garde writer might have given 30 years ago.

[3] He would certainly have referred to himself as a highbrow. Not without irony, but seriously nevertheless, he would have distinguished himself from the middle-brow, the ape of culture, and from the lowbrow or no-brow, that philistine hater of all that was good and beautiful in the modern tradition. This is not to say that the highbrow writer invariably loved his isolation and that he rejected the great public out of pride or decadent class-feeling. On the contrary, the division of cultures into high and low caused much bitterness and was considered by many highbrows to be dangerous to society and to civilization as a whole.

From *The New York Times,* July 10, 1966. © 1966 by The New York Times Company. Reprinted by permission.

[4] Perhaps overlooking the humiliations of the poet under pa-
20 tronage, the vanguardist of the thirties was often nostalgic for the
18th century and the small, refined and aristocratic public of that
age of masterpieces. In his view the 19th-century public was already
fully vulgarized—enthusiastic, perhaps, but coarse-grained, an audience of shopkeepers. The weaknesses of this public were aggravated
25 by commercial exploitation, by promoters who made great fortunes
in cheap novels, bringing mass culture into the world. The vanguard
minority, by this vanguard account, grew smaller and smaller. The
specialist now appeared, the technician, a new sort of intellectual with
little or no understanding of art and small sympathy for the life of
30 the mind.

[5] Finally, in the 20th century, to state the case as it was stated
by a brilliant critic and observer, the late Wyndham Lewis, an authentic high-brow civilization cut itself in two, driving into pens and
reservations all that was most creative and intelligent. The vanguard
35 artist, like the American Indian, was shut up in barren places, se-
questered in the ivory tower, deprived of human contact and influence. Probably all this would end in the total liquidation of intellectuals. Only a few twilight masterpieces by men like Joyce or Paul
Klee would remain, and we would reach the stage of final degrada-
40 tion, the era of brutal unrelieved stupidity.

[6] This in some ways resembles the description of the bourgeois
situation given by the 19th century romantic, not wholly unjustified
but containing certain exaggerations. The romantic saw himself cut
off from society, held in contempt by its rulers, separated from the
45 people and longing to be reunited with them.

[7] Wyndham Lewis was a thoughtful and original observer, but it
is apparent that he made any number of wrong guesses. Intellectuals
have not been liquidated. On the contrary they have increased in
number and in influence. They are now spoken of with respect, even
50 with awe, as indispensable to the government, as makers of educated
opinion, as sources of symbolic legitimacy—replacing the clergy. Old
Walt Whitman, announcing, "The priest departs, the divine literatus
arrives," does not sound as unhinged as he did 30 years ago.

[8] I do not speak of the *quality* of these literati (that is another
55 matter; they are still a little remote from divinity) but of the growth
of their power.

[9] On the eve of World War II the highbrow public was indeed
very small. This is no longer the case. We now have a growing class
of intellectuals or near-intellectuals. There are millions of college

graduates. A college degree may not mean much. It does, however, 60
indicate exposure to high culture. And the literary culture to which
these students are exposed was the creation of highbrow geniuses—
disaffected, subversive, radical. The millions who go to art museums
today admire there the strangely beautiful, powerful paintings of artists who worked in what Lewis called the thickening twilight of 65
modernism. The millions who take courses in literature become acquainted with the poems and novels of men who rejected the average
preferences of their contemporaries.

[10] The minority public is no longer that handful of connoisseurs
that read Transition in the twenties or discussed "significant form." 70
We have at present a large literary community and something we can
call, *faute de mieux,* a literary culture, in my opinion a very bad one.

[11] For one thing, the universities have now embraced modern
literature. Stony old pedants two generations ago refused to discuss
anyone newer than Browning, but their power was broken in the 75
thirties, and all universities permit the study of contemporary writers.
Thousands of teachers turn out millions of graduates in literature.
Some of these teachers, a very small minority, are quite useful; others
are harmless enough, textual editors, antiquarians and fuddyduddies.
Others are influential interpreters. Or misinterpreters. 80

[12] It is in the universities that literary intellectuals are made,
not on Grub Street, not in Bohemia. The mass media and the univer-
sity-sponsored quarterlies have between them swallowed up literary
journalism. The salaried professor will supply literary articles cheaply
and has all but wiped out his professional competitors. Bohemia, 85
too, has been relocated in new quarters, near to university campuses.

[13] The university therefore is producing quantities of literary
intellectuals who teach, write or go into publishing houses. So far as
I can see this new group, greatly influenced by the modern classics,
by Joyce, Proust, Eliot, Lawrence, Gide, Valéry, etc., have done little 90
more than convert these classics into other forms of discourse, trans-
lating imagination into opinion, or art into cognitions. What they do
is to put it all differently. They redescribe everything, usually making it less accessible. For feeling or response they substitute acts of
comprehension. 95

[14] Sometimes they seem to be manufacturing "intellectual history," creating a sort of subculture more congenial to them and to
their students than art itself. Sometimes I think they are trying to
form a new model of the civilized intelligence for the 20th century,
an intelligence to which a more worthy art will one day be offered— 100

the *zeitgeist* permitting. Perhaps the "dehumanization of art" of which Ortega speaks reflects the demands made upon art by literary intellectuals. It may in part be a result of the pressure they put upon it for meanings.

105 [15] Redescription can be intriguing and useful, and succeeding generations must, like Adam and Eve in the Garden of Eden, rename their beasts. Molière revealed the comic possibilities of this when M. Jourdain discovered that all his life he had been speaking prose. We Americans take great satisfaction in this comedy of terms. We 110 pay psychologists to penetrate our characters and redescribe them to us scientifically, rationalizing consciousness on the verbal level at least. We are delighted to hear that we are introverted, fixated, have a repression here, a cathexis there, are attached to our mothers thus and so. Such new accounts seem valuable in themselves, worth the 115 money we pay for them.

[16] Yet what our literary intelligentsia does is to redescribe everything downward, blackening the present age and denying creative scope to their contemporaries. They assume themselves to be the only heirs of the modern classical writers. Our most respected men 120 of letters identify themselves with Joyce, Proust, et cetera, and present themselves as the distinguished representatives, indeed the only representatives of these masters. The agents, managers or impresarios (popularizers) of James or the French symbolists consider themselves the only successors of these writers. Thus they enjoy a certain gen-125 teel prestige. They are the happy few. And they are not unlike the old pretorians faithful to the remains of poor Browning. But the scale of operations is much greater.

[17] There are clear signs that intellectuals in what American universities call the humanities are trying to appropriate literature for 130 themselves, taking it away from writers. These intellectuals are like the British princess who said to her husband during the honeymoon, "Do the servants do this too? Much too good for them." Literature is too good for contemporary novelists, those poor untutored drudges.

[18] And what do these intellectuals do with literature? Why, they 135 talk about it; they treasure it; they make careers of it; they become an élite through it; they adorn themselves with it; they make discourse of it. It is their material, their capital. They take from it what they need for their own work in culture history, journalism or criticism of manners producing hybrid works, partly literary, sometimes 140 interesting in themselves, but postulating almost always the decadence or obsolescence of contemporary literature. They want to use the

literature of the modern tradition to make something far better; they project a higher, more valuable mental realm, a realm of dazzling intellectuality.

[19] Let me direct your attention to other consequences of the 145 teaching of modern literature. In his latest book, "Beyond Culture," Prof. Lionel Trilling tells us that we now have a sizable group of people in the United States educated in the modern classics. He thinks they have not turned out very well. One sees his point.

[20] They seem to have it both ways. On the one hand these 150 teachers, editors or culture-bureaucrats have absorbed the dislike of the modern classic writers for modern civilization. They are repelled by the effrontery of power and the degradation of the urban crowd. They have made the Waste Land outlook their own. On the other hand they are very well off. They have money, position, privileges, 155 power; they send their children to private schools; they can afford elegant dental care, jet holidays in Europe. They have stocks, bonds, houses, even yachts, and with all this, owing to their education, they enjoy a particular and intimate sympathy with the heroic artistic life. Their tastes and judgments were formed by Rimbaud and D. H. Law- 160 rence. Could anything be neater?

[21] Yet this may be the way things are in the modern world, a consequence perhaps of the decline in belief, or of certain doubts about the value of human actions. Thus in a short life one feels free to combine all things of value. People pursue luxury but try to keep 165 by some means values conceived in austerity. They combine private security with rebellious attitudes, monogamy with sexual experiment, conventional family life with bohemian attitudes, the *dolce vita* with the great books. Vice presidents during the working day, they may be anarchists or utopians at cocktail time. In the higher income 170 brackets, insulated from the dirt and danger of New York, they retain as a matter of course all the sentiments of alienation, honor-bound to be sullen, ungrateful, dissatisfied, suspicious and theoretically defiant of authority.

[22] There is nothing very new in this. Dostoevsky observed that 175 people who recited Schiller's odes with tears in their eyes were also very good at managing their bureaucratic careers. No wonder Professor Trilling is upset. He sees that a literary education may be a mixed blessing, and that the critics, writers and executives sent into the world by English departments have not turned out very well. 180

[23] What important function might they be performing? That question is answered by Irving Kristol in a recent number of The

Public Interest. He points out that the literary intellectuals help shape the opinions of the educated classes and play a crucial role in defin-
185 ing the moral quality of our society. He says, "There is surely no more important task than to question or affirm the legitimacy of a society's basic institutions, to criticize or amend the original assumptions on which political life proceeds. How well equipped are our literary intellectuals for this job? Not, it must be confessed, as well
190 equipped as they ought to be."

[24] This then is the situation. Critics and professors have declared themselves the true heirs and successors of the modern classic writers. They have obscured the connection between the contemporary writer and his predecessors. They have not shaped the opinions
195 of the educated classes. They have done nothing to create a new public. They have miseducated the young. They are responsible for a great increase in what Veblen called "trained incapacity."

[25] Furthermore, they have projected the kind of art and literature that suits them and have the power to recruit painters and novel-
200 ists who will meet their requirements. Novels are written which contain attitudes, positions or fantasies pleasing to the literary intelligentsia. These are of course given serious consideration, though they may be little more than the footnotes of fashionable doctrines.

[26] Literature is becoming important for what one can do with
205 it. It is becoming a source of orientations, postures, life-styles, positions. These positions are made up of odds and ends of Marxism, Freudianism, existentialism, mythology, surrealism, absurdism, *undsoweiter*—the debris of modernism, with apocalyptic leftovers added.

[27] I am speaking of educated and indeed supercivilized people
210 who believe that a correct position makes one illusionless, that to be illusionless is more important than anything else, and that it is enlightened to expose, to disenchant, to hate and to experience disgust. Wyndham Lewis had an excellent term for this last phenomenon—he spoke of the vulgarization of once aristocratic disgust by the modern
215 romantics. One might add that the skepticism of the Enlightenment has also been vulgarized, and that it is at present thought blessed to see through to the class origins of one's affection for one's grandfather, or to reveal the hypocritical weakness and baseness at the heart of friendships.

220 [28] Nevertheless there are friendships, affinities, natural feelings, rooted norms. People do on the whole agree, for instance, that it is wrong to murder. And even if they are unable to offer rational arguments for this, they are not necessarily driven to commit gratuitous

acts of violence. It seems to me that writers might really do well to start thinking about such questions again. Evidently they will have 225 to do this without the aid of the critics. The critics are too romantic to deal with these problems.

[29] A final word about the avant-garde. To labor to create vanguard conditions is historicism. It means that people have been reading books of culture-history and have concluded retrospectively that 230 originality is impossible without such conditions. But genius is always, without strain, avant-garde. Its departure from tradition is not the result of caprice or of policy but of an inner necessity.

[30] As for the highbrow public of an earlier time, it has now been assimilated by our literary culture and transformed into some- 235 thing else. For the time being the writer will have to do without it. He will have to believe that what he writes will evoke a public, that the new forms he creates will create a new public, summoned up by the force of his truth.

Every writer has a point of view toward his subject—an attitude toward it, a slant—which makes the treatment of the subject his own. One could write an article about teen-agers from a point of view sympathetic to them, believing in their innocence, and say that their faults are really the faults of their parents. Or one could write from the teenagers' own perspective, about the world and its perils. Or one could possibly treat the same subject from the point of view of irate, or bemused, or shocked, or "superior" and condescending adults. Each of these points of view would cause the writer to use a particular tone, select incidents or details as examples, order his material, even choose particular words and phrases. In fact, the writer's point of view shapes the raw material into a piece of writing: helps him to formulate his guiding purpose and limit his topic.

1. As editor for a major publishing house, Maxwell Perkins was called upon to reply to a reader's letter criticizing F. Scott Fitzgerald's novel, *The Great Gatsby*. He might have written from any one of several points of view. He might have taken the position that "the customer is always right"; his letter then would have been apologetic. Or he might have written—indignantly—from the point of view of an editor outraged at the audacity of a reader criticizing a book which he had not finished reading. From what point of view does Perkins actually write? On what statements in his letter do you base your answer?

2. Reconstruct the main points that seem to have been made in the "letter in criticism of *The Great Gatsby*" to which Perkins' letter

replies. Indicate at least two points of view (other than those mentioned in question 1) from which Perkins might have written his reply. What would the tone be of each of the letters written from these points of view? How would each of these letters differ from Perkins' letter in specific items of content?

3. In the last paragraph of his letter, Perkins says, "Such people maintain that it would be better not to inform the public about evil or unpleasantness. Certainly this position has a strong case." Indicate two points of view from which you might make the "strong case." Then, to show how point of view affects content, list briefly the arguments you would muster from each of the points of view.

4. Saul Bellow reflects a point of view throughout his article: a point of view toward the writer, the public, literary intellectuals, and "rooted norms." Find a sentence for each of these four groups or concepts in which he states or reveals his point of view.

5. Restate the first paragraph in your own words. What tone does it reflect? How is that tone appropriate to Bellow's point of view?

6. Why does or does not Bellow violate unity by the inclusion of paragraphs 3 through 8? What, if anything, is the relationship between those paragraphs and paragraphs 9 and 10?

7. What does he mean by "a literary culture"? What is its relationship to literary intellectuals? intellectual history?

8. What is "redescription"? How does the simile in paragraph 15 reflect Bellow's point of view toward "redescription"?

9. How are the sentence structure and repetition in paragraph 18 reflective of Bellow's point of view?

10. Comment on the structure of paragraph 20. How do the beginning and ending of the paragraph reflect Bellow's point of view? What is the relationship between paragraph 20 and 21?

11. What, according to Bellow, should be the role of the literary intellectual? Which literary intellectuals that you know of attempt to fulfill that role? Does Bellow? If so, how does he? Or, if not, how does he fail?

12. Study the first sentence of paragraph 27. Restate it. What is Bellow's point of view in it? How do you know? Do you think Maxwell Perkins is one of the people described in that sentence? Why or why not?

13. In the last paragraph, Bellow speaks of "a new public." Define this new public. Does Bellow believe there will be a new public such as he describes? How is his attitude consistent or inconsistent with his point of view throughout? Why is or is not this paragraph a good one with which to end the article?

14. What would Bellow think of this series of questions on his article?

Alternate selections for the study of Point of View: Robert
Benchley, "How I Create"; Henry James, "The London Theatres";
George Bernard Shaw, "Personal Animosity."

Theme Assignment: Write a theme on teen-agers—their problems, their attitudes, their behavior—from any one of a number of
points of view. You can write as a teen-ager defending your own generation or criticizing it; you can write as an atypical teen-ager—one
with a strongly rooted home and close family ties—or as a typical
teen-ager in rebellion against your parents' generation; you can write
as an adult (or near adult) with an adult's point of view on "the
younger generation"; or you can write as a potential parent, expressing
what you hope to do for, with, against your own teenage children.
Formulate a guiding purpose that will clearly reflect the point of view
you have chosen, and then write the theme.

or

If you have read *Herzog* by Saul Bellow, or if your instructor asks
you to read it, write a theme in which you discuss the relevance of
that novel to this essay. In what way or ways does Moses Herzog
typify the people described in this essay? How does what happens to
him in the novel pertain to the essay and the point of view reflected
in it?
If you have not read *Herzog,* or are not asked to read it, select a
novel, play, or poem written in the past year or two with which you
are familiar. Write a theme in which you discuss the relevance of
Bellow's essay to that novel, play, or poem. You may find that there
is no relevance: that is, that the writer does not fill the role Bellow
would have him fill. If that is so, you may describe the role which
the writer does fill and discuss whether or not that role is worthwhile.
You may approach this question from either your own point of view
or Bellow's.

Unity

The Gettysburg Address

GILBERT HIGHET

[1] *Fourscore and seven years ago* . . .

[2] These five words stand at the entrance to the best-known monument of American prose, one of the finest utterances in the entire language, and surely one of the greatest speeches in all history.
5 Greatness is like granite: it is molded in fire, and it lasts for many centuries.

[3] Fourscore and seven years ago . . . It is strange to think that President Lincoln was looking back to the 4th of July 1776, and that he and his speech are now further removed from us than he himself
10 was from George Washington and the Declaration of Independence. Fourscore and seven years before the Gettysburg Address, a small group of patriots signed the Declaration. Fourscore and seven years after the Gettysburg Address, it was the year 1950 (in November 1950 the Chinese had just entered the war in Korea), and that date
15 is already receding rapidly into our troubled, adventurous, and valiant past.

[4] Inadequately prepared and at first scarcely realized in its full importance, the dedication of the graveyard at Gettysburg was one of the supreme moments of American history. The battle itself had been

a turning point of the war. On the 4th of July 1863, General Meade 20
repelled Lee's invasion of Pennsylvania. Although he did not follow
up his victory, he had broken one of the most formidable aggressive
enterprises of the Confederate armies. Losses were heavy on both
sides. Thousands of dead were left on the field, and thousands of
wounded died in the hot days following the battle. At first, their burial 25
was more or less haphazard; but thoughtful men gradually came to
feel that an adequate burying place and memorial were required.
These were established by an interstate commission that autumn, and
the finest speaker in the North was invited to dedicate them. This
was the scholar and statesman Edward Everett of Harvard. He made 30
a good speech—which is still extant: not at all academic, it is full of
close strategic analysis and deep historical understanding.

[5] Lincoln was not invited to speak, at first. Although people
knew him as an effective debater, they were not sure whether he was
capable of making a serious speech on such a solemn occasion. But 35
one of the impressive things about Lincoln's career is that he constantly strove to *grow*. He was anxious to appear on that occasion
and to say something worthy of it. (Also, it has been suggested, he
was anxious to remove the impression that he did not know how to
behave properly—an impression which had been strengthened by a 40
shocking story about his clowning on the battlefield of Antietam the
previous year.) Therefore when he was invited he took considerable
care with his speech. He drafted rather more than half of it in the
White House before leaving, finished it in the hotel at Gettysburg
the night before the ceremony (not in the train, as sometimes re- 45
ported), and wrote out a fair copy next morning.

[6] There are many accounts of the day itself, 19 November 1863.
There are many descriptions of Lincoln, all showing the same curious
blend of grandeur and awkwardness, or lack of dignity, or—it would
be best to call it humility. In the procession he rode horseback: a tall 50
lean man in a high plug hat, straddling a short horse, with his feet
too near the ground. He arrived before the chief speaker, and had to
wait patiently for half an hour or more. His own speech came right
at the end of a long and exhausting ceremony, lasted less than three
minutes, and made little impression on the audience. In part this was 55
because they were tired, in part because (as eyewitnesses said) he
ended almost before they knew he had begun, and in part because he
did not speak the Address, but read it, very slowly, in a thin high
voice, with a marked Kentucky accent, pronouncing "to" as "toe"
and dropping his final R's. 60

[7] Some people of course were alert enough to be impressed. Everett congratulated him at once. But most of the newspapers paid little attention to the speech, and some sneered at it. The *Patriot and Union* of Harrisburg wrote, "We pass over the silly remarks of the 65 President; for the credit of the nation we are willing . . . that they shall no more be repeated or thought of"; and the London *Times* said, "The ceremony was rendered ludicrous by some of the sallies of that poor President Lincoln," calling his remarks "dull and commonplace." The first commendation of the Address came in a single 70 sentence of the Chicago *Tribune,* and the first discriminating and detailed praise of it appeared in the Springfield *Republican,* the Providence *Journal,* and the Philadelphia *Bulletin.* However, three weeks after the ceremony and then again the following spring, the editor of *Harper's Weekly* published a sincere and thorough eulogy of the 75 Address, and soon it was attaining recognition as a masterpiece.

[8] At the time, Lincoln could not care much about the reception of his words. He was exhausted and ill. In the train back to Washington, he lay down with a wet towel on his head. He had caught smallpox. At that moment he was incubating it, and he was stricken down 80 soon after he re-entered the White House. Fortunately it was a mild attack, and it evoked one of his best jokes: he told his visitors, "At last I have something I can give to everybody."

[9] He had more than that to give to everybody. He was a unique person, far greater than most people realize until they read his life 85 with care. The wisdom of his policy, the sources of his statesmanship—these were things too complex to be discussed in a brief essay. But we can say something about the Gettysburg Address as a work of art.

[10] A work of art. Yes: for Lincoln was a literary artist, trained 90 both by others and by himself. The textbooks he used as a boy were full of difficult exercises and skillful devices in formal rhetoric, stressing the qualities he practiced in his own speaking: antithesis, parallelism, and verbal harmony. Then he read and reread many admirable models of thought and expression: the King James Bible, the essays 95 of Bacon, the best plays of Shakespeare. His favorites were *Hamlet, Lear, Macbeth, Richard III,* and *Henry VIII,* which he had read dozens of times. He loved reading aloud, too, and spent hours reading poetry to his friends. (He told his partner Herndon that he preferred getting the sense of any document by reading it aloud.) There-100 fore his serious speeches are important parts of the long and noble

classical tradition of oratory which begins in Greece, runs through Rome to the modern world, and is still capable (if we do not neglect it) of producing masterpieces.

[11] The first proof of this is that the Gettysburg Address is full of quotations—or rather of adaptations—which give it strength. It is partly religious, partly (in the highest sense) political: therefore it is interwoven with memories of the Bible and memories of American history. The first and the last words are biblical cadences. Normally Lincoln did not say "fourscore" when he meant eighty; but on this solemn occasion he recalled the important dates in the Bible—such as the age of Abraham when his first son was born to him, and he was "fourscore and six years old" (Gen. 16:16; cf. Exod. 7:7). Similarly he did not say there was a chance that democracy might die out: he recalled the somber phrasing of the Book of Job—where Bildad speaks of the destruction of one who shall vanish without a trace, and says that "his branch shall be cut off; his remembrance shall perish from the earth" (Job 18:16–17; cf. Jer. 10:11, Micah 7:2). Then again, the famous description of our State as "government of the people, by the people, for the people" was abumbrated by Daniel Webster in 1830 (he spoke of "the people's government, made for the people, made by the people, and answerable to the people") and then elaborated in 1854 by the abolitionist Theodore Parker (as "government of all the people, by all the people, for all the people"). There is good reason to think that Lincoln took the important phrase "under God" (which he interpolated at the last moment) from Weems, the biographer of Washington; and we know that it had been used at least once by Washington himself.

[12] Analyzing the Address further, we find that it is based on a highly imaginative theme, or group of themes. The subject is—how can we put it so as not to disfigure it?—the subject is the kinship of life and death, that mysterious linkage which we see sometimes as the physical succession of birth and death in our world, sometimes as the contrast, which is perhaps a unity, between death and immortality. The first sentence is concerned with birth:

Our *fathers brought forth* a *new* nation, *conceived* in liberty.

The final phrase but one expresses the hope that

this nation, under God, shall have a *new birth* of freedom.

And the last phrase of all speaks of continuing life as the triumph over death. Again and again throughout the speech, this mystical contrast and kinship reappear: "those who *gave their lives* that that nation might *live*," "the brave men *living* and *dead*," and so in the

140 central assertion that the dead have already consecrated their own burial place, while "it is for us, the *living*, rather to be dedicated . . . to the great task remaining." The Gettysburg Address is a prose poem; it belongs to the same world as the great elegies, and the adagios of Beethoven.

145 [13] Its structure, however, is that of a skillfully contrived speech. The oratorical pattern is perfectly clear. Lincoln describes the occasion, dedicates the ground, and then draws a larger conclusion by calling on his hearers to dedicate themselves to the preservation of the Union. But within that, we can trace his constant use of at least

150 two important rhetorical devices.

[14] The first of these is *antithesis:* opposition, contrast. The speech is full of it. Listen:

> The world will little *note*
>   nor long *remember*   what *we say* here
> but   it can never *forget*   what *they did* here.

And so in nearly every sentence: "brave men, *living and dead*"; "to *add or detract.*" There is the antithesis of the Founding Fathers and

155 the men of Lincoln's own time:

> Our *fathers brought forth* a new nation . . .
> now *we* are testing whether that nation . . . can *long endure.*

And there is the more terrible antithesis of those who have already died and those who still live to do their duty. Now, antithesis is the figure of contrast and conflict. Lincoln was speaking in the midst of a great civil war.

160 [15] The other important pattern is different. It is technically called *tricolon*—the division of an idea into three harmonious parts, usually of increasing power. The most famous phrase of the Address is a tricolon:

>   government of the people
>   by the people
>   and   for the people.

The most solemn sentence is a tricolon:

> we cannot dedicate
> we cannot consecrate
> we cannot hallow   this ground.

And above all, the last sentence (which has sometimes been criticized 165
as too complex) is essentially two parallel phrases, with a tricolon
growing out of the second and then producing another tricolon: a
trunk, three branches, and a cluster of flowers. Lincoln says that it
is for his hearers to be dedicated to the great task remaining before
them. Then he goes on.   170

> that from these honored dead

—apparently he means "in such a way that from these honored
dead"—

> we take increased devotion to that cause.

Next, he restates this more briefly:

> that we here highly resolve . . .

And now the actual resolution follows, in three parts of growing
intensity: 175

> that these dead shall not have died in vain
> that this nation, under God, shall have a new birth of freedom

and that

> (one more tricolon)
>   government of the people
>   by the people
>   and   for the people
>   shall not perish from the earth.

Now, the tricolon is the figure which, through division, emphasizes
basic harmony and unity. Lincoln used antithesis because he was
speaking to a people at war. He used the tricolon because he was
hoping, planning, praying for peace.   180

[16] No one thinks that when he was drafting the Gettysburg Address, Lincoln deliberately looked up these quotations and conciously chose these particular patterns of thought. No, he chose the theme. From its development and from the emotional tone of the
185 entire occasion, all the rest followed, or grew—by that marvelous process of choice and rejection which is essential to artistic creation. It does not spoil such a work of art to analyze it as closely as we have done; it is altogether fitting and proper that we should do this: for it helps us to penetrate more deeply into the rich meaning of the
190 Gettysburg Address, and it allows us the very rare privilege of watching the workings of a great man's mind.

[For treatment of this selection, see pp. 55–56.]

Education by Poetry

ROBERT FROST

[1] I am going to urge nothing in my talk. I am not going to advocate. I am going to consider a matter, and commit a description. And I am going to describe other colleges than Amherst. Or, rather say all that is good can be taken as about Amherst; all that is bad will be about other colleges. 5

[2] I know whole colleges where all American poetry is barred —whole colleges. I know whole colleges where all contemporary poetry is barred.

[3] I once heard of a minister who turned his daughter—his poetry-writing daughter—out on the street to earn a living, because he 10 said there should be no more books written; God wrote one book, and that was enough. (My friend George Russell, "Æ", has read no literature, he protests, since just before Chaucer.)

[4] That all seems sufficiently safe, and you can say one thing of it. It takes the onus off the poetry of having to be used to teach chil- 15 dren anything. It comes pretty hard on poetry, I sometimes think,— what it has to bear in the teaching process.

[5] Then I know whole colleges where, though they let in older poetry, they manage to bar all that is poetical in it by treating it as

From *Selected Prose of Robert Frost* edited by Hyde Cox and Edward Connery Lathem. Copyright © 1966 by Holt, Rinehart and Winston, Inc.

20 something other than poetry. It is not so hard to do that. Their reason I have often hunted for. It may be that these people act from a
kind of modesty. Who are professors that they should attempt to deal
with a thing as high and as fine as poetry? Who are *they?* There is a
certain manly modesty in that.

25 [6] That is the best general way of settling the problem; treat all
poetry as if it were something else than poetry, as if it were syntax,
language, science. Then you can even come down into the American
and into the contemporary without any special risk.

[7] There is another reason they have, and that is that they are,
30 first and foremost in life, markers. They have the marking problem
to consider. Now, I stand here a teacher of many years' experience
and I had rather mark anyone for anything—for his looks, carriage,
his ideas, his correctness, his exactness, anything you please,—I
would rather give him a mark in terms of letters, A, B, C, D, than
35 have to use adjectives on him. We are all being marked by each other
all the time, classified, ranked, put in our place, and I see no escape
from that. I am no sentimentalist. You have got to mark, and you
have got to mark, first of all, for accuracy, for correctness. But if I
am going to give a mark, that is the least part of my marking. The
40 hard part is the part beyond that, the part where the adventure begins.

[8] One other way to rid the curriculum of the poetry nuisance
has been considered. More merciful than the others it would neither
abolish nor denature the poetry, but only turn it out to disport itself,
45 with the plays and games—in no wise discredited, though given no
credit for. Any one who liked to teach poetically could take his subject, whether English, Latin, Greek or French, out into the nowhere
along with the poetry. One side of a sharp line would be left to the
rigorous and righteous; the other side would be assigned to the
50 flowery where they would know what could be expected of them.
Grade marks were more easily given, of course, in the courses concentrating on correctness and exactness as the only forms of honesty
recognized by plain people; a general indefinite mark of *X* in the
courses that scatter brains over taste and opinion. On inquiry I have
55 found no teacher willing to take position on either side of the line,
either among the rigors or among the flowers. No one is willing to
admit that his discipline is not partly in exactness. No one is willing
to admit that his discipline is not partly in taste and enthusiasm.

[9] How shall a man go through college without having been
60 marked for taste and judgment? What will become of him? What

will his end be? He will have to take continuation courses for college graduates. He will have to go to night schools. They are having night schools now, you know, for college graduates. Why? Because they have not been educated enough to find their way around in contemporary literature. They don't know what they may safely like 65 in the libraries and galleries. They don't know how to judge an editorial when they see one. They don't know how to judge a political campaign. They don't know when they are being fooled by a metaphor, an analogy, a parable. And metaphor is, of course, what we are talking about. Education by poetry is education by metaphor. 70

[10] Suppose we stop short of imagination, initiative, enthusiasm, inspiration and originality—dread words. Suppose we don't mark in such things at all. There are still two minimal things that we have got to take care of, taste and judgment. Americans are supposed to have more judgment than taste, but taste is there to be dealt 75 with. That is what poetry, the only art in the colleges of arts, is there for. I for my part would not be afraid to go in for enthusiasm. There is the enthusiasm like a blinding light, or the enthusiasm of the deafening shout, the crude enthusiasm that you get uneducated by poetry, outside of poetry. It is exemplified in what I might call "sun- 80 set raving." You look westward toward the sunset, or if you get up early enough, eastward toward the sunrise, and you rave. It is oh's and ah's with you and no more.

[11] But the enthusiasm I mean is taken through the prism of the intellect and spread on the screen in a color, all the way from hy- 85 perbole at one end—or overstatement, at one end—to understatement at the other end. It is a long strip of dark lines and many colors. Such enthusiasm is one object of all teaching in poetry. I heard wonderful things said about Virgil yesterday, and many of them seemed to me crude enthusiasm, more like a deafening shout, many of them. 90 But one speech had range, something of overstatement, something of statement, and something of understatement. It had all the colors of an enthusiasm passed through an idea.

[12] I would be willing to throw away everything else but that: enthusiasm tamed by metaphor. Let me rest the case there. En- 95 thusiasm tamed to metaphor, tamed to that much of it. I do not think anybody ever knows the discreet use of metaphor, his own and other people's, the discreet handling of metaphor, unless he has been properly educated in poetry.

[13] Poetry begins in trivial metaphors, pretty metaphors, "grace" 100 metaphors, and goes on to the profoundest thinking that we have.

Poetry provides the one permissible way of saying one thing and meaning another. People say, "Why don't you say what you mean?" We never do that, do we, being all of us too much poets. We like to talk in parables and in hints and in indirections—whether from diffidence or some other instinct.

[14] I have wanted in late years to go further and further in making metaphor the whole of thinking. I find some one now and then to agree with me that all thinking, except mathematical thinking, is metaphorical, or all thinking except scientific thinking. The mathematical might be difficult for me to bring in, but the scientific is easy enough.

[15] Once on a time all the Greeks were busy telling each other what the All was—or was like unto. All was three elements, air, earth, and water (we once thought it was ninety elements; now we think it is only one). All was substance, said another. All was change, said a third. But best and most fruitful was Pythagoras' comparison of the universe with number. Number of what? Number of feet, pounds, and seconds was the answer, and we had science and all that has followed in science. The metaphor has held and held, breaking down only when it came to the spiritual and psychological or the out of the way places of the physical.

[16] The other day we had a visitor here, a noted scientist, whose latest word to the world has been that the more accurately you know where a thing is, the less accurately you are able to state how fast it is moving. You can see why that would be so, without going back to Zeno's problem of the arrow's flight. In carrying numbers into the realm of space and at the same time into the realm of time you are mixing metaphors, that is all, and you are in trouble. They won't mix. The two don't go together.

[17] Let's take two or three more of the metaphors now in use to live by. I have just spoken of one of the new ones, a charming mixed metaphor right in the realm of higher mathematics and higher physics: that the more accurately you state where a thing is, the less accurately you will be able to tell how fast it is moving. And, of course, everything is moving. Everything is an event now. Another metaphor. A thing, they say, is an event. Do you believe it is? Not quite. I believe it is almost an event. But I like the comparison of a thing with an event.

[18] I notice another from the same quarter. "In the neighborhood of matter space is something like curved." Isn't that a good one! It seems to me that that is simply and utterly charming—to

you do not have to write it up to make it poetry; it is ready-made
for you. But, I don't know—the poetry written in that city might not
seem like poetry if read outside the city. It would be like the jokes
made when you were drunk; you have to get drunk again to appreciate them.)   310

[48] But as I say, there is another way to come close to poetry,
fortunately, and that is in the reading of it, not as linguistics, not as
history, not as anything but poetry. It is one of the hard things for a
teacher to know how close a man has come in reading poetry. How
do I know whether a man has come close to Keats in reading Keats? 315
It is hard for me to know. I have lived with some boys a whole year
over some of the poets and I have not felt sure whether they have
come near what it was all about. One remark sometimes told me.
One remark was their mark for the year; had to be—it was all I got
that told me what I wanted to know. And that is enough, if it was the 320
right remark, if it came close enough. I think a man might make
twenty fool remarks if he made one good one some time in the year.
His mark would depend on that good remark.

[49] The closeness—everything depends on the closeness with
which you come, and you ought to be marked for the closeness, for 325
nothing else. And that will have to be estimated by chance remarks,
not by question and answer. It is only by accident that you know
some day how near a person has come.

[50] The person who gets close enough to poetry, he is going to
know more about the word *belief* than anybody else knows, even in 330
religion nowadays. There are two or three places where we know belief outside of religion. One of them is at the age of fifteen to twenty,
in our self-belief. A young man knows more about himself than he is
able to prove to anyone. He has no knowledge that anybody else will
accept as knowledge. In his foreknowledge he has something that is 335
going to believe itself into fulfilment, into acceptance.

[51] There is another belief like that, the belief in someone else, a
relationship of two that is going to be believed into fulfilment. That is
what we are talking about in our novels, the belief of love. And the
disillusionment that the novels are full of is simply the disillusionment 340
from disappointment in that belief. That belief can fail, of course.

[52] Then there is a literary belief. Every time a poem is written,
every time a short story is written, it is written not by cunning, but
by belief. The beauty, the something, the little charm of the thing to
be is more felt than known. There is a common jest, one that always 345
annoys me, on the writers, that they write the last end first, and then

work up to it; that they lay a train toward one sentence that they think is pretty nice and have all fixed up to set like a trap to close with. No, it should not be that way at all. No one who has ever come
350 close to the arts has failed to see the difference between things written that way, with cunning and device, and the kind that are believed into existence, that begin in something more felt than known. This you can realize quite as well—not quite as well, perhaps, but nearly as well—in reading as you can in writing. I would undertake to
355 separate short stories on that principle; stories that have been believed into existence and stories that have been cunningly devised. And I could separate the poems still more easily.

[53] Now I think—I happen to think—that those three beliefs that I speak of, the self-belief, the love-belief, and the art-belief, are
360 all closely related to the God-belief, that the belief in God is a relationship you enter into with Him to bring about the future.

[54] There is a national belief like that, too. One feels it. I have been where I came near getting up and walking out on the people who thought that they had to talk against nations, against national-
365 ism, in order to curry favor with internationalism. Their metaphors are all mixed up. They think that because a Frenchman and an American and an Englishman can all sit down on the same platform and receive honors together, it must be that there is no such thing as nations. That kind of bad thinking springs from a source we all know.
370 I should want to say to anyone like that: "Look! First I want to be a person. And I want you to be a person, and then we can be as interpersonal as you please. We can pull each other's noses—do all sorts of things. But, first of all, you have got to have the personality. First of all, you have got to have the nations and then they can be as in-
375 ternational as they please with each other."

[55] I should like to use another metaphor on them. I want my palette, if I am a painter, I want my palette on my thumb or on my chair, all clean, pure, separate colors. Then I will do the mixing on the canvas. The canvas is where the work of art is, where we make
380 the conquest. But we want the nations all separate, pure, distinct, things as separate as we can make them; and then in our thoughts, in our arts, and so on, we can do what we please about it.

[56] But I go back. There are four beliefs that I know more about from having lived with poetry. One is the personal belief,
385 which is a knowledge that you don't want to tell other people about because you cannot prove that you know. You are saying nothing about it till you see. The love belief, just the same, has that same

shyness. It knows it cannot tell; only the outcome can tell. And the national belief we enter into socially with each other, all together, party of the first part, party of the second part, we enter into that to bring the future of the country. We cannot tell some people what it is we believe, partly, because they are too stupid to understand and partly because we are too proudly vague to explain. And anyway it has got to be fulfilled, and we are not talking until we know more, until we have something to show. And then the literary one in every work of art, not of cunning and craft, mind you, but of real art; that believing the thing into existence, saying as you go more than you even hoped you were going to be able to say, and coming with surprise to an end that you foreknew only with some sort of emotion. And then finally the relationship we enter into with God to believe the future in—to believe the hereafter in. 390 395 400

When we say that a piece of writing is unified or that a writer has achieved unity in his work, we do not, of course, mean that the writing says only one thing over and over again. We do mean that all the elements that make up the writing work harmoniously toward the single end of achieving the writer's purpose. Each idea in a piece of writing, each example or illustration or detail, each description or exchange of dialogue must be integral to the whole and must make its contribution to the total meaning. Practically all the elements of writing treated in this book have a part, in one way or another, in achieving unity. If ideas are not placed in proper order, if point of view and tone are not consistent, if less important elements are not subordinated to more important elements, if relations among ideas are not made clear, if irrelevant materials are included, unity is bound to be adversely affected.

Unity in writing, as in all the arts, results, not in monotony, but in harmony. The painter does not achieve unity by using a single color or a single shape: his colors, his shapes, his lines, his masses all work together to produce a unity of effect which is a major source of the viewer's pleasure. Similarly, the composer does not achieve unity by using a single note or even necessarily by writing in a single key or tempo; the unity of his work, like that of painting and writing, comes from the integration of all the elements of which his music is comprised. The Highet and Frost selections provide an opportunity for seeing how diverse elements can be welded into a unified whole.

1. Give in one sentence the guiding purpose of the Gilbert Highet essay. Where in the selection does the author most directly state his guiding purpose? Why do you think he chose to place his statement

where he did? Compare Highet's positioning of his guiding purpose with Frost's. How do you account for the difference?

2. In the first paragraph, Highet says "greatness is like granite: it is molded in fire, and it lasts for many centuries." Show how the author has demonstrated each of the two parts of this simile throughout the selection. What does your answer suggest to you about the unity of the essay?

3. Do you think that paragraphs 2 and 3, in which the author presents historical background about the battle of Gettysburg, violate the unity of the piece? Justify your answer.

4. How has Highet made Lincoln's reported "clowning" at Antietam relevant to his guiding purpose?

5. What is the function of paragraph 5?

6. What purpose is served by mentioning the negative intial reactions to the speech?

7. Lincoln's attack of smallpox seems at first glance to have nothing to do with the greatness of the Gettysburg Address, yet the first sentence of paragraph 8 justifies Highet's mention of the attack. Explain.

8. If, as Highet says in paragraph 8, the "wisdom of . . . [Lincoln's] policy, the sources of his statesmanship" are "too complex to be discussed in a brief essay," why does he mention them? Is he cluttering up his essay with two major purposes? If you think not, show how the two dovetail and present your evidence to prove that one theme is subordinated to the other.

9. Highet mentions three oratorical devices which Lincoln studied: antithesis, parallelism, and verbal harmony. But before discussing them, he spends the rest of paragraph 9 on the classical tradition of oratory and paragraphs 10, 11, and 12 on presenting his evidence that the Gettysburg Address is part of that tradition. Explain why this seeming digression is or is not a violation of unity.

10. What structural outline does the remainder of the selection follow?

11. What contribution does the ending make to the unity of the whole selection?

12. In the first paragraph of "Education by Poetry," Robert Frost says he is going to "consider a matter, and commit a description." He also tells the reader what he is *not* going to do: he is not going to urge anything. What matter does he consider; what description does he "commit"? Does he, indeed, "urge nothing"? Having answered these questions, and thought about the whole selection, explain why you do or do not consider this first paragraph relevant to his purpose and effective.

13. Describe as accurately as possible the tone Frost uses in para-

graphs 2 through 8. How does he achieve that tone? Explain its appropriateness to his guiding purpose.

14. Is the subject of marking a violation of unity? Why or why not?

15. Paragraph 9 warrants close study. Justify the heavy use of rhetorical devices in the paragraph: of questions, repetition, sameness of sentence structure. What is the function of the paragraph?

16. If the title of the selection is truly descriptive—if this is an essay about education by poetry—why does Frost devote so much of the essay to a discussion of metaphor? Select three of the subjects he considers to be metaphors and explain in your own words how they are or are not metaphoric. Based on your explanations, justify the inclusion of the description of these subjects in the selection.

17. What contribution to the total meaning does the dialogue in paragraphs 24 through 34 make?

18. Throughout the selection, Frost himself uses metaphors. He speaks, for example, of "the prism of the intellect" (paragraph 11) "a gathering metaphor" (paragraph 38); he says, "I want my palette on my thumb . . . all clean, pure, separate colors" (paragraph 55). Select five of his own metaphors and explain, in Frost's words, why they do or do not "break down": are they apt? Why or why not? What does each contribute to unity? to Frost's tone? to his guiding purpose?

19. What are the four beliefs of which Frost speaks? Why is it appropriate to speak of them? to end with them?

Alternate selections for the study of Unity: E. M. Forster, from "The Ivory Tower"; Theodore Dreiser, from *A Book about Myself;* Lewis Mumford, "The Case against Modern Architecture."

Theme Assignment: Select one of the following ideas which Frost propounds:

1. A student should be marked on his taste and judgment. Often one remark he makes during the semester can and should determine his grade in the course.

2. Education by poetry is education by metaphor.

3. All knowledge is metaphor. (Or select one branch of knowledge.)

4. Poetry is enthusiasm tamed by metaphor. Write a theme in which you (a) explain what Frost means and (b) agree or disagree with him in some detail. Your problem will be to keep your theme from breaking in two: to keep it unified.

or

"The old and the new" is a subject of endless fascination for all of us, and it appears as a theme everywhere from family debates to the choruses of Greek tragedies. While the debates which take place usually give voice to extreme positions, seemingly opposed, there are often many points of similarity between old and new.

Write a theme in which you compare and contrast old and new in one specific area. You must, first of all, carefully delineate and limit that area in your guiding purpose. For example, you may select the general store and the supermarket, the old and the new "woman's place," the English Tudor house and the split-level ranch. You will then have to determine your organization; it would be possible, for example, to explore the *old* fully before describing the *new,* to describe the new and then the old, to mention all points of dissimilarity and then all points of similarity between old and new, or to maintain throughout your theme a continuing point-for-point comparison between the two. The method of organization should be determined by your ultimate purpose and point of view. Your major writing problem will be one of unity—the merging, in this particular theme, of seemingly disparate elements into a whole. For the solution of this problem, the importance of a clearly defined and carefully limited guiding purpose, explicitly stating your point of view, cannot be overemphasized.

Ordering
of Ideas

Do We Go to the Theatre for Illusion?   TYRONE GUTHRIE

[1] Most of the new theaters in North America with any serious policy have been built with an open stage. Stratford, Canada; the Arena in Washington, D.C.; the Alley in Houston; the Tyrone Guthrie in Minneapolis; the Vivian Beaumont in the Lincoln Center, and the new theater being built at Ithaca, N.Y., all have "open" or 5 "thrust" stages. That is to say, the stage sticks out into the auditorium, so that the audience partly surrounds the actors.

[2] No more than 20 years ago it would have been taken for granted that a new theater would be built on the lines almost universally accepted since the middle of the 17th century: a horse-shoe 10 shaped auditorium facing, not surrounding, a stage; and a stage divided from the auditorium by a proscenium arch. This arch is, in effect, a frame which encloses the stage picture; indeed, in many theaters it is decorated like a picture frame with gilt moulding. Just inside the proscenium arch hangs a curtain, behind which scenery 15 and stage effects can be prepared unseen and, in theory, unheard by

From *The New York Times,* January 16, 1966. © 1966 by The New York Times Company. Reprinted by permission of *The New York Times* and Tyrone Guthrie.

the audience. Then, when all is ready, up goes the curtain and . . .
Lo and Behold!

[3] Theaters were not always built on this plan. In Elizabethan
20 England, the audience sat almost completely around the stage, which
jutted out into the auditorium. Shakespeare's plays were written for
such a stage; and it was primarily to grapple with the great difficulties inherent in producing Shakespeare on a proscenium stage that
the Festival Theater at Stratford, Ontario, a landmark in theatrical
25 design, was planned in 1952.

[4] But the open stage goes back far further into history than
Shakespeare's time. The classic theaters of Greece and Rome had
open stages and the Elizabethan theater was an evolution from the
Greek, involving only minor changes of plan. About 1650, this sort
30 of theater went out of favor and theaters with proscenium arches
came in, for two reasons—one practical, one theoretical.

[5] The practical reason was the vogue, which spread from Italy
all over Europe, for musical works, or opera. In opera, it is desirable
that the singers see their conductor. He stands in the orchestra, fac-
35 ing the stage; they face the audience and at the same time face the
conductor and so "get the beat." It follows that the audience should
be arranged facing the stage, watching the faces of singers, actors or
dancers, and the back of the conductor. When theaters began to be
built in conformity with the conventions of Italian opera, not only
40 did the audience and actors now face one another but a great gulf
was fixed between them. In this gulf, or pit, sat the orchestra grouped
around its conductor.

[6] This was only partly a matter of convenience. It also marked
the social chasm, which separated a predominantly courtly and aristo-
45 cratic audience from the socially inferior persons who were paid to
entertain it. The separation was reinforced by yet another barrier,
practical and symbolic—of fire, or footlights. From the 17th century
until the installation of electric light in the 1880's, these footlights,
naked flames, were a perpetual source of danger. Fires, followed by
50 panic, were not uncommon and there came into force everywhere a
whole budget of precautionary regulations, including yet another barrier, the iron curtain, now a world-famous symbol of political separation.

[7] With the whole stage picture firmly isolated from the audi-
55 ence, and set against a painted and obviously artificial background;
with the grouping and utterance of the performers stylized to the

requirements of opera, an immense emphasis was thrown onto artifice.

[8] But meantime another tendency was at work. Acting, writing and production were all aiming to be a closer imitation of real life. Thus a paradoxical situation was created: the theater was trying, with more and more artifice, to be more and more natural.

[9] Realism has for more than 300 years been the dominant aim of theatrical productions in Europe and America. Yet it can readily be seen that this aim cannot be very thoroughly or consistently achieved. It is hard to get very near to realism in exterior scenes. These are, at best, a rather uneasy mixture of three-dimensional elements (imitation rocks, tree trunks, house fronts) with representational painting. But you can, it is true, within a proscenium arch achieve a very plausible imitation of a domestic interior. Such a scene, however, has one or two markedly unreal features: one side of it has no wall, and a thousand or more people are looking in. Also the sunshine of this unreal real scene comes not from a real sun but from a number of powerful lamps.

[10] Similarly, realistic acting can only be realistic within limits; even secrets must be spoken loud enough to be heard by all those people out there in the dark. Every significant action must be sufficiently emphatic for them all to see. Even a quick glance must register. The script of a realistic play must eliminate most of the dull, irrelevant remarks of which real conversation mostly consists, and must stick with quite unrealistic logic to the matter in hand. In brief, even the most realistic productions of the most realistic plays are not fully realistic. They are an elaborate exercise in style, in the selection and emphasis of certain elements of real life, the suppression of others and the precisely realistic imitation of only a very few.

[11] For about 50 years now the view has been gaining currency that Shakespeare's plays can best be produced in a theater which at least approximates the kind for which his plays were written—that is to say, for an auditorium arranged not *in front of* the stage, but, to a greater or less extent, wrapped *around* the stage. Usually, when the audience completely surrounds it, the stage is called Arena, and the performance is called Theater-in-the-Round. When the auditorium only partly surrounds it, the stage is called a Thrust or an Open Stage.

[12] Few people would deny the logic of producing Shakespeare on such a stage. There is, however, a good deal of doubt as to its

adaptability to a varied repertory since the proscenium enables more elaborate scenic and lighting effects to be achieved; it is capable of creating a greater degree of illusion. Arguably, however, scenic elabo-
100 ration is not a desirable end in the sort of drama where the text demands concentrated attention. As to illusion, the matter will be discussed later in this piece. Whatever may be the drawbacks of the open stage, it has, I think, three very solid advantages over the proscenium.

105 [13] The first is artistic: it is a fact that by gathering the audience *around* rather than spreading it *in front* of the actors, many more people can be close to the actors. Between 1,500 and 2,000 people can be seated around an open stage, none of them more than 50 feet from the stage, and no seat father than 15 rows from the front. A
110 proscenium house of equal intimacy could seat barely half that number.

[14] Therefore the relation between actor and audience can, with an open stage, be far more intimate. Furthermore, intimacy can be combined with a rather large total number of spectators. This is im-
115 portant. Shakespeare, Greek or French tragedy, Goethe's "Faust" or Ibsen's "Peer Gynt," in fact almost all the big shots of the classical repertory demand the warmth and excitement which only a large audience can generate.

[15] I must, in honesty, admit that an open stage poses acoustical
120 problems. All the actors for part of the time have their backs turned to one side or other of the house. When an actor's face cannot be seen, it is inevitably harder to hear what he is saying. The solution of this problem lies partly in the skill with which an actor can turn; so that, without seeming to fidget, his face is never turned away
125 more than momentarily from any one part of the audience; partly in the skill with which the face of a listening actor reflects what his colleague is saying; but chiefly in the vocal technique of the speaking.

[16] The open stage does make great demand upon the actor's accomplishment, but no greater than is required for an actor to be
130 heard in a large proscenium theater without sounding noisy and false. The good actor is largely distinguishable from the less good by being totally audible, whether on an open stage or within a proscenium, without ranting, seeming in fact, to speak "naturally."

[17] The second advantage of the open stage is economic and also
135 relates to the fact that arranging the audience *around* the actors is a more economic use of the cubic space of the auditorium: larger capacity makes possible large takings. For instance, the Festival

Theater at Stratford accommodates over two thousand people. Receipts, therefore, from a full house, at prices very much lower than those which prevail on Broadway, still exceed those of any Broad- 140
way house of comparable intimacy.

[18] The third advantage is philosophic and may seem to some people to be no advantage but a drawback. People sitting around an open stage cannot but be aware of other people doing likewise on the opposite side of the house. Behind and beyond the lighted 145
stage you can descry, albeit dimly, other members of the audience. If you allow your attention to wander, you may even recognize them: between Hamlet and Horatio—no . . . yes, I thought so . . . the McKinstrys—and just to the left of Queen Gertrude's left ear, little Miss Gimpel who keeps the corner store. 150

[19] But this is only if you let your attention wander. And even in a proscenium house, if you let your attention wander, you'll get some pretty irrelevant and incongruous impressions.

[20] But, you may say, even if I don't actually identify the Mc-Kinstrys or Miss Gimpel, the mere fact of *people* in the background, 155
spectators all around the castle of Elsinore, or wherever it may be, is destructive of illusion. Granted. But do we really go to the theater in search of illusion, in order to be convinced that a palpable fiction is reality?

[21] I think not. After the mental age of about 8, we are no longer 160
"taken in" by the theater. We no longer believe that the undoubtedly female personage slung on an easily perceptible wire is a boy called Peter Pan. We know perfectly well that it is a splendid little lady called Mary Martin, who is highly paid to *pretend* to be Peter Pan and to *pretend* to fly. 165

[22] Does this knowledge detract from our pleasure? Surely not; it enhances it. Why else do we read the program; and why else have we taken some trouble to see Mary Martin doing Peter Pan rather than some other equally nice, but totally unknown little lady? Surely, therefore, our pleasure in the theater is occasioned by something 170
other than illusion.

[23] It is true, of course, that a play can be so absorbing that you are temporarily quite lost to reality. You are, as it were, rapt, spellbound. But the very same thing can happen when you are reading a novel. Is this illusion? I think not. Has it not often been your ex- 175
perience, when reading a book, to be thus rapt? But does it therefore

follow that you are apt to mistake figment for reality? Does the rapt beholder of Leonardo's "Virgin of the Rocks" think that he is really in the presence of those holy beings, that he is really in that golden 180 and brown landscape? When great music conjures, as they say, the soul out of your body, is there any question of illusion? You probably lose for a while all sense of time and place, but you do not suppose things to be really taking place, which are not, in fact, taking place.

185 [24] Likewise, in the theater you may be rapt, rendered unaware of your immediate surroundings. But there is no illusion. You know perfectly well that you are at a play, that the events are fictitious, the characters mere players and you just your same old self, who has been for a short time, like Bottom, translated.

190 [25] The method of transport is Ritual. A play is a ritual re-enactment of events arranged to form an intelligible and significant pattern. This pattern is re-created, in predetermined, ritual form, by the actors for the audience every time a performance is given.

[26] The appreciation of Ritual is greatly enhanced if you are 195 aware of its performance as a social act, aware of being one of many who are "assisting" at the performance, as the French so accurately describe the function of an audience.

[27] This social, shared aspect of performance is emphasized if you are aware, though not too much aware, of your fellow members 200 in the audience. To my mind, the members of an audience dimly seen beyond a brightly lighted open stage suggest this sociable idea with just the right emphasis. You are constantly, but not in the least insistently, reminded that one and all are sharing the same occasion, taking part in the same rites.

205 [28] I can understand that there are those who want to believe that theatergoing is just fun, and that it is fun to be again a child of 8, childishly thrilled by the make-believe, childishly surrendering to the illusion. For such people, the open stage will tend to be less satisfactory than the proscenium. Those who take the theater more 210 seriously will, I believe, prefer open-stage presentation.

[29] Let me say again: I do not think that the open stage should, or will, replace the proscenium. The latter is more suitable for many kinds of entertainment; but not for any and every kind. It is not, and will not become, a substitute for the proscenium. It is a valuable, and 215 in some instances, indispensable alternative.

[For treatment of this selection, see p. 71.]

✐ Climates of Criticism

MOSES HADAS

[1] Unless a craftsman is both rich and obsessed he must make his work acceptable to a public. If his products are in the nature of tools or instruments, any experienced user and any fellow-craftsman can judge their effectiveness and hence their acceptability. If they are not instruments but themselves final ends to be consumed, like 5 food or music, the element of taste enters in. Taste is variable and subjective, and therefore susceptible to refinement or debasement. Here the ordinary consumer, or even producer, is not necessarily the best judge. A man who cannot himself cook a meal or write a poem may be a better critic of such matters than cooks or poets. 10 The further artifacts are removed from the elementary needs of physical survival, the greater the scope for informed judgment. When we call the exercise of informed judgment by its Greek name "criticism," we recognize its claim to be an independent and specialized activity with a particular function—to safeguard quality and to purify 15 taste.

[2] The history of criticism is almost as old as the history of the arts it serves, and it has proven a salutary adjunct to cultural productivity in all categories and at all levels. Because it is rooted in tradition and uses the choicest experience of the past as its gauge, 20 it may tend, in the hands of dull practitioners, to propagate conservatism. But imaginative critics encourage innovation, provided it exhibits quality and taste; the object of their vigilance is not nonconformity but the dishonest and the tawdry and the lunatic.

[3] Where a product is exotic or revolutionary and addressed to a 25 limited and homogeneous audience of sophisticates, criticism interposes a useful barrier against these qualities but affects the general level of taste only indirectly. But where the product is of a traditional kind and its audience large and heterogeneous, criticism becomes an essential safeguard. Inside the laboratory a pinch of a questionable 30

substance is enough to establish its character; outside, mass itself is an important factor in determining effects. The audience of a televised play of Sophocles or Shakespeare or Shaw is greater than the aggregate of all its previous audiences; microscopic deviations, up-
35 ward or downward, are multiplied a millionfold, and the effect on the total direction of quality and taste is therefore substantial.

[4] The television audience is not only unprecedentedly large; it is also heterogeneous and it includes many novices. People do not go to theater or concert or art exhibitions and do not buy a book with-
40 out some antecedent knowledge of the genre and therefore some basis for judgment. But to look at a television screen requires no effort or expense or even social pressure, and some who do so may have little antecedent experience to inform judgment. The larger and more indiscriminate the audience, the greater the need to safeguard
45 and purify standards of quality and taste.

[5] That so potent a medium of communication can profitably be served by criticism is therefore a truism. But what should the scope of television criticism be? Who should exercise it? How can it be made effective? Experience in other areas, to which we normally turn
50 for answers to such problems, cannot supply a complete model because the challenge is unexampled; but it can at least clarify the issues and perhaps help us formulate a solution. Among contemporary cultural activities, those in which quality and taste are most decisively affected by criticism are drama and literature. Drama is closer to
55 television because it is presented orally and involves spectacle; but dramatic criticism, as we shall see, is too restricted to serve as a pattern. Literature offers a more fruitful analogy: its range is wide and the responses—which the challenge posed by the invention of printing evoked—may suggest appropriate responses to closely simi-
60 lar challenges posed by the invention of television. We shall look first at literary criticism, therefore, and notice how it was transformed upon the invention of printing.

[6] From Aristotle onward and well into the Humanist age criticism was mainly a philological study. It began by analyzing estab-
65 lished classics in order to demonstrate desirable or faulty techniques and effects, and proceeded, like its modern counterpart, to the enucleation of hitherto unobserved devices and significances. Occasionally, as in Horace's *Art of Poetry,* it centered on aesthetic taste. More often it judged books for their educational usefulness—in
70 forming character, for example, as in Plato; or in training eloquent

and resourceful lawyers, as in Quintilian. Such criticism was addressed mainly to cognoscenti with an avowed interest in books, but it served to influence a general climate of quality and purpose. In classicizing periods, as in late antiquity or the Humanist age, the dicta of recognized critics acquired almost canonical prestige, and sometimes hampered rather than promoted creativity.

[7] Acceptance or rejection of criticism proffered by individuals remained a private matter, however, for there was between producer and consumer no third agent interested in securing conformity to a prescribed standard. The influence of such middlemen as there were was negligible, for hand-written editions were, perforce, small and there was no copyright to protect investment. An artist might then alter a line in a poem or painting or musical composition in deference to a critical dictum, or he might stand by his independent creation and await more intelligent or favorable criticism. No profit and loss for himself or his publisher was at stake.

[8] By multiplying audiences manyfold printing also enhanced the importance of the middleman, for publishing involves large investment and elaborate organization. Even when a publication was sponsored by a wealthy patron (as is still the case with learned books and with television programs), the conscientious middleman had to assure himself that the product would be acceptable. Reputable publishers, out of a sense of public responsibility, themselves sponsor exceptional works which are sure to lose money—in effect, as a sort of sustaining program. But the area of publishing which gave rise to the kind of criticism which is our present concern is that of so-called trade books, which depend for their success on their acceptance by large numbers of men in the street.

[9] We can see the transition to modern usage in the decades following the invention of printing. Some of the earlier Humanists deplored the innovation as opening the gates to vulgarization and insisted on using only manuscript books; we can see now that their posture was as misguided and essentially anti-Humanist as is that of their latter-day analogues who deplore the advent of television. The maturer Humanists, whose principal concern was the dignity of man, welcomed easy multiplication of the means of culture as promoting general enlightenment. It is interesting to observe that a privilege granted Aldus Manutius by Pope Leo X stipulated that his admirable editions must be low in price.

[10] Manutius and other pioneers employed and heeded the very best critical talents available to ensure that their products should be,

as they are, as good as possible. But with the proliferation of books and readers, independent critics, like the redoubtable Scaliger, took it upon themselves to shape a climate of critical opinion which it was
115 prudent for the middleman to heed. In course of time, audiences have increased in size and in independence, with concomitant increase in the power of the critic. Before he risks his investment, the middleman seeks expert advice on the probable reaction of critics and hence of purchasers. The author himself may be persuaded to
120 design or alter his product to promote a favorable critical reaction. Normally (though striking exceptions are easy to cite) a book damned by critics will fail, and one praised will have a chance of success.

[11] Here a distinction must be drawn between the specialist kind
125 of criticism which is cultivated for its own sake and which may be highly subjective and esoteric, and the kind which affects circulation figures. The critic whose work means success or failure for a book speaks not so much for himself as for the prevailing critical climate. This is not to imply that he is a cipher or a hack; if he is competent
130 and honest, as he normally is, he does serve to safeguard quality and taste. The critical climate which he articulates will affect many persons who never see his words. He himself knows well enough that critical climate is subject to change. Another generation may discover merits in a book which contemporaries overlooked or which only an
135 esoteric minority appreciated. Acclaim of a later work may call attention to an author's undeservedly neglected early work. A book once printed, in short, may manage to survive hostile criticism.

[12] In drama, by contrast, the power of the critic is nearly absolute. Original plays are produced only in the metropolis, and at-
140 tendance at theater is expensive. Virtually the whole of the play-going public knows and heeds the judgment of the handful of reputable critics. In consequence only plays commended by critics can have a successful run; those damned shut down. What gives the critic of drama his power, and what makes his task different from the super-
145 ficially similar task of the television critic, is the fact that the play he discusses is expected to be repeated night after night for a period of months, and it can be repeated only if spectators have been sufficiently convinced of its merit to pay the high cost of admission.

[13] The television critic has no such power, for it is not expected
150 that the production he discusses will be repeated. Furthermore— possibly because productions are seldom repeated or possibly because

the spectator spends no money—the proportion of the total audience which reads television criticism is negligible in comparison to the proportion that reads drama criticism. That is why so few organs publish television criticism (though the little that appears is often very good), and why there is nothing like so tangible a critical climate in television as there is in literature. Desirable as criticism of television may be, therefore, it seems that there are no adequate channels to make it effective.

[14] But we must avoid the mistake of generals who prepare for a past war. Television is revolutionary, and the problems it imposes upon the critic are different from those which confront the critic of drama. The premises of television are that its audience is almost coextensive with the population, that its subject matter embraces almost the entire spectrum of human interest, and that box-office receipts are not in question. Because he is not directly determining profit and loss, because he is contemplating a range of subject matter almost unlimited in scope and has regard to an audience almost as large and varied, the critic of television is in effect dealing with universals and hence he must cultivate the philosophical approach. To have validity, universals must, of course, be solidly grounded in particulars, and our critic must obviously be expert in various relevant techniques; but these are ancillary to his larger aims. The larger aims are, in a word, educational. And education in its fullest sense, not schooling alone, is the single most important enterprise of civilized society.

[15] A truer analogy than drama, therefore, is literature, which has traditionally held the general educational mandate television has now come to share. In literature, too, the scope is vast, the audience coextensive with literacy, and the benefits need not involve cash expenditure. In literature, as we have observed, there is a tangible critical climate, guided and made articulate by professional critics, perhaps, but shaped by all who take books seriously and write and talk about them. The critical climate, in turn, determines what books are made available; no writer who wishes to be heard and no sane publisher will fly in the face of it. A similar critical climate must be created for television; all who take education seriously in its larger sense—and not the professed critics alone—should talk and write about television as they do about books. Nor would any television producer ignore TV's climate of criticism if it were as tangible as in the field of books. He is not, as determined romantics main-

tain, a conscious party to a conspiracy against integrity and taste, but rather like a rich old lady who grows headstrong in her caprice be-cause no one ventures to cross her. And although the producer—if
195 not his audience—is ultimately dependent upon financial considera-tions, he has freedom to venture beyond the traditionally profitable.

[16] So lofty a program does not imply that the critic must banish from the screen anything which is not suitable for discussion in a Great Books study group. In the world of books, too, there are many
200 that do not aspire to that high dignity, but are meant to fill an idle hour agreeably. Such books, and such television programs, have their legitimate place, and only a prig says "a mere picaresque novel" or "a mere Western." Actually, heightened critical awareness has pro-duced marked improvement even in books designed for filling an
205 idle hour, and heightened critical awareness can improve analogous television offerings also.

[17] Neither hammock reading at one end of the publishing spectrum nor technical and learned works at the other is the principal concern of literary criticism (though it ultimately affects these also),
210 but the solid mass in between, which is addressed to the normally intelligent and curious layman, and so it should be with television criticism. Society has long recognized the essentially educational function of the printed word, and those responsible for making books available acknowledge the usefulness of the critical function
215 in safeguarding standards painfully achieved and in encouraging honest innovation. The essentially educational function of television, which is as effective as print in compassing some of the goals of edu-cation, has not yet been so universally recognized. An intelligent climate of criticism will first convince society, as the open-eyed Hu-
220 manists convinced their traditionalist brethren, that a new means of human enlightenment has come into the world, and then ensure, as its Humanist avatars began to do, that the new means realize its potentialities most effectively.

The skillful writer, keenly aware of the various relationships among the ideas about which he is going to write, must establish the order in which he is going to deal with the ideas. Logic, of course, may deter-mine order. Premises may have to be dealt with before conclusions can be drawn. Certain facts may have to be explained before other facts can be made meaningful. Or the writer's material may lend itself to chronological order; explaining how to change a tire, for example, might best be done chronologically. Moving from less important material to more important material or from easier to more difficult material or from left to right or front to back (in describing a room, for example) or from less controversial to more controversial or from simple to complex are all commonly used means of ordering materials. An adequately formulated guiding purpose plays a major role in determining the order of ideas.

1. Indicate at least five additional orders which may be imposed on ideas.

2. Formulate Guthrie's guiding purpose.

3. Is the title of the article a clue to the relative weight of the major ideas in the article? Why or why not?

4. In the light of your answer to question 3, evaluate your formulation of Guthrie's guiding purpose and, if necessary, reformulate the guiding purpose.

5. The article can be roughly divided into three parts: the first deals with the proscenium or "picture frame" stage; the second with the open or arena stage; and the last with the audience's response in the theater. Exactly how is the last part related to the first two? Where in the essay do you find this relationship most explicitly expressed?

6. Indicate at least two other orders which Guthrie might have chosen for his three sections.

7. By discussing the alternative orders, indicate in some detail why you think Guthrie's order is or is not the best for his purpose.

8. On the basis of what criteria do you think Guthrie established his order?

9. Justify the order in which Guthrie chose to discuss the "three very solid advantages [which the open stage has] over the proscenium" (paragraph 12).

10. Professor Hadas' article is a compressed and closely reasoned piece of writing in which the order of ideas is particularly important. Summarize the major ideas contained in the first section of the essay (paragraphs 1 through 5). What considerations do you think made Hadas decide to open the section with the material in paragraph 1? What would have been gained or lost had this material been put elsewhere in the section?

11. To what large subject is the second section of the essay (paragraphs 6 through 11) devoted? Why does the chronological order in this section serve Hadas' purposes particularly well?

12. In paragraph 5, Hadas briefly discusses criticism of drama and criticism of literature (as they relate to criticism of TV) and then says, "We shall look first at literary criticism. . . ." Why do you suppose Hadas decided to look at literary criticism before dramatic criticism?

13. The third section of the essay (paragraphs 12 through 13) discusses criticism of drama vis-à-vis criticism of TV. The final section (paragraphs 14 through 17) returns to literature again as supplying a better analogy to TV than does drama. Why do you suppose Hadas placed section 3 where he did? Where else in the essay might he have placed it? Would it have been more or less effective there? Explain.

Alternate selections for the study of Ordering of Ideas: Jacques Barzun, "The Decay of Conversation"; Harold C. Schonberg, "Equating Turner with Music"; Rex Stout, "Watson Was a Woman."

Exercise: For each of the following topics indicate two possible ways in which the relevant materials might be ordered. For each of the topics, discuss which of the two orders you think would be more effective.

a. A description of the exterior of a large building
b. A résumé of the content of a specific college course
c. An explanation of how a one-cylinder gasoline engine works
d. Directions for driving a car
e. An explanation of how to read a weather map
f. An explanation of the major differences between the Democratic and Republican parties
g. An evaluation of a television program
h. An account of your vocational plans
i. The qualities of your ideal husband or wife
j. A comparison of life in colonial days with life today

Theme Assignment: Write a theme in which you describe a particular place—a room in your home, the lobby of a large theatre, the student cafeteria, a sports arena, a business office, a drugstore—to show the relationship between the physical layout of the place and the use or uses to which it is put. Your fully formulated guiding purpose should indicate whether you think the place is suitable or unsuitable for the uses to which it is put. You will have to plan carefully not only to establish the order of the details needed to make your description vivid to the reader but also to determine just where in the theme you will introduce and discuss suitability.

or

If we accept Hadas' cogent argument establishing the need for TV criticism, we are left with a dilemma that has been much discussed but not satisfactorily resolved. When should the TV critic function, when should his criticism of a given program be published—before or after public presentation of the program? If before, he can certainly supply the public with guidance, judgment, critical evaluation; but his criticism may constitute a form of censorship. If after, his opportunity of improving public taste, of meeting his essentially educational function may be seriously impaired.

Write a theme on this dilemma. You may wish to support one position and refute the other, or you may wish to attempt to clarify the issues involved. Whatever your guiding purpose is, pay particular attention to the order of your ideas.

Coherence

✍ The Experience of Writing History   GEORGE F. KENNAN

[1] I just want to make a few very informal observations about the nature of history as a subject and about the condition of the historian. My excuse for doing so is simply that I came to this work unusually late in life, after a quarter of a century, in fact, in a wholly
5 different sort of occupation. The impressions I have gained of these matters have something of the quality of the naïve. And since the naïve is occasionally amusing, whether or not it is instructive, I thought you might just possibly like to hear what these impressions are.
10 [2] One of the first things that dismayed me, as I tried to put pen to paper with a view to relating historical events, was to discover the hopeless open-endedness of the subject of history itself: its multi-dimensional quality, its lack of tidy beginnings and endings, its stubborn refusal to be packaged in any neat and satisfying manner. I
15 was soon brought to realize that every beginning and ending of every historical work is always in some degree artificial and contrived. No matter what you told, there was always something that had gone before, or came afterward, which you didn't have time to tell about,

From *The Virginia Quarterly Review,* Spring 1960, and reprinted with its permission.

or which you didn't know about, and which was nevertheless essential to the completeness of the tale.   20

[3] This open-endedness of the historical subject applied, I was brought to realize, not just to the longitudinal dimension of chronology, but also to the latitudinal dimension of related subjects and related happenings. No matter what field of human activity you selected for treatment, there were always a dozen other fields that   25 had something to do with it, which you couldn't treat. And wherever you tried to draw the boundary between what you could write about and what you couldn't, it was always an artificial boundary, doing violence in some degree to the integrity of the presentation itself.

[4] The perfect historical work, in other words, could not be   30 written. If you were a great enough historian, if you were sufficiently learned in the environment of your subject as well as in its central core, then you might be able to do a good job of concealing from all but the most perceptive of your readers the untidiness of the outer limits of your presentation. But the untidiness would be   35 there, nevertheless. There would always be a border, however well concealed, beyond which the firmness of your knowledge trailed off into the obscurity of your ignorance, or where the obvious limits on the patience of publishers and readers made it impossible for you to tell all you knew.   40

[5] In addition to this diffuse quality of the subject, I was startled to discover how rigorous, when you stopped to think of it, were the limitations of perspective. History, it seemed, besides being openended, partook also of the nature of a sphere. You couldn't see it from all directions at once. You could see it only from some tiny,   45 fixed point in its ample stratosphere. This point was always arbitrary in relation to the subject. An infinite number of other points could conceivably have been selected. Each would have revealed something which you, from the perspective of your particular point, were unable to reveal. Every point was, therefore, severely limited in its   50 possibilities. Not only that, but there was a real question as to what latitude you really had in selecting the point you were going to use —whether, in fact, it was not already substantially selected for you.

[6] This brought up, as you will readily see, the whole perplexing question of subjectivity. I had naïvely supposed, before I tackled this   55 work, that there was a body of unrevealed or unappraised historical fact lying scattered around, like so many archeological fragments, in the archival and bibliographical sediment of the ages, and that the

historian's task was only to unearth these fragments, to order them,
60 to catalog them, and to arrange them in a manner that would permit
them to tell their own tale. I was soon to learn that it was not this
simple. These fragments were there, all right; but they had, it seemed,
no single, definitive tale to tell. They could be arranged in an infinite
number of ways, and each had its specific implications. Much was
65 left to the powers of insight of the arranger. He had to do this arranging on the strength of his own good conscience, and to take personal
responsibility for the product. This was the task of analysis and interpretation. And this meant that the fixed point from which one viewed
history was actually none other than one's own self—one's self in the
70 most intimate personal sense.

[7] The describing of historical events, in other words, was partly
an act of the creative imagination of the writer. You might know the
bare skeleton of circumstance: that such and such occurred on such
and such a day. The fact remains: you weren't there; you didn't see
75 it. To arrive at its true significance—to understand its atmosphere, its
meaning for those who experienced it, its relation to other events—
you had to put yourself in the place of the people who were there;
you had to apply to the historical record something which, however
you tried to make it informed and dispassionate, was still an act of
80 the imagination.

[8] But then the question arose: was your imagination not the
product of what you yourself had known in life? Of things you had
seen and experienced, as the inhabitant of a specific historical age?
And if so, could you really visualize the happenings of another age?
85 Could you conceive of things outside the range of your own experience? If not, then were you not really imposing a distorting lens
upon the stuff of history by the very act of attempting to describe it?
Was it not history which was serving as a framework for the product
of your own imagination, rather than your imagination which was
90 serving to illumine the facts of history?

[9] I recall once seeing a performance of Gogol's Revisor (The
Inspector) in one of the leading theatres in Stockholm. It was Gogol's
old classic, all right. The words were correctly translated. The script
was faithfully followed. Yet what was represented was not Russia but
95 Sweden. Gogol's profound and despairing caricature of bureaucratic
life in a Russian provincial administrative center of the early nineteenth century, with all its sad and despairing humor, had been
somehow transformed into a jolly, colorful little Swedish fairy tale,
with characters who were like painted dolls—a very creditable per-

formance, a very enjoyable and creative one, in its way; but it was Sweden, not Russia. 100

[10] One was obliged to wonder whether this was not substantially what one did to any historical subject one touched, no matter how objective one tried to be. I wrote two volumes about certain phases of international life in 1917 and 1918. I did my best to describe things as I thought they looked to the actors in that drama. Sometimes I thought I had succeeded in tolerable degree. But I also had panicky moments of wonder as to whether I had done anything closer to reality than a sort of historical novel. In any case, I was forced to realize, when I looked at the volumes in retrospect, that however revealing they were as a record of the time to which they pertained, they were probably more revealing as a record of our own time—of the outlook and manner of thought of a citizen of the 1950's. I realized then why someone was once caused to remark that all history was contemporary history. 115

[11] On the other hand, I did see that it was possible to do better or worse in this respect. It was possible to enhance one's capacity for visualizing history by means of the very effort of studying it. One thing supported another. The more you steeped yourself in the environment of your subject—the more, let us say, you supported a study of political events with a parallel study of the art, the religious beliefs, the folklore, the economics, and the manners of the times— the more your imagination could rise to the task. You could, in other words, lift yourself, to a degree, by your own intellectual bootstraps. But this meant that if you really wanted to get near to your subject, it was yourself you had to change. The mere amassing of more data would not do it. To understand a past episode, you had to make yourself to some extent a citizen of the epoch in question. You had to make its spirit, its outlook, its discipline of thought, a part of your own nature. 130

[12] But this was something which you did only at a certain personal price; and the nature of this price was again one of the things that struck me very strongly about the writing of history. It was something which I can only describe—and I hope the term will not sound too bizarre to you—as its loneliness. 135

[13] I do not mean to use this term in any self-pitying way. I have enjoyed no less than anyone else the company of my colleagues in the academic life—their company, that is, in the sense of the association one has with them in the odd moments of relaxation: over luncheon tables, and that sort of thing. I even discovered that schol- 140

ars, so long as they have not constituted themselves a committee to deal with academic-administrative affairs (in which case something very strange indeed happens to them), are the most amusing and companionable of men. I should also like to stress that what I am
145 about to say applies only to the studying and writing of history, not to the teaching of it. But it does appear to me that the studying and writing of history is a relatively lonely occupation.

[14] The historian is lonely, first of all, vis-à-vis the historical personages who are the objects of his study. He lives for long periods
150 among these people. They absorb his attention, his thoughts, sometimes even his sympathies and antipathies. Yet generally speaking, they are not really his companions. They surround him, silently and inscrutably, like figures in a wax museum. He can see them to one extent or another, in the literal sense, depending upon the stage of
155 pictorial or photographic representation in the period when they lived. But they are inanimate. He sees them only frozen in poses—in a series of *tableaux morts*. Sometimes, to be sure, words are to be seen issuing from their mouths, hovering above their heads, so to speak, like the bubbles of utterance that emerge from characters in a comic
160 strip. But one does not actually hear the voices; and one is often not sure whether the words were really theirs or those of the author of the comic strip. In any case, the human context of the utterance: the elusive nuances of circumstances, of feeling, of environment, of intuition and telepathy—the things that made that particular moment
165 unlike any other moment that ever was or will be—all this is seldom to be recaptured. Only, perhaps, in case of the most profound and selfless and erudite identification of the historian with the period of his study does there occur that intimacy of acquaintance which permits historical personages really to become alive again in their own
170 right—not as products of the arbitrary imagination of the writer, but in reasonable resemblance to what they really were.

[15] But even where such people become real for the historian, he, let us remember, does not become real for them. Their mutual relationship is a one-way street. *He* takes an interest in *them*. He supports
175 them. He becomes their posthumous conscience. He tries to see that justice is done them. He follows their trials and experiences, in many instances, with greater sympathy and detachment than any of their egocentric and jealous contemporaries ever did.

[16] But do *they* support *him?* Not in the least. They couldn't
180 care less. Most of them would snort with contempt if they were to be made aware of the identity of those who would later undertake

the effort to interpret their lives and strivings to future generations. Statesmen often conceive themselves to be working for posterity in the abstract, but they have little real respect for individual members of it, in a world where youth is never what age was and where the good old times will never be recaptured. Historical characters would have little solicitude for the brash member of a future generation who takes upon himself so presumptuously the burden of interpreting *their* doings and *their* difficulties.

[17] The historian assists then, like a disembodied spirit, at the activities of his characters. To them, he has a duty, a responsibility, of understanding and of sympathy. But he himself remains unseen, unknown, unaided. This, for my money, is loneliness.

[18] And it is not only vis-à-vis the inhabitants of the past that the historian is lonely. The study of history is something that cuts one off from the age in which one lives. It represents—let us face it— a certain turning of one's back on the interests and preoccupations of one's own age, in favor of those of another. This association with the past cannot occur, if only for reasons of time, otherwise than at the expense of the association with the present.

[19] This is something which one's contemporaries, polite as they may be, rarely really understand or forgive. Every age is egocentric —and fiercely so. Every age thinks itself to be the most important age that ever occurred. Is not the present generation, after all, the occupant of that incomparably most important place in human history— the area between the past and the future? The very idea that one of the members of this generation should turn away from its absorbing and unprecedented concerns to give his attention, professionally and at length, to the affairs of people who suffer from the obvious inferiority of not being alive at all: this, to any normal and full-blooded contemporary, is little short of insulting. It implies that there were people long ago whose lives were so much more important and interesting than our own that the mere contemplation of them from a distance is held preferable to a direct participation in the affairs of our own age, despite all its obvious glories and mysteries. What body of the living, intoxicated by the illusion of progress and the belief in the uniqueness of its own experience, would ever forgive *that*?

[20] The historian too often finds himself, I fear, in the position of the man who has left the noisy and convivial party, to wander alone on cold and lonely paths. The other guests, whom he has left behind, murmur discontentedly among themselves: "Why should he have left? Who does he think he is? Obviously, he doesn't like our

company. He thinks us, plainly, a band of frivolous fools. But we are many; he is one of very few. We therefore are clearly right, and he is wrong. The devil take him. Let him sulk." So they say. And so he does.

[21] So much for the historian's loneliness. Let me just mention one more thing that has grown upon me in the course of this work. It is the realization of how deeply one has to dig to find the justification for what one is doing. There are, after all, so many discouragements.

[22] A librarian friend of mine told me the other day that it was most doubtful, in view of the inferior quality of present-day American paper, that anything I, or any of my colleagues, had recently written would still be legible fifty years hence. Since one of the few real consolations of writing history is the faint hope that perhaps one has accomplished something for the ages, this was a shattering thought.

[23] Then, too, there is the atom, with all its grisly implications. I find it hard to forget that we live in an age when all sorts of people who haven't got the faintest concern for history—who don't even know, in fact, what it is—have it already in their power to put an end not only to great portions of the historical record (this, various military characters have done very successfully at frequent intervals in the past), but to both the writers and the readers. It is an uncomfortable reflection that this entire work of the study of the past—its subject, its rationale, its practitioners, its customers, its meaning—that all this is vulnerable, or soon will be, to the whims of brother Khrushchev or brother Mao or even certain of our American brethren that I could name, not to mention others who may, with time, come into the power of disposition over these apocalyptic weapons.

[24] Even if men manage to avoid, by some unaccountable good fortune, the plunge over this particular abyss, one sees that humanity is now living, anyway, in the midst of some sort of a biological and technological explosion, by which the terms of life are being altered at an ever-increasing pace. A part of this explosive process is the multiplication of the historical record, particularly the recent one. Even the major events of the present century—events which appeared to people at the moment to be of major, headline significance—have accumulated in such volume as to place them quite beyond the apprehension of the layman. It is the rarest of persons who today has any comprehension of the series of events which, just in his own time and that of his father, has brought him where he is today. Even the historian feels increasingly inadequate to this task. He can only wan-

der around, like a man with a tiny flashlight amid vast dark caverns, shining his little beam here and there for a moment on a tiny portion of the whole, but with the darkness always closing up behind him as it recedes ahead. More history is probably written today than at any time in the past; and with respect to distant ages, once largely lost to historical knowledge, we are no doubt making progress. But with respect to the doings of our fathers and grandfathers, or even our elder brothers, we are, I fear, fighting a losing battle. The dizzy pace of change is carrying us into the future faster than we can pay out the delicate thread of historical scholarship that is our only link to the past.

[25] What, then, is the use? Has this pursuit of history become no more than a superfluous habit—something that people assume their children ought to study in school simply because this has always been done within their memory? Are the conditions of our lives being altered with such rapidity that the record of the past would have little to tell us even if we could keep up with the explosive expansion of its volume?

[26] Each of us, I suppose, has to answer these questions for himself. I am personally convinced that they must be answered in the negative. It may be true that it is becoming increasingly difficult to reconstruct an adequate record of the past. It may be true that there never was a time when history was less susceptible of apprehension, in its entirety, by the layman. It may be true that we are condemned to explore only tiny and seemingly unrelated bits of a pattern already too vast for any of us to encompass, and rapidly becoming more so. All these things, to my mind, merely make the effort of historical scholarship not less urgent but more so.

[27] It is clear that the spectacular mechanical and scientific creations of modern man tend to conceal from him the nature of his own humanity and to encourage him in all sorts of Promethean ambitions and illusions. It is precisely this person who, as he gets carried along on the dizzy pace of technological change, needs most to be reminded of the nature of the species he belongs to, of the limitations that rest on him, of the essential elements, both tragic and helpful, of his own condition. It is these reminders that history, and history alone, can give; for only history can expose the nature of man as revealed in simpler and more natural conditions where that which was elemental was less concealed by artificialities. And to the supplying of these reminders, which is the historian's task, it is not necessary that one should know or understand the whole uncon-

305 scionable and spreading panorama of history. A little bit, looked at
hard and honestly, will do. In this little bit will be found, in the
measure of the devotion applied to it, the compensation for all the
essential imperfection of the historical art, for all the struggle with
subjectivity, for all the loneliness, for all the questioning as to whether
310 anyone will ever read what you wrote or whether it would do them
any good if they did.

[For treatment of this selection, see p. 94.]

Editing the Writings of Walt Whitman: A Million Dollar Project Without a Million Dollars   GAY WILSON ALLEN

[1] In 1955 Mr. Allan Angoff, who was then the chief editor of
the New York University Press, asked me if I could suggest a major
project for the Press. I replied that I could, but that it would need
a million-dollar endowment for research, editing, and printing. Un-
5 daunted, Mr. Angoff said he would like to know what it was anyway,
and I told him a collected edition of Walt Whitman's writings.

[2] "But isn't there already such an edition?" Mr. Angoff asked.
"There is a ten-volume set of books," I admitted, "called *The Complete Writings of Walt Whitman,* but it is not complete, it was
10 published in 1902 by amateur scholars, and was not definitive even
when published. It has long been out of date."

[3] In recent years several outstanding scholars have remarked
that not a single major American author has had a scholarly, really
definitive, collected edition of his writings. At the present time several
15 are in preparation, such as the Franklin at Yale and Hawthorne at

Reprinted from *Arts & Sciences* (Winter, 1962/1963) by permission.

Ohio State, both adequately financed. And there are also several heavily-endowed, well-organized staffs of scholars working on editions of American statesmen-authors, notably (besides Franklin) Jefferson, Hamilton, and Madison.

[4] But the New York University Press is unique in undertaking a 20 collected edition of a major writer without an endowment or a large grant from a foundation. Furthermore, editing and printing such an edition for Walt Whitman is probably the most difficult, gigantic, and problem-haunted undertaking in the whole field of American letters. Why it is so large and difficult, and how the difficulties are being 25 overcome, is a very interesting story of courage (even bordering on foolhardiness), unselfish cooperation among scholars, sacrifice of time and effort, and—crucially important—the generosity of a great collector, Charles E. Feinberg, who owns the greatest number of unpublished Whitman letters, manuscripts, notebooks, and other holo- 30 graphs. Without permission to use his vast resources, no new collected edition would have been possible. Fortunately, he loves Whitman, and has made collecting him a life-avocation; consequently, he was quite willing to have his holdings used, although most collectors believe that an unpublished manuscript is more valuable than a published 35 one. Having secured Mr. Feinberg's cooperation, we found little difficulty in getting permission to use the valuable collections in university libraries at Yale, Duke, Pennsylvania, Texas; also Library of Congress, the New York Public Library, and several others, as well as a number of smaller personal collections. 40

[5] The problems which Whitman's editors have to wrestle with today began over a century ago when the poet had his first edition of *Leaves of Grass* printed in 1855 at his own expense by friends of his, the Rome Brothers, in Brooklyn, because no commercial publisher would accept the book. At a time when Longfellow was the 45 most admired poet in America, Whitman's unrhymed, unmetrical poems and uninhibited diction seemed to most editors, critics, and readers not poetry at all, and probably indecent. This story is too well known to need rehearsing. But the fact that Whitman had to be his own publisher throughout most of his literary life has created 50 nightmares for his bibliographers and editors. He did have two commercial publishers, the Boston firm of Thayer and Eldridge in 1860, which soon afterward went bankrupt, though not because of publishing Whitman; and another Boston firm, James R. Osgood, in 1881, which dropped *Leaves of Grass* after a threat of prosecution unless 55

certain sexual passages were removed, which the poet refused to do. This edition was promptly taken over by a Philadelphia firm, Rees Welsh (later David McKay), though actually more as a distributor than as a real publisher.

60 [6] But this is far from the whole bibliographical story. In his lifetime Whitman printed or published nine distinctly separate editions of *Leaves of Grass*. Until 1881 (the seventh edition) he continued to revise and add to the original (1855) poems until he had over three hundred. He also complicated matters for bibliographers 65 in almost every conceivable manner, changing titles, regrouping (with new group titles), splitting and combining poems, even discarding entirely some poems. Whether he improved or injured his poems by this constant "tinkering" is still debated by the critics. But that is another story too. What is pertinent here is that *Leaves of Grass* is 70 the title of nine different books written by Whitman.

[7] Since most of the time Whitman was his own publisher, he kept extra sheets of each printing, and frequently had batches of these bound up for special distribution. It was easy, therefore, for him to vary the contents of these small batches, and how many "issues," or 75 variants, exist for some editions is still not definitely known. The bibliographer needs to examine hundreds of copies to find out. The University of Pennsylvania Library, for example, owns an 1876 *Leaves* with some new poems *pasted in* (clipped from galley proofs). This may be a unique copy, or Whitman may have "fixed up" other 80 copies in the same way at the same time.

[8] Throughout his poetic career Whitman was also writing prose, some of which he later collected in several volumes variously entitled *Prose Works, Complete Prose,* etc. In early life, as is well known, he was a journalist and newspaper editor. Before printing the 85 first *Leaves of Grass* he had published many conventional poems and sentimental stories in popular magazines and newspapers, and a prohibition novel called *Franklin Evans*. In old age he collected some of these in an appendix to his *Prose Works,* not because he was proud of them but simply as samples of his juvenilia. He did not collect 90 any of his editorials, and not nearly all his essays written after 1855. Though his prose does not exist in so many versions as his poems, finding all the versions is a big task. Worse yet is identifying unsigned editorials and articles, or those he published under pseudonyms. Much of this prose has very slight literary value, though some 95 biographical; but many of his Civil War newspaper articles do have considerable value both as history and literary art. In fact, some of

Whitman's prose, especially in *Specimen Days,* can be called major American literature.

[9] As if these are not complications enough, Whitman was also all along creating others. He was thought by many of his contemporaries to be lazy, but in truth he was one of the most industrious authors in literary history. He wrote constantly: diaries, notebooks, workbooks, plans and outlines for poems and essays, and trial versions. Even casual letters he worded first in rough drafts, which he corrected and copied, keeping the original for his file, before the day of typewriters and carbon copies. And to judge by the stack of manuscript material that has survived, he never destroyed anything. He was a regular magpie! It is hard to believe that one man wrote so much, and that so much of it has survived. Sometimes his exhausted editors almost wish that he had had two or three good house fires, and considering the houses he lived in, it is also astonishing that he did not.

[10] Having spent a lifetime struggling for recognition, publishing in any way possible, Whitman cannily selected his literary executors and left them, at his death in 1892, his great storehouse of printed editions, proof sheets, and holographs. These literary executors were, of course, personal friends, and rather an odd mixture, but he could not have chosen more devoted or conscientious men. They were Dr. Richard Maurice Bucke, a Canadian psychiatrist; Thomas Harned, a highly respected Philadelphia lawyer; and Horace Traubel, a young bank clerk, who professed to be a socialist and wrote sententious journalism and poems crudely imitating Whitman's. Harned was a practical, level-headed, completely dependable man. Traubel was a disciple, emotional, partisan, but a man of integrity. Dr. Bucke was something of a mystic himself, who wrote a book on mysticism called *Cosmic Consciousness* which has survived and was recently reprinted in a paperback edition. He also wrote a biography of Whitman approved by the poet himself.

[11] These men began dividing Whitman's literary hoard even before the funeral was over. To judge by their later publications, Dr. Bucke got the lion's share, though Harned received Whitman's correspondence with Mrs. Anne Gilchrist, the distinguished British widow who tried to marry the poet, and miscellaneous manuscripts which Harned later gave to the Library of Congress. Traubel had already been given a vast batch of letters received by Whitman, which he later quoted in *With Walt Whitman in Camden* (to date four volumes published and three still in manuscript). Dr. Bucke edited

and published *Calamus* (1897), Whitman's letters to a young street-car conductor, Peter Doyle; *The Wound-Dresser* (1898), containing
140 letters and newspaper articles written during the War while Whitman was working in the army hospitals; and *Notes and Fragments* (1899), consisting of preparatory notes and passages of poems and prose. Harned edited *Letters Written by Walt Whitman to His Mother from 1866 to 1872* (1902).

145 [12] Meanwhile these literary executors were preparing *The Complete Writings of Walt Whitman,* which was published in 1902 by G. P. Putnam and Sons in ten volumes, on heavy paper, in various de luxe bindings, limited to less than 1000 sets. It contained *Leaves of Grass* (supposedly the final, or "deathbed" text, authorized by the
150 poet); the prose which Whitman himself had collected in *Prose Works;* and the recent books of "uncollected" writings edited by Harned and Bucke (none of Traubel's had yet appeared). This edition also contained a "Variorum Readings" of *Leaves of Grass* compiled by Professor Oscar Lovell Triggs, of the University of Chicago,
155 but it was not complete, or entirely accurate even for published texts, and contained only sporadic manuscript versions. It also contained a bibliography, reliable for books published by Whitman, though with meager descriptions, and without a checklist of his extensive periodical publications. All things considered, this was a handsome
160 memorial to the poet, conscientiously prepared and luxuriously printed. Probably even professional editors could not have done much better in 1902. After 1902 the editing of Whitman's uncollected writings continued, with *Walt Whitman's Diary in Canada* (1904), edited by William Sloane Kennedy; *An American Primer* (1904),
165 containing notes on style and the American language, edited by Traubel; and the very important *Uncollected Poetry and Prose of Walt Whitman* (1921) by Emory Holloway. For three decades Holloway continued to search out and republish Whitman's journalistic writings, and other editors added nearly a dozen volumes containing
170 all sorts of uncollected writings except personal letters.

[13] When the New York University Press became interested in a new collected writings of Whitman, I estimated that it would contain at least a fourth more material than the 1902 ten-volume edition. In addition to the "uncollected" items already gathered into some twenty
175 books (which would need re-verification, reorganizing, and uniform editorial apparatus), a great many manuscripts still awaited transcription. All known letters must be collected and edited. Fortunately,

thanks to Mr. Feinberg's indefatigable collecting, this could now, for the first time, be done. The Variorum needed to be re-done entirely. The most authoritative text for *Leaves of Grass* and such major prose as *Specimen Days* must be established. Finally, all this should be capped by a definitive bibliography. How could all this vast labor and voluminous printing be accomplished without a large sum of money?

[14] The officials of the Press decided that the project could be undertaken if we could secure editors for the job who would rely mainly on their own institutions for support of their research and editing. The volumes could be published at the rate of two or three a year without subsidy, and income from the sales of these volumes would help defray the expenses of printing additional volumes. To my surprise, the leading Whitman scholars agreed to cooperate on such a plan as this. First we were able to secure a distinguished Advisory Editorial Board, consisting of, besides myself: Roger Asselineau, University of Paris; Harold W. Blodgett, Union College; Sculley Bradley, University of Pennsylvania; Charles E. Feinberg, the Detroit collector of Whitman; Clarence Gohdes, Duke University; Emory Holloway, Queens College (now emeritus); Rollo G. Silver, Simmons College; and Floyd Stovall, University of Virginia.

[15] In the beginning I acted as editor-in-chief, but I soon began to foresee that when the manuscripts for the various volumes began to come in, I would have more than I could handle alone. Fortunately, Professor Sculley Bradley, even though he had just become Vice-Provost for the University of Pennsylvania (with responsibility for educational policy), consented to become co-editor with me, agreeing to serve as general editor for the manuscripts if I would organize the edition, determine the contents of each volume, secure editors, act as liaison between the Press and the editors, and be available at all times for bibliographical consultation. After several years of letter writing, consultations, and conferences at MLA meetings, my duties have become less time-consuming as Bradley's have increased —so much so that he plans to take a temporary leave from his University position next January.

[16] Publication of *The Collected Writings of Walt Whitman* began in the summer of 1961 with the first two volumes of *The Correspondence . . . 1842–1867* and . . . *1868–1875,* edited by Edwin Haviland Miller, who started his editing while at Simmons College but is finishing it as Professor of English at New York University. He was chosen because he and his wife, Rosalynd, had already compiled a checklist of Whitman's letters, and in his other publications had

shown himself to be a meticulous and competent scholar. The unani-
220 mous praise of the *Correspondence* so far published has confirmed
the wisdom of choosing him. *The Library Journal* called the publication of these volumes "the most important event of the year in
American scholarship." Almost all reviewers also praised the beautiful printing and the handsome designing by Andor Braun, who is
225 widely regarded as one of the best in the business.

[17] Meanwhile Miller has continued editing Whitman letters,
which will probably make three more volumes instead of the two
anticipated. Even as he works, new letters are discovered. In July,
1962, Mr. Feinberg bought forty-one letters and twenty-one postcards
230 hitherto unknown to scholars—paying, incidentally, $10,000 for
them. Possibly some letters may be discovered in obscure places even
after all volumes of the *Correspondence* are in print, but the number
is not likely to be large, and two thousand letters should make an
edition extensive enough for the needs of Whitman students and
235 scholars. But this situation shows how nearly impossible it is to have
an absolutely complete edition.

[18] The next published unit of *The Writings* will be *Specimen
Days and Other Prose* and *Collect and Other Prose,* edited by Floyd
Stovall, of the University of Virginia, who has been well known as a
240 Whitman scholar for many years. The manuscript is ready for the
printer, and publication is planned for January, 1963. Although these
volumes will contain prose collected by the poet himself in his *Prose
Works,* the text will be based on a collation of the texts published
by Whitman, with full annotations. Introductions and notes will in-
245 dicate the background and importance of each title.

[19] A volume of Whitman's *Fiction and Early Poems* (the poems
being pre–*Leaves of Grass*) will be published simultaneously with
Stovall's volumes. This has been edited by Professor Thomas Brasher,
of San Marcos State College, Texas. (The wide geographical distri-
250 bution of the editors is entirely coincidental, but might be said to
symbolize the scope of the project.) Although Emory Holloway collected the early poems in his *Uncollected Poetry and Prose . . . ,* and
Thomas O. Mabbott most of the stories in *The Half-Breed and Other
Stories,* Brasher has gone back to the originals and has made some
255 discoveries which will make his edition the most complete and authoritative one. This volume will also contain Whitman's prohibition
novel, *Franklin Evans.* Despite the fact that Whitman's early fiction
and conventional poetry showed little promise of the great poet he
was to become, his juvenilia nevertheless throw light on his develop-

ment, and on the 1840-decade in American history, when most of 260
these poems and stories were written.

[20] As already remarked, *Leaves of Grass* is not one book but
many, deceptively bearing the same title. Which provides the best
text for the definitive *Writings?* Should it not be the 1892 "deathbed"
text, which Whitman authorized as his choice, commanding in a 265
preface that henceforth no other be reprinted? For half a century all
editors and most scholars have assumed this to be the best. And
they have also assumed that this was the text printed by the literary
executors in the 1902 so-called *Complete Writings.* But Bradley has
discovered that the executors had the 1902 text set in new type, from 270
which new plates were made (which soon disappeared and no trace
has been found of them), and the text actually printed in 1902 was
not entirely faithful to the 1892 text. The bibliographical details are
far too complicated to enumerate here, but the important fact is that
the completely authentic "deathbed" text has not ever been reprinted, 275
despite the fact that several editions have been so advertised. The
New York University Reader's Edition of *Leaves of Grass* will be
printed from photographic copy of the 1892 text, and, with meticulous proof-reading, will be absolutely authentic.

[21] Actually, the New York University Press *Collected Writings* 280
will contain two texts of *Leaves of Grass,* the genuine "authorized"
text in the Reader's Edition, and a second, with the poems arranged
chronologically, in the Variorum Edition. The latter will use the
1881–1892 text as a base, but will also record all variants from both
printed and unprinted sources. Both editions are being prepared by 285
Blodgett and Bradley. The present schedule calls for the publishing
of the Reader's Edition in 1963, and the Variorum a year later.

[22] The Reader's Edition will also contain more than one hundred poems not in any edition hitherto published. Some of these have
never been printed anywhere and exist only in manuscripts, while 290
others have been rescued from Bucke's *Notes and Fragments,* which
Triggs only partly employed in his "Variorum Readings." The new
Variorum Edition will include many manuscript fragments whose relationship to *Leaves of Grass* Triggs did not perceive; furthermore,
the Reader's Edition will present many fragments of poems that are 295
outside Leaves of Grass, being compositions which Whitman decided
not to admit to his canon. Whitman also, for some reason, dropped
a few poems after his 1860 edition, and these will be restored in the
Reader's Edition.

300 [23] Some of the "rescued" poems, particularly those so-called fragments which make better sense printed as separate poems, reveal new dimensions of Whitman's art and thought, such as "Scantlings":

> White, shaved, foreign, soft-fleshed, shrinking,
> Scant of muscle, scant of love-power,
> Scant of gnarl and knot, modest, sleek in costumes,
> Averse from the wet of rain, from the fall of snow,
>   from the grit of the stones and soil,
> A pretty race, each one just like hundreds of the rest,
> Race of scantlings from the strong growth of America.

Whitman is not known as a satirist, but the incisive bite of these lines shows he had the ability to write effective satire.

305 [24] Another of the "new poems" has the formal balance and finish of a *haiku:*

> O I must not forget!
> To you I reach friendly—
> O I must not forget
> To you I adhere!—
> I do not flatter—I am not polite—
>   but I adhere to you
> Baffled, exiled, ragged, gaunt.

[25] The problems Blodgett and Bradley face and are solving in the preparation of the Variorum Edition are stupendous. To begin with, few if any poets have left so many published versions of their 310 poems. Bradley, with the help of a staff of assistants at the University of Pennsylvania, is recording every line of all poems in *Leaves of Grass* (all editions and issues) on 6 by 10 inch cards. Though still not complete, these cards, filed compactly, already measure over thirty-eight feet.

315 [26] Blodgett's files are not so visibly spectacular, but he has performed an equally heroic job, without any assistants. One year he was a Fulbright scholar to Iran, but he took a trunk full of photostats with him and continued recording variants in Teheran. And in addition to his research in manuscripts, he has also summarized all 320 critical interpretations of any consequence of individual poems, which he will draw upon in notes for the Reader's Edition.

[27] Both Bradley and Blodgett will collaborate on the General Introduction for the Variorum Edition, Blodgett concentrating on the

"growth" of the *Leaves* and Bradley on the history of their publication. Whitman fondly believed that his book had grown like the rings of a tree, but these editors will show that it was not so simple as that. The poet did not have a clear, lifelong plan. He fumbled and experimented and improvised. Now, with the vast data accumulated by these two editors, the whole story can be told, clearly and accurately for the first time. The literary executors attempted this in the 1902 edition, but they did not have sufficient data or knowledge.

[28] After publication of the two editions of *Leaves of Grass,* the remaining volumes of *The Collected Writings* may seem anticlimactic, but they will be important to the complete edition. And the problems of the editors will scarcely be less difficult, though of course different, from those encountered by Blodgett and Bradley. The remaining manuscript material (notebooks, diaries, prose fragments) is being edited by Professor Edward Grier, of the University of Kansas, and Professor William White, of Wayne State University. White is working in Mr. Feinberg's collection, which contains over 500 manuscripts. Grier has attempted to locate and obtain photocopies of all other manuscripts (excluding letters, poems, and fiction assigned to other editors). He sent out 1500 letters to libraries and private collectors, and located and obtained photostats of approximately 1800 manuscripts of varying length.

[29] One big detail still to be settled is how much of all the "vast batch left to oblivion," as Whitman called his unused manuscripts, should be printed. At first the editorial staff hoped to print everything, so that the *Collected Writings* could be called absolutely "complete." But some items, as Miller discovered for the letters, will probably continue to come to light for years to come. Moreover, many of the miscellaneous manuscripts are hardly more than lists of words, names, addresses, trial titles, and trivial memoranda. Is a poet's laundry list worth publishing? This is not a rhetorical question, for maybe it should be. But the question is still being debated by the editors of the *Collected Writings* and the New York University Press.

[30] In some ways, the most baffling of all problems are those faced by the remaining editor, Professor Herbert Bergman, of Michigan State University, who is trying to assemble Whitman's journalistic writings. Despite the fact that Holloway and others have already collected a great number of editorials and newspaper articles and published them as Whitman's, it is still not certain how many of these Whitman actually wrote—unless he signed them with his own name

or a known pseudonym. Many of the articles are signed, but almost
365 none of the editorials. Can we assume that all editorials printed in
the Brooklyn *Eagle* and Brooklyn *Times* while he was editor were
his? This has been the assumption of previous editors, without other
evidence. Bergman is doing painful research to discover, if possible,
some objective means of identifying Whitman's work. Style and ideas
370 give indications of authorship, but other criteria need to be found.

[31] Bergman's volumes (probably two) will be the final unit in
The *Collected Writings* except for a Bibliography, which William
White is preparing. Aside from having done extensive bibliographical
work, he was also the logical choice for this assignment because he
375 has catalogued Mr. Feinberg's library, and will have constant access
to it as well as the owner's extensive knowledge. He will not complete his manuscript until Blodgett and Bradley have published their
Variorum, thus being able to make use of their discoveries.

[32] From the very first this project has been a truly cooperative
380 endeavor. The editors have been able to carry on their research and
editing because most of them have been supported by their own
institutions with grants, released time, or assistants. I was able to use
funds granted me by our own Graduate School of Arts and Science
to pay for photostats for editors who did not have institutional sup-
385 port. Several editors also secured grants from the American Council
of Learned Societies and the American Philosophical Society, both of
which have been generous. The ACLS also granted Miller a fellow-
ship which released him from teaching for a year. The Union College
Library bought microfilm and photostats for Blodgett. Most generous
390 of all has been the University of Pennsylvania, which supported
Bradley's work with renewed grants in aid from year to year, with
the annual appointment of a research assistant, a generous allocation
of space as editorial headquarters for the project in the Rare Book
Division of the Library, and purchases of Whitman first editions to
395 be consumed in the editorial process.

[33] The University of Virginia supported Stovall's research with
grants, as has also, on a smaller scale, Michigan State University for
Bergman, San Marcos State College for Brasher. Grier writes: "I
have been generously supported by the Graduate Research Fund and
400 the General Research Fund of the University of Kansas, and I should
appreciate special mention of both funds, for they have been extraordinarily good to me." He also adds that I need not mention that
he has worn out a set of tires on his car in pursuit of manuscripts.

[34] Thus, even though we have not had a large grant from any foundation, we have had financial aid for individual editors. The New York University Press has not had funds available for more than a few conference lunches, but the officials have been very cooperative in every way possible. When Mr. William Harvey became Director of the Press in 1958, he knew nothing about this huge commitment, but he immediately recognized its importance and set about supporting it in any way he could.

[35] The present editor of the Press, Mr. Robert T. King, has had the labor and the honor of seeing the first volumes through the publication processes. Though all the academic men connected with this edition wish him great success in his profession, they hope that no commercial firm entices him away until the last volume of *The Collected Writings of Walt Whitman* is printed—which, it is hoped, will be in 1965.[1]

[36] In the first year of publication over 1200 sets of the *Correspondence,* at $20 a set, have been sold, and orders continue to come in. The Press does not expect to make money on this project, but the original optimistic hope that the sale of published volumes would help considerably to defray the cost of printing forthcoming volumes seems not to have been visionary. But what especially pleases me is that we are succeeding in publishing this huge and difficult scholarly edition without a large endowment, but with unending cooperation and effort. I think we are erecting a monument to academic courage, faith, generosity, and scholarly work.

Good writing has the quality of "hanging together"—of coherence —from sentence to sentence, from paragraph to paragraph, from section to section. Coherence is basically a matter of having the parts of a piece of writing in the right order (logical, chronological, climactic, etc.) with the relations among the parts made clear to the reader. Often enough these relations are obvious, but just as often they must be pointed up for the reader. One way of doing this is to raise a question at the end of one section and answer it in the following section or sections. Another way of achieving coherence is to indicate at the end of a section the over-all direction the thinking will take in subsequent sections. Sometimes a paragraph is used—a paragraph of one or

[1] Seven of the projected fifteen volumes have been published to date (Fall 1966). The present editor of the Press, Mr. William B. Harvey, indicates that publication will be completed in 1970.

several sentences—to show the relation of what has been said to what is about to be said. Ideas may even be labeled "first," "second," "third" to keep the reader aware of their progression. Constantly valuable for increasing coherence are such transitional words or expressions as *however, nevertheless, in addition, consequently, but, indeed, finally, as a result, in contrast to, in spite of, again, most of all, least of all.* Coherence may also be achieved through judicious repetition of key words and expressions and through pronouns which, by referring back to their antecedents, may link one section or paragraph or sentence to another.

1. In the last paragraph of Kennan's essay, he gives us his own outline. He has been talking, he says, about "the essential imperfections of the historical art, . . . the struggle with subjectivity, . . . the loneliness, . . . [and] the questioning as to whether anyone will ever read what you wrote or whether it would do them any good if they did." These four points form the body of his essay, and are taken up in paragraphs 2 through 26. Fill in this outline, indicating which paragraphs are devoted to each of the four points.

2. What is Kennan's guiding purpose? Where is it stated?

3. What is his conclusion and where is it stated?

4. Justify, in terms of Kennan's guiding purpose and conclusion, the order of the four parts of the selection.

5. In each of paragraphs 2 through 11, find the words or phrases that Kennan uses to link the paragraphs to one another.

6. Find two key places in the essay in which Kennan uses the device of repetition for the purpose of coherence.

7. Point out all the means by which internal coherence is achieved within paragraph 5.

8. Justify the statement that paragraph 7 is part summary and part transition.

9. What is the function of the questions in paragraph 8?

10. Paragraph 12 introduces the subject of loneliness. How? How does the paragraph contribute to the coherence of the piece?

11. Paragraph 21 is a paragraph of transition. How do you know this? Has Kennan made his guide posts too obvious here? Why or why not?

12. What is Kennan's answer to the over-all question he raises in the essay? Why is it placed where it is? How does its placement contribute to coherence?

13. Allen's article is divided into six sections—paragraphs 1 through 4, 5 through 12, 13 through 19, 20 through 27, 28 through 31, and 32 through 36. In one carefully worded sentence for each, summarize the content of each of the sections.

14. What determined the order of the first five sections? Just how does this order contribute to the coherence of the article?

15. Point out those places in which Allen uses explicit transitions between sections. Comment on each of the transitions to show how it contributes to coherence.

16. How does the first sentence of paragraph 6 contribute to coherence? the first sentence of paragraph 9?

17. How does Allen effect a transition between paragraphs 10 and 11? between 11 and 12?

18. What is the function of the last sentence of paragraph 13?

19. Point out all explicit transitional devices in paragraphs 15 through 19, commenting on the effectiveness of each.

20. Analyze the last section of the article to determine all the means by which Allen achieves coherence within the section.

Alternate selections for the study of Coherence: John Mason Brown, "The Camera Creative"; James A. Perkins, "Should the Artist Come to the Campus?"; Richard Franko Goldman. "The Wonderful World of Culture or: A Strictly Highbrow and Artistic Subject."

Exercise: The items below suggest a common situation. Using all of the items, write at least three paragraphs in which you achieve coherence within and between paragraphs by reordering the items and supplying adequate transitions:

>   newly licensed driver
>   bus
>   important date
>   flat tire
>   heavy rains
>   two telephone calls
>   irate parent
>   borrowed money
>   pet shop

Theme Assignment: We have seen that in this essay Kennan has taken a long look at his own profession. He has considered it as a subject and has attempted to justify it as a lifetime endeavor. This task requires the perspective of a practitioner. However, each of you has made at least some tentative choice of a major field of study and some even more tentative choice of an occupation within that field.

Write a theme on the subject in which you plan to major, as you see it from your own perspective, and give your reasons for having selected an occupation related to it. This is, as you will readily see, a topic which requires considerable planning and considerable use of the tools of coherence to keep it from falling apart into half a dozen different topics.

or

Allen's article supplies the reader with insights into the problems and complexities of scholarly editing. From the insights you have gained, write a theme describing the particular qualities of training, talent, personality that you feel a scholarly editor must have to do his job well. Pay particular attention to coherence, underlining for your instructor's benefit all the transitional devices you were skillful enough to use.

Logic

✐ *Love Is a Fallacy* MAX SHULMAN

Charles Lamb, as merry and enterprising a fellow as you will meet
in a month of Sundays, unfettered the informal essay with his memorable *Old China* and *Dream Children*. There follows an informal
essay that ventures even beyond Lamb's frontier. Indeed, "informal"
may not be quite the right word to describe this essay; "limp" or   5
"flaccid" or possibly "spongy" are perhaps more appropriate.

Vague though its category, it is without doubt an essay. It develops
an argument; it cites instances; it reaches a conclusion. Could Carlyle
do more? Could Ruskin?

Read, then, the following essay which undertakes to demonstrate   10
that logic, far from being a dry, pedantic discipline, is a living, breathing thing, full of beauty, passion, and trauma.

—AUTHOR'S NOTE

Cool was I and logical. Keen, calculating, perspicacious, acute and
astute—I was all of these. My brain was as powerful as a dynamo, as
precise as a chemist's scales, as penetrating as a scalpel. And—think   15
of it!—I was only eighteen.

It is not often that one so young has such a giant intellect. Take,

for example, Petey Burch, my roommate at the University of Minnesota. Same age, same background, but dumb as an ox. A nice enough
20 fellow, you understand, but nothing upstairs. Emotional type. Unstable. Impressionable. Worst of all, a faddist. Fads, I submit, are the very negation of reason. To be swept up in every new craze that comes along, to surrender yourself to idiocy just because everybody else is doing it—this, to me, is the acme of mindlessness. Not, how-
25 ever, to Petey.

One afternoon I found Petey lying on his bed with an expression of such distress on his face that I immediately diagnosed appendicitis. "Don't move," I said. "Don't take a laxative. I'll get a doctor."

"Raccoon," he mumbled thickly.

30 "Raccoon?" I said, pausing in my flight.

"I want a raccoon coat," he wailed.

I perceived that his trouble was not physical, but mental. "Why do you want a raccoon coat?"

"I should have known it," he cried, pounding his temples. "I
35 should have known they'd come back when the Charleston came back. Like a fool I spent all my money for textbooks, and now I can't get a raccoon coat."

"Can you mean," I said incredulously, "that people are actually wearing raccoon coats again?"

40 "All the Big Men on Campus are wearing them. Where've you been?"

"In the library," I said, naming a place not frequented by Big Men on Campus.

He leaped from the bed and paced the room. "I've got to have a
45 raccoon coat," he said passionately. "I've got to!"

"Petey, why? Look at it rationally. Raccoon coats are unsanitary. They shed. They smell bad. They weigh too much. They're unsightly. They—"

"You don't understand," he interrupted impatiently. "It's the thing
50 to do. Don't you want to be in the swim?"

"No," I said truthfully.

"Well, I do," he declared. "I'd give anything for a raccoon coat. Anything!"

My brain, that precision instrument, slipped into high gear. "Any-
55 thing?" I asked, looking at him narrowly.

"Anything," he affirmed in ringing tones.

I stroked my chin thoughtfully. It so happened that I knew where to get my hands on a raccoon coat. My father had had one in his undergraduate days; it lay now in a trunk in the attic back home. It also happened that Petey had something I wanted. He didn't *have* it exactly, but at least he had first rights on it. I refer to his girl, Polly Espy.

I had long coveted Polly Espy. Let me emphasize that my desire for this young woman was not emotional in nature. She was, to be sure, a girl who excited the emotions, but I was not one to let my heart rule my head. I wanted Polly for a shrewdly calculated, entirely cerebral reason.

I was a freshman in law school. In a few years I would be out in practice. I was well aware of the importance of the right kind of wife in furthering a lawyer's career. The successful lawyers I had observed were, almost without exception, married to beautiful, gracious, intelligent women. With one omission, Polly fitted these specifications perfectly.

Beautiful she was. She was not yet of pin-up proportions, but I felt sure that time would supply the lack. She already had the makings.

Gracious she was. By gracious I mean full of graces. She had an erectness of carriage, an ease of bearing, a poise that clearly indicated the best of breeding. At table her manners were exquisite. I had seen her at the Kozy Kampus Korner eating the specialty of the house—a sandwich that contained scraps of pot roast, gravy, chopped nuts, and a dipper of sauerkraut—without even getting her fingers moist.

Intelligent she was not. In fact, she veered in the opposite direction. But I believed that under my guidance she would smarten up. At any rate, it was worth a try. It is, after all, easier to make a beautiful dumb girl smart than to make an ugly smart girl beautiful.

"Petey," I said, "are you in love with Polly Espy?"

"I think she's a keen kid," he replied, "but I don't know if you'd call it love. Why?"

"Do you," I asked, "have any kind of formal arrangement with her? I mean are you going steady or anything like that?"

"No. We see each other quite a bit, but we both have other dates. Why?"

"Is there," I asked, "any other man for whom she has a particular fondness?"

"Not that I know of. Why?"

I nodded with satisfaction. "In other words, if you were out of the picture, the field would be open. Is that right?"

100   "I guess so. What are you getting at?"

"Nothing, nothing," I said innocently, and took my suitcase out of the closet.

"Where are you going?" asked Petey.

"Home for the weekend." I threw a few things into the bag.

105   "Listen," he said, clutching my arm eagerly, "while you're home, you couldn't get some money from your old man, could you, and lend it to me so I can buy a raccoon coat?"

"I may do better than that," I said with a mysterious wink and closed my bag and left.

110   "Look," I said to Petey when I got back Monday morning. I threw open the suitcase and revealed the huge, hairy, gamy object that my father had worn in his Stutz Bearcat in 1925.

"Holy Toledo!" said Petey reverently. He plunged his hands into the raccoon coat and then his face. "Holy Toledo!" he repeated
115 fifteen or twenty times.

"Would you like it?" I asked.

"Oh yes!" he cried, clutching the greasy pelt to him. Then a canny look came into his eyes. "What do you want for it?"

"Your girl," I said, mincing no words.

120   "Polly?" he said in a horrified whisper. "You want Polly?"

"That's right."

He flung the coat from him. "Never," he said stoutly.

I shrugged. "Okay. If you don't want to be in the swim, I guess it's your business."

125   I sat down in a chair and pretended to read a book, but out of the corner of my eye I kept watching Petey. He was a torn man. First he looked at the coat with the expression of a waif at a bakery window. Then he turned away and set his jaw resolutely. Then he looked back at the coat, with even more longing in his face. Then he turned
130 away, but with not so much resolution this time. Back and forth his head swiveled, desire waxing, resolution waning. Finally he didn't turn away at all; he just stood and stared with mad lust at the coat.

"It isn't as though I was in love with Polly," he said thickly. "Or going steady or anything like that."

135   "That's right," I murmured.

"What's Polly to me, or me to Polly?"

"Not a thing," said I.

"It's just been a casual kick—just a few laughs, that's all."

"Try on the coat," said I.

140   He complied. The coat bunched high over his ears and dropped

all the way down to his shoe tops. He looked like a mound of dead raccoons. "Fits fine," he said happily.

I rose from my chair. "Is it a deal?" I asked, extending my hand. He swallowed. "It's a deal," he said and shook my hand.

I had my first date with Polly the following evening. This was in the nature of a survey; I wanted to find out just how much work I had to do to get her mind up to the standard I required. I took her first to dinner. "Gee, that was a delish dinner," she said as we left the restaurant. Then I took her to a movie. "Gee, that was a marvy movie," she said as we left the theater. And then I took her home. "Gee, I had a sensaysh time," she said as she bade me good night.

I went back to my room with a heavy heart. I had gravely underestimated the size of my task. This girl's lack of information was terrifying. Nor would it be enough merely to supply her with informaiton. First she had to be taught to *think*. This loomed as a project of no small dimensions, and at first I was tempted to give her back to Petey. But then I got to thinking about her abundant physical charms and about the way she entered a room and the way she handled a knife and fork, and I decided to make an effort.

I went about it, as in all things, systematically. I gave her a course in logic. It happened that I, as a law student, was taking a course in logic myself, so I had all the facts at my finger tips. "Polly," I said to her when I picked her up on our next date, "tonight we are going over to the Knoll and talk."

"Oo, terrif," she replied. One thing I will say for this girl: you would go far to find another so agreeable.

We went to the Knoll, the campus trysting place, and we sat down under an old oak, and she looked at me expectantly. "What are we going to talk about?" she asked.

"Logic."

She thought this over for a minute and decided she liked it. "Magnif," she said.

"Logic," I said, clearing my throat, "is the science of thinking. Before we can think correctly, we must first learn to recognize the common fallacies of logic. These we will take up tonight."

"Wow-dow!" she cried, clapping her hands delightedly.

I winced, but went bravely on. "First let us examine the fallacy called Dicto Simpliciter."

"By all means," she urged, batting her lashes eagerly.

"Dicto Simplicter means an argument based on an unqualified

generalization. For example: Exercise is good. Therefore everybody should exercise."

"I agree," said Polly earnestly. "I mean exercise is wonderful. I mean it builds the body and everything."

185 "Polly," I said gently, "the argument is a fallacy. *Exercise is good* is an unqualified generalization. For instance, if you have heart disease, exercise is bad, not good. Many people are ordered by their doctors *not* to exercise. You must *qualify* the generalization. You must say exercise is *usually* good, or exercise is good *for most people.*
190 Otherwise you have committed a Dicto Simpliciter. Do you see?"

"No," she confessed. "But this is marvy. Do more! Do more!"

"It will be better if you stop tugging at my sleeve," I told her, and when she desisted, I continued. "Next we take up a fallacy called Hasty Generalization. Listen carefully: You can't speak French. I
195 can't speak French. Petey Burch can't speak French. I must therefore conclude that nobody at the University of Minnesota can speak French."

"Really?" said Polly, amazed. "*Nobody?*"

I hid my exasperation. "Polly, it's a fallacy. The generalization is
200 reached too hastily. There are too few instances to support such a conclusion."

"Know any more fallacies?" she asked breathlessly. "This is more fun than dancing even."

I fought off a wave of despair. I was getting nowhere with this girl,
205 absolutely nowhere. Still, I am nothing if not persistent. I continued. "Next comes Post Hoc. Listen to this: Let's not take Bill on our picnic. Every time we take him out with us, it rains."

"I know somebody just like that," she exclaimed. "A girl back home—Eula Becker, her name is. It never fails. Every single time we
210 take her on a picnic—"

"Polly," I said sharply, "it's a fallacy. Eula Becker doesn't *cause* the rain. She has no connection with the rain. You are guilty of Post Hoc if you blame Eula Becker."

"I'll never do it again," she promised contritely. "Are you mad
215 at me?"

I sighed deeply. "No, Polly, I'm not mad."

"Then tell me some more fallacies."

"All right. Let's try Contradictory Premises."

"Yes, let's," she chirped, blinking her eyes happily.

220 I frowned, but plunged ahead. "Here's an example of Contra-

dictory Premises: If God can do anything, can He make a stone so heavy that He won't be able to lift it?"

"Of course," she replied promptly.

"But if He can do anything, He can lift the stone," I pointed out.

"Yeah," she said thoughtfully. "Well, then I guess He can't make 225 the stone."

"But He can do anything," I reminded her.

She scratched her pretty, empty head. "I'm all confused," she admitted.

"Of course you are. Because when the premises of an argument 230 contradict each other, there can be no argument. If there is an irresistible force, there can be no immovable object. If there is an immovable object, there can be no irrisistible force. Get it?"

"Tell me some more of this keen stuff," she said eagerly.

I consulted my watch. "I think we'd better call it a night. I'll take 235 you home now, and you go over all the things you've learned. We'll have another session tomorrow night."

I deposited her at the girls' dormitory, where she assured me that she had had a perfectly terrif evening, and I went glumly home to my room. Petey lay snoring in his bed, the raccoon coat huddled like 240 a great hairy beast at his feet. For a moment I considered waking him and telling him that he could have his girl back. It seemed clear that my project was doomed to failure. The girl simply had a logic-proof head.

But then I reconsidered. I had wasted one evening; I might as well 245 waste another. Who knew? Maybe somewhere in the extinct crater of her mind, a few embers still smoldered. Maybe somehow I could fan them into flame. Admittedly it was not a prospect fraught with hope, but I decided to give it one more try.

Seated under the oak the next evening I said, "Our first fallacy 250 tonight is called Ad Misericordiam."

She quivered with delight.

"Listen closely," I said. "A man applies for a job. When the boss asks him what his qualifications are, he replies that he has a wife and six children at home, the wife is a helpless cripple, the children have 255 nothing to eat, no clothes to wear, no shoes on their feet, there are no beds in the house, no coal in the cellar, and winter is coming."

A tear rolled down each of Polly's pink cheeks. "Oh, this is awful, awful," she sobbed.

"Yes, it's awful," I agreed, "but it's no argument. The man never 260 answered the boss's question about his qualifications. Instead he appealed to the boss's sympathy. He committed the fallacy of Ad Misericordiam. Do you understand?"

"Have you got a handkerchief?" she blubbered.

265 I handed her a handkerchief and tried to keep from screaming while she wiped her eyes. "Next," I said in a carefully controlled tone, "we will discuss False Analogy. Here is an example: Students should be allowed to look at their textbooks during examinations. After all, surgeons have X-rays to guide them during an operation, 270 lawyers have briefs to guide them during a trial, carpenters have blueprints to guide them when they are building a house. Why, then, shouldn't students be allowed to look at their textbooks during an examination?"

"There now," she said enthusiastically, "is the most marvy idea 275 I've heard in years."

"Polly," I said testily, "the argument is all wrong. Doctors, lawyers, and carpenters aren't taking a test to see how much they have learned, but students are. The situations are altogether different, and you can't make an analogy between them."

280 "I still think it's a good idea," said Polly.

"Nuts," I muttered. Doggedly I pressed on. "Next we'll try Hypothesis Contrary to Fact."

"Sounds yummy," was Polly's reaction.

"Listen: If Madame Curie had not happened to leave a photo- 285 graphic plate in a drawer with a chunk of pitchblende, the world today would not know about radium."

"True, true," said Polly, nodding her head. "Did you see the movie? Oh, it just knocked me out. That Walter Pidgeon is so dreamy. I mean he fractures me."

290 "If you can forget Mr. Pidgeon for a moment," I said coldly, "I would like to point out that the statement is a fallacy. Maybe Madame Curie would have discovered radium at some later date. Maybe somebody else would have discovered it. Maybe any number of things would have happened. You can't start with a hypothesis 295 that is not true and then draw any supportable conclusions from it."

"They ought to put Walter Pidgeon in more pictures," said Polly. "I hardly ever see him any more."

One more chance, I decided. But just one more. There is a limit to what flesh and blood can bear. "The next fallacy is called Poison- 300 ing the Well."

"How cute!" she gurgled.

"Two men are having a debate. The first one gets up and says, 'My opponent is a notorious liar. You can't believe a word that he is going to say.' . . . Now, Polly, think. Think hard. What's wrong?"

I watched her closely as she knit her creamy brow in concentration. Suddenly a glimmer of intelligence—the first I had seen—came into her eyes. "It's not fair," she said with indignation. "It's not a bit fair. What chance has the second man got if the first man calls him a liar before he even begins talking?"

"Right!" I cried exultantly. "One hundred percent right. It's not fair. The first man has *poisoned the well* before anybody could drink from it. He has hamstrung his opponent before he could even start. . . . Polly, I'm proud of you."

"Pshaw," she murmured, blushing with pleasure.

"You see, my dear, these things aren't so hard. All you have to do is concentrate. Think—examine—evaluate. Come now, let's review everything we have learned."

"Fire away," she said with an airy wave of her hand.

Heartened by the knowledge that Polly was not altogether a cretin, I began a long, patient review of all I had told her. Over and over and over again I cited instances, pointed out flaws, kept hammering away without let up. It was like digging a tunnel. At first everything was work, sweat, and darkness. I had no idea when I would reach the light, or even *if* I would. But I persisted. I pounded and clawed and scraped, and finally I was rewarded. I saw a chink of light. And then the chink got bigger and the sun came pouring in and all was bright.

Five grueling nights this took, but it was worth it. I had made a logician out of Polly; I had taught her to think. My job was done. She was worthy of me at last. She was a fit wife for me, a proper hostess for my many mansions, a suitable mother for my well-heeled children.

It must not be thought that I was without love for this girl. Quite the contrary. Just as Pygmalion loved the perfect woman he had fashioned, so I loved mine. I determined to acquaint her with my feelings at our very next meeting. The time had come to change our relationship from academic to romantic.

"Polly," I said when next we sat beneath our oak, "tonight we will not discuss fallacies."

"Aw, gee," she said, disappointed.

"My dear," I said, favoring her with a smile, "we have now spent five evenings together. We have gotten along splendidly. It is clear that we are well matched."

"Hasty Generalization," said Polly brightly.

345 "I beg your pardon," said I.

"Hasty Generalization," she repeated. "How can you say that we are well matched on the basis of only five dates?"

I chuckled with amusement. The dear child had learned her lessons well. "My dear," I said, patting her hand in a tolerant manner,
350 "five dates is plenty. After all, you don't have to eat a whole cake to know that it's good."

"False Analogy," said Polly promptly. "I'm not a cake. I'm a girl."

I chuckled with somewhat less amusement. The dear child had
355 learned her lessons perhaps too well. I decided to change tactics. Obviously the best approach was a simple, strong, direct declaration of love. I paused for a moment while my massive brain chose the proper words. Then I began:

"Polly, I love you. You are the whole world to me, and the moon
360 and the stars and the constellations of outer space. Please, my darling, say that you will go steady with me, for if you will not, life will be meaningless. I will languish. I will refuse my meals. I will wander the face of the earth, a shambling, hollow-eyed hulk."

There, I thought, folding my arms, that ought to do it.

365 "Ad Misericordiam," said Polly.

I ground my teeth. I was not Pygmalion; I was Frankenstein, and my monster had me by the throat. Frantically I fought back the tide of panic surging through me. At all costs I had to keep cool.

"Well, Polly," I said, forcing a smile, "you certainly have learned
370 your fallacies."

"You're darn right," she said with a vigorous nod.

"And who taught them to you, Polly?"

"You did."

"That's right. So you do owe me something, don't you, my dear?
375 If I hadn't come along you never would have learned about fallacies."

"Hypothesis Contrary to Fact," she said instantly.

I dashed perspiration from my brow. "Polly," I croaked, "you mustn't take all these things so literally. I mean this is just classroom stuff. You know that the things you learn in school don't have any-
380 thing to do with life."

"Dicto Simpliciter," she said, wagging her finger at me playfully.

That did it. I leaped to my feet, bellowing like a bull. "Will you or will you not go steady with me?"

"I will not," she replied.

"Why not?" I demanded.   385

"Because this afternoon I promised Petey Burch that I would go steady with him."

I reeled back, overcome with the infamy of it. After he promised, after he made a deal, after he shook my hand! "The rat!" I shrieked, kicking up great chunks of turf. "You can't go with him, Polly. He's   390 a liar. He's a cheat. He's a rat."

"Poisoning the Well," said Polly, "and stop shouting. I think shouting must be a fallacy too."

With an immense effort of will, I modulated my voice. "All right," I said. "You're a logician. Let's look at this thing logically. How   395 could you choose Petey Burch over me? Look at me—a brilliant student, a tremendous intellectual, a man with an assured future. Look at Petey—a knothead, a jitterbug, a guy who'll never know where his next meal is coming from. Can you give me one logical reason why you should go steady with Petey Burch?"   400

"I certainly can," declared Polly. "He's got a raccoon coat."

[For treatment of this selection, see p. 108.]

✍ From *Notes on Opera as Basic Theatre*   GIAN-CARLO MENOTTI

[1] Although the accusation that opera is unrealistic is an indiscriminate one, I have been assailed with it too often not to wish to dispose of it now. If by realistic, people mean a literal duplication of life, what art can be called truly realistic? Literal photographic techniques are, as far as I am concerned, the very negation of art.   5

[2] But it is curious how most people, once they accept the conventional limitations of an art form, are unconscious of its unrealistic pattern. I have been asked again and again why characters should sing instead of talk. Why, then, should they dance instead of speak?

From *The New York Times Magazine*, January 2, 1955. Reprinted by permission of The New York Times.

10 Or why, as in a Shakespearean play, should people express themselves in pentameter instead of ordinary speech?

[3] Even the cinema, which is generally upheld as the very essence of realistic art, has imposed upon an audience unaware of it the most extraordinarily unrealistic conventions. Huge faces, fifty times 15 the size of normal ones, are flashed at us without alarming us in the slightest. Hundred-piece orchestras, supposedly hidden behind the sofa, spin out sugary melodies while Van Johnson kisses Jennifer Jones in the living room, and in the flick of an eyelash we are transported, without the slightest explanation, from Ma's kitchen to the 20 very top of K-2.

The selection by Max Shulman is not merely fun; its purpose is self-explanatory. Much prose writing consists of the presentation of ideas and arguments. The order and validity of this presentation are of great importance; the reader must be led along the path of reason to a valid conclusion. To be able to lead him successfully, the writer must be aware of pitfalls and avoid them. Some of the more common of these pitfalls are explained in "Love Is a Fallacy."

Once you have become aware of these pitfalls or fallacies, you will begin to see examples of them in print. They are used—sometimes innocently and sometimes not so innocently—most frequently in persuasive writing, writing that attempts to convince the reader that some stand or point of view or action is correct.

1. Give an example, either imaginary or based on your own experience, of each of the fallacies described by Shulman.

2. Bring to class an example of one type of fallacy drawn from your reading of newspapers, magazines, or any other printed source. Be prepared to explain the fallacy in the selection you find and to determine, if possible, the motive for its use.

3. Which of the fallacies named by Shulman does Menotti use? Explain.

Alternate selections for the study of Logic: Edward J. Steichen, from "The Living Joy of Pictures"; Sinclair Lewis, from *Babbitt;* Rex Stout, "Watson Was a Woman."

Theme Assignment: Assume that you have been hired by one or another political party to write campaign literature—throwaways to be distributed in your local precinct. This is a party with which you are in sympathy, and the men and women in charge of the campaign are sincere and well meaning. You may be asked to write copy about your candidate's position on a balanced budget; deductions from income taxes for tuition costs at institutions of higher learning; making sixteen the age throughout the country at which a driver's license may be obtained; federal loans to aid local communities to improve hospitals and nursing homes; legislation which would make it a criminal offense to threaten falsely that a bomb has been set in a public place; extending the minimum-wage law to cover a greater number of men and women; reducing the voting age to eighteen.

Write a theme presenting your candidate's views (pro or con) on any one of these issues. Remember that this leaflet will be read by your neighbors—the voters—and that its ultimate objective is to convince them to vote for your candidate. Remember, too, that you are to avoid fallacies in logic; your candidate is an honorable man!

Emphasis

✐ Of the Librarian's Profession

ARCHIBALD MACLEISH

[1] Nothing is more difficult for the beginning librarian than to discover in what profession he is engaged. Certain professions define themselves. Others are defined by those who practice them. The librarian's profession is of neither nature. A librarian is so called not
5 for what he does, as the farmer who farms or the lawyer who laws, but from the place in which he does it. And the definitions of the librarians, though they are eloquent in describing the librarian's perfections, are reticent in saying what the librarian's perfections are for.

[2] Hugo Blotius, the sixteenth-century librarian of the Hofbiblio-
10 thek in Vienna, defined his profession by saying that a librarian should be learned in languages, diligent and quiet—adding, by way of reminder to his master, the Emperor, that "if not of noble blood he should be given a title to enhance the dignity of his office." Cotton des Houssayes told the general assembly of the Sorbonne in 1780
15 that when he reflected "on the qualifications that should be united in your librarian" they presented themselves to his mind in so great a number, and in such character of perfection, that he distrusted his ability not only to enumerate but even to trace a true picture of

hem. Pressing himself to the point, however, the learned orator (who spoke, it should be noted, in the Latin tongue) supplied the follow- 20 ng description of the office: "Your librarian should be above all, a learned and profound theologian; but to this qualification, which I shall call fundamental, should be united vast literary acquisitions, an exact and precise knowledge of all the arts and sciences, great facility of expression, and lastly, that exquisite politeness which conciliates 25 he affection of his visitors while his merit secures their esteem."

[3] One gathers that M. des Houssayes thought well of the librarian's office, but beyond that, and a certain conviction of personal inadequacy, one is little wiser than before. To be at once a profound and learned theologian, the possessor of vast literary acqui- 30 sitions, the exact and precise master of all the arts and all the sciences, a facile writer and a charming gentleman possessed of that exquisite politeness which wins heads as well as hearts, is to be an unusual and admirable human being—but even to be all these things at once is scarcely a profession. 35

[4] And yet it is largely in the vein of the orator of the Sorbonne and the librarian of the Holfbibliothek that the profession of the librarian is presented. Modern librarians—perhaps because they do not speak in Latin—have never been as eloquent as Cotton des Houssayes, but even modern librarians write as though the profes- 40 sion of the librarian had been defined when the scholarly attainments and linguistic achievements of the, perhaps, ideal librarian have been described.

[5] The consequence is that the beginning librarian is thrown upon his own resources, upon the dictionary, and upon the familiar 45 sentences of the great founder of the Bodleian Library at Oxford. From Sir Thomas Bodley, besides learning that a librarian should not be "encumbered with marriage nor with a benefice of cure" and that he should be "a personable scholler and qualified, if it may be, with a gentlemanlike speeche and carriage . . . able to interteine commers 50 in aswel of other nations as our owne, with meete discourses for the place," the apprentice librarian will learn that a librarian is a keeper of a library. From the dictionary he will learn that a library is "a large collection of books, public or private." And by his own resources he will attempt to deduce what the keeper of a large collec- 55 tion of books, public or private, may, in actionable and intelligible language, be. Keeper, but how a keeper? Of books—but what, then, in this context is a book?

[6] It is not an altogether simple question, and for this reason.

60 There are two meanings of the word "book," and two relations, therefore, between a book and the man entrusted with its keeping. There is one meaning which signifies a physical object made of certain physical materials in a physical shape. There is another meaning which signifies an intellectual object made of all materials or of no
65 materials and standing in as many shapes as there are forms and balances and structures in men's minds. The two meanings overlap and are confused. Readers associate the intellectual book with the physical book, thinking of Plato's vision of the world in terms of dark green linen and a gilded name. Collectors associate the physical
70 book with the intellectual book, imagining that because they possess a rare edition of a poet's work they somehow have possessed the poem. But the two meanings are nevertheless distinct. The physical book is never more than an ingenious and often beautiful cipher by which the intellectual book is communicated from one mind to an-
75 other, and the intellectual book is always a structure in the imagination which may hang for a time above a folio page in ten-point type with a half-calf binding only to be found thereafter on a different page above a different type and even in another language.

[7] When it is said, therefore, that a librarian is a keeper of
80 books, it must be determined first of which of these two books he is the keeper. Is he, for one example, the keeper of the small, cloth-bound object of 110 pages of text and 6 of front matter manufactured by Macmillan & Co., Ltd., in London in 1928 and called *The Tower,* by W. B. Yeats? Or is he the keeper of that very differ-
85 ent object created in many men's minds before, and now in yours, by this—these words, these symbols, images, perceptions—

> That is no country for old men. The young
> In one another's arms, birds in the trees,
> —Those dying generations—at their song,
> The salmon falls, the mackerel-crowded seas,
> Fish, flesh or fowl, commend all summer long
> Whatever is begotten born and dies.
> Caught in that sensuous music all neglect
> Monuments of unaging intellect.

[8] It makes a difference whether the book is the cloth and paper or the intellectual image. If it is the physical book of which a librarian is keeper, then the character of his profession is obvious
90 enough. He is a custodian as all keepers of physical objects are cus-

:odians, and his obligations are a custodian's obligations. He is a sort
of check boy in the parcel room of culture. His duty is to receive the
priceless packages confided to him by the past and to redeliver them
:o the future against the proper stub. To perform that obligation he
nust be reliable, orderly, industrious, and clever. He must devise in- 95
allible and complicated ticket systems to find the parcels on the
shelves. He must read the notations of origin and ownership in a
dozen tongues. He must guard the wrappers from the risk of time
and theft and matches and men's thumbs. He must be courteous and
patient with the claimants. And for the rest he has no duty but to 100
wait. If no one comes, if no one questions, he can wait.

[9] But if it is not the physical book but the intellectual book of
which the librarian is keeper, then his profession is a profession of a
very different kind. It is not the profession of the custodian, for the
intellectual book is not a ticketed parcel which can be preserved by 105
keeping it from mice and mildew on a shelf. The intellectual book
s an imagined object in the mind which can be preserved only by
preserving the mind's perception of its presence. Neither is the librarian's profession the profession of the check boy who receives
and guards and redelivers—receives from the past, guards against the 110
present, and redelivers to the future—for the intellectual book is not
a deposit of the past which the future has a right to call and claim.
The intellectual book is a construction of the spirit, and the constructions of the spirit exist in one time only—in that continuing and
endless present which is now. If it is the intellectual book rather than 115
he physical book of which the librarian is keeper, then the profession of the librarian is not and cannot be the neutral, passive, nega-
ive profession of the guardian and fiduciary, but must become instead the affirmative and advocating profession of the attorney for a
cause. For the intellectual book is the word. And the keepers of the 120
word, whether they so choose or not, must be its partisans and
advocates. The word was never yet protected by keeping it in storage
in a warehouse: the preservation of the word is now, as it has always
been, a cause—perhaps the greatest—not, I think, the least in danger in this time. 125

[10] It makes a difference, therefore—a very considerable difference in the understanding of the librarian's profession—which of
hese two meanings of the book is taken. Both are held. The librarian
who asserts that the sole and single strength of his profession in a
distracted world is its disinterested objectivity, meaning its negative 130
and custodial detachment from the dangers which beset the Word,

thinks of the book necessarily as a physical object on his shelves for which, in its intellectual aspects, he accepts no share of risk or credit. The library trustee or the moralizing editor who demands of
135 librarians that they stick to the job of pasting on the labels and handing out the loans accepts, but with less honesty, the same assumption—less honesty because he speaks, not from love of the librarian's profession, but from hatred of the Word, and fear of its persuasions.

140 [11] Those who love the power of the Word and who defend it take the opposite position. Shortly after William Dugard was released, through the efforts of John Milton, from Newgate prison, he published two letters by John Dury, deputy keeper in 1649 of the King's medals and library, which put the case with eagerness and
145 passion: "For if librairie-keepers did understand themselves in the nature of their work, and would make themselves, as they ought to bee, useful in their places in a publick waie; they ought to become agents for the advancement of universal learning. . . . The end of that imploiment, in my conception, is to keep the publick stock of
150 learning, which is in books and mss., to increas it, and to propose it to others in the waie which may bee most useful unto all. His work then is to bee a factor and trader for helps to learning, and a treasurer to keep them, and a dispenser to applie them to use or to see them well used, or at least not abused."

155 [12] As between these two conceptions of the profession, a man can choose only for himself and not for those who practice the profession with him. But there are, notwithstanding, certain considerations which even a novice among librarians may propose. The chief of these considerations is the nature of the times in which men live.
160 In a different time from ours—such a time as men a generation ago considered natural and normal—it made relatively little difference whether a librarian behaved himself as a custodian of volumes or as a "factor and trader for helps to learning, and a treasurer to keep them, and a dispenser to apply them to use." A generation ago the
165 word, the life of the mind, the monuments of unaging intellect, were not under attack. It was agreed by all civilized nations, by all governments in power, that the cultural tradition was a common treasure, that truth was an end to be sought equally by all men, and that the greatest glory and final justification of human life was the creative-
170 ness of the human spirit. In such a world the librarian who considered himself a custodian, who devoted himself to the perfection of his catalog and the preservation of his bindings, and who wait~

for the calls of those who had business with his collections, was not only prudent but entirely wise. There was no need for him to advocate the cause of learning or to assert the supreme importance of the contents of his library, for no one doubted the one or challenged the other. The librarian who presented himself in the years before the Great War as a champion of culture would have received the ironic welcome he deserved. What was required of him then—and what he practiced—was discretion, dignity, and a judicial calm.

[13] But the world in which we live is not that world. The world in which we live is a world that world would have believed impossible. In the world in which we live it is no longer agreed by all governments and citizens that truth is the final measure of men's acts and that the lie is shameful. There are governments abroad, and there are citizens here to whom respect for truth is naïve—governments and individuals who, when it is proved they lie, have not been shamed "either in their own or in their neighbors' eyes." In the world in which we live it is no longer agreed that the common culture is a common treasure. There are governments abroad, and there are citizens here to whom the common culture which draws the peoples of the West together is a common evil for which each nation must now substitute a private culture, a parochial art, a local poetry, and a tribal worship. In the world in which we live it is no longer agreed that the greatest glory and final justification of human history is the life of the human mind. To many men and many governments the life of the human mind is a danger to be feared more than any other danger, and the word which cannot be purchased, cannot be falsified, and cannot be killed is the enemy most hunted for and hated. It is not necessary to name names. It is not necessary to speak of the burning of the books in Germany, or of the victorious lie in Spain, or of the terror of the creative spirit in Russia, or of the hunting and hounding of those in this country who insist that certain truths be told and who will not be silent. These things are commonplaces. They are commonplaces to such a point that they no longer shock us into anger. Indeed it is the essential character of our time that the triumph of the lie, the mutilation of culture, and the persecution of the word no longer shock us into anger.

[14] What those who undertake to keep the libraries must consider—or so it seems to me—is whether this profound and troubling alteration of the times alters also their profession. Granted that it was not only possible but desirable for the librarian to think of his profession in negative and custodial terms in the quiet generations when

the burning of books was a medieval memory, is it still possible for
215 librarians to think of their profession in these passive terms in a
time in which the burning of the books is a present fact abroad and
a present possibility at home?

[15] Granted that it was not only prudent but wise as well for the
librarian to admit no positive, affirmative duty to the cause of learn-
220 ing in a time when learning was universally honored and the works of
great art and great scholarship were admired monuments, is it still
wise for librarians to admit no positive duty to learning in a time
when governments abroad teach ignorance instead of knowledge to
their people, and fanatical and frightened citizens at home would, if
225 they could, obliterate all art and learning but the art and learning they
consider safe?

[16] In a division which divides all men, because it is a division
drawn through everything that men believe, can those who keep the
libraries—those who keep the records of belief—avoid division? In a
230 struggle which is truly fought, whatever the economic interpreters and
the dialectical materialists may say to the contrary, across the countries of the spirit, can those who hold those countries remain neutral?
In an attack which is directed, as no attack in history ever was
directed, against the intellectual structures of the books, can those
235 who keep the books contend their books are only objects made of
print and paper?

[17] I can answer only for myself. To me the answer is not doubtful. To me the changes of the time change everything. The obligations
of the keepers of the books in such a time as ours are positive obliga-
240 tions because they have no choice but to be positive. Whatever the
duty of the librarian may have been in a different world and a more
peaceful generation, his duty now is to defend—to say, to fight, and
to defend. No one else—neither those who make the books nor those
who undertake to teach them—is bound as he is bound to fight in
245 their behalf, for no one else is charged as he is charged with their
protection. No one as much as he must say, and say again, and still
insist that the tradition of the written word is whole and single and
entire and cannot be dismembered. No one is under obligation as
he is under obligation to meet the mutilators of the word, the
250 preachers of obscurantism, the suppressors—those who would cut off
here and ink out there the texts their prejudices or their parties or
their churches or their fears find hateful. And these obligations are
not obligations which are satisfied by negatives. The books can be
protected from the preaching demagogues and the official liars and the

terrorizing mob not by waiting for attack but by forestalling it. If the ₂₅₅ cultural tradition, the ancient and ever-present structure of the mind, can still be saved, it can be saved by reconstructing its authority. And the authority of art and learning rests on knowledge of the arts and learnings. Only by affirmation, only by exhibiting to the people the nobility and beauty of their intellectual inheritance, can that inherit- ₂₆₀ ance be made secure.

[18] Some years before his elevation to the bench Mr. Justice Brandeis referred to himself as "counsel for the situation." The librarian in our time, or so it seems to me, becomes the counsel for the situation. His client is the inherited culture entrusted to his care. ₂₆₅ He—he more than any other man—must represent this client as its advocate. Against those who would destroy the tradition he must bring the force of the tradition. Against those who would mutilate the monuments he must bring the beauty of the monuments. Against those who would limit the freedom of the inquiring mind he must ₂₇₀ bring the marvels of the mind's discoveries.

[19] Keepers of books, keepers of print and paper on the shelves, librarians are keepers also of the records of the human spirit—the records of men's watch upon the world and on themselves. In such a time as ours, when wars are made against the spirit and its works, ₂₇₅ the keeping of these records is itself a kind of warfare. The keepers, whether they so wish or not, cannot be neutral.

Archibald MacLeish's eloquent statement about the librarian's pro-fession and the world in which we live is as relevant today as when it was written over twenty years ago. Part of its effectiveness comes from its organization and the emphasis given to certain ideas.

1. MacLeish devotes the first four paragraphs to the difficulties in defining and describing—both in the past and the present—the li-brarian's profession. Just what are the difficulties? What do the quo-tations from Hugo Blotius and Cotton des Houssayes contribute to your understanding of the librarian's profession and the difficulties in adequately describing it?

2. How is paragraph 5 related to the first four paragraphs and to the rest of the essay?

3. In your own words, explain the "two meanings of the word 'book' " (paragraph 6).

4. What is the function of paragraph 7?

5. Paragraphs 8 and 9 contrast the librarian's profession in terms of the two meanings of book—the "cloth and paper" book and the

"intellectual image." Paragraph 9 is considerably longer than paragraph 8. What does this suggest about the emphasis MacLeish wants placed on the librarian as keeper of the "intellectual book"? Show how the following contrasting sentences (contrasting in both diction and figures of speech) contribute to emphasizing the librarian as keeper of the "intellectual book":

> "He is a sort of check boy in the parcel room of culture" (paragraph 8).

> "If it is the intellectual book rather than the physical book of which the librarian is keeper, then the profession of the librarian is not and cannot be the neutral, passive, negative profession of the guardian and fiduciary, but must become instead the affirmative and advocating profession of the attorney for a cause" (paragraph 9).

Find additional contrasting sentences in paragraphs 8 and 9 which serve the same purpose as those above.

6. Ideas are contrasted again in paragraphs 10 and 11. What are the two ideas? Upon which one is more emphasis placed? Discuss the means by which MacLeish places the emphasis.

7. MacLeish's feelings about the "world in which we live" are communicated emphatically in paragraph 13. Part of the emphasis is achieved through the contrast between this world and the world "in a different time from ours" (paragraph 12). What additional means does MacLeish use to achieve emphasis in paragraph 13?

8. What functions are served by the three questions which constitute paragraph 16?

Alternate selections for the study of Emphasis: Robert Frost, "Education by Poetry"; John Ciardi, "Angel-Fluffs, Savages, and Dispensable Adults."

Theme Assignment: There is a vast difference between the librarian as portrayed by MacLeish and the librarian as seen by the elementary and high school student. Similarly the child's view of the policeman or the railroad conductor or the physician or the airline pilot that "he wants to be when he grows up" is vastly different from reality.

Write a theme—perhaps based on your own early ambitions—in which you contrast the child's view of a profession or occupation with the profession or occupation in reality. You will have to decide whether to give equal emphasis to the two views or greater emphasis to one and then organize your theme accordingly.

Subordination

Harold Ober: Literary Agent

CATHERINE DRINKER BOWEN

[1] He was tall and lean, with deep-set, serious blue eyes, a big nose, a high color, and, when I first knew him, a head of handsome gray hair which he wore parted on one side and carefully brushed down. He had the figure of a polo player; his clothes and his elegant big brown shoes were made to order on Bond Street and he was apt 5 to carry a rolled umbrella. He looked, in short, like nothing in the known world of New York literary business; he was neither slick nor shaggy and the wonder was that with his disposition and natural propensities he managed to develop one of the biggest and best-known literary agencies in the world. An agent spends half his time 10 reading manuscript; Harold even had a defect of vision—without his glasses he saw two trees where only one stood. Once, driving two neighbor children and me, he ran spang into a car standing by a Scarsdale curb.

[2] What with the rolled umbrella and the Bond Street clothes, 15 his London partner, Edmund Cork, liked to say that Harold was more British than a duke. Actually he was as New Hampshire as the town of New Ipswich (population, four hundred), where his roots lay. He used four syllables for the word "pneumoni-a"; his *a*'s had more

From *The Atlantic Monthly*, July 1960. Copyright © 1960 by Catherine Drinker Bowen. Reprinted by permission of Harold Ober Associates, Incorporated.

20 than a touch of the flat Maine *ah*. He said the name Ober sounded
like a German cornet player; actually it was French and had originally been spelled Aubert. Physically, Harold was strong and not a
little vain about it. He was born nearly eighty years ago; the legend
is that when young he walked on Sundays from Tenth Street, New
25 York, where he lived, out to Scarsdale for lunch with Paul Reynolds.
In his late sixties, Harold was still skiing every winter with his sons.
I remember when at sixty-four he broke a leg on the slopes and told
me irritatedly that a middle-aged woman came down the mountain
and crashed into him. He persisted in climbing ten flights to the
30 office floor; he said it strengthened his leg muscles. His partners were
afraid he might collapse on the way; at the appointed time one of
them would sneak out and stand guard at the stairwell.

[3] He never liked the word "agent"; he said it sounded as if he
made soap or sports cars. Thirty years ago, when I first came to him,
35 the heading on his office paper read "Harold Ober, Author's Representative." Later on it changed to plain "Harold Ober Associates,"
without the "Representative." But he was right about those words:
neither of them came near to describing his function. His clients
ranged from Scott Fitzgerald, William Faulkner, John Gunther, Faith
40 Baldwin, Adlai Stevenson, Paul Gallico, Walter D. Edmonds, Philip
Wylie, Agatha Christie, Agnes de Mille, J. D. Salinger, Dean Brelis,
John Brooks, Berton Roueché to the newest recruit who had walked
in with a manuscript which the partners considered promising.

[4] It was quite a stable to keep in order. Aside from actual busi-
45 ness and the making of contracts, Harold looked after certain of his
authors as if they were his children—stood up at their marriages,
helped them through their divorces, got them to the doctor when they
were sick, and lent them money out of his own pocket when they
were broke. Once I saw a pile of laundry in the office hallway; Harold
50 said it belonged to a woman writer who lived in the country—she
picked it up on Thursdays. The only thing Harold would not do was
take his authors to psychiatrists when they needed it. "I don't believe
in that stuff," he would say. He was very stiff about it; he said
people should be able to discipline themselves and not pay somebody
55 twenty-five dollars an hour to do it for them. With the license
of an old association I used to try to argue him out of this. I said
it was antediluvian and no wonder his ulcer kept coming back; his
kind of self-discipline was bad for ulcers. But I got nowhere.

[5] It was seldom, I believe, that any of us spoke to Harold about
60 himself; always the relationship was the other way around. For my

part it was Harold Ober who advised me whether or not to send my thirteen-year-old son to boarding school, helped me decide on colleges for my son and daughter, told me what to do when my springer bitch whelped, what to say to the neighbors when a community storm blew up, and whether to marry my second husband. ("If you marry this doctor, do you think you will keep on writing?") I don't know how many years Scott Fitzgerald was Harold's client, but it is well known that Scott's daughter, Scotty, lived with the Obers in Scarsdale and also that before Fitzgerald died Harold had given him not only a long and loyal friendship but had lent him, in all, twenty thousand dollars.

[6] One afternoon in the early thirties I ran into Harold Ober in the Pennsylvania Station. He looked frantic and said there were two authors in the building, both drunk; he had been trying to get them out and home. One of them was Scott Fitzgerald. Harold worried more about Fitzgerald than any other author he ever took care of, and with reason. Yet even when Fitzgerald's drinking had brought him to near ruin, Harold kept on with him, hoping against hope. Once I walked into the office at 40 East 49th Street and found Harold at his desk, reading manuscript and looking depressed, a condition unusual with him. When I asked the reason, he passed me some typed sheets and asked what I could make of them. The pages were interlined, written over in red ink, blotched, almost illegible, and made no sense at all. Harold said that was the way Scott's stories had been coming in lately. He got up and stood with his back to me, looking out the window; I saw him take out his handkerchief and blow his nose. I think it was as though one of his own sons had defected and gone past the point of no return.

[7] I have met many literary agents, and Harold was markedly different from the rest of them. I do not mean to stress here his elegance, because that had a sturdy New England quality, altogether without affectation. But there was no city push or rush about him, no smooth manipulative techniques; he never pressured his authors. His office reflected this attitude. One met there no chrome or slingbacked chairs, no hurry and noise of typewriters, though much business flowed through this place. When you needed to talk to Harold you sat in his quiet corner room, where books were shelved to the ceiling and the telephone did not ring. Agents and publishers are forever asking writers to go out and speak at book and author lunches, preside at book fairs, attend literary cocktail parties, or in other ways show their faces in public. Harold operated the other way

around. When an author was engaged in a book that Harold believed in, he simply sheared away petty annoyances or business responsibilities and left the writer in a vacuum until the work was done. "You
105 don't have to make that speech or attend that meeting," he would say. "Just give me the telephone numbers and I'll get you out of it." The miracle was that Harold accomplished these missions without offense at the other end. It was the business of a writer to write, Harold maintained. Let publishers take care of the advertising.

110   [8] In 1937, after six hard-working and entirely obscure years with Harold's office, I published a biography of Tchaikovsky which was chosen by the Book-of-the-Month Club. I must have been feeling my oats, because I asked Harold if he didn't think it a good thing for a writer to be part of the general literary scene. What was the use
115 of my languishing in the Philadelphia suburbs, and would he please introduce me to some New York authors? The answer was in the negative and, for Harold, very eloquent. The gist of it was that most New York writers sat up all night talking their books instead of writing them, and I had much better stay in Bryn Mawr, where I
120 belonged. Didn't I realize how lucky I was to have a decent roof over my children's and my heads, plenty of daylight writing time, and no pressing need to go out and get a job teaching or copy reading? Actually, I had once tried for a job with the *Woman's Home Companion;* at my insistence Harold had even made me an appointment
125 with Miss Roberts, one of the editors. Miss Roberts said she couldn't hire me; they didn't need anybody. But she commissioned me to write six articles on music at a price I had never before commanded, and I went out of the place on wings. Years later, Harold confessed that he had asked Miss Roberts not to take me on. "I knew in the end
130 you'd do better financially, writing books," he said blandly.

[9] I think Harold was the only survivor in the New York literary business who called people by their last names. He always referred to his partners as Miss Olding and Mr. Von Auw, even when everybody else was calling them Dorothy and Ivan. There was an old-
135 fashioned courtesy about him even when he was young. Yet Harold could take a writer down with aim as deadly as the legendary Tell. He was impatient with the prima donna type. More than once I have heard him say that writers were an egotistical, maddening breed and he wondered how he had happened to get mixed up with them
140 in the first place. As a matter of fact, I wondered a little myself. His early education had been in the New England public schools, from whence he had gone in due course to Harvard, where he stroked

the varsity crew. After that he went to Paris for a year. When I asked him why he went abroad and stayed so long he told me, looking embarrassed, that he had wanted to be a writer, and in those days 145 people who wanted to be writers went to Paris.

[10] Harold was a shrewd trader, with the mark of worldliness about him; when bargaining was in process one rejoiced to be on his side. I think there was something in him which disarmed publishers and editors, even when they had known him for a long time. Perhaps 150 "deceived" is the better word, though the deception was unconscious on Harold's part. He carried in his bearing no hint of Madison Avenue and the hard tough marts of trade. Indeed it seemed scarcely right to mention money to Harold at all. When John Gunther first came over to the agency he asked me one day if Harold Ober wasn't 155 perhaps too much the gentleman to be a good businessman. I repeated this to a magazine editor, at a moment when his magazine was settling terms with Harold for a feature article they wanted me to write. The editor made a loud derisive noise. "Harold Ober, too much the gentleman to drive a bargain?" he said. "Has he told you what he 160 is getting out of us, in his gentlemanly way, for your piece?"

[11] The lunch table is, of course, the confidential conference place of the publishing world. Yet Harold Ober was offish about inviting people to lunch, though on occasion he would favor old clients or out-of-town authors. I first met Harold in 1930. I had come from 165 Easton, Pennsylvania, where I then lived, and I had never been to lunch in a New York restaurant in my life. I carried three notebooks I had brought along, with pieces of paper stuck in, about things I wanted to write next. Harold led me into a restaurant, and we were ushered to our seats. I got out the notebooks and put them on the 170 table in front of me; the pieces of paper fell out, and Harold helped me pick them off the floor. Then he smiled and said, "Suppose we wait till we have something to eat?" I put away the notebooks, ate my oysters, and looked around. The walls were oak-paneled, but the room was bright; there was an air of ease and gaiety. I said, "Where 175 are we, Mr. Ober, what is this place?" He said, "This place? Why, this is the Ritz."

[12] At once I felt reassured; in fact I felt wonderful. Nobody, I reasoned, gets fed at the Ritz unless he is worth something to the person who feeds him. Mr. Ober had read the manuscript of my 180 novel; he must think it pretty good. He hadn't said so, it was true, but then he hadn't said much of anything. Harold, I was to discover, possessed a genius for knowing just how much encouragement and

discouragement to give a writer, how much of what William James
called "No no!"—and how much of comfort. With the latter he was
chary. I remember when my first novel was published in 1934,
Harold said kindly that perhaps I would like to walk down with him
to Putnam's and see my book on the stands. But he felt he must tell
me something: When an author's first novel comes out, the author
thinks it is going to change the world. And then it doesn't. Nothing
happens. "Actually, the world pays very little attention to first
novels."

[13] Long afterward, when other books of mine had been published, I thanked Harold for that remark. He said he remembered
it well and that he had hated saying it. But it was better to be frank
with beginning authors; it saved them worse suffering in the end.
In thirty years of association, I remember just three letters of professional comment that Harold showed me. All three had a profound
effect, and there is no doubt that Harold knew they would and had
calculated it out to the last twinge. The first came from Fanny
Heaslip Lea, the novelist and short story writer, who had introduced
me to Harold after reading the manuscript of my novel. My manuscript had amateurish places in it, Fanny's letter said, but she thought
that I could learn to write. The juxtaposition of those two remarks
was enough to set a writer off like a time bomb and Harold knew it.
I took the letter home with me and went to work.

[14] The second letter came a few years later and it was from
Frederick Lewis Allen, then editor in chief of *Harper's* magazine. I
was trying to write personal essays, eventually to be published as a
small collection called *Friends and Fiddlers.* But the unfamiliar form
crippled me; I was stiff and self-conscious. Harold offered two of the
essays to *Harper's,* which already had published several things of
mine. The essays were rejected. Harold sent them back with a brief
note saying that he was enclosing Fred Allen's covering letter, which
I was not supposed to see. But he thought it might be wise to send it
on. "What is the matter with Mrs. Bowen?" Allen's letter said. "She
writes like a disgruntled schoolteacher." I put that letter on the floor
beside my typewriter, where it stared up at me. In anger and chagrin
—all stiffness knocked out of me—I began to rewrite. Once again,
Harold had known exactly what he was doing.

[15] The third letter I mention because Harold Ober's accompany-
ing note was so characteristic. The letter had come to Harold from
Hamish Hamilton, my English publisher, who had just received the
manuscript of my biography of Chief Justice Sir Edward Coke, on

which I had been at work for six years. Hamilton was pleased with 225
the book and said so. "When you read this you won't turn into a
conceited author, will you?" Harold wrote. I used to tell Harold he
was just like John Adams. If on Saturday night there was joy, on
Sunday morning Adams turned it into cause for sober thought and
future self-improvement. 230

[16] Harold was indeed so reserved that I wondered, sometimes,
how he managed in conference with publishers and with the lawyers
who took care of his clients' income tax returns and plagiarism suits
and all the tangled affairs of the literary business. When he did take
an author to lunch, he could sit for ten minutes straight without 235
anybody saying a word. One morning I told the same Miss Roberts
of the *Woman's Home Companion* that I was to lunch at noon with
Mr. Ober. She shook her head and inquired what on earth we would
find to talk about. "That New Hampshireman can say nothing for
longer periods than the great Buddha." Yet, as soon as one found 240
out that these silences did not make Harold Ober uneasy, they ceased
also to make other people uneasy. After the smooth volubility of
editors and publishers, Harold's silence had a reassuring quality.

[17] In politics he was liberal, a strong supporter of Franklin D.
Roosevelt, and thereby fell into difficulties with his far-to-the-right 245
neighbors of Westchester County. At a big Scarsdale dinner party
the talk became viciously anti-Semitic. Harold endured it as long as
he could. ("I didn't know what to say, it's hard to break into a conversation like that.") Finally he put his napkin on the table, got up,
and left the dining room and the house. "My wife came along later," 250
he told me vaguely. When I asked if he had mentioned the incident
afterward to his host and hostess, called up or anything, Harold said,
"No, what would there be to say?"

[18] We didn't talk about business much, though we discussed at
length what I was currently writing and what I had better plan to 255
write next. Harold plainly considered me feeble-minded where money
was concerned. He told me sharply never to make terms with editors
or publishers, but let him do it for me. Once he astonished me with
a check for $5000 from Hollywood; he said it was an option on
Yankee from Olympus. The option covered eighteen large single- 260
spaced pages, and it specified that the production could include
singing and dancing. The notion of Justice Holmes *en ballet* charmed
me (even aside from the $5000), and I begged Harold to complete
the deal. How did the office think I'd do in Hollywood? Harold said
he would think it over. 265

[19] I never heard another word about Hollywood and Holmes. Before I knew it I was deep in a biography of John Adams. Looking back, I am sure it was no accident that this pattern kept repeating itself, and that for thirty years under Harold's direction I wrote straight out of one book into another. Sometimes, at the end of a book, I would inquire if any publishers had sent in ideas for a new biography I might write. Last time I asked was just after *The Lion and the Throne* was finished. Harold said Yes, he had a list of a dozen or so ideas from different publishers; he had held them back until I finished writing. Actually I never saw the list because I started right in on a new book of my own choosing.

[20] I don't know how it was with his other authors, but for me the greatest service Harold did was to keep me at work. Of course every writer is confronted, sooner or later, by false prophets who urge him to change publishers or agents. The farthest pastures are greenest, and look how much that new agent, Harry Smithers, made for So-and-so on his last novel, what with digests and paperbacks. I remember one remark of Harold's that alone was worth thirty years at 10 percent. We were walking along Forty-ninth Street toward his office. At this particular time I wanted to break away from books on music, of which I had published three, and write about Justice Oliver Wendell Holmes. Most authors overtalk their points. I had talked mine down to incoherence, tormenting myself with obvious logic against the venture, arguing counter to my own desires and then demanding of Harold why he didn't say something. Was it that old Yankee caution? What did he really think—should I try this book about a judge and the law? Suppose I ended up, fire years later, flat on my face?

[21] Harold did not pause in his stride or glance around. He looked straight ahead, and he was frowning. "People should gamble on their abilities," he said. He repeated it. "Kitty, you must gamble on yourself."

[22] It was the sheer integrity of his character, I think, that made Harold's pronouncements so impressive—when he made them. Again, he was sparing of that kind of thing. His letters were triumphs of reticence. "Dear Kitty: Here is your Chapter 21 and it is a very nice one. Any comments I have are inconsequential. Filacer and prothonotary on page 17 stumped me but perhaps lawyers will know them. Isn't *fenny* a little far fetched, wouldn't marshy do as well? Sincerely, Harold."

[23] That was in 1955, when I was writing the biography of Sir

Edward Coke, with fourteen chapters still ahead of me. Long before, in 1941 or 1942, I remember sending Harold the first seven chapters of *Yankee from Olympus*—about twenty-five thousand words which were concerned entirely with Justice Holmes's ancestors and his father and mother. I waited anxiously for Harold's reply. "I am sure," he wrote, "that your book is going to be very interesting. Your books are always interesting. But how can I judge seven chapters of a biography when the hero isn't even born yet?"

[24] Authors are exigent; there is no end to the sympathy they need and can absorb. A good agent knows it. During the final year of my successive biographies, my telephone would ring at exactly the right moment in the morning's work. "How is it coming?" the cheerful, even voice would ask. Plainly, Harold Ober was not worried about my book, so why should I be so everlastingly anxious? He was strongly against hurry in writing—a trait unusual in a profession which is forever sighting deadlines and whipping up ideas for books that can be written in six months, articles that can be produced in two weeks. "Never mind if the publishers are pushing you," Harold said. "Take another five months if you need it. Take another year. Good books aren't written in a hurry."

[25] It was my great good fortune to have a literary agent with a passion for history. Harold thought the writing of biography was "worth while," and he did not hesitate to use that comfortable, outmoded phrase. As he grew older, Harold stayed much in New York and let his young partners make the necessary trips to see his Hollywood and London affiliates. For his writers it was marvelous to know that Harold was in New York and available. Most agents and publishers seem forever to be somewhere else—flying to Paris to round up French authors, to England for play contracts. Or it is August and they are in Maine. For an author with a manuscript to be read, these absences are unreasonable, unforgivable, and altogether crushing.

[26] As he grew older, Harold became more exacting about the quality of manuscripts submitted. It must have been hard on his partners. He told me ruefully that he could no longer judge the magazine fiction that came to his office. "I take home a serial, and next day I tell Miss Olding it's horrible, not fit to print. Then she reads it and sells it to some woman's magazine for thirty thousand dollars." In his last years he read much for his own pleasure: history, philosophy—Carlyle, Froude, Santayana, Trevelyan, Burckhardt. He said he had given up reading manuscript on the commuters' train and read printed books instead. Right up to the end he continued to work

in his Scarsdale garden. He had wonderful strawberries, and four thousand gladioli which he crossbred for new species; his wife, Anne,
350 complained that he would break his back digging trenches for asparagus.

[27] Harold did not like getting old; the fact of it seemed to embarrass him, as if he had done something a bit off-color that ought to be suppressed. Over the rafters in his living room was the big oar
355 he had won as stroke at Harvard, with his name and class painted on it; he kept it rolled over so no one could see the date. When his sons came home from college for the holidays, they used to turn the oar around, to tease him. "Yesterday was my birthday," Harold would announce, standing in the office hallway. "I am getting very old."
360 He would look quickly to see what we would say. I always made the same reply. "Harold, I know exactly how old you are. I have known for thirty yeas." This seemed at the same time to surprise and relieve him. "Why, I had no idea you knew my age!" he would exclaim.

365 [28] Beginning in 1956 he had several heart attacks, one of which sent him to the hospital. But he never talked about his health. Some months after the first attack, I ventured to ask Harold how he had really felt about it. From his manner one would think heart attacks were part of normal daily life. Hadn't he been under any strain at
370 all? Was he scared, apprehensive? Harold shook his head quickly. "I felt humiliated," he said.

[29] The summer before he died, some of us had driven down through New Hampshire with him and had prevailed on him to stop at New Ipswich and call on his Cousin Caroline. Cousin Caroline was
375 eighty-five; she lived in a brick-ended clapboard house not far from the common. We drove up to the back door after the New England fashion; Miss Caroline was in the kitchen putting up beans. She had on a big apron and a cap which entirely covered her hair; she lived alone and she spoke with Harold's exact accent. We sat in the front
380 room while the two of them talked, exchanging stories. Obviously there was mutual affection and respect. Miss Caroline showed a quick interest in everything pertaining to the world of books. It was the only time I ever heard Harold expand into anecdote—homely stories about the region, about his grandfather's friend, for instance
385 who was up shingling the roof and all of a sudden called out, "By the gods, I'm going to fall!" Then he said, "By the gods, I'm falling!" And then, "By the gods, I've fallen!" And he picked himself up and limped off.

[30] We left Miss Caroline and walked along a tree-lined road to the cemetery. Four stones bore the name of Ober; they were small stones, and they looked out over the valley and hills to the south. There was a big pond in the cemetery; boys were fishing in it. As we drove out of town we passed a little house, very old and set deep in a green slope. Harold said it had belonged to his great-grandfather.

[31] All of us were glad, afterward, that we had gone there and seen the gravestones, Cousin Caroline, and the old house built in the green bank. They explained Harold Ober, defined him as New York City and Scarsdale could never define him: spare and kind, cautious yet believing, a gentleman of the old school who kept his sights high and his bargaining wits about him—above all a man country bred, in whose hands an author could feel safe.

The proper subordination of the parts of any piece of writing contributes much to the total effectiveness of the writing. Though it is impossible to create a set of rules which, when followed, will result in correct subordination, the skillful writer manages his materials so that the reader is made fully aware of what is of major importance, what of subordinate importance, what a mere example, and what a basic idea.

In writing her sketch of Harold Ober, Catherine Drinker Bowen faced the problem of portraying both Ober the man and Ober the literary agent. The typical reader of the sketch could not be expected to know much about literary agents and their work habits, their methods, their relationships with their clients. Consequently, to do justice to her material, Mrs. Bowen had to supply information about literary agents in general so that the specific characteristics of Ober would be understandable to the reader. But the general information had to be subordinated to the more specific information.

The amateur writer might have solved this problem in subordination by opening his sketch with several paragraphs about literary agents and their work. Mrs. Bowen, however, is far more skillful.

1. Why does Mrs. Bowen begin her sketch with a physical description of Harold Ober? What is the relevance of his appearance to his being a literary agent? What information about literary agents emerges in the first paragraph? Why does Mrs. Bowen place the incident of the automobile accident at the end of the first paragraph?

2. What is the significance of the list of authors in paragraph 3? What insight do you get about Harold Ober from learning that he numbered among his clients "the newest recruit who had walked in with a manuscript . . ."?

3. What conclusions can you draw about literary agents in general from what you learn about Ober in paragraph 4?

4. To use the material about herself in paragraphs 5 and 8, Mrs. Bowen had to solve the problem of keeping herself subordinate to Ober. How did she solve the problem in each of the paragraphs? Do you think she succeeded in each? Why or why not?

5. How does Mrs. Bowen manage to give the reader a picture of a typical literary agent and his office in paragraph 7 without ever letting Harold Ober leave "the center of the stage"?

6. Mrs. Bowen is clearly interested not in running down literary agents in general but rather in paying a deeply felt tribute to Harold Ober. Suppose, however, that her purpose had been to concentrate on the bad qualities of agents in general and to use Ober merely as a subordinate element for the purpose of contrast. Rewrite paragraph 7 from this suppositious point of view; use the information in the paragraph but feel free to make whatever changes are necessary to achieve the "upside-down subordination."

7. Make a list of the items of information you learn about literary agents in general in paragraphs 9 through 25. Which of the items does Mrs. Bowen communicate directly? Which indirectly? Discuss the means by which the items are communicated indirectly. What conclusions can you draw about the relationship between indirection and subordination?

Alternate selections for the study of Subordination: Robert Allen Durr, from "The Last Days of H. L. Mencken"; H. L. Mencken, "Literature and the Schoolma'm"; William Butler Yeats, from *Reveries over Childhood and Youth*.

Theme Assignment: Your analysis of the Bowen sketch should have made you aware of the problem of subordination and of various solutions to it. The following assignments test your skill in solving the problem in your own writing.

One of the marks of maturity is knowing that few opinions can be held without awareness of some validity in an opposing opinion. For example, a man may believe passionately that television is a major instrument of education; but he may, at the same time, be aware that much television broadcasting is an utter waste of time. Or a person who believes that travel is a major source of pleasure may nevertheless admit that travel can be an unmitigated bore. Partisans of athletics as an integral part of a liberal arts education may still realize that time spent in athletic endeavor is taken away from serious intellectual pursuits. People who feel strongly that advertising is a necessary public service may also be aware that advertising can be a public menace.

Write a theme in which you take a strong position in favor of one of the opinions indicated above, taking into account nevertheless the validity of the opposing position which should be kept subordinate but related to your main argument. You will not, of course, be guilty of using any fallacies in logic.

or

The way in which a person engages in an activity—even an everyday, routine activity—frequently reveals much about his personality. Choose a person whom you know well—a parent, a friend, a roommate, an employer, a local storekeeper or service-station attendant, a barber—and show, in a theme of at least four paragraphs, what is revealed of his personality by the way in which he engages in some one specific activity. To make the individual real and alive to the reader, you will have to describe him in some detail engaging in the activity, but the activity itself should be kept clearly subordinate to the personality trait or traits he reveals.

Beginning
and Ending

Editorial Disorder and Early Sorrow   MEG GREENFIELD

[1] The first publication I ever worked for was a newspaper that was co-owned and co-edited by me. It was called the *El-Jo DeLuxe* in honor of my middle name, which is Ellen, and my partner's name, which was Josephine. We were nine years old at the time, and this
5 kind of fair-sharing arrangement was the agreed-upon basis of our partnership, although we were less faithful in observing it whenever cash was at stake. Our frequent discord over the division of our income was resolved in a series of meetings that I remember chiefly for the unusual amount of kicking, biting, and scratching they entailed
10 —not to mention the consequent shrieking. Josephine was tall and featured knees. I was short and wore an inverted soup-bowl haircut to which there was loosely affixed at all times a gigantic taffeta ribbon. Ghastly as it was to observe, we never went anywhere but arm in arm. We were best friends.

15   [2] Since our principles also required that we have offices in each of our houses, the paper was planned in Josephine's closet and printed in my basement, where our work was not without its hazards. The

From *The Reporter,* February 10, 1966. Copyright 1966 by The Reporter Magazine Company. Reprinted by permission of the author.

least of these was envelopment by wet laundry, and the worst is still beyond my power to describe—it involved the fact that the machine on which we typed our stencil was emplaced directly beneath my brother's punching bag. Still, we fought for the right to do the typing, since whoever got there first at once inscribed herself as "editor-in-chief," leaving the other in the unenviable role of "distributor." The distributor delivered not only our twenty subscription copies, which were legibly reproduced in purple ink, but also half a dozen others we continued to run off well after the stencil had given out. These were printed in a watery orchid hue that a court of law might or might not have declared to be in fact invisible, and they were stuffed under the doors of nonsubscribing neighbors by the distributor, who presented herself the next day and demanded five cents payment. From time to time, we made a nickel this way, but on the whole it was unrewarding work. And that is why, as the editor typed away, the distributor would sit on the cold cement floor and sulk.

[3] It was in that basement not long ago, now minus the apparatus of childhood, that I came across some copies of the *El-Jo DeLuxe* while my brother and I were going through family papers, prior to the sale of the house. Unlike the other memorabilia we encountered, the sight of it suffused me with a sense of Significance and Woe. Twice in its brief existence from 1940 to 1941, I recalled, the *El-Jo DeLuxe* had had to be suppressed and its printing machinery to be seized. Moreover, the second of these episodes had involved some large and basic truths about the function of the press in a free society. The story of the *El-Jo DeLuxe* is a turbulent one, but it is full of morals for our time—if only we are brave enough to face them.

[4] I see by an issue from the autumn of 1940 that the McIntyres had just come home. Here is the complete story: "FLASH! The McIntyres of 21st avenue north are back from eleven months on business in the east. In their opinion, this is the best city. Warm regards, McIntyres!!" I cite this story in full because it expresses the sum of our editorial policy: eternal solicitude for our subjects (almost all our stories ended with a dispensation of regards), and local pride bordering on mania. Not from the McIntyres alone but from all returning travelers, we exacted something like a municipal loyalty oath; and we were very stingy with our allegiance, extending it only to the barest minimum of persons and places that we had been assured were worthy. These, as any child of the period could tell you, included Finland, because she had paid her First World War debt; Haile

Selassie; King Zog of Albania; and—grudgingly—Great Britain, who
had not paid her war debt but in whose behalf anyway we often
60 stood in Josephine's closet and sang, "Don't give up, Tommy Atkins
—Be a stout fellow! Chin up! Cheerio! Carry on!"

[5] Neither our foreign nor domestic policy, however—the one
extremely cranky, the other a little damp with good will—reveals
itself upon scrutiny of the paper to have been our principal inspira-
65 tion as publishers. We were moved by the profit motive, as I may
have already made plain, and there is evidence throughout the *El-Jo
DeLuxe* that we were quite slipshod about maintaining the line between editorial content and commercial self-interest that is supposed
to be the first ethic of publishing. "If you have noticed a slick cream
70 auto on Crescent Drive Wednesday morn," one of our typical news
accounts begins, "it belongs to Mrs. and Mr. Jack Kilbey of Belling-
ham. Mrs. Kilbey subscribed to the *El-Jo DeLuxe* and more of you
ought to follow her example."

[6] To rouse our readers' curiosity in what often turned out to be
75 house ads, we of course had to provide some news. And we knew
our market well. For the most part it consisted of housewives who
counted on us to supply missing parts of a picture they could only
make out dimly from behind a twitching living-room curtain: the
name of the family who had moved in, what "he" did for a living,
80 the ages and grades in school of the children, the extent to which
certain houses had been remodeled, which of the neighbors planned
to repaint in the spring. Josephine and I were meticulous about providing the answers to such questions, although we probably didn't
always emphasize the things our matronly readers cared about most.
85 "The dog-house," we would tell them, for example, "is large enough
to accommodate three children and has two windows which adds to
its attractiveness." Still, we were trying; and if we failed, it was only
for lack of news. Very little ever happened in that neighborhood, a
problem we only partially succeeded in disguising by beginning all
90 our items—including fillers and birthday messages to my great-aunts
in Ohio—with "FLASH!" Our fillers themselves tell the sad story.
Usually they were full-length articles we left untitled because we had
plagiarized them from the local press. One such filler, an analysis of
Walt Disney by Sidney Skolsky, went on for two consecutive issues
95 in their entirety.

[7] In Washington, I have since learned, there is nothing government press officers fear more than what is called a "news vacuum"—
a dull stretch in which reporters, desperate for a story, may pick up

anything that comes along and overplay it beyond recognition. We, of course, lived in a permanent news vacuum; and in almost every edition of the *El-Jo DeLuxe* one can see the frantic quest for "the story"—the sixth-grade teacher "almost" had a bad skid in her automobile; a fifth-grade pupil "practically" fainted from Clorox fumes. It was only a matter of time until it happened, but since our parents were not press officers, they could not be expected to know what was coming. What came was a description, in all its repellent detail, of what we called the "near fatal nosebleed" of Josephine's younger brother—a story that began memorably as follows: "Most people think a nosebleed is nothing, but what would you say if clots of blood four inches long came out of your nose?" Speaking strictly professionally, I do not think I have ever surpassed that as a lead sentence. But my enthusiasm was not widely shared. The printing machine disappeared from the basement. Publication of the paper was suspended. And perhaps—I can't remember—we were even slammed around a little bit.

[8] Well, as the history of the free press amply demonstrates, you can't keep a good newspaper down; much less a bad one. We were back in business in about six months, owing to the baseless optimism of our parents, who believed we were appreciably more mature at ten than we had been at nine and that we had "learned something" from our experience. This time we only lasted for two issues.

[9] The trouble the second time around involved charges a good deal more serious than mere sensationalism, and it concerned a real public issue. Some time earlier that year, the school board had announced its decision to create a junior high school out of the Henry Wadsworth Longfellow Elementary School. Seventh- and eighth-grade students from four schools in our area would attend it, and the displaced younger children from Longfellow would, in turn, be sent to us. The stir that followed this announcement was no less real for being subterranean in nature. Where the other four schools existed in comfortable middle-class neighborhoods, Longfellow was in the poor, tough part of town. Its pupils were largely Negroes, and there had been no Negroes in our school before.

[10] I have searched my memory to be careful about all this. I had probably never even met a Negro, and the word had not come down from Josephine's parents or from mine. Where did we hear the talk? Specifically, I recall one of our teachers as a source, and also the old lady with whom we haggled over candy in the school store

and who was, in this pursuit, an equal match to our joint talents.
But there were others. We heard of remarks allegedly made by the
principal of one school, of do-or-die resistance being planned in another. When we sat down to immortalize the situation, there is no
doubt in my mind that we were reflecting faithfully—if crudely and
starkly—the prevalent attitude in our neighborhood. "FLASH!," it
naturally began: "Children From Stevens, Lowell, T. T. Minor, and
Montlake will go to Longfellow which will be East Center Junior
High in the fall. Although no one wants their children to go to Longfellow or visa versa due to the negroes, that is what is going to happen say the school board." Josephine and I rooted around in the
current folklore, came up with a suitable tag line, and gave it just
that extra little shove. "Said the principal of Montlake school," I
typed, "we don't want those niggers coming here."

[11] The routine manner in which we filled the rest of the paper
with our heartfelt regards for persons who were having their windows
washed, and distributed it to our subscribers and our nonsubscribing
victims, leads me to believe that we were innocent of what we had
done and unsuspecting of the uproar to follow. We were—and yet, in
some small way, we weren't. Before I knew exactly what was going
on, but when my parents' expressions and the whole atmosphere of
our house had already become ominous, I think I could have told
you that the gathering storm had something to do with me and the
El-Jo DeLuxe. And as I marched down the stairs on my way to an
exchange of views with my father, by whom I was finally summoned,
I believe I could also have pointed out the offending article and its
most offensive passages.

[12] I will not pretend to remember all that was said on that occasion, but I will never forget the highlights, much as I'd like to.
Roughly, the charges against me were (1) lying and (2) the pos-
session of ridiculous and ignorant opinions. My defense followed a
complicated course: Yes, I had too heard the principal say it, although, no, it was true I had never even laid eyes on him, but
Josephine knew him well and she heard him say it, or at least that's
what she told me, but she may have made it all up, and in any
event, the whole thing was her fault. My problem was that I still
didn't know precisely what the "fault" was, since I continued to assume that my father and I and that poor maligned principal were
in agreement on the fundamentals. So, to reinforce our common
bond, I asked him whether he thought the "niggers" ought to come
to our school. He chose that moment to advise me that the word I

wanted was "Negro," and—perhaps because I saw the whole tight structure of my various patriotisms and loyalties being challenged—I remember that this remark enraged me. "Nee-gro," I began to mimic with exaggerated care, and then, seeing the look on his face, I abruptly feigned a racking cough, so he would attribute my enunciation to ill-health rather than insolence. "Nee-gro-ho-ho-ho-awgh," I fairly choked, and, lest he had any doubt about my good faith in the matter or the probability of my immediate death, I went through it for him a second time—"Nee-hee-awgh-awgh-awgh. . . ."

[13] He was unimpressed, as I had reason to know he would be. The Camille thing had never been much use in our family, although I tried it out repeatedly in moments of great danger, of which, I suddenly realized, this was one. But with the superior wisdom of age, my father took this show for what it was: a confession of guilt and a surrender. He more or less set aside the charge of lying and sought to convince me that I had somehow misinterpreted what people thought and that it would be too bad if I based my editorial judgments on such cockeyed information. This approach had the virtue of permitting me to reconstruct the event as a dreadful misunderstanding in which I was blameless. I leapt at the opportunity and could hardly remember ever thinking what, in fact, I had been thinking five minutes before. The discussion dwelt briefly on newspaper retractions, and this interested me enormously. I had no way of knowing the subject was academic, since I didn't know he had already decided that the world had seen enough of the *El-Jo DeLuxe*.

[14] You may wonder where my partner was at such a critical time. She was probably home facing similar music. Whenever there was trouble of this magnitude, Josephine and I were separated for at least a full week, each set of parents being of the opinion that the other child was the bad influence. Accordingly, I set about what I considered the very glamorous task of preparing a retraction on my own. The only thing Josephine and I shared that week was the unrelieved hostility of the neighborhood. We were outcasts. Indeed, you would have thought we had invented racism in my basement. Most people didn't even talk to us, and those who did lectured us on what was known simply as "brotherhood" in those days. Notably, their number included the same persons who had given us our original *sub rosa* guidance. That teacher, for instance, fixed me with a terrible stare when she delivered some tender thoughts to the class about the family of man and how it had been created equal.

220 [15] If I had been a sufficiently sensitive child, this turn of events might have led me to a more memoir-like conclusion. I would have been able to record that my youthful encounter with adult hypocrisy had disillusioned me in an interesting sort of pastel-tinted, melancholy way. Far from it; I was exhilarated. Each new lecture and 225 every sly recantation only seemed to confirm the truth of the document I was composing; and if my mentors assured me that the Negro race was supposed to be right up there with Finland and Albania, that was all right with me. I only wished they had made it so explicit sooner. The burden of my retraction was that the entire article in 230 the previous week's paper had been due to some unspecified "error" on the part of some similarly unspecified "reporter." But mostly it was taken up with another fictitious quotation from the principal of Montlake School, this time to the effect that he could hardly wait for the proposed merger to take place. I had worked very hard on that 235 quotation and was extremely disappointed to discover that I no longer had a newspaper to publish it in.

[16] In my twilight years I have taken to thinking that Josephine and I alone were responsible for the orderly desegregation of our city's school system in 1941—a daydream that I find as irresistible 240 as it is preposterous. At most, we managed to destroy resistance in one neighborhood by having done nothing more virtuous than the wrong thing. Still, in our inadvertent and ignoble way, we caused policy to be made as I have so often seen it made since—by outright denial of that which had been true. More than my experience 245 with the *El-Jo DeLuxe* has convinced me that it is a foolish journalist who will underestimate the fallibility of his own reporting, the unreliability of his sources, the Pecksniffery of his public, and—taken together—their tremendous potential as a force for good. Over the long term, anyway, the worst seems to be for the best and hypocrisy 250 its own reward. One thinks about these things.

A piece of writing is a unit. It has architecture—structure, order. It has parts which must be developed separately but which must be made to hold together. The relationships among these parts must be clear, and the parts must be weighted appropriately. Also, this organized, ordered whole has strategic, sensitive spots. It is mere common sense that the beginning and ending are strategic.

1. Beginnings and endings, of course, need not be held to one para-

graph each. How long is the beginning of "Editorial Disorder and Early Sorrow"? How do you know?

2. What tone does the author set in her first sentence? in the beginning of the article as you have determined it? If your answers to these questions differ from one another, account for that difference in terms of the guiding purpose of the selection.

3. Presumably beginnings not only set a tone, but are useful in enticing the reader to continue. The enticement may be accomplished in numerous ways: for example, the author may raise a question or present a problem, he may create suspense by a dramatic or startling statement or situation, he may present a character who is immediately engaging, he may make a direct appeal to emotion by addressing the reader, or he may use some combination of these or other devices. What device or devices does Greenfield use to engage the reader's attention and encourage the reader to continue?

4. What is the relevance to the article of the emphasis placed upon "the profit motive" (paragraph 5)?

5. Comment on the effectiveness of the sentence in paragraph 7 of which Meg Greenfield wrote ". . . I do not think I have ever surpassed that as a lead sentence."

6. What is the function of paragraph 8? of the first sentence of the paragraph? Account for your answer.

7. Why has the author included both incidents of the suppression of the *El-Jo De Luxe*? What would have been gained or lost had the first of the two incidents been omitted?

8. In the last paragraph, Greenfield says, "More than my experience with the *El-Jo DeLuxe* has convinced me . . ." Presumably, then, she could have cited many more incidents in support of her position. What would have been gained or lost had she done so?

9. A conclusion should be the outgrowth and summation of what has preceded it. In what ways are these functions met by the last paragraph of the article?

10. Restate in your own words the third sentence of the last paragraph. What would have been gained or lost had this sentence appeared at the beginning of the article?

11. What is the function of the last sentence of the article?

Alternate selections for the study of Beginning and Ending: Carl Sandburg, "How to Read a Newspaper"; E. B. White, "How to Tell a Major Poet from a Minor Poet."

Theme Assignment: Write a theme in which you discuss the pros and cons of the statement ". . . it is a foolish journalist who will underestimate the fallibility of his own reporting, the unreliability of his sources, the Pecksniffery of his public, and—taken together—their tremendous potential as a force for good" (paragraph 16). You will want to relate this statement to what *you* take to be "the function of the press in a free society." You may include an illustration or illustrations in support of your own point of view (which you will have to determine clearly before writing your theme). Remember to pay particular attention to the beginning and ending.

or

Write a theme illustrating and elaborating upon the statement that policy is often made "by outright denial of that which had been true." You may want to use as illustration an incident from your own childhood, a campus incident, or an incident of local or national political significance. Remember that you are not merely reporting an incident, you are demonstrating a statement. The beginning and ending of your theme should be useful to you in solving this writing problem.

or

Write a theme in which you say the opposite of what you mean. Thus you will be persuasive in an indirect way; you will employ humor; you will adopt—tongue in cheek—a point of view entirely different from your own. For example, if you believe that weight is a medical problem, and that everyone should keep his weight down (or up) to a certain figure, assume the attitude that weight is of no importance, and that everyone should eat whatever and whenever he likes. Or, if you believe that rock and roll is here to stay, adopt—exaggeratedly—the position that rock-and-roll music disgusts and bores you. If you think that going steady is not harmful to teen-age development, write as though you thought it most harmful. Keep your theme short, and make full use of the possibilities of the beginning and ending. Keep your tone light: this is not weighty disputation, but argument by indirection.

Concreteness

Literature and the Schoolma'm

H. L. MENCKEN

[1] With precious few exceptions, all the books on style in English are by writers quite unable to write. The subject, indeed, seems to exercise a special and dreadful fascination over schoolma'ms, bucolic college professors, and other such pseudo-literates. One never hears of treatises on it by George Moore or James Branch Cabell, but the 5 pedagogues, male and female, are at it all the time. In a thousand texts they set forth their depressing ideas about it, and millions of suffering high-school pupils have to study what they say. Their central aim, of course, is to reduce the whole thing to a series of simple rules—the over-mastering passion of their melancholy order, at all 10 times and everywhere. They aspire to teach it as bridge whist, the American Legion flag-drill and double-entry bookkeeping are taught. They fail as ignominiously as that Athenian of legend who essayed to train a regiment of grasshoppers in the goose-step.

[2] For the essence of a sound style is that it cannot be reduced 15 to rules—that it is a living and breathing thing, with something of the devilish in it—that it fits its proprietor tightly and yet ever so loosely, as his skin fits him. It is, in fact, quite as securely an integral

From *Prejudices: Fifth Series* by H. L. Mencken. Reprinted by permission of Alfred A. Knopf, Inc. Copyright 1926 by Alfred A. Knopf, Inc.

part of him as that skin is. It hardens as his arteries harden. It has
20 *Katzenjammer* on the days succeeding his indiscretions. It is gaudy
when he is young and gathers decorum when he grows old. On the
day after he makes a mash on a new girl it glows and glitters. If
he has fed well, it is mellow. If he has gastritis it is bitter. In brief, a
style is always the outward and visible symbol of a man, and it
25 cannot be anything else. To attempt to teach it is as silly as to set
up courses in making love. The man who makes love out of a book
is not making love at all; he is simply imitating someone else making love. God help him if, in love or literary composition, his pre-
ceptor be a pedagogue!

30   [3] The schoolma'm theory that the writing of English may be
taught is based upon a faulty inference from a sound observation.
The sound observation is that the great majority of American high-
school pupils, when they attempt to put their thoughts upon paper,
produce only a mass of confused and puerile nonsense—that they
35 express themselves so clumsily that it is often quite impossible to
understand them at all. The faulty inference is to the effect that what
ails them is a defective technical equipment—that they can be trained
to write clearly as a dog may be trained to walk on its hind legs.
This is all wrong. What ails them is not a defective equipment but a
40 defective natural equipment. They write badly simply because they
cannot think clearly. They cannot think clearly because they lack the
brains. Trying to teach them is as hopeless as trying to teach a dog
with only one hind leg. Any human being who can speak English
understandably has all the materials necessary to write English
45 clearly, and even beautifully. There is nothing mysterious about the
written language; it is precisely the same, in essence, as the spoken
language. If a man can think in English at all, he can find words
enough to express his ideas. The fact is proved abundantly by the
excellent writing that often comes from so-called ignorant men. It is
50 proved anew by the even better writing that is done on higher levels
by persons of great simplicity, for example, Abraham Lincoln. Such
writing commonly arouses little enthusiasm among pedagogues. Its
transparency excites their professional disdain, and they are offended
by its use of homely words and phrases. They prefer something more
55 ornate and complex—something, as they would probably put it, demanding more thought. But the thought they yearn for is the kind,
alas, that they secrete themselves—the muddled, highfalutin, vapid
thought that one finds in their own text-books.

   [4] I do not denounce them because they write so badly; I merely

record the fact in a sad, scientific spirit. Even in such twilight regions of the intellect the style remains the man. What is in the head infallibly oozes out of the nub of the pen. If it is sparkling Burgundy the writing is full of life and charm. If it is mush the writing is mush too. The late Dr. Harding, twenty-ninth President of the Federal Union, was a highly self-conscious stylist. He practiced prose composition assiduously, and was regarded by the pedagogues of Marion, Ohio, and vicinity as a very talented fellow. But when he sent a message to Congress it was so muddled in style that even the late Henry Cabot Lodge, a professional literary man, could not understand it. Why? Simply because Dr. Harding's thoughts, on the high and grave subjects he discussed, were so muddled that he couldn't understand them himself. But on matters within his range of customary meditation he was clear and even charming, as all of us are. I once heard him deliver a brief address upon the ideals of the Elks. It was a topic close to his heart, and he had thought about it at length and *con amore*. The result was an excellent speech—clear, logical, forceful, and with a touch of wild, romantic beauty. His sentences hung together. He employed simple words, and put them together with skill. But when, at a public meeting in Washington, he essayed to deliver an oration on the subject of the late Dante Alighieri, he quickly became so obscure and absurd that even the Diplomatic Corps began to snicker. The cause was plain: he knew no more about Dante than a Tennessee county judge knows about the Institutes of Justinian. Trying to formulate ideas upon the topic, he could get together only a few disjected fragments and ghosts of ideas—here an ear, there a section of tibia, beyond a puff of soul substance or other gas. The resultant speech was thus enigmatical, cacophonous and awful stuff. It sounded precisely like a lecture by a college professor on style.

[5] A pedagogue, confronted by Dr. Harding in class, would have set him to the business of what is called improving his vocabulary—that is, to the business of making his writing even worse than it was. Dr. Harding, in point of fact, had all the vocabulary that he needed, and a great deal more. Any idea that he could formulate clearly he could convey clearly. Any idea that genuinely moved him he could invest with charm—which is to say, with what the pedagogues call style. I believe that this capacity is possessed by all literate persons above the age of fourteen. It is not acquired by studying text-books; it is acquired by learning how to think. Children even younger often show it. I have a niece, now eleven years old, who already has an

excellent style. When she writes to me about things that interest her —in other words, about the things she is capable of thinking about— she puts her thoughts into clear, dignified and admirable English. Her vocabulary, so far, is unspoiled by schoolma'ms. She doesn't try to
105 knock me out by bombarding me with hard words, and phrases filched from Addison. She is unaffected, and hence her writing is charming. But if she essayed to send me a communication on the subject, say, of Balkan politics or government ownership, her style would descend instantly to the level of that of Dr. Harding's state papers.

110 [6] To sum up, style cannot go beyond the ideas which lie at the heart of it. If they are clear, it too will be clear. If they are held passionately, it will be eloquent. Trying to teach it to persons who cannot think, especially when the business is attempted by persons who also cannot think, is a great waste of time, and an immoral
115 imposition upon the taxpayers of the nation. It would be far more logical to devote all the energy to teaching, not writing, but logic— and probably just as useless. For I doubt that the art of thinking can be taught at all—at any rate, by school-teachers. It is not acquired, but congenital. Some persons are born with it. Their ideas flow in
120 straight channels; they are capable of lucid reasoning; when they say anything it is instantly understandable; when they write anything it is clear and persuasive. They constitute, I should say, about one-eighth of one percent of the human race. The rest of God's children are just as incapable of logical thought as they are incapable of jumping over
125 the moon. Trying to teach them to think is as vain an enterprise as trying to teach a streptococcus the principles of Americanism. The only thing to do with them is to make Ph.D.'s of them, and set them to writing handbooks on style.

[For treatment of this selection, see pp. 153–154.]

From *Epstein: An Autobiography*   JACOB EPSTEIN

[1] In my portraits it is assumed that I start out with a definite conception of my sitter's character. On the contrary, I have no such conception whatever in the beginning. The sitter arrives in the studio, mounts the stand, and I begin my study. My aim, to start with, is entirely constructive. With scientific precision I make a quite coldly 5 thought out construction of the form, giving the bony formations around the eyes, the ridge of the nose, mouth, and cheek-bones, and defining the relation of the different parts of the skull to each other. As the work proceeds, I note the expression, and the changes of expression, and the character of the model begins to impress itself on 10 me. In the end, by a natural process of observation, the mental and physiological characteristics of the sitter impose themselves upon the clay. This process is natural and not preconceived. With close and intensive study come subtleties and fine shades. From turning the work around so as to catch every light, comes that solidity that makes 15 the work light-proof, as it were. For in a work of sculpture the forms actually alter with the change of light, not as in a painting or drawing, where the forms only become more or less visible. In Ibsen's *When We Dead Awaken* there is a sculptor depicted as a disillusioned, embittered man, who is, I should say, the contrary of what a 20 sculptor should be. I will quote what he says of his sitters (Act 1):

MAIA. Do you think it is better then—do you think it is worthy of you to do nothing at all but a portrait-bust now and then?

PROF. RUBEK (*with a sly smile*). They are not exactly portrait-busts that I turn out, Maia.

MAIA. Yes indeed they are—for the last two or three years—ever since you finished your great group and it got out of the house . . .

PROF. RUBEK. All the same they are no mere portrait-busts, I assure you.

MAIA. What are they then?

PROF. RUBEK. There is something equivocal, something cryptic, lurking in and behind these busts—a secret something, that the people themselves cannot see.

MAIA. Indeed?

PROF. RUBEK (*decisively*). I alone can see it. And it amuses me unspeakably. On the surface I give them the striking likeness, as they call it, that they all stand and gape at it in astonishment—(*lowers his voice*)—but at the bottom they are all respectable, pompous, horse-faced, and self-opinionated donkey muzzles, and lop-eared, low-browed dog-skulls, and fatted swine-snouts—and sometimes dull brutal bull-fronts as well.

MAIA (*indifferently*). All the dear domestic animals in fact.

PROF. RUBEK. Simply the dear domestic animals, Maia. All the animals which men have bedevilled in their own image—and which have bedevilled men in their turn. (*Empties his champagne glass and laughs.*) And it is these double-faced works of art that our excellent plutocrats come and order of me. And pay for in all good faith—and in good round figures too—almost their weight in gold as the saying goes.

[2] Naturally, a sculptor like this could never arrive at the truth about a person. It is said that the sculptor as an artist always depicts himself in his work, even in his portraits. In only one sense is this
25 true, that is in the sense in which the artist's own nature colours his outlook. To illustrate what I say, take a portrait of Franz Hals. We observe that his outlook on humanity is cold and detached, he observes his models without any emotions, and never warms to them. He seemed unfortunate in his sitters; as human beings they evidently
30 aroused in him no feeling of sympathy, and he turned to their clothes with greater pleasure than he got from their faces. He obviously enjoyed his own technique and revelled in his marvellous skill.

[3] With Rembrandt the opposite seems the case. His great heart seemed to warm towards the men and women who sat for him, and
35 he seemed to penetrate into their inner selves, and reveal their very souls—in children their lively joy, and in grown-ups the burden of living, their sorrow and disappointments. There is a great wisdom in him, and his people look out of his canvases, human beings whose trades and businesses you cannot tell, but they have deep human
40 thoughts; they are not just tradesmen and shrews, as in Hals. A beggar in the hands of Rembrandt is some ancient philosopher, a Diogenes content in his tub; a manservant in a borrowed cloak be-

comes a King of the East with splendour wreathing him round. So with the portraits of Goya. His men are witty, cynical, brutal, and his women lovely, gallant, and lecherous.

[4] Rarely have I found sitters altogether pleased with their portraits. Understanding is rare, and the sitter usually wants to be flattered. How Goya ever "got away" with his superb portraits of the Spanish Royal Family is still an inexplicable mystery.

[5] I recall the naïve expression of one of my sitters who asked me if his nose was as I depicted it, and when I assured him that it was so, cajolingly exclaimed, "Can't you cheat nature a little?"

[6] Another will feel the bump at the back of his neck and look ruefully at my bust. On the whole, men sitters are more vain than women sitters. Shaw was terribly nervous about his bust, so was Priestley, and I have found that rarely does a wife see eye to eye with the artist. Always the artist "has just missed something" that she wants in or he has "put in something" that she has never observed.

[7] My best portraits, of course, have been those of friends and people I have asked to sit for me. The model who just sits and leaves the artist to his own thoughts is the most helpful one. Not the model who imagines she is inspiring the artist. It seems to me that Mona Lisa said nothing, that "enigmatic" smile was quite enough for Leonardo to bother about.

[8] I should like to say here that with most of my men portraits, I have been asked to work from them when they were very old, the reason for that being, I suppose, that they had not attained a fame worthy of commemoration earlier. What a relief it would be were I to be asked to do some notable person, say, in the hey-day of his physical and mental powers. Often my models, after a few minutes on the stand, go to sleep, and all I can see of them is the tops of their bald heads.

[9] For the art of the portrait, I have noticed on the part of art critics a certain contempt. Sculptors themselves do not feel this contempt. On the contrary, it is the ambition of many sculptors to do a fine portrait, which they know is not easily arrived at. It is well not to be too dogmatic as to what is sculpture and what is not, for one must estimate as the highest expression of sculpture those Egyptian works, which were never meant to be anything but portraits; the Cephren in Cairo, or the Sheik El Beled. Personally I place my work in as important a category as I place any other work of mine, and I am content to be judged by it.

[10] The successful portrait sculptor or painter for that matter
needs a front of brass, the hide of a rhinoceros, and all the guile of a
courtier. While I have done a certain number of portraits, the history
of those portraits is for the most part a story of failure to please the
sitters or their relatives. Even my dealers are distrustful, and in one
instance where I had exhibited the bust of a man and an inquiry was
made with a view to purchasing a replica, the gallery was so sceptical
about the sincerity of this inquiry that they coolly informed me they
had not even taken the address of the inquirer. This, mind you, was
one of my best portraits. When it comes to the statue of a famous
man for commemoration, I will instance the Thomas Hardy memorial. When this memorial was under consideration I was approached
informally by a member of the committee, with whom I discussed
the project, and undertook to do the work, stating my fee. I heard
nothing further about it, and one morning read in *The Times* that
the memorial had been entrusted to a sculptor. A memorial to
Thomas Hardy would have been a work that would test all the
powers of the portrait sculptor, and I had really looked forward to
the commission. To have portrayed the great novelist, so that not
only his essential physical characteristics were shown, but also some
sense of the over-burdening pessimism of his soul, something of the
feeling of human frustration, was a work to call out all one's forces
of evocation, also some suggestion of that elemental nature that is the
background for Hardy's tragic characters. The statue produced was
more than unfortunate. Hardy was represented as a dejected market
gardener, with a trilby hat, seated, as he might appear on a Sunday
morning, deploring a bad crop of spinach. Colonel T. E. Lawrence
who was on the Committee of the memorial, wrote early on to Sir
Sidney Cockerell of Cambridge (August 29th, 1927) concerning the
proposed memorial to Hardy. "Statues are so difficult, unless someone quite first-rate does them. Epstein is the obvious choice." Yet
after the first half-hearted approach I was passed over.

[11] Sometimes the sitter impresses his own conception of himself
upon the artist. This can never result in a successful work—one that
renders the character of the model. Sir Hugh Walpole was one of
these sitters. He insisted in sitting to me like a Pharaoh, with head
held high and chin stuck out. In reality, Sir Hugh was the most
genial of men with sparkling, twinkling, humour in his eye, and his
mouth wreathed in a kindly and genial smile. But with the rigidity
of Sir Hugh's pose I could do nothing. I knew that the head was
well modelled, but as for a portrait of my model's real self, I never

thought it was that for a moment. It was Sir Hugh Walpole in the 125
rôle of Benito Mussolini.

JOSEPH CONRAD

[12] Muirhead Bone had arranged that I should do a bust of
Conrad for him. I had desired, ten years before, to work from him
and had spoke to Richard Curle about it, but had been informed
by him that Conrad could not sit for me owing to the intervention 130
of a painter "friend." At the time I was deeply disappointed and
dropped the idea, but in 1924 the commission was finally arranged.
My admiration for Conrad was immense, and he had a head that
appealed to a sculptor, massive and fine at the same time, so I
jumped at the idea of working from him at last. After a meeting in 135
London it was arranged with him that I should go down to his place
at Oswalds, near Canterbury, and—at my suggestion—should live in
an inn in a nearby village while working on the bust. This arrangement always suits me best, as I prefer to be free outside my working
hours. 140

I set out from London on a cold March morning, feeling somewhat ill and down-hearted. I hated working away from my studio,
amidst uncertain and perhaps disagreeable conditions. Before beginning a work I am timid and apprehensive. What will the lighting
be? A good start is everything, and with a subject like Conrad I 145
wanted to do justice to myself. My taxi contained my working materials, stands, clay, and working tools. It seemed a long journey to
Kent, I arrived towards dark with snow falling. Conrad met me and
we arranged the room in which I should work, where I unpacked
my baggage. I was then conducted across a park to the village of 150
Bridge and the inn where I was to stay. This inn seemed to be of
the gloomiest and coldest type. The whole mood of the place, with
the sodden country-side, promised a cheerless beginning.

[13] The next morning I began the work. At the end of the sitting
I did not know what to think of it, and felt altogether wretched. In 155
the evening I wired for my five-year-old Peggy Jean to come. The
second day, on the arrival of Peggy Jean, things looked better. Conrad was an absorbing study. He took posing seriously and gave me
good long sittings until one o'clock, when we lunched and talked.
Conrad from the beginning called me Cher Maître, embarrassing me 160
by this mode of address from a much older man who was a great
master of his own craft. His manners were courtly and direct, but
his neurasthenia forced him at times to outbursts of rage and irrita-

bility with his household which quickly subsided. I already had a
165 fairly clear notion as to how I should treat the bust. A sculptor had
previously made a bust of him which represented him as an open-
necked, romantic, out-of-door type of person. In appearance Conrad
was the very opposite. His clothes were immaculately conventional,
and his collar enclosed his neck like an Iron Maiden's vice or gar-
170 rotter's grip. He was worried if his hair and beard were not trim
and neat as became a sea captain. There was nothing shaggy or
Bohemian about him. His glance was keen despite the drooping of
one eyelid. He was the sea captain, the officer, and in our talks he
emphasised the word "responsibility." Responsibility weighed on him
175 and weighed him down. He used the word again and again and one
immediately thought of *Lord Jim*—the conscience suffering at the
evasion of duty. It may have been because of my meeting him late
in life that Conrad gave me a feeling of defeat; but defeat met with
courage.
180 [14] He was crippled with rheumatism, crotchety, nervous, and ill.
He said to me, "I am finished." There was pathos in his pulling out
of a drawer his last manuscript to show me that he was still at work.
There was no triumph in his manner, however, and he said that he
did not know whether he would ever finish it. "I am played out," he
185 said, "played out."
[15] We talked after the sittings, mostly in the afternoons when
we had tea together and Conrad was full of reminiscences about
himself. We were usually alone. There, in this country house, he
seemed to live alone although the house was filled with servants. A
190 few visitors came at the weekends, but he appeared a lonely, brooding man, with none too pleasant thoughts.
[16] He was a good sitter, always strictly punctual, and he stuck
to the stand, giving me plenty of opportunity for work and study. I
was with him for twenty-one days. Once, while posing, he had a
195 heart attack, and felt faint. His manservant brought him a stiff whisky
and he insisted on renewing the sitting. I had no hesitations while at
work, owing to his very sympathetic attitude. A doubtful, or critical
attitude of the sitter will sometimes hang like a dark cloud over the
work and retard it. Conrad's sympathy and good-will were manifest,
200 and he would beam at me with a pleased expression and forget his
rheumatism and the tree outside the window at which he railed.
The tree was large and beautiful, but to Conrad it was a source of
misery.

[17] The house was roomy, and set among low hills. To Conrad it was a prison set in a swamp. He must move. He must find another house. He would set out in his car. One step from the door to the sealed vehicle to search for the new house. No outdoors for him. The sea captain hated out of doors, and never put his nose into it.

[18] To return to the bust; Conrad had a demon expression in the left eye, while his right eye was smothered by a drooping lid, but the eyes glowed with a great intensity of feeling. The drooping, weary lids intensified the impression of brooding thought. The whole head revealed the man who had suffered much. A head set on shoulders hunched about his ears. When he was seated, the shoulders gave the impression of a pedestal for the head. His gnarled hands were covered with woollen mittens, and his habit of tugging at his beard when in conversation or in thought gave me the idea of including the hands in the bust, but Conrad recoiled from so human a document.

[19] On anything connected with the plastic arts Conrad frankly confessed ignorance, although perhaps to flatter me he attempted to draw a parallel between the processes of building up a work of sculpture and that of writing a novel. Of music he said he knew nothing, nor did it interest him; but he admitted being impressed by the sound of drums coming across the waters in Africa at night.

[20] The walls of his house carried a few indifferent family portraits in oil. He turned over lovingly the family portrait album of his ancestors. His father, Korzeniowski, was a distinguished literary Pole, who had suffered under the Czar, photographs of himself very young; these showed him as being extremely handsome.

[21] We usually had tea in his small, cosy study. On one occasion, as there was company, I recall having tea in a large, grand, shuttered room with French furniture very conventionally arranged. Conrad was strongly feudal in his ideas and when I complained of the servile attitude of the villagers round about, he said that they were happier so. My reference to the villagers was occasioned by an incident which happened at Bridge. I had remarked on the astonishing velocity of a racing-car which had driven through the village at race-track speed scattering children and chickens. At the local barber's I mentioned this, and ventured to remark that the children were in danger of their lives. The barber said that in fact several children had been killed, but that the racing magnate had paid the parents handsomely, and all the villagers looked to him for employment. The re-

port that Conrad refused a knighthood because it was offered by a
245 Socialist Government, would, if true, bear out my observation about
his feudal cast of mind.

[22] I looked at Conrad's bookshelf. He had not many books. In
no sense a library. A complete edition of Turgeniev in English. We
talked of books and, expecting him to be interested in Melville's
250 *Moby Dick,* I mentioned it, and Conrad burst into a furious denun-
ciation of it. "He knows nothing of the sea. Fantastic, ridiculous," he
said. When I mentioned that the work was symbolical and mystical:
"Mystical my eye! My old boots are mystical." "Meredith? His characters are ten feet high." D. H. Lawrence had started well, but had
255 gone wrong. "Fifth. Nothing but obscenities." For Henry James he
had unqualified admiration. Of his own novels he said it was a toss
up at one time as to whether he would write in English or French.
He emphasised the amount of labour he gave to a novel to get it to
satisfy himself.

260 [23] At a few of the sittings Conrad dictated letters to the secretary. His English was strongly foreign with a very guttural accent, so
that his secretary frequently failed to get the right word, which made
Conrad growl. I would try to detach myself from the work to listen.
His composition was beautiful. Sentence followed sentence in classic
265 "Conrad," totally unlike his conversational manner, which was free,
easy, and colloquial.

[24] The work on the bust was nearing completion. One day at
the end of the sittings, Mrs. Conrad appeared at the door to see it.
She gave one glance and fled. A wife, a lover, can perhaps never see
270 what the artist sees. The fact, at any rate, is that they rarely ever do.
Perhaps a really mediocre artist has more chance of success in this
respect. When George Bernard Shaw was sitting to me, I asked him
why he had given sittings to a very incompetent artist. Shaw exclaimed: "Why, he is a fine portrait painter—my wife, on entering
275 the room where the portrait was, actually mistook it for myself."

[25] Conrad's own opinion about my portrait of himself was conveyed in a letter he wrote to Richard Curle, his biographer and literary executor. "The bust of Ep. has grown truly monumental. It is a
marvellously effective piece of sculpture, with even something more
280 than a masterly interpretation in it. . . . It is wonderful to go down to
posterity like that." Later Sir Muirhead Bone offered the bust to the
National Portrait Gallery. It was refused.

[26] At last the bust was completed. I wired my moulder to come

and carry it away to London to be cast. I said good-bye to the old Master and travelled with the bust. Five months later I opened a 285 newspaper and read that Joseph Conrad was dead.

If you ask a waiter in a restaurant to provide you with some nourishment, you have, perhaps, let him know that you are hungry, but you have not given him any guidance in choosing one or more of the scores of dishes available in the kitchen. To put the matter in another way, you have used an abstract term, "nourishment," when concrete terms—"medium-rare T-bone steak with onion rings and French-fried potatoes"—were needed.

Ideas, people, places, "things" may be dealt with—in writing and speaking—in the abstract. We can say that democracy is good, that parents love their children, that lakes are good for fishing, that cars travel fast. Though each of these statements communicates some meaning (just as "nourishment" did above), the communication is essentially vague, ineffective, even possibly inexact and inaccurate. Just what is "democracy" and just what does "good" mean? "Good" for whom? Economically "good" or socially "good"? "Good" for all time or only under certain circumstances? Do cars travel "fast" compared with jet planes? Do parents who spoil their children and give them a skewed view of reality "love" them?

It should be obvious—but writers too often overlook the point—that concreteness is a necessary ingredient in exact, accurate, and efficient communication. In organizing his material, a writer must be constantly aware of abstractions that need to be made concrete, of general statements that need to be made specific.

1. Formulate Mencken's guiding purpose to show that this primary interest in this selection is in style rather than in schoolma'ms.

2. Style—as used to describe a certain quality of writing—is essentially an abstraction. Does the introduction of "schoolma'ms, bucolic college professors, and other such pseudo-literates" help to make the abstraction at all concrete? Why or why not?

3. In paragraph 2, Mencken grapples with the problem of making "the essence of a sound style" concrete enough so that the reader can fully and precisely understand what Mencken means by style. What is the chief means by which he solves the problem? What additional means does he use in this paragraph? How well do you think he succeeds in solving the problem? Justify your answer. What is the function of the last sentence in the paragraph?

4. In referring to Abraham Lincoln as an example of an admirable stylist, Mencken neither supplies illustrative quotations from Lin-

coln's writing nor refers to specific writings of Lincoln. Yet he makes concrete several qualities of Lincoln's style. How does he do this?

5. What is Mencken's purpose in devoting most of paragraph 4 to President Harding? What, specifically, do you learn about Mencken's concept of style from the treatment of Harding's "message to Congress," "address upon the ideals of the Elks," and "an oration on the subject of the late Dante Alighieri"? Does the material on Mencken's niece in paragraph 5 add to your understanding of style or does it merely repeat what you had learned from the Harding material?

6. In each of the following paired statements, show which is the better statement and why; use as your criteria the fullness, relevance, and effectiveness of specific details.

a. (1) "They aspire to teach it [style] as bridge whist, the American Legion flag-drill and double-entry bookkeeping are taught."

(2) They aspire to teach style as certain activities governed by rules are taught.

b. (1) "The sound observation is that the great majority of American high-school pupils, when they attempt to put their thoughts on paper, produce only a mass of confused and puerile nonsense—that they express themselves so clumsily that it is often quite impossible to understand them at all."

(2) The sound observation is that the great majority of American high-school pupils, when they attempt to put their thoughts on paper, write extremely badly.

c. (1) "The resultant speech was thus enigmatical, cacophonous and awful stuff."

(2) The resultant speech was thus enigmatical, cacophonous, factually inaccurate, and critically immature.

d. (1) "She doesn't try to knock me out by bombarding me with hard words, and phrases filched from Addison."

(2) She doesn't try to impress me with her learned style.

e. (1) "Trying to teach them to think is as vain an enterprise as trying to teach a streptococcus the principles of Americanism."

(2) Trying to teach them to think is as vain an enterprise as trying to teach a philosophic principle to a bacterium.

7. Mencken says, ". . . a style is always the outward and visible symbol of a man. . . ." What of the man Mencken is revealed to you by his style in this essay? Compare and contrast your impressions of Mencken gained from his style with those given you by Durr (pp.10–13).

8. In the first paragraph of "Portraits," the author, Jacob Epstein,

the noted sculptor, describes the process of portrait sculpture. How has (or has not) concreteness contributed to the effectiveness of his description?

9. In the excerpt from Ibsen's *When We Dead Awaken,* to what purpose or purposes does Ibsen use concreteness? Justify Epstein's inclusion of the quotation.

10. Identify five passages in which the author makes an artist's or a sculptor's style come alive by means of concreteness.

11. Is the concrete description of the author's trip to Kent relevant?

12. Make a list of all the concrete terms Epstein uses to describe Joseph Conrad's appearance, personality, and artistry. Based on your list, but not quoting from it, write a paragraph giving your impressions of Conrad. Be specific.

13. Based upon your reading of the entire selection, write a similar paragraph of your impressions of Epstein. Once again, be specific.

Alternate selections for the study of Concreteness: Walter Pater, "Notre-Dame de Chartres"; Françoise Gilot and Carlton Lake, from *Life with Picasso;* James Agee, "Comedy's Greatest Era."

Theme Assignment: Choose a teacher from any of the schools you have attended to whom you reacted strongly. You may have liked him intensely or disliked him intensely. You may have been fascinated or repelled by his mannerisms or dress or attitude toward his students. You may have thought him your best teacher or your worst. In order to explain your reaction, write a theme describing the teacher in action; remember that avoiding vague generalities and including relevant specific details can make your reaction credible and the teacher alive to the reader.

or

In our daily communication with other people, we are constantly using abstractions, words which stand for broad concepts, intangible emotions, or elaborate processes. Some of these terms are "beauty," "harmony," "academic freedom," "centrifugal force," "love," "teleology," "patriotism," "equation," "atomic energy," and "provincialism." If we were called upon to explain these terms and to make them meaningful to people who had never heard them, we could do so only by drawing upon concrete details familiar to these people.

Select one of these terms or another of your own choosing. Write a theme in which you explain it to your readers in specific, concrete terms. In formulating your guiding purpose, clarify in your own mind and, if it seems appropriate to you, include in your theme some delineation of the audience you are addressing.

or

Write a theme in which you explain a process familiar to you but assumed to be unfamiliar to the reader. Remember that you will not only take the reader step by step through the process in a logical order but may also have to define some of your terms, give examples and details, explain cause-and-effect relations. Above all, you will want to use concreteness to make your process real and vivid for the reader. For example, if you are explaining how your college newspaper is produced, you will not only want to tell the reader what happens first, second, and third. You may also want to define an editor in chief, a staff reporter, a "stringer" and compare the roles of each. You may want to explain something of the printing process, contrast the editorial office at deadline time with the office the day after the paper comes out. You may want to touch upon your college's policy toward the press as it affects the putting together of the paper.

Relevance

Angel-Fluffs, Savages, and Dispensable Adults   JOHN CIARDI

[1] I didn't always have children. To begin with, in fact, I was a child myself. I suppose any intelligent person who has survived such a beginning should know better than to get involved in that sort of thing all over again. Nevertheless, there came a season of enthusiasm, my wife was co-operative, the weather of our mood was a bit balmy, 5 we ourselves were a bit balmy, and the first thing we knew we had made parents of ourselves. And then again. And then again.

[2] I haven't consulted the latest opinion polls and I don't know what average parents think they got out of the genetic grab bag. We got savages. Three of them—a girl, a boy, and a Martian, in that 10 order.

[3] Savages, of course, come in all sorts of tribal denominations. Some, I have read, can be civilized more or less easily. Others take to the bushes at the least sign of approaching civilization. Ours, I have long since discovered, are deep-bush savages. By now Benn is 15 10, Jonnel (John L.) is 12, and Myra is 13 going on 18, with no real signs as yet that anything like civilization is setting in. Their emotions, their vocabularies, their imagery, and their rhythms are naturally violent. There are, nevertheless, compensations, for like all deep-bush savages, they have a natural affinity for poetry. 20

157

[4] With such a throbbing jungle built into the house, it was inevitable that I should turn to writing children's poetry. Few invitations from this world's deep, may I say, have given me more joy. I found myself reveling in the healthy child's appetite for poetry. And
25 I found myself reveling in my own rediscovered childhood. As a matter of fact, I no longer pretend that I am writing for my children. I am always happy, to be sure, when they seem to approve of what I write, but they are beginning to be a little afraid of seeming childish. They are in a hurry to grow up. I, on the other hand, have dis-
30 covered that I have no such compulsion upon me. I intend to make my childhood last as long as possible. Much longer than theirs.

[5] These, I submit, are indispensable discoveries, and may every adult come to them before he has taken himself seriously forever. For in the course of publishing my first nine children's books (and may
35 there be ninety-nine still to come) I also made some highly dispensable discoveries about highly dispensable adults. An adult becomes dispensable, let me suggest, when he has taken himself with entire seriousness, when he thinks that children are little angel-fluffs, or when he thinks the natural emotional diet of children calls for
40 little sugar-coated moralities. I should have supposed that Mother Goose, the Brothers Grimm, and Lewis Carroll had put an end to any such nonsense about children. Or that an elementary introspection would prove the bogey man to be a better imaginary character than the Good Fairy. But the truly dispensable adult is beyond sup-
45 posing: he *knows* what children like, whether they like it or not.

[6] Two of the most dispensable adults I have ever met made themselves known to me soon after I had published a book of poems called *You Read to Me, I'll Read to You.*

[7] Children's books, as most parents know, consist of read-to-
50 me-out-of's and I-can-read-it-myself's. The idea of this book was to make bedtime reading a two-way street by alternating the poems. The odd-numbered poems (printed in black ink) are for the parent to read to the child, and the even-numbered poems (printed in blue ink) are built on a simplified vocabulary for the child to read to the
55 parent. The first poem in the book reads this way:

ABOUT THE TEETH OF SHARKS

The thing about a shark is—teeth.
One row above, one row beneath.

Now take a close look. Do you find
It has another row behind?

Still closer—here, I'll hold your hat:
Has it a third row behind that?

Now look in and . . . Look out! Oh my,
I'll *never* know now! Well, goodbye.[1]

[8] This bit of deep-sea dental research seemed to be right down the center of this family's taste but it provoked a howl from two Flat-Footed and Indignant Virtues who stalked me at the Bread Loaf Writers' Conference soon after the book had appeared.

[9] "Do you get any pleasure out of disturbing children?" they demanded, taking position in front of me like an armored division.

[10] Bread Loaf is generally a civilized place and not above a certain amount of well-enacted horseplay. I assumed they were joking. "Only when I think they need it," I said.

[11] I had made a mistake. They were not joking. They were, they let me know, teachers in the New York School System. My book had appeared in the school library. The children in their classes had read it. And the results, I soon gathered, had been frightful. Some of the children had even had nightmares because of the poem, and all had been upset, badly upset, if I could believe my two Indignant Virtues. They were, as it turned out, in a considerable hurry to tell me how much grief I had caused them and their children. Nor did they fail to make it clear that I was not—repeat: not ever—to write such frightful poems for children.

[12] I hadn't been braced for such an assault and I fumbled a bit. What they were talking about sounded like no child I had ever known. Had they come up with a new breed, I wondered. "What unknown breed of human child *do* you teach?" I finally managed to ask.

[13] "I'll have you know that we do special guidance work," said Virtue One.

[14] "With disturbed children," said Virtue Two.

[15] I hope I know when a conversation is over. "Goodbye," I said.

[16] Heaven knows there is nothing funny about a disturbed child. May every sick chick be tended in love and mercy. They are, in a way, like the very young, who must be fed specially strained foods.

But the whole point of such a diet is to get them ready for the ordinary foods of good health. The only reasonable function of pab-
90 ulum is to prepare for the day when the child can eat charcoal-broiled steak. To eat pabulum for its own sake is to offend every natural diet of mankind.

[17] The healthy child's appetite for imaginary violence is part of its natural roaring energy, but that child always knows the difference
95 between "real" and pretend. He is a sick child exactly when he no longer recognizes that difference. And if he is sick, he does need a specially selected diet for his imagination. But if the child is not sick, what can be better for him than to convert his natural taste for violence into the rhymes, the images and the jingles of poetry—to
100 take a natural chaos of the imagination and to make a pleasurable formality of it? Such a conversion of wild energy into happy form is the healthiest diet of the healthy.

[18] What my two dispensable, if virtuous, adults were proposing was nothing less than a universal pabulum: because there are some
105 children who can eat nothing but mush, all children must be fed only mush.

[19] And if theirs seems an impoverished logic, I am bound to report that I have met worse.

[20] Of them all, my most dispensable adult was one I had met a
110 few years earlier. Houghton Mifflin Company, publishers of one of my college texts, had suggested to me that I try a book of poems based on a limited vocabulary for first graders, and since my daughter was then about to enter the first grade, the idea took hold of me at once: I would write the first book she read all the way through.
115 [21] The challenge of the limited vocabulary is simple enough for the writer: he hopes to stay within the 420 words of the minimum first-grade reading list and to come up with something a bit more interesting than "Look! Dick. Look!" Which is, I submit, rather dull stuff, though if spelled backwards, it does come out as "Kool!
120 Kcid. Kool!" There is at least that much advantage to being retrogressive rather than progressive.

[22] The progressive ones are up to two-syllable names and that dialogue runs about so:

"Look! Alice. Look!"
"Where, Jerry? Where?"
"See! See the pup!"
Jerry sees the pup.

Alice sees the pup.
Pretty, pretty pup!

[23] And what can come of that sort of thing except a gibber at the schoolhouse door as teacher locks up and staggers her brain-washed way home muttering "Drat, children! Drat!"? My daughter, in any case, and her two brothers listening in, were not about to sit still for any such mindlessness. I set out to see what I could do to liven up the program and in short order the book had practically written itself and was published as *I Met a Man,* since most of the poems—riddles, games, and whatnot—opened with that phrase.

[24] Soon, too, the book had appeared in a number of classrooms, and though some teachers seemed to like it, many others were writing me to let me know it absolutely would not do. One particularly indignant schoolman who was in charge of elementary education for a Massachusetts school district even went so far as to offer to disclose my sins to me, and since a second edition was soon due, I decided to fly up to Boston to hear what he had to say. Even if he turned out to be no help, the trip would be a chance to visit my mother and my sisters, all of whom still live in and around Boston.

[25] We met at the Sheraton-Plaza and with a minimum preamble my volunteer tutor opened the book to a poem that read:

I MET A MAN WHO WAS TRYING TO WHITTLE[2]

I met a man that was trying to whittle
A ship from a stick, but little by
little
The ship he whittled grew littler and
littler.
Said he with a sigh, "I'm a very bad
whittler!
I've whittled my ship till it's small
as a boat.
Then I whittled a hole in it—how
will it float?"
So he threw it away and cut his throat.

[26] As I see it, a man that has whittled himself into such a situation hasn't many choices of action left to him, and of them all cutting

[2] From *I Met a Man Who Was Trying to Whittle,* © by John Ciardi, published by Houghton Mifflin Company.

145 his throat strikes me as eminently the most reasonable. My tutor, however, read that last line with doleful disapproval.

[27] "No good?" I said, a bit unnerved by his tone.

[28] He shook his head sadly.

[29] "That throat-cutting, huh?" I asked, eager to show that I
150 knew a doleful disapproval when I heard one.

[30] He cleared his throat and said something that sounded like "optimum archetypal behavioral patterns." There was more to it than that, but though all of it was at least as good as the sample, the sample was as much as I could rescue from it.

155 [31] "You mean," I said, to sum up, "all the kiddies will be tempted to buy switchblades and start cutting throats?"

[32] He cleared his throat again. "Well, of course, not exactly, but—" And thereupon he was off into some more of that optimum-archetypal-behavior sort of thing.

160 [33] I'll say this for him: he was a stylist. In fact, I was so carried away by my admiration of his style that my own language-pump began working and I came up with a bright idea. "How about this," I said—"suppose I add two lines to it and make it a happy ending?"

[34] And I wrote:

> And when he saw his head was gone,
> He whittled another and put that on.[3]

165 Which is how the poem appeared in the second edition and in every edition since.

[35] My mentor nodded a bit, his enthusiasm, if any, restrained. "It is at least a more positive associative reinforcement of socially constructive attitudes," he said.

170 [36] I wanted to tell him how happy he made me by thinking such round thoughts about my poems, but he had already turned to a longer poem, a sort of house-that-Jack-built rhythm, and he was reading the first lines.

> I met a man that lived in a house
> With a cat, and a dog, and a bird,
>   and a mouse,
> And a big gold fish, and a little
>   brown louse.[3]

[3] From *I Met a Man Who Was Trying to Whittle*, © by John Ciardi, see p. 161.

[37] His tone as he came to the last word delivered its own verdict.   175

[38] "Louse?" I said.

[39] "Very socially negative associations," he said.

[40] "But," I said, "it was on the word list I was given."

[41] "Well," he said, "we don't encourage it."

[42] I did try to argue. I pointed out that, semantically speaking, 180 words have both referents and connotations. For most children, "louse" is pure connotation, a way of making an unhappy noise in your sister's direction when she "has done something." Why wouldn't it be educational to teach the young that the word has a firmly identifiable animalcule as a referent? I even grew a bit stylistic 185 in my own turn. But though I had admired his style, he was not about to return the compliment. Instead, he was already bringing up a new poem:

THE CAT HEARD THE CAT-BIRD[4]

One day, a fine day, a high-flying-
    sky day,
A cat-bird, a fat bird, a fine fat
    cat-bird
Was sitting and singing on a stump
    by the highway.
Just sitting. And singing. Just
    that. But a cat heard.

A thin cat, a grin-cat, a long thin
    grin-cat
Came creeping the sly way by the
    highway to the stump.
"O cat-bird, the cat heard! O cat-
    bird scat!
The grin-cat is creeping! He's going
    to jump!"

—One day, a fine day, a high-flying-
    sky day
A fat cat, yes, that cat we met as
    a thin cat
Was napping, cat-napping, on a stump
    by the highway,

[4] From *The Cat Heard the Cat-Bird* © by John Ciardi, published by Houghton Mifflin Company.

And even in his sleep you could see
he was a grin-cat.

Why was he grinning?—He must have
had a dream.
What made him fat?—A pan full of
cream.
What about the cat-bird?—What bird,
dear?
I don't see any cat-bird here.

[43] By now I had come to recognize the mental aroma of this
190 particular dispensability and was not surprised to learn that it was—
among other things—"unadaptive" to let children read about cats
eating birds.

[44] I still, however, had not given up all hope of reason. I
pointed out that the poem was built on its pairing of sounds, and
195 that the trick was to see how many such pairs could be made to
work. My first half-formed notion, in fact, had been to have the bird
fly into an oak and drop an acorn on the cat, saying "Take that and
scat fat cat." The first idea had run into trouble because I couldn't
keep the sounds paired off and still get the cat fattened up for the
200 last line. I had had finally to let the pairings go in their own direction. If anything had eaten the bird, therefore, it was the poem itself. Nor had I said that the cat had eaten the bird. Instead I had
been careful to explain exactly what it was that had fattened up the
cat. And besides, which child doesn't know that cats stalk birds, that
205 they sometimes catch them, and that, having caught them, they sometimes eat them? At my house, I wanted him to know, we ate a lot
of birds, and much bigger ones, usually stuffed and roasted. And the
United States, I summed up, has even gone so far as to declare a
special holiday for bird-eating, and to call it Thanksgiving.

210 [45] I was even ready, as may be seen, to ring in patriotism in the
name of reason. He, however, stood firm to his own views.

[46] "Definitely inconducive to the ideal classroom function
atmosphere-wise," he said.

[47] And he turned to another poem—this one a simple double
215 limerick I had been especially happy about, for although it used less
than thirty first-grade words, I thought it caught a good child-like
sort of imagination, that it moved along well, and that it even came
up with a mild tongue-twister at the end.

WHEN I WENT TO GET A DRINK[5]

I said to a bug in the sink,
"Are you taking a swim or a drink?"
    "I," said the bug,
    "Am a sea-going tug.
Am I headed for land do you think?"
"What a silly!" I said. "That's
    no sea—
It's a sink!"—"A sink it may be.
    But I'd sooner, I think,
    Be at sea in the sink
Than sink in the sea, sir," said he.

[48] As I say, I had begun to recognize the aroma of high dispensability—or the high aroma of dispensability—in that man's mind. But even I was not prepared for the objection he came up with this time.

[49] "It makes the American home sound unsanitary," he said.

[50] I didn't wait for him to turn to another poem. It was in any case getting on to lunch time. The morning had been destroyed: why ruin lunch?

[51] In mercy, let me say that I don't really think of him as representing the school system, but rather as a private disaster that had gotten itself publicly affiliated. The trouble is that I visit a lot of schools on lecture tours and I do keep running into one of him here and there across the country, and usually at the fringes of a school system. No, thank heaven, not often. About as often, say, as I turn up a real angel-fluff of a child without discovering that it's in the hands of a psychiatrist. One at a time and far between is just about enough for my taste.

[52] I like it better with the archetypal minimally adaptive savages. I like to think we're getting the better of it. At least it's more fun here—and, I suspect, just a bit closer to the human race.

In a unified piece of writing, all items of content must be relevant to the guiding purpose. They may contribute to the meaning by enhancing it, furthering it, exemplifying it, presenting a comparison or contrast which heightens it; but they must in some way be relevant to it. Often enough, however, the relevance of material may not be immediately apparent unless the writer—aware of the necessity for letting his reader in on the "secret"—makes it apparent. Occasionally,

---

[5] From *When I Went to Get a Drink* © by John Ciardi, published by Houghton Mifflin Company.

seemingly irrelevant material may be introduced for humor or even surprise: when the seemingly irrelevant suddenly becomes relevant, the reader may be amused or shocked. But in expository writing, the main intent is normally not to be funny or shocking; the student writer will do well not only to exclude the irrelevant but also to keep his reader aware at all times of the relevance of the material included.

1. The title of Ciardi's article takes on meaning only in the light of the article itself. Explain the title and justify your evaluation of it as a title, making clear the criteria on which you base your judgment.

2. The title does not mention the poems that are quoted in the article. Is this a weakness in the title? Explain.

3. What purpose or purposes do the poems in the article serve? In the light of your answer, comment on the relevance of the poems to the article as a whole.

4. What is the relevance of Ciardi's children to the article as a whole? Where in the article is their relevance made most explicit?

5. The first three paragraphs serve several purposes, one of which is to supply a sprightly, humorous opening for the article. What additional purposes do they serve? Do these purposes firmly establish the relevance of these paragraphs to the article or could Ciardi have started just as effectively with the materials in paragraphs 4 and 5? Explain your answer.

6. Indicate some of the means or techniques by which Ciardi achieves humor in the opening paragraphs. Where else in the article does he use these techniques to achieve humor? Where in the article is humor achieved in other ways? What are the ways? Where does relevance (or the lack of it) contribute to humor?

7. Formulate Ciardi's guiding purpose, taking into account the title of the article, your answers to questions 1 through 5, and the fact that the article was written for *Woman's Day*, a popular magazine addressed to the American homemaker and sold through supermarkets.

8. What is the relevance of the humorous passages taken as a whole —or, if you will, the humor in the article—to Ciardi's guiding purpose?

Alternate selections for the study of Relevance: Catherine Drinker Bowen, "Harold Ober: Literary Agent"; Jacob Epstein, from *Epstein: An Autobiography*.

Theme Assignment: Each of the adages below has withstood the test of time presumably because each contains some element of truth; at the same time, the validity of each is open to serious question. Though a hasty marriage, for example, may result in leisurely repentance, it is far from inevitable that it do so.

Write a theme dealing with the idea embodied in one of the adages. You may focus on the validity of the idea or its lack of validity; you may show the applicability of the idea to a significant problem; or you may deal with a not-so-obvious implication of the idea. Be sure that your central thesis is so adequately developed that your reader will fully realize its significance and perhaps even be convinced of its validity. Be sure, also, to make the most of specific, concrete, and relevant details and examples.

Marry in haste and repent at leisure.
A bird in the hand is worth two in the bush.
He who hesitates is lost.
Penny wise, pound foolish.
Fine words butter no parsnips.
A stitch in time saves nine.
The early bird gets the worm.
Pride goeth before destruction.
A shoemaker should stick to his last.
Nothing ventured, nothing gained.

or

Read or reread Rumer Godden, "Last of the Great Fairy-Talers" (pp. 16–19) and write a theme comparing Godden's view of children and their response to literature with Ciardi's. You may wish to include what you consider to be the function (or functions) of children's literature. Draw specifically on the content of both essays to support your points. Your instructor will be particularly interested in the relevance of your supporting material to your guiding purpose.

or

Write a theme in which you make clear your ideas about the nature of humor, taking into account the three statements below. You may draw illustrative material from the Ciardi essay; from other published sources; from radio, TV, and motion pictures; or from situations or incidents you have experienced. Pay particular attention to the relevance of your illustrative material to your guiding purpose.

Humour is odd, grotesque and wild,
Only by affectation spoil'd;
'Tis never by invention got,
Men have it when they know it not.
(Jonathan Swift)

The most perfect humour and irony is
generally quite unconscious.
(Samuel Butler)

Humour is the juxtaposition of incongruities.
(Henry Bergson)

THE
PARAGRAPH

Topic Sentence

Pieter Bruegel the Elder

VIRGIL BARKER

[1] The subject-matter of Bruegel's great paintings is limited only by the world and life. The whole cycle of nature is in them—the seasons as they pass over mountain, plain and moving waters; the dazzling beauty of the southern sea, the northern cold. The entire range of human life is in them; somewhere in these multitudes every 5 emotion finds its expressive gesture. Even all the animals that are intimately a part of human life are given in their degrees of individuality. These pictures seem to set before the eye every experience possible to man.

[2] In Bruegel's time story-telling in pictures generally was still 10 one of the principal means of communicating ideas—even, perhaps mainly, ideas that were not inherently pictorial; prints were still the nearest things to books in popular circulation. Moreover, a nation living under the necessity of never speaking out openly on either politics or religion naturally resorted to symbol, the concrete proverb 15 or the image that said one thing and meant another. The print of the big and little fish not only meant that the great oppressed the small but carried an idea beyond the words of the proverb in showing the

From *The Arts Magazine*, September 1926.

big fish ripped up and disgorging; and upon a people so apt at in-
20 terpreting images the significance of that would not be lost. This people could not only take a hearty enjoyment of the good things of life
but they could also face the whole of it without shrinking from any
part of it, whether of grossness or of terror. For the latter, indeed,
they even had a gusto and the former they laughed away with a sav-
25 ing healthiness. The distinguishing mark of their living and their
thinking was a robust realism.

[3] In Pieter Bruegel there emerged from among them a man of
genius in complete sympathy with their realistic attitude towards
life; knowing it from childhood, he gave it in his art a more com-
30 plete expression than it had ever had before. The whole originality
and fertility of his mind were for long expended upon feeding the
popular taste not only for the familiar or exotic beauty of nature
but also for a rough philosophy, unorganized but none the less genuine; and a habit so well established in him by years of labor would
35 not vanish all at once even when more purely painter-like interests
assumed for him a major importance. His predecessors in painting
had been realistic in their measure; in them, however, realism was
largely confined to details of execution and was more than counter-
balanced by markedly idealistic conceptions.

40 [4] To examine the *Proverbs* in detail is to get a feeling of being
among mad folks because so many of the sayings here illustrated turn
upon outlandish actions; but as a picture it is a piece of masterly
realistic sanity showing a whole village, in which some of the inhabitants happen to be crazy, intensely busy about its own affairs.
45 The *Triumph of Death,* so far from being a piece of wild and gross
fancy, is actually the lucid statement of an idea as true as any gesture
in the picture; it is precisely the relentlessness of its realism in
thought as well as in embodiment which frightens people into calling
it untrue. The latter two paintings only show that if an artist is real-
50 ist enough, if he penetrates sufficiently into the actual, he necessarily
becomes imaginative; they only reiterate and strengthen Breugel's
right to be considered the supreme realist in painting.

[5] Part of his realism is his refusal to depict what he did not feel.
Part of his realism is the robust laughter which is the only solution
55 for the fix in which human beings find themselves. It is the spirit
that animated Rabelais in describing the birth of his hero and
Shakespeare in creating Falstaff. To come closer home to Bruegel,
perhaps, it is the spirit of *Till Eulenspiegel,* whose gross pleasantries
were probably relished by the painter along with the rest of his gen-

eration. Bruegel's passion for completeness in his realism abolishes ₆₀
privacy, and the state of affairs brought to pass by this slicing away
of all walls is saved only by humor. Humor is the safety-valve for a
spirit resolute to probe life to its last refuge—to probe life, but not to
break through by main force, as attempted by later realists so-called.

[6] Another element in Bruegel's realism is the objectivity of his ₆₅
work. Van Mander's anecdote, often quoted, shows that Bruegel
went among the peasants, not as a professional artist in search of
material, but as a participator in their life; and the great pictures
themselves strikingly bear this out. This is not to say that Bruegel
never worked directly from life, for there are many drawings which ₇₀
could not have been done otherwise—a team of horses resting, soldiers standing in the way, old market-women squatting beside their
wares. But when he came to paint the great pictures, Bruegel worked
from a memory stocked with the gestures and actions of people who
are unconscious of being watched. Bruegel's mind was centered upon ₇₅
their life and he was concerned with technic hardly beyond the point
where it would enable him to crowd all their life into his given space
and shape. His concentration upon the story he was telling, from
the encyclopedic narrative of the early works to the simple and
straightforward emotionalism of the *Months,* put him on the crest ₈₀
of a wave of energy which carried him through many an undertaking
that would have been impossible for a more self-conscious man. We
who see the pictures now are unconscious of the painter because he
was himself lost in his subject; and because of this, also, we are unconscious of ourselves. "No glance ever strays across the footlights to ₈₅
the audience," wrote Meier-Graefe of Hogarth's scenes. In Bruegel's work there are no actors, no footlights and no audience. There
is only life and participation in life by painter and by us.

[7] And everywhere in these pictures it is the life of Bruegel's
own time. His predecessors had clothed religious themes in con- ₉₀
temporary dress, but the outer and the inner remained separate
things; Bruegel, retaining the outer, put into it its own proper content. He ousted religious stories by contemporary stories. These he
painted so completely that a thorough sociological knowledge of the
age might be founded upon or tested by his pictures. The whole life ₉₅
of the time is set down by a hand that never falsifies, that swerves
neither to the right of idealization nor to the left of caricature.

[8] Yet to leave him as a painter of contemporary manners only
would be almost as false to his greatness as to consider him only as
Bruegel the Droll. For he penetrates below the temporary appear- ₁₀₀

ances of his time to the permanent in human nature. His pictures can be a means of access to the life of his age, to be sure; but no lover of them would think of using them in this fashion. The important thing is that they give access to a life that is of more than one age; under the costume of the time exists the same humanity that now wears another dress.

[9] In giving himself over so unreservedly to the impermanent, Bruegel took what was for him the only way to the permanent. This cannot be captured by going out after a vague and unlocalized something called life in general; what is presented to the artist for his use is always life in particular. There is an all-life in the study and swelling succession of human generations; but the only means of access to that is the now-life. The great artist's major accomplishment lies in revealing the universal through the particular, the permanent through the transitory, the inevitable through the accidental.

[10] This Bruegel does; and how well he does it is to be found by analyzing the thought behind his varied rendering of events and people. Even in his early pictures each creature has his own individuality and yet is part of the crowd, which remains a crowd in spite of all detail; each individual retains his own value of personality and yet is integrated into a collective being. Bruegel's minute accuracy of drawing expresses his love for the individual as such; his great masses of people express his desire to see life largely and as an interwoven whole.

[11] The *Months* sum up his life's endeavor both in the material he had all along been dealing with and in the conceptions between which all along he had been alternating. They are full of motives and incidents taken from his earlier works—the church he drew so often, children at their games, the great stretches of landscape that he loved. But all things are adjusted to one another in a new way; the people are seen neither too large nor too small, but in a perfect relationship to an immensely embracing nature; and each picture is pervaded by an unbroken harmony of mood. This set marks the attainment of final insight into everything that had concerned him; they constitute his acceptance and affirmation of life.

[12] The more Bruegel's work is studied the stronger grows the feeling that almost everything may be attributed to him. To go to Vienna and through that group of fifteen pictures to come into direct contact with his mind across three hundred and fifty years is to be convinced that his is one of the inexhaustible minds of the world. The material brilliancy of the painting is more than matched by the

brilliancy of the creative soul behind them. Whether he himself was conscious of all that can now be perceived in his work does not much matter; whether it came there with him aware or unaware, it is enough to make him superbly great. But this much is true: the more 145 his mind is apprehended, the more vast and purposeful it appears.

[13] He was fortunate in finding his means of expression in what was then a popular art; everything about that art was so alive that it drew to itself some of the greatest minds of the time. There existed a tremendous amount of give-and-take between the artist and his 150 age, and this degree of interaction it was which had most to do with endowing both art and artist with vitality; they were fed from sources outside of and larger than themselves. Thus it was that Bruegel attained to so comprehensive an expression of himself and his age together that his work has become one of the permanent things of art. 155

[14] There are purer painters, but for the purity of their art they pay the price of going without something of importance to a complete life. And even their gain in intensity seems hardly a gain in the face of Bruegel's intensity on all the levels of his completeness. He transposes all life into his pictures in a scale of relative relationship 160 that preserves the values of human life itself. Every other painter lacks something or has something in excess. Bruegel is the most comprehensive and the best balanced, the most energetic and the mellowest. Of all painters he is the greatest realist, and of them all the most humane. 165

A paragraph may be defined as a group of sentences that develop a single idea. In spite of the definition, there are occasionally reasons for using a one-sentence paragraph: the idea may need merely to be stated rather than developed, or a writer may want to give an idea special emphasis and so lets it stand alone, with its development in a following paragraph. A one-sentence paragraph may serve as a transition between sections of an essay; dialogue frequently contains one-sentence paragraphs, a new paragraph being used to indicate each change of speaker. Normally, however, a paragraph contains a group of sentences.

The topic sentence states the idea developed in the paragraph. (For a discussion of methods of paragraph development, see pages 179–180.) Although most often the topic sentence is the first sentence, it may be placed anywhere in the paragraph, depending on the method or methods of development. For example, a writer may give certain bits of evidence leading inescapably to a logical conclusion; the statement of the conclusion at the end of the paragraph would be the topic sentence. Or he might prefer to state his conclusion first and then supply the supporting evidence or even give some of the evidence, state the conclusion, and then give the rest of the evidence. Judicious placement of the topic sentence is one factor in writing good paragraphs; some variety in placement from paragraph to paragraph lends variety to a piece of writing as a whole.

The development of an idea in some paragraphs may make the actual statement of the idea unnecessary; the idea emerges, then, by implication. Such paragraphs are said to have implied topic sentences. A paragraph with an implied topic sentence should be so carefully organized and developed that a reader would have no difficulty in formulating an explicit topic sentence.

1. What is the topic sentence of the first paragraph? Is the paragraph about two qualities of Bruegel's paintings or about one? Explain. What is the relationship between the topic sentence and the last sentence of the paragraph?

2. The topic sentence of the second paragraph is implied. Formulate a topic sentence for the paragraph. Where in the paragraph does your topic sentence belong? Why?

3. Explain why Bruegel's is "a nation living under the necessity of never speaking out openly on either politics or religion . . ." (paragraph 2). Does the topic sentence you formulated provide for this description of Bruegel's nation? If not, revise your formulation.

4. Is the topic sentence of paragraph 3 stated or implied? If stated, identify it; if implied, formulate it. What is the function of the last sentence in the paragraph?

5. What is the meaning of "more purely painter-like interests" (paragraph 3)?

6. Identify the topic sentence of paragraph 4 and comment on the order of the parts of the paragraph.

7. At first glance, the first sentence of paragraph 5—because of its position—might seem to be the topic sentence, but it is not. Identify the topic sentence. Does the first sentence violate the unity of the paragraph? Explain.

8. Comment on the opening of paragraph 7. Why is the use of "And" in the first sentence particularly effective?

9. Comment on the placement of the topic sentence in paragraph 8.

10. Is the topic sentence of paragraph 9 stated or implied? Justify your answer.

11. What two functions are served by the first sentence of paragraph 10?

12. Identify (or formulate, if implied) the topic sentences of the

last two paragraphs of the essay and comment on the order of materials in the final paragraph.

Alternate selections for the study of Topic Sentence: George F. Kennan, "The Experience of Writing History"; Theodore Dreiser, from *A Book about Myself.*

Theme Assignment: Imagine yourself with unlimited means to furnish a large living room in your home. Write a well-developed paragraph in which you describe the kind of furnishings you would select and your reasons for selecting them. You will have to be careful to avoid violating paragraph unity. Organize the paragraph so that the topic sentence appears at or near the beginning. Then rewrite the paragraph so that the topic sentence logically belongs at or near the end. Avoid a mere mechanical rearrangement; there is a considerable difference in structure between a paragraph which opens with a topic sentence and one which closes with a topic sentence.

or

Write a single paragraph in which you describe a relationship between two people. They may be people whom you know or literary or historic personages such as Edith Wharton and Henry James, Franklin Roosevelt and Harry Hopkins, Romeo and Juliet. It is your task to capture the essence of a human relationship in one paragraph, showing the meaning each of the two people had for the other. You may either state this meaning as your topic sentence or imply it.

or

Select an artist whose work you have come to know reasonably well. You may select a painter, a sculptor, a novelist, a poet, a playwright, a composer. In a well-constructed paragraph, evaluate the artist you have selected on the basis of Barker's statement that "the great artist's major accomplishment lies in revealing the universal through the particular, the permanent through the transitory, the inevitable through the accidental." If your topic sentence is stated, underline it; if implied, formulate it and submit it with your paragraph.

Methods of
Paragraph Development

ACCUMULATION OF DETAIL

The Raw Material of Poetry

RAINER MARIA RILKE

I think I ought to begin to do some work, now that I am learning
to see. I am twenty-eight years old, and almost nothing has been
done. To recapitulate: I have written a study on Carpaccio which
is bad, a drama entitled "Marriage," which sets out to demonstrate
5 something false by equivocal means, and some verses. Ah! but verses
amount to so little when one writes them young. One ought to wait
and gather sense and sweetness a whole life long, and a long life if
possible, and then, quite at the end, one might perhaps be able to
write ten lines that were good. For verses are not, as people imagine,
10 simple feelings (those one has early enough),—they are experiences.
For the sake of a single verse, one must see many cities, men and
things, one must know the animals, one must feel how the birds fly
and know the gesture with which the little flowers open in the morn-

ing. One must be able to think back to roads in unknown regions, to unexpected meetings and to partings one had long seen coming; to 15 days of childhood that are still unexplained, to parents whom one had to hurt when they brought one some joy and one did not grasp it (it was a joy for someone else); to childhood illnesses that so strangely begin with such a number of profound and grave transformations, to days in rooms withdrawn and quiet and to mornings by 20 the sea, to the sea itself, to seas, to nights of travel that rushed along on high and flew with all the stars—and it is not yet enough if one may think of all this. One must have memories of many nights of love, none of which was like the others, of the screams of women in labor, and of light, white, sleeping women in childbed, closing again. 25 But one must also have been beside the dying, must have sat beside the dead in the room with the open window and the fitful noises. And still it is not yet enough to have memories. One must be able to forget them when they are many and one must have the great patience to wait until they come again. For it is not yet the memories themselves. 30 Not till they have turned to blood within us, to glance and gesture, nameless and no longer to be distinguished from ourselves—not till then can it happen that in a most rare hour the first word of a verse arises in their midst and goes forth from them.

It has been pointed out that a paragraph contains one basic idea and consists of sentences which develop this basic idea as it is expressed in a topic sentence or as it emerges by implication throughout the paragraph. However, there are many methods of developing an idea. Some paragraphs combine two or more methods of development; others seem to defy analysis. But several methods have emerged (or perhaps simply have been observed) as most useful and therefore most frequently employed; among these methods are accumulation of detail, exemplification, definition, comparison (which may include the use of contrast), and relating cause to effect.

It should be noted that professional writers do not sit at their desks and ask themselves, "Now what type of paragraph shall I use today?" any more than philosophers ask themselves what school of thought they belong to. But students of writing are not "writers." It is useful to study the methods of paragraph development and even, at first, to employ them consciously, to understand and master them.

Furthermore, it is well to keep in mind that ideas need not be fully developed within a single paragraph, but that the methods of development used for single paragraphs apply as well to larger units—a group of paragraphs, perhaps, or even a whole theme or essay. So you will find that you may apply these principles of development in the planning and executing of themes as well as single paragraphs.

Probably the most common method of paragraph development is accumulation of detail. The multiple details may support a central thesis; describe a person, place, or thing; make a general statement specific and concrete; or in any other way substantiate the topic sentence.

1. Rilke's paragraph, an excerpt from the notebooks of a fictitious writer—a partial disguise for Rilke himself—has an implied topic sentence. Formulate a sentence of your own which contains the central idea of the paragraph.

2. What do all the details Rilke uses to develop this idea have in common?

3. What order can you detect in his presentation of the details? How do you justify the order?

4. Why is accumulation of detail an apt method for the development of the central idea of this particular paragraph? Specifically, why must the author present many details to make his point?

5. What purposes are served by Rilke's writing "to mornings by the sea, to the sea itself, to seas"? How do these three details differ from one another?

6. Do the last four sentences violate the unity of the paragraph? Why or why not?

7. Do you agree or disagree with Rilke? Justify your answer, perhaps bringing to class a poem which seems to you to illustrate your own position.

8. Any one of the details which Rilke mentions might itself be expanded into a paragraph developed by the same method. Select one of the details which is particularly familiar to you and write a paragraph about it, using accumulation of details as your method of development.

[For assignment, see pp. 207–208.]

EXEMPLIFICATION

☞ *Writers and Talkers*

THOMAS BAILEY ALDRICH

[1] As a class, literary men do not shine in conversation. The
scintillating and playful essayist whom you pictured to yourself as
the most genial and entertaining of companions turns out to be a
shy and untalkable individual, who chills you with his reticence when
you chance to meet him. The poet whose fascinating volume you 5
always drop into your gripsack on your summer vacation—the poet
whom you have so long desired to know personally—is a moody and
abstracted middle-aged gentleman, who fails to catch your name on
introduction, and seems the avatar of the commonplace. The witty
and ferocious critic whom your fancy had painted as a literary canni- 10
bal with a morbid appetite for tender young poets—the writer of
those caustic and scholarly reviews which you never neglect to read
—destroys the un-lifelike portrait you had drawn by appearing before
you as a personage of slender limb and deprecating glance, who stam-
mers and makes a painful spectacle of himself when you ask him his 15
opinion of "The Glees of the Gulches," by Popocatepetl Jones. The
slender, dark-haired novelist of your imagination, with epigrammatic
points to his mustache, suddenly takes the shape of a short, smoothly-
shaven blond man, whose conversation does not sparkle at all, and
you were on the lookout for the most brilliant of verbal fireworks. 20
Perhaps it is a dramatist you have idealized. Fresh from witnessing
his delightful comedy of manners, you meet him face to face only
to discover that his own manners are anything but delightful. The
play and the playwright are two very distinct entities. You grow
skeptical touching the truth of Buffon's assertion that the style is the 25

man himself. Who that has encountered his favorite author in the flesh has not sometimes been a little, if not wholly, disappointed?

[2] After all, is it not expecting too much to expect a novelist to talk as cleverly as the clever characters in his novels? Must a drama-
30 tist necessarily go about armed to the teeth with crisp dialogue? May not a poet be allowed to lay aside his singing-robes and put on a conventional dress-suit when he dines out? Why is it not permissible in him to be as prosaic and tiresome as the rest of the company? He usually is.

[For treatment of this selection, see p. 186.]

✒ The Painter's Hands

LEONARDO DA VINCI

If the painter wishes to see enchanting beauties, he has the power to produce them. If he wishes to see monstrosities, whether terrify-ing, or ludicrous and laughable, or pitiful, he has the power and au-thority to create them. If he wishes to produce towns or deserts, if
5 in the hot season he wants cool and shady places, or in the cold season warm places, he can make them. If he wants valleys, if from high mountaintops he wants to survey vast stretches of country, if beyond he wants to see the horizon on the sea, he has the power to create all this; and likewise, if from deep valleys he wants to see high
10 mountains or from high mountains deep valleys and beaches. Indeed, whatever exists in the universe, whether in essence, in act, or in the imagination, the painter has first in his mind and then in his hands. His hands are of such excellence that they can present to our view simultaneously whatever well-proportioned harmonies real things
15 exhibit piecemeal.

[For treatment of this selection, see p. 186.]

From "Notebooks of Leonardo da Vinci" as reprinted in *Artists on Art*, edited by Robert Goldwater and Marco Treves, and published by Pantheon Books, Inc. Reprinted by permission of Harcourt, Brace & World, Inc.

From *Some Unsentimental Confessions of a Nature Writer*

JOSEPH WOOD KRUTCH

[1] A few years ago I first laid myself open to the charge of being a "nature writer." Perhaps in time I shall know better what it is that I am trying to do and why I do it. At the moment I still do not know precisely what a "nature writer" is.

. . . .

[2] Man is after all a part of nature. Life is a mystery and an 5 adventure which he shares with all living things. The only clew to himself is in them. The universe is divided into two parts: that which is living and that which remains dead. We ought to be fully aware of which side we are on and of what it means to be on that side.

[3] Yet as civilization becomes more complicated we have less and 10 less to do with the things which are on our side. We live in cities surrounded by dead things. We deal far more with machines than we do with animals. The principal context of our lives has come to be dead matter, not living matter. And under these circumstances we tend more and more to lose sight of what we are and of what we 15 are like.

. . . .

[4] The question used to be whether or not men had souls. The question now seems to be whether or not they are alive at all; but that is seldom asked any more. In a city we may doubt it. In the presence of nature we cannot. 20

[5] I do not mean that we should all go live on Walden Pond. I am not any kind of crank or any kind of Utopian reformer. I do not believe that the solution to the world's ills is a return to some previous age of mankind. But I do doubt that any solution is possible unless we think of ourselves in the context of living nature. 25

From the New York *Herald Tribune Book Review,* June 15, 1952. Reprinted by permission of the New York *Herald Tribune* and the author.

[6] Perhaps that suggests an answer to the question what a "nature writer" is. He is not a sentimentalist who says that "nature never did betray the heart that loved her." Neither is he simply a scientist classifying animals or reporting on the behavior of birds just because
30 certain facts can be ascertained. He is a writer whose subject is the natural context of human life, a man who tries to communicate his observations and his thoughts in the presence of nature as part of his attempt to make himself more aware of that context. "Nature writing" is nothing really new. It has always existed in literature. But it
35 has tended in the course of the last century to become specialized partly because so much writing that is not specifically "nature writing" does not present the natural context at all; because so many novels and so many treatises describe man as an economic unit, a political unit, or as a member of some social class but not as a living
40 creature surrounded by other living things.

[7] There are few men who have never looked at a kitten and thought it was cute or looked at the stars and felt themselves small. Whoever has done either has been aware of the context of nature and that is good as far as it goes. But it does not go very far and
45 there is little in modern life, not too much in modern literature or modern art, to make him go further. What the "nature writer" is really asking him to do is to explore what such thought and such feelings mean. Nearly everyone admits that literature and art have something to say that science and sociology cannot. But nature in her
50 turn has something to say beyond the reach of literature and art. To that something the nature writer asks us to open our minds and our hearts precisely as another kind of writer asks us to open them to art or music or literature.

[8] That is, at least, what I am asking myself to do when I write
55 about a year in Connecticut or a year in the desert, about the courtship of lizards, or the desert toad who seems to spend four-fifths of his life holed up in the sand not dreading but waiting for a rainy day. He is interesting primarily because he is playing his part in an inconceivable adventure in which we are all somehow involved.

60 [9] One of the things which I remember best from my year in the West is a day spent alone on a mountain top looking down at a desert. Half seriously I said to myself that this was my great chance. Moses and Zarathustra did just that. Most of the prophets have retired either to a mountain or to a desert. If ever, I thought, you are
65 to get The Answer it ought to be now.

[10] I did not get it. These days, I suppose, no one ever does.

This is not an age when men appear to hear the voice of God. But I do not think that I ever before understood myself so well and with the understanding came a conviction. We cannot understand other people or the world unless we do understand ourselves first. It is presumption and folly to advise, and direct, and legislate unless we at least know our own selves. But we do not understand ourselves unless we have been alone with ourselves and with that nature of which we are more a part than we usually seem to remember.

[11] Alone on a mountain top no one ever believed that Man is nothing but the product of economic forces or that production per man hour is a reliable index of human welfare. And surely no man on a mountain top ever believed that Good and Evil are nothing except the prejudices of a given society. Such dismal, such deadly, opinions are possible only to those who do not know human beings because they do not know themselves and do not know themselves because they have never been alone with themselves. This will never be a world in which a good life is possible for most people as long as dismal and deadly opinions predominate. And the nature writer, like the poet and like the priest, is their enemy.

[12] I do not mean to suggest that the nature writer always is or always should be on the mountain tops, either literally or figuratively. No one who actually looks at nature rather than at some fancy projected upon or read into her can ever fail to realize that she represents some ultimate things-as-they-are, not some ideal of things-as-he-thinks-they-ought-to-be. There is in her what we call cruelty and also, even more conspicuously, what we call grotesqueness and what we call comedy. If she warns the so-called realist how limited his conception of reality is she is no less likely to bring the sentimentalist back, literally, to earth.

[13] How much of the cruelty, of the grotesqueness, or of the sublimity any given man will see depends no doubt to some considerable extent upon his own temperament and I suppose it is some indication of mine when I confess that what I see most often and relish the most is, first, the intricate marvel and, second, the comedy. To be reminded that one is very much like other members of the animal kingdom is often funny though it is never, like being compared to a machine, merely humiliating. I do not too much mind being somewhat like a cat, a dog, or even an insect but I resent having it said that even an electronic calculator is like me.

[14] Not very long ago I was pointing out to a friend the courtship of two spiders in a web just outside my door. Most people know

that the male is often much smaller than his mate and nearly everybody knows by now that the female of many species sometimes eats
110 her husband. Both of these things were true of the common kind
beside my door and the insignificant male was quite obviously torn
between ardor and caution. He danced forward and then darted back.
He approached now from one side and now from the other. He would
and he wouldn't.

115 [15] My friend, no nature student and not much given to observing such creatures, was gratifyingly interested. Presently he could
contain himself no longer.

[16] "You know," he said thoughtfully, "there is only one difference between that spider and a human male. The spider knows it's
120 dangerous."

[17] That, I maintain, both is and ought to be as much grist for a
nature writer's mill as a sunset or a bird song.

Another method of developing the central thesis expressed in a
paragraph is exemplification. In practice, this method is sometimes
difficult to distinguish from the method of accumulation of detail; in
fact, they overlap in structure and function. The only meaningful
distinction between the two is that details elaborate upon, describe,
or embellish the central thesis, whereas examples illustrate it. When a
writer uses details, the very weight of numbers is a necessary concomitant; when he uses exemplification, the writer may limit himself
to a single example or may present several examples. The topic sentence may appear before or after the examples; it may, particularly if
the entire paragraph is a single example, be implied rather than stated.

1. What is the topic sentence of the first paragraph of the Aldrich
selection?

2. How many types of authors does Aldrich give as examples?

3. What is the pattern of each example?

4. Point out as many ways as you can in which Aldrich achieves
variety among the examples.

5. What is the structure of paragraph 2? What is its function?

6. In what ways is humor achieved throughout the selection?

7. What is Da Vinci exemplifying?

8. Do his examples prove his point? Explain.

9. Account for the difference in placement within the paragraph
of the examples in the Aldrich and Da Vinci selections.

10. State in one carefully worded sentence the central thesis of the
Krutch selection.

11. Where do you first find exemplification used to develop the

thesis? With what other method of development is exemplification combined in the paragraph you have identified? Explain.

12. What two extended examples does Krutch use for the further development of his thesis? Which of the two do you consider the more effective? Why? In just what way is each effective?

[For assignment, see pp. 207–208.]

DEFINITION

From *What Is a Classic?*

C. A. SAINTE-BEUVE

[1] A true classic, as I should like to hear it defined, is an author who has enriched the human mind, increased its treasure and caused it to advance a step; who has discovered some moral and not equivocal truth, or revealed some eternal passion in that heart where all seemed known and discovered; who has expressed his thought, ob- 5 servation, or invention, in no matter what form, only provided it be broad and great, refined and sensible, sane and beautiful in itself; who has spoken to all in his own peculiar style, a style which is found to be also that of the whole world, a style new without neologism, new and old, easily contemporary with all time. 10

.   .   .   .   .   .

[2] It is necessary to make a choice, and the first condition of taste, after obtaining knowledge of all, lies not in continual travel, but in rest and cessation from wandering. Nothing blunts and destroys taste so much as endless journeyings; the poetic spirit is not the *Wandering Jew.* However, when I speak of resting and making choice, 15 my meaning is not that we are to imitate those who charm us most among our masters in the past. Let us be content to know them, to penetrate them, to admire them; but let us, the late-comers, en-

deavour to be ourselves. Let us have the sincerity and naturalness of
20 our own thoughts, of our own feelings; so much is always possible.
To that let us add what is more difficult, elevation, an aim, if possible,
toward an exalted goal; and while speaking our own language, and
submitting to the conditions of the times in which we live, whence
we derive our strength and our defects, let us ask from time to time,
25 our brows lifted toward the heights and our eyes fixed on the group
of honored mortals: *what would they say of us?*

[3] But why speak always of authors and writings? Maybe an age
is coming when there will be no more writing. Happy those who read
and read again, those who in their reading can follow their un-
30 restrained inclination! There comes a time in life when, all our jour-
neys over, our experiences ended, there is no enjoyment more
delightful than to study and thoroughly examine the things we know,
to take pleasure in what we feel, and in seeing and seeing again
the people we love: the pure joys of our maturity. Then it is that the
35 word classic takes its true meaning, and is defined for every man of
taste by an irresistible choice. Then taste is formed, it is shaped and
definite; then good sense, if we are to possess it at all, is perfected
in us. We have neither more time for experiments, nor a desire to go
forth in search of pastures new. We cling to our friends, to those
40 proved by a long intercourse. Old wine, old books, old friends. We
say to ourselves with Voltaire in these delightful lines:—

[4] "Let us enjoy, let us write, let us live, my dear Horace! . . .
I have lived longer than you: my verse will not last so long. But
on the brink of the tomb I shall make it my chief care—to follow the
45 lessons of your philosophy—to despise death in enjoying life—to
read your writings full of charm and good sense—as we drink an old
wine which revives our senses."

[5] In fact, be it Horace or another who is the author preferred,
who reflects our thoughts in all the wealth of their maturity, of some
50 one of those excellent and antique minds shall we request an interview
at every moment; of some one of them shall we ask a friendship
which never deceives, which could not fail us; to some one of them
shall we appeal for that sensation of serenity and amenity (we have
often need of it) which reconciles us with mankind and with our-
55 selves.

[For treatment of this selection, see p. 191.]

What Is a Poet?

WILLIAM WORDSWORTH

What is a Poet? To whom does he address himself? And what language is to be expected from him?—He is a man speaking to men: a man, it is true, endowed with more lively sensibility, more enthusiasm and tenderness, who has a greater knowledge of human nature, and a more comprehensive soul, than are supposed to be 5 common among mankind; a man pleased with his own passions and volitions, and who rejoices more than other men in the spirit of life that is in him; delighting to contemplate similar volitions and passions as manifested in the goings-on of the Universe, and habitually impelled to create them where he does not find them. To these qualities 10 he has added a disposition to be affected more than other men by absent things as if they were present; an ability of conjuring up in himself passions, which are indeed far from being the same as those produced by real events, yet (especially in those parts of the general sympathy which are pleasing and delightful) do more nearly resemble 15 the passions produced by real events than anything which, from the motions of their own minds merely, other men are accustomed to feel in themselves:—whence, and from practice, he has acquired a greater readiness and power in expressing what he thinks and feels, and especially those thoughts and feelings which, by his own choice, or 20 from the structure of his own mind, arise in him without immediate external excitement.

[For treatment of this selection, see p. 191.]

✐ What Is a Poem?

SAMUEL TAYLOR COLERIDGE

[1] A poem is that species of composition, which is opposed to works of science, by proposing for its *immediate* object pleasure, not truth; and from all other species—(having *this* object in common with it)—it is discriminated by proposing to itself such delight from
5 the *whole,* as is compatible with distinct gratification from each component *part.*

[2] Controversy is not seldom excited in consequence of the disputants attaching each a different meaning to the same word; and in few instances has this been more striking, than in disputes concerning
10 the present subject. If a man chooses to call every composition a poem, which is rhyme, or measure, or both, I must leave his opinion uncontroverted. The distinction is at least competent to characterize the writer's intention. If it were subjoined, that the whole is likewise entertaining or affecting, as a tale, or as a series of interesting reflec-
15 tions, I of course admit this as another fit ingredient of a poem, and an additional merit. But if the definition sought for be that of a *legitimate* poem, I answer, it must be one, the parts of which mutually support and explain each other; all in their proportion harmonizing with, and supporting the purpose and known influences of
20 metrical arrangement. The philosophic critics of all ages coincide with the ultimate judgment of all countries, in equally denying the praises of a just poem, on the one hand, to a series of striking lines or distiches, each of which, absorbing the whole attention of the reader to itself, becomes disjoined from its context, and forms a
25 separate whole, instead of a harmonizing part; and on the other hand, to an unsustained composition, from which the reader collects rapidly the general result unattracted by the component parts. The reader should be carried forward, not merely or chiefly by the mechanical impulse of curiosity, or by a restless desire to arrive at the final solu-
30 tion; but by the pleasurable activity of mind excited by the attractions of the journey itself. Like the motion of a serpent, which the Egyptians made the emblem of intellectual power; or like the path of sound

through the air;—at every step he pauses and half recedes, and from the retrogressive movement collects the force which again carries him onward.

35

Definition is a fairly formularized process. In order to define a term, it is necessary to place it in its proper category (*genus*) and then delineate it from other members of that category by giving its unique qualities or characteristics (*differentiae*). For example, the *American College Dictionary* defines a dive bomber as "an airplane [*genus*] of the pursuit type which drops its bombs while diving at the target [*differentiae*]."

1. Show how Wordsworth's definition of a poet does or does not include both *genus* and *differentiae*.

2. Definition frequently appears in combination with other methods of paragraph development. Why do you think it does? Which of the methods you have studied do you think would combine effectively with the method of definition? Why?

3. Does the paragraph in which Wordsworth defines a poet employ a combination of methods? Explain.

4. In his definition of a classic, Sainte-Beuve supplies a rather large number of *differentiae*. List them and suggest what may have determined the order which Sainte-Beuve has established for them.

5. What other method or methods of paragraph development does he employ?

6. Explain why Sainte-Beuve says that it is only in maturity that "the word classic takes its true meaning." How does this elaboration of the definition add to your understanding of the word "classic" as he defines it?

7. Select a work which you think fulfills Sainte-Beuve's definition of a classic and justify your choice by applying his criteria (or *differentiae*) to it.

8. Do you consider Coleridge's definition of a poem adequate? Why or why not?

9. What other definitions does Coleridge mention in paragraph 2? Does he use the classic form of definition for them? Explain. What method or methods of paragraph development do you find in paragraph 2?

10. "Controversy is not seldom excited in consequence of the disputants attaching each a different meaning to the same word," Coleridge says. From your reading of the newspaper, cite an example of such a controversy from current-day events. Write a one-paragraph definition, which you consider accurate, of the word you have selected.

11. In paragraph 2, Coleridge compares the reader of poetry with

two other things. What are they? Why do you consider these comparisons apt or inept? Why does comparison or analogy so often accompany definition?

12. In "Some Unsentimental Confessions of a Nature Writer," Krutch avowedly is defining what he means by a nature writer. To what extent does his definition meet the requirements of formal definition?

[For assignment, see pp. 207–208.]

COMPARISON AND CONTRAST

✍From *Culture and Snobbism*

ROGER FRY

[1] Can we distinguish between culture and snobbism? In both a certain religious attitude of worship is evident, and they are concerned largely with the same values. In both, too, communion with fellow worshippers is a matter of supreme importance, so that it
5 is not always an easy matter to say of a particular act of devotion or article of faith to which Church it belongs. It may, indeed, partake of both, since these are not mutually exclusive doctrines.

[2] There is, however, I think, a difference of mental attitude which the words enable us to distinguish. The snobbist, by his
10 pilgrimage to the "right" picture gallery at the "right" moment, and his display there of the "right" enthusiasm before the "right" works of art is really upheld by the consciousness that those acts bring him into close communion with a certain group of people, and it is not altogether remote from his consciousness, although, perhaps, kept
15 below its surface, that those people are socially influential. His acts

tend to make certain that he will be "in the swim." It is this subtle connection between a certain esthetic creed and its social adherents that is, perhaps, too frankly revealed by the word "snobbism." The man of culture, on the other hand, lives in a world more detached from these considerations. His communion is not only with the living. By his acts of devotion he unites himself to a long line of historical precedents. He upholds the tradition which sensitive and contemplative spirits have handed on from generation to generation. And, since the verdicts of esthetic sensibility have a tendency to violent fluctuations, this traditional esthetic doctrine has called to its aid the steadying influence of learning and scholarship. So that the devotees of culture often acquire more merit by what they know about the history of a work of art than by what they feel in front of it. To them an artist does not become a serious artist until a learned monograph has been consecrated to his life work. Thus the cultured, linked to the past by a long line of predecessors and filled with a sense of responsibility for the future, tend to adopt a conservative attitude to contemporary art. Their imprimatur must not be lightly given. They yield in the end, and become the guardians of what they resisted, judging, perhaps rightly, that only its irresistibility justifies this consecration. The snobbist, on the other hand, whilst always respectful of learning, is too anxious to know the latest word to await its judgment. He tends, therefore, to march in step with the vanguard of any esthetic movement as soon as its victory is no longer in doubt. Until victory is fairly in view the movements of the true snobbist afford a fascinating spectacle, he—or perhaps she, for, thanks to the quicker social sense of women, they form the greatest and most devout part of the communion—shows the greatest anxiety and trepidation. A too overt adherence to the new doctrine at such a moment would precipitate him along a social blind alley and leave him in a position from which recovery is too difficult and sometimes slightly ridiculous. On the other hand, to be left behind on the right track, though a fault more easily repaired, is to miss a supreme opportunity.

[For treatment of this selection, see p. 198.]

✑From *The Defense of Poesy*

SIR PHILIP SIDNEY

Our comedians think there is no delight without laughter, which is very wrong; for though laughter may come with delight, yet cometh it not of delight, as though delight should be the cause of laughter; but well may one thing breed both together. Nay, rather in
5 themselves they have, as it were, a kind of contrariety. For delight we scarcely do, but in things that have a conveniency to ourselves, or to the general nature; laughter almost ever cometh of things most disproportioned to ourselves and nature. Delight hath a joy in it either permanent or present; laughter hath only a scornful tickling. For
10 example, we are ravished with delight to see a fair woman, and yet are far from being moved to laughter; we laugh at deformed creatures, wherein certainly we cannot delight. We delight in good chances; we laugh at mischances. We delight to hear the happiness of our friends and country, at which he were worthy to be laughed
15 at that would laugh; we shall, contrarily, sometimes laugh to find a matter quite mistaken, and go down the hill against the bias, in the mouth of some such men as for the respect of them one shall be heartily sorry he cannot choose but laugh, and so is rather pained than delighted with laughter. Yet deny I not but that they may go
20 well together; for as in Alexander's picture well set out we delight without laughter, and in twenty mad antics we laugh without delight: so in Hercules, painted, with his great beard and furious countenance, in a woman's attire, spinning at Omphale's commandment, it breeds both delight and laughter; for the representing of so strange a power
25 in love procures delight, and the scornfulness of the action stirreth laughter. But I speak to this purpose, that all the end of the comical part be not upon such scornful matters as stir laughter only, but mix with it that delightful teaching which is the end of poesy.

[For treatment of this selection, see p. 198.]

Equating Turner with Music

HAROLD C. SCHONBERG

[1] So the other morning we went to see the Turner exhibition at the Museum of Modern Art. The idea was to get there early, have the place to ourself, wander from painting to painting. You know what happened, of course. There was a crowd waiting for the doors to open. Busload upon busload of the art-hungry kept pulling up. 5 Schoolchildren by the hundreds, herded by desperate teachers, arrived to get their culture. Not since V-J Day in Times Square has there been an equal tumult. Inside, we peeked over shoulders, trod on toes and were trod upon, elbowed and were elbowed. But we saw the Turners. 10

[2] It was worth it. That fierce concentration on pigment and pure color! That ability to see things in a unique way! Whether or not Turner was The Father of Us All, he certainly had an amazing vision for his day (1775–1851) and one that few figures in any art can parallel. We kept thinking, while looking at the seascapes, of 15 our own field. What composer would be a near-equivalent? The name of Berlioz, who was a contemporary of Turner, automatically came to mind. Berlioz, too, used tones in a manner somewhat similar to the way Turner used pigment. Berlioz, too, had the kind of imagination that could take a naturalistic scene and transfigure it. 20

Parallel

[3] There is indeed a parallelism. Turner, for instance, manipulated nature, rather than let nature manipulate him. He did not copy a universe; he created one for himself. Similarly Berlioz did not let the materials of music manipulate him. A minor composer is content to take the rules as handed down. A major composer breaks them, as 25 Berlioz did. If, in music, the diatonic scale and the tonic-dominant derivatives correspond to "nature," then Berlioz was Turneresque in

From *The New York Times*, April 17, 1966. © 1966 by The New York Times Company. Reprinted by permission.

his defiance of natural rule. One thinks of the enharmonic horn notes in the "Pilgrim's March" of "Harold in Italy." No other composer
30 of the time, not even Schumann, would have so dared to introduce those enharmonic notes, which have no grammatical reason for being. But how expressive they are!

[4] What other composer? Certainly not ultra-realists like Wagner and Strauss. Not Debussy, who was much more allied to the French
35 impressionists; and impressionistic painting is a carefully composed affair, objective, full of attention to detail and basically quite different from Turner's approach. But it occurred to us that in one piece of music a composer who normally would be in a different camp approached Turner more closely than any other musical figure. The
40 composer was Arnold Schoenberg, and the work in question is the third of his Five Orchestral Pieces, the one called "Summer Morning by a Lake (Colors)." Even the title is Turneresque (though Schoenberg originally named it "The Changing Chord").

[5] You remember those Turner seascapes, in which ocean merges
45 into sky without even a hint of the horizon; in which great areas of color come together; and in which there is infinitely subtle variation within those great areas. Schoenberg's piece works much the same way. It is a study on a single chord—C, G sharp, B, E and A—and its possibilities for orchestral color within the permutations of the
50 chord. "The change of chords in this piece," wrote the composer in the score, "has to be executed with the greatest subtlety, avoiding accentuation of entering instruments, so that only the difference in color becomes noticeable."

[6] In this piece of music there is no "horizon," but only one
55 pulsating slab of shifting color. There does not seem to be a top, bottom, sides. It starts with pure color and ends with pure color; and if ever a musical score can be identified with the product of another art, Schoenberg's No. 3 of the Five Orchestral Pieces is a late Turner.

[7] One wonders how well Schoenberg knew his Turner. As is well
60 known, he himself dabbled in painting, He was a Sunday painter of the expressionist school, and was closely identified with the expressionist group. Indeed, he was almost a charter member of Der Blaue Reiter in Berlin. Toward the end of 1911, Marc, Klee, Chagall and Kandinsky, among others, put out a publication that was an ex-
65 pressionist manifesto, and Schoenberg was a contributor to the first issue. By that time he had begun to take painting quite seriously, and between 1907 and 1910 had turned out a rather large number of

canvases. On Oct. 8, 1910, he had an exhibition at the book store and art gallery of Hugo Heller in Berlin.

Theories

[8] All of this painting was done during the composition of the 70
Five Orchestral Pieces in 1909. Now, music must be judged as music and not in terms of another art. But theories do go into musical composition, and it is clear that Schoenberg was strongly influenced by the Berlin expressionists. The expressionists were intensely sub- jective, they were great ones for the subconscious, and they would 75
never think of reproducing a subject exactly as they saw it. Instead they emphasized the ego, the unconscious, the elements which to them (and often to them alone) signified the spiritual nature of the subject. Said one sitter for an expressionistic portrait, in 1910: "Kokoschka has made a painting of me. It is quite possible that those 80
who know me will not recognize me. But it is certain that those who do not know me will recognize me." Spiritual truth, in short, rather than physical likeness.

[9] And so we come back to Turner: spiritual truth rather than physical likeness. Turner was one of the first to discard realism, mere 85
copying, in favor of expression, thus arriving almost at a form of super-realism, a Platonic realism. He may or may not have done this instinctively. In music, Schoenberg did the same thing, but quite de- liberately. In his essay in Der Blaue Reiter, he concerned himself with the relationship between text and music. He pointed out that he 90
had fully understood a Schubert song, in its deepest implications, without knowing the text. He went on to quote a Kandinsky essay on the spiritual in art, and then expressed the hope "that those who ask about the text, about the subject matter, will soon ask no more."

[10] He went one step further. The outward manifestation be- 95
tween music and text, he said, has but little to do with the "inward correspondence" of music, and "belongs to the same stage of primi- tive imitation of nature as the copying of a model." Indeed we do come back to Turner!

In the method of comparison and contrast, two or more units may be compared in the same paragraph, or separate paragraphs may be devoted to each unit. Strictly, the purer example of the form is the single paragraph which combines the units.

There is a meaningful distinction between the terms "comparison" and "contrast"; comparison implies similarity, while contrast suggests dissimilarity between or among the units. Of course, items may be both similar in certain ways and dissimilar in others. For example, a plum and peach are both fruits, both round, both sweet, both juicy. But they have striking dissimilarities: one has smooth skin and the other has fuzzy; one is red and the other is multicolored—green and yellow and "peach." Both comparison and contrast, then, may be relevant to the development of the topic sentence or the guiding purpose.

1. The passage by Roger Fry is singularly useful for our purposes here since it consists of one paragraph of comparison and one of contrast. Explain this statement, making detailed references to the text.

2. In paragraph 2, Fry speaks of a difference in attitude between the snobbist and the man of culture. What is that difference? What methods of development does Fry employ to make clear the difference?

3. Why does it seem to you that Fry found it advisable to go into some detail about the attitude of one man before discussing the attitude of the other?

4. Upon which is more emphasis placed, the snobbist or the man of culture? How do you know?

5. Is Fry's attitude the same or different toward the two? If it is different, in what way or ways does it differ? Justify your answer.

6. Is the Sidney paragraph primarily one of comparison or of contrast? How does Sidney himself tell you so? Where is the other element (*i.e.*, comparison, if your answer to the first part of this question was contrast; or contrast, if your answer was comparison) present in the paragraph?

7. How does the Sidney paragraph differ in organization from paragraph 2 of the Fry selection? Why do you think Sidney found his procedure of organization useful?

8. What, if any other method of paragraph development does Sidney also use? Explain.

9. Where does Sidney tell us his reason for writing this paragraph? Why is his statement placed where it is?

10. Since Harold Schonberg set out to find a composer who might be "a near-equivalent" to Turner, it was inevitable that his article would be built on comparison rather than contrast. Nevertheless, contrast is involved in the development of the first paragraph. Explain. What additional method or methods are used to develop this paragraph? Where else in the article does Schonberg use contrast?

11. What is the function of the first sentence of paragraph 3? of paragraph 4?

12. Which of the remaining paragraphs (5 through 10) are developed primarily through comparison? In which paragraph (or paragraphs) is comparison implicit rather than explicit?

13. What additional methods of paragraph development are used in paragraphs 5 through 10; indicate in which paragraph or paragraphs you find each.

14. Though Schonberg deals with the painting of Turner, the theories of the Berlin expressionists, and the music and painting of Arnold Schoenberg, he has not violated unity of the whole. Taking into account Schonberg's guiding purpose, justify the preceding statement.

[For assignment, see pp. 207–208.]

CAUSE AND EFFECT

Penny Arcades to Cinematic Cathedrals

BUDD SCHULBERG

In 1900, hundreds of thousands were introduced to movies when vaudeville managers used them to break the first theatrical strike. But the return of the rebellious actors left the movies out in the cold, a homeless child of four. The displaced medium was taken in by penny-arcade owners who added films to the shooting galleries, the 5 midgets, and the traffic in French postcards. Whereas in France the approach of the pioneer Méliès was closer to that of artists in more established media, in America the movie was a gutter child growing up without guidance or traditions in an atmosphere of opportunistic commercialization of the cheap thrill. It has been a long, impressive 10

From "Movies in America: After Fifty Years," *The Atlantic Monthly,* 1947.

climb from those crummy arcades to magnificent cinematic cathedrals like the Music Hall. But psychologists will tell you it's the first ten years that mold our characters, and it could be that this applies to our films as well. For despite their spectacular development in tech-
15 nique and the occasional film of real beauty, it may be that they have yet to outgrow their penny-arcade origin and point of view.

[For treatment of this selection, see p. 204.]

✐ From *The Language of Business* WILLIAM H. WHYTE, JR.

[1] Not so long ago, the businessman used to take his language pretty much for granted. He could afford to. His place was respected his authority unquestioned. And so he bought, he sold, he collected his bills, made an occasional speech perhaps—and if the public,
5 the workers, or the government didn't quite understand what he was up to, well, so much the better for all concerned.

[2] But no longer. Acknowledging the fact—and the necessity—of others' scrutiny, he has made the interchange of facts and ideas with them one of his principal jobs. The house organ, the interoffice memo,
10 the press release, the press conference, the annual report—the range of his efforts has grown enormous. So widespread, indeed, that business has become almost as extensive a publisher as the government itself.

[3] Is the language of business up to the job? The news—and
15 refreshing news it is—is that the American businessman himself has begun to conclude that it is not. Some, in fact, have gone so far as to assert that the pomposity of management prose is the "root ill of our communication troubles." While that may be an overexcited judgment, management's surveys have demonstrated that a large
20 amount of its language has been not only incomprehensible to the people it is trying to reach, but enormously expensive in money, time, and misunderstanding as well. "It is high time the American businessman discovered the English language—it would be very use-

From *Fortune*, November 1950. Courtesy of Fortune Magazine.

ful to him" . . . "We've turned our offices into paper mills" . . . "We love curt clear correspondence—but damned few of us know how to write it." Everywhere the chorus of self-criticism is growing. 25

[4] The positive results of this self-examination have been impressive. In company after company, executives have been setting up "writing clinics" to scour management copy, staging correspondence-improvement courses, holding schools in conference and public-speaking techniques, and, at the very least, peppering subordinates with "For-God's-sake-won't-you-people-learn-to-use-English-around-here" memos. All of which is clearly to the good. At the same time —and not so clearly to the good—a school of experts has come forward to help the businessman by redesigning the language of industry. To accomplish this, the experts have developed a scientific method that, as we shall see later, has some disturbing implications. Meanwhile, a look at the anatomy of this language that is to be redesigned. 30 35

[5] First, the written variety—and that infamous jargon, which, for want of a better term, we'll call businesese. Its signal characteristic, as the reader and all other critics of businesese will recognize, is its uniformity. Almost invariably, businesese is marked by the heavy use of the passive construction. Nobody ever *does* anything. Things *happen*—and the author of the action is only barely implied. Thus, one does not refer to something, reference is made to; similarly, while prices may rise, nobody *raises* them. To be sure, in businesese there is not quite the same anonymity as is found in federal prose, for "I" and "we" do appear often. Except when the news to be relayed is good, however, there is no mistaking that the "I" and "we" are merely a convenient fiction and that the real author isn't a person at all but that great mystic force known as the corporation. 40 45 50

[6] Except for a few special expressions, its vocabulary is everywhere quite the same. Midwesterners are likely to dispute the latter point, but a reading of approximately 500,000 words of business prose indicates no striking differences—in the Midwest or anywhere else. Moreover, in sounding out a hundred executives on the subject, *Fortune* found that their views coincided remarkably, particularly so in the matter of pet peeves (principally: "please be advised," "in reference to yours of . . .," "we wish to draw attention," "to acknowledge your letter"). The phrases of businesese are everywhere so uniform, in fact, that stenographers have a full set of shorthand symbols for them. 55 60

[7] Because of this uniformity, defenders of businesese can argue

65 that it doesn't make for misunderstanding. After all, everybody knows the symbols, and, furthermore, wouldn't a lot of people be offended by the terseness of more concise wording? There is something to this theory. Since businesese generally is twice as wordy as plain English, however, the theory is rather expensive to uphold. By the
70 use of regular English the cost of the average letter—commonly estimated at 75 cents to $1—can be cut by about 20 cents. For a firm emitting a million letters a year, this could mean an annual saving of $200,000. Probably it would be even greater; for, by the calculations of correspondence specialist Richard Morris, roughly 15
75 percent of the letters currently being written wouldn't be necessary at all if the preceding correspondence had been in regular English in the first place.

[8] Where do the terms of businesese come from? Most, of course, are hand-me-downs from former generations of businessmen, but
80 many are the fruit of cross-fertilization with other jargons. A businessman who castigates government bureaucrats, for example, is at the same time apt to be activating, expediting, implementing, effectuating, optimizing, minimizing, and maximizing—and at all levels and echelons within the framework of broad policy areas. Similarly,
85 though he is amused by the long-hairs and the social scientists, he is beginning to speak knowingly of projective techniques, social dynamics, depth interviewing, and sometime soon, if he keeps up at this rate, he will probably appropriate that hallmark of the sound sociological paper, "insightful." Businesese, in fact, has very nearly become
90 the great common meeting ground of the jargons.

[9] Why do people who in private talk so pungently often write so pompously? There are many reasons: tradition, the demands of time, carelessness, the conservative influence of the secretary. Above all is the simple matter of status. Theorem: the less established the status
95 of a person, the more his dependence on jargon. Examine the man who has just graduated from pecking out his own letters to declaiming them to a secretary and you are likely to have a man hopelessly intoxicated with the rhythm of businesese. Conversely, if you come across a blunt yes or no in a letter, you don't need to glance further
100 to grasp that the author feels pretty firm in his chair.

[10] The application of euphemism, a favored device of businesese, further illustrates this status principle. Take the field of selling. At the top of the ladder you will find a great many people in it: *sales* managers, vice presidents for *sales,* etc. As you go down the ranks,
105 however, it becomes difficult to find people in this line of work. Field

underwriters, estate planners, merchandising apprentices, social engineers, distribution analysts, and representatives of one kind or another, yes. But *sales*men? Rarely.

[11] Not only does businesese confer status, it protects it as well, by its magnificent usefulness for buck passing and hedging. "All you have to remember," one executive says, "is the one basis which characterizes all such intracommunication: let the language be ambiguous enough that if the text be successfully carried out, all credit may be claimed; but if the text be unsuccessfully carried out, a technical alibi can be set up out of the text itself."

[12] For this purpose there is a regular subglossary of businesese. Most notable terms: "in the process of," "at this time," "under consideration," "in the not-too-distant future," "company policy," and, when one is unable to explain something properly, "obviously." People who have to submit periodic reports to their superiors are particularly dependent on such terms—salesmen, for example, would have a hard time if they couldn't report of some prospects that they were "very impressed." ("I am allergic to that word," says one sales manager. "It results in so few orders.")

[13] The full application of businesese to hedging occurs when more than two heads are put to work on a problem. As the members of top management sit around the table, a relatively simple policy statement is introduced for discussion. This is kicked around a bit, as the saying goes, for though it certainly is a fine statement, couldn't agree with it more, there are just a few little angles and suggestions that maybe ought to be noted. Thereupon each executive, much as a baseball captain grasps a bat in choosing up sides, adds his qualification, until finally the original statement has been at once pointed up, toned down, given more dignity, made more forceful, altered to anticipate possible objections, concretized, amended, and resolved. Now no longer a mere statement but a philosophy, or collection of philosophies, it is turned over to the Public Relations Department to give to the waiting public. There is nothing, as so many people say, quite like what you get when everybody on the team works together.

A fifth method of paragraph development is that of cause and effect. There may be one cause with many effects or many causes of a single effect. Thus either the cause or the effect may be the central thought of the paragraph and may be placed either at the beginning or at the end.

1. State in your own words the cause (or causes) and effect (or effects) discussed in the Schulberg paragraph.

2. To which does Schulberg devote more space, the cause or the effect? Why do you think this distribution of space was necessary?

3. This is a highly compressed paragraph. What points might be included in an elaboration of it? Make an outline of a theme for which this paragraph states the guiding purpose.

4. Justify the placement of the topic sentence in this paragraph. Or, if you think the topic sentence is implied, state it in your own words.

5. What is the relevance of the comparison of the movies to the first ten years of a child's life? Point out specifically where and how the author has prepared us for this comparison—or figure of speech—earlier in the paragraph.

6. What is meant by the phrase "penny-arcade point of view"? Give several examples which either demonstrate or refute Schulberg's contention that the movies have not outgrown this point of view.

7. Work your examples into a paragraph.

8. Paragraph 4 of "The Language of Business" consists largely of effects. In what paragraph is the cause of these effects stated? Why were the two paragraphs not combined? What is the function of sentence 1 of paragraph 4?

9. What method of development is used in paragraph 5? Why is this method appropriate to the central thought of the paragraph? Where else in the selection do you find the same method of paragraph development?

10. The question raised in paragraph 9 is answered largely through the cause-and-effect method of development. How adequately is the question answered; that is, are the causes sufficient to account for the effect? Why or why not?

[For assignment, see pp. 207–208.]

COMBINED METHODS

On Individual Style

LAFCADIO HEARN

If you look at the dictionary you will find various definitions of the word *style,* but all these can be reduced to two. The first, or general style, is simply rhetorical; it means the construction of sentences according to a complete set of rules, governing the form and proportion of every part of the sentence. This once was style. 5 There was a time when everybody was supposed to write according to the same rules, and in almost exactly the same way, We might expect that work done by different individuals according to such rules would be all very much alike; and as a matter of fact, there was a great likeness in the styles of French and English writers during the 10 time that classical rules of composition were in force. I suppose you know that by *classical* I mean rules obtained from study of the Greek and Latin writers. The effort of Western men of letters during the late seventeenth and early eighteenth centuries was to imitate the old classics. So they had rules and measures for everything, for every part 15 of a sentence, and for the position of every word. Therefore the styles did greatly resemble each other. In France the similarity I refer to was greater than in England, the French being a more perfect language, and much closer to Latin than English. For example, you would find it very hard to distinguish the style of a story written by 20 Diderot from the style of a story written by Voltaire. The Encyclopedists, as they are called, wrote very much after the same fashion. But a fine critic could detect differences, nevertheless. For no matter how exact the rules might be, the way of obeying them would differ according to differences of character, mental character; I need 25

scarcely tell you that no two minds think and feel in exactly the same way. These differences of individual thinking and feeling necessarily give a slightly different tone to the work of each writer, even in the most rigid period of classical style. And this difference of tone is what
30 we call style today—after the old classical rules have been given up. But there is still much popular error upon the subject of individual style. People still think with the ideas of the eighteenth century. They think that there are rules for individual style, because there are rules for classical style. They think that when we talk of the style of
35 Macaulay or Froude, of Arnold or of De Quincey, we mean certain rules of composition by which the literary method of one man can be known from that of another. I should like to see any man living attempt to define these rules. The authors themselves could not define them. There are no such rules. This is altogether an error—and a
40 very serious error. The differences are not due to any definable rules at all; they are due entirely to individual differences of character. And therefore I say that style, in the modern meaning of the word, is character.

Paragraphs may, of course, combine several methods of development; they may employ any number of methods not analyzed here. Some of these additional methods are repetition, division into components (for example, a step-by-step description of a process), and analogy. The number of possible combinations begins to be astronomical and had best be left to the realm of the computing machine. It will be enough to sample these combinations of methods in the selection by Lafcadio Hearn; you will, in your own writing, employ many of the possible combinations.

1. Which of the methods of paragraph development discussed in the preceding sections do you find in the Hearn paragraph? Point out precisely where each method is used.

2. Point out the sentences, words, or phrases in this selection which explain or explicitly state the methods of development employed. List other such words or phrases which might appear in paragraphs combining methods of development.

3. Which method, if any, do you think predominates in this paragraph? Explain your answer in terms of the implied or explicit topic sentence.

4. Comment on Hearn's own style, in both the "classical" and the "modern" sense in which he uses the term.

5. Bring to class three paragraphs which you find in print. Be prepared to explain which method or methods of development each em-

ploys and to suggest another possible method for developing the topic sentence of each paragraph.

6. List six topics each of which lends itself well to development by a combination of methods; indicate what the combinations might be.

Alternate selections for the study of Methods of Development: Gay Wilson Allen, "Editing the Writings of Walt Whitman: A Million Dollar Project Without a Million Dollars"; Saul Bellow, "Cloister Culture"; Rumer Godden, "Last of the Great Fairy-Talers."

Assignment: The following topic sentences lend themselves to any number of possible methods of paragraph development. Suggest alternate methods for developing each of the sentences into paragraphs, indicating what material of your own invention you would include for each method selected.

Select one of the sentences, and write three separate paragraphs developing it in three different ways.

or

Write one paragraph for each of three of the sentences, employing different methods of development for each.

"Astronomy hath excellent uses."—Ralph Waldo Emerson, *The Journals*

"Politics, as a practice, whatever its professions, had always been the systematic organization of hatreds. . . ."—Henry Adams, *The Education of Henry Adams*

"The most sensitive barometer of what is going on at a college is the extracurriculum."—Frederick Rudolph, "Neglect of Students as a Tradition"

"John F. Kennedy was a happy president."—Theodore Sorensen, *Kennedy*

"Hard work, trouble in life does, it seems, after all beautify, to one with an eye at all trained to see beauty."—Sherwood Anderson, *Puzzled America*

"History is a bath of blood."—William James, "The Moral Equivalent of War"

"Freedom is in its very nature always relative and never absolute."—Harry D. Gideonse, "The Purpose of Higher Education"

"Books are the best of things, well used; abused, among the worst."—Ralph Waldo Emerson, "The American Scholar"

"A work that aspires, however humbly, to the condition of art should carry its justification in every line."—Joseph Conrad, "Preface" to *The Nigger of the Narcissus*

"It is the luxurious and dissipated who set the fashions which the herd so diligently follow."—Henry David Thoreau, *Walden*

"It would be a shallow kind of optimism to assume that the introduction of the art of inventing has been an immediate and unmixed blessing to mankind."—Walter Lippmann, *Interpretations*

"That a mild amount of exercise—a very mild amount—may be good for a man, I am not fool enough to deny."—George Jean Nathan, *The Intimate Notebooks of George Jean Nathan*

". . . it is high time to challenge the assumption that education takes place only when the student is physically present in a classroom."—James B. Conant, *The Education of American Teachers*

"Every generation is privileged to stand on the shoulders of its predecessors, and it is taller by what they accomplished."—Brander Matthews, *Inquiries and Opinions*

"Hero-worship is a dangerous vice . . ."—E. M. Forster, *Two Cheers for Democracy*

Unity

From *The Living Joy of Pictures*   EDWARD J. STEICHEN

[1] In speculating about the creation of art and the enjoyment of art, we have to begin by trying to understand the fundamentals. Let's start with the one form of creation about which there is no speculation or argument: the woman who conceives and bears a child. I sometimes wonder about the guy who stands out in the meadow with an easel or with a camera and sees the daisies nodding their heads and the wind blowing the clouds in the sky, and makes a picture of that and thinks he's created something. I wonder if he shouldn't have his head examined. I think we should stop and think of the original creative force that exists in all living organisms and that is so beautifully expressed in the Bible: "Be fruitful and multiply." I think we should visualize what goes on within a woman during the weeks and months when she's carrying a child, and then think of that wondrous moment when the baby is being born, and the triumph when all that happens. It's just a little difficult to put that kind of test up to any artist when we talk about "creation." There are not many artists who can measure up to that, and those are and have been, I think, the great artists of all time. Those artists go through the same pains and struggle in the production of a work of art, whether it's music or poetry or painting or photography. When the work has the quality which lives, there's been a terrific ordeal.

From *Holiday*, March 1956. Reprinted by permission of the author.

[2] Down in the garden of the Museum of Modern Art here, we now have a statue of Balzac that Auguste Rodin made. When it was finished, the committee that had commissioned it said that it was
25 nothing but a head stuck on a sack, and turned it down. And a long, long time afterward, all of the mass of studies and the sketches that Rodin had made for that statue were unearthed, and you could see the struggle and travail that gave form to a masterpiece. I remember one of Matisse's greatest paintings, called *The Dance*. At that time
30 I was seeing a great deal of him, and I watched that painting from the first outlines on the canvas right straight through to the finish. I saw the effort and turmoil and the changes and changes that he made. It was gradual, almost as gradual as the development of the baby that's under a woman's apron. And then came the final burst of
35 passion. Within a few days he changed the whole painting; the figures became brilliant vermilion, the background a deep Prussian blue. It was a moment of exaltation—a child being born! A work of art being born!

[For treatment of this selection, see p. 212.]

✍From *Words and Behavior*

ALDOUS HUXLEY

Words form the thread on which we string our experiences. Without them we should live spasmodically and intermittently. Hatred itself is not so strong that animals will not forget it, if distracted, even in the presence of the enemy. Watch a pair of cats, crouching
5 on the brink of a fight. Balefully the eyes glare; from far down in the throat of each come bursts of a strange, strangled noise of defiance; as though animated by a life of their own, the tails twitch and tremble. What aimed intensity of loathing! Another moment and surely there must be an explosion. But no; all of a sudden one of the two

From *The Olive Tree* by Aldous Huxley. Reprinted by permission of Harper & Row, Publishers.

creatures turns away, hoists a hind leg in a more than fascist salute 10
and, with the same fixed and focussed attention as it had given a moment before to its enemy, begins to make a lingual toilet. Animal love
is as much at the mercy of distraction as animal hatred. The dumb
creation lives a life made up of discrete and mutually irrelevant episodes. Such as it is, the consistency of human characters is due to 15
the words upon which all human experiences are strung. We are purposeful because we can describe our feelings in rememberable words,
can justify and rationalize our desires in terms of some kind of argument. Faced by an enemy we do not allow an itch to distract us from
our emotions; the mere word "enemy" is enough to keep us reminded 20
of our hatred, to convince us that we do well to be angry. Similarly
the word "love" bridges for us those chasms of momentary indifference and boredom which gape from time to time between even
the most ardent lovers. Feeling and desire provide us with our motive
power; words give continuity to what we do and to a considerable 25
extent determine our direction. Inappropriate and badly chosen words
vitiate thought and lead to wrong or foolish conduct. Most ignorances
are vincible, and in the greater number of cases stupidity is what the
Buddha pronounced it to be, a sin. For, consciously or subcon-
sciously, it is with deliberation that we do not know or fail to under- 30
stand—because incomprehension allows us, with a good conscience,
to evade unpleasant obligations and responsibilities, because ignorance is the best excuse for going on doing what one likes, but
ought not, to do. Our egotisms are incessantly fighting to preserve
themselves, not only from external enemies, but also from the assaults 35
of the other and better self with which they are so uncomfortably
associated. Ignorance is egotism's most effective defense against that
Dr. Jekyll in us who desires perfection; stupidity, its subtlest stra-
tagem. If, as so often happens, we choose to give continuity to our
experience by means of words which falsify the facts, this is because 40
the falsification is somehow to our advantage as egoists.

In order to achieve unity, a paragraph must contain one central
thesis—specific, carefully delineated, and capable of development—
and that thesis must be fully and methodically developed. But there
is more to the problem. Perhaps the easiest approach to the subject
of paragraph unity is a negative approach. A unified paragraph does
not contain material irrelevant to the central idea: it does not veer
off on tangential material, however interesting that material may be;
it does not get so wound up in one of the subdivisions of the topic

or in one of the methods of development that it fails to complete the development of the central thesis.

1. In paragraph 1, Steichen blends a variety of ideas into a wholly unified paragraph. What are the main ideas which emerge in the paragraph? Is the last sentence the topic sentence, or is the topic sentence implied? If you think it is implied, write a topic sentence for the paragraph. What contribution does Steichen's topic sentence (either stated or implied) make to the unity of the paragraph? What devices of coherence within the paragraph contribute to unity?

2. In his second paragraph, Steichen makes his central point by means of two examples. What is his central point? How does he avoid violating paragraph unity?

3. What central thesis does Huxley develop in his paragraph?

4. If you have formulated Huxley's thesis correctly, you will be aware that he faced a difficult problem in unity. What, in terms of his thesis, is the problem?

5. At what point in the paragraph does the relevance of the cats to the central thesis become evident? Does the material about the cats violate paragraph unity or contribute to it? Explain.

6. What figure of speech does Huxley use to help achieve unity in the paragraph? Comment on its appropriateness in terms of the central thesis.

7. If Huxley had chosen to use two paragraphs to develop his thesis, at what point do you think he would have split the paragraph? Would he have needed a transitional sentence? Why or why not? Had Huxley used two paragraphs, what would have been gained or lost?

Alternate selections for the study of Unity: H. L. Mencken, "Literature and the Schoolma'm"; Brooks Atkinson, "Jargon" and "Enemies of Jargon."

Assignment: Write a paragraph showing the many ways in which a creative photographer might undergo the "terrific ordeal" that Steichen speaks of. You might consider such matters as choice of subject, control of subject, limitations of the camera, and technical problems of developing, printing, enlarging, and mounting. Your problem is to construct out of a diversity of materials a thoroughly unified paragraph. Should you feel that you do not know enough about the photographic process, you may substitute any one of the arts about which you do have information.

Coherence

The Decay of Conversation

JACQUES BARZUN

[1] In private life, the counterpart of public debate is conversation. The word sounds old-fashioned and its meaning is blurred, because in the years since conversation was given a name and made an ideal, its nature has changed as much as that of public debate—and for the same reasons. Yet whether we use the word to mean all 5 forms of verbal exchange or, more narrowly, the sociable sifting of opinion for pleasure, conversation is the testing ground of manners. This is so because manners are minor morals which facilitate the relations of men, chiefly through words. When those verbal relations are deliberately staged, for no other purpose than pleasure, men find 10 themselves engaged in an intellectual exercise that is one of the delights of life. Manners, therefore, are not solely a clue to the deeper moral assumptions of an age, they are also a strong or weak guardian of Intellect at its most exposed.

[2] Conversation being difficult, the reality of it has always been 15 inferior to the ideal. We can nevertheless deduce almost as much from the ideal—or the lack of it—as from the audible reality. The reader will have noticed that I did not speak of sociable conversation as the *exchange,* but as the *sifting* of opinion. The "exchange"

213

20 view is a nearly correct description of modern practice: A delivers an opinion while B thinks of the one he will inject as soon as he decently can. It is an exchange in the same sense that we "exchange" greetings: we offer a formula and are offered another, but generally go off with our own.

25 [3] In this rudimentary game Intellect plays a small role. It contents itself with finding words adequate to the belief or impression of the moment, while navigating a passable course among other ideas suspected of being afloat in the vicinity. The genuine exercise or true conversation sifts opinion, that is, tries to develop tenable positions

30 by alternate statements, objections, modifications, examples, arguments, distinctions, expressed with the aid of the rhetorical arts— irony, exaggeration, and the rest—properly muted to the size and privateness of the scene.

[4] In modern life this discovery of opinion by conversing is supposed

35 to have more than pleasurable uses. We are addicted to "panels" and "forums" and "round tables" on given topics. When broadcast, such performances are supposed to interest, and even instruct, millions of listeners and viewers, also in living rooms. That these conversations in public most often fail is a proof of the lack of

40 conversational skill among the educated. After one such failure on a national network, an introspective member of the group, a psychiatrist, tried to state the causes, for the use of program directors. He blamed the latter as well as the speakers: "Every one . . . did a bad job. Our inept efforts at discussion reminded me of a lot of falling-

45 down drunks trying to shake hands." He then listed the requisites of success: "not a group of yes-men, but of men who are on a par in their knowledge of the field . . . so that they can communicate without such purely verbal confusions as clouded our interchange. I will say flatly that unless any panel . . . is given lots of prebroadcast time

50 for free discussion, and repeatedly, the group cannot be expected to talk effectively in front of the camera. . . . An unrehearsed polydisciplinary group lack a common language. . . . We had assembled for an hour and a half before the broadcast, but failed to take advantage even of that meager time. This was because after about ten min-

55 utes of groping talk, further discussion was halted lest we become stale. . . . Similarly, during the conduct of the discussion, just as we would begin to join issue around some problem, our moderator would abruptly change the topic. . . . Everybody on the panel felt increasingly frustrated and the audience was confused and unenlightened."

60 [5] Most participants in public conversations would agree with the

critic and would welcome one or two hours of warming up. But in a practiced conversationalist a prolonged rehearsal would kill interest and spontaneity before the broadcast. The director's fear of staleness was therefore justified; his error was to suppose that his experts— lecturers and writers though they were—were conversationalists. Our use of panels and other discussion groups offers a curious instance of a social form that does not produce its adepts. The cause must lie in the existence of a stronger contrary force. In a discussion of "Political Communication and Social Structure in the United States," Mr. David Riesman makes clear that the eliciting of opinion, notably by interviewers, is universally considered the very opposite of conversation. That name is reserved for "chit-chat about health, personal relations, the job."

[6] A German writer, noting recently that in the title of the latest edition of Brockhaus, the term "Konversations-lexicon" has been dropped, attributes the general decay of conversation to the lack of an idle class, or more simply, of leisure. But leisure is increasing, and enough time, surely, is spent by persons with a college degree in "exchanging" ideas, on social as well as on public occasions. It cannot be our material circumstances alone that hamper us, but rather our manners, that is to say, at bottom, our emotions.

[7] For the starting point of conversation is contradiction, and this democratic manners do not tolerate. Contradiction implies that one or another of the conversing group must be wrong, and under modern manners, as I said earlier without trying to explain it, peculiar feelings cling to error. Perhaps science has made small accuracy sacred to all, though everybody thinks that to be caught in a mistake is necessary to prove that one is human. Or again it may be that business and industry lead us to overestimate the interest of facts, about which contradiction is foolish. I think it more likely that the fear of being wrong which prohibits contradiction has in view, not error as an intellectual mishap, but the punishment that follows a breach of group unity. If your hostess says that the latest play by Mr. Kentucky Jones is very fine, and you contradict her, no matter how sweetly, one of you will have the majority in opposition. And this, regardless of who is the odd man out, nobody will enjoy. The reasoning goes: you are one against several = you are wrong = you are a fool. In some companies, the series of inferences would run: perverse = showing off = a snob; and the rejection would be no less complete.

[8] In either form, the syllogism is bound to be hard to refute

when the first premise of a society is that the voice of the people, ascertained by majority vote, is the voice of God. All the great men since Socrates may have asserted the contrary, but their assertion was 105 evidently self-serving. Virtue in modern politics is against the solitary dissident. It is assumed that he too wants the backing of a majority, and having gained it will enjoy power. This is never allowable in a populist culture. Even in the Soviet Union the "cult of personality" has been denounced, which is comic but indicative.

110   [9] By confining conversation to facts or to the exchange of bland opinions, trouble is avoided. This is elementary self-protection in a system where the absence of fixed place and privilege puts one at the mercy of the group. When we quote what Tocqueville said: "I know of no country in which there is so little independence of mind and 115 real freedom of discussion as in America," we must not ascribe wholly to timidity what is in part sensible self-restraint. Even in the great days of militant liberalism it was decreed that politics and religion should be excluded from general conversation. This is a tribute to the power of words, in that people take them as the signs of instant 120 action, of treason, rape, sacrilege. One does not know whether to wonder more at the imagination of the listener who is so readily hurt and alarmed, or at the skill of the speaker who over a cup of tea can with a few phrases produce flushed faces and the grim ardor of a militia defending hearth and home. However it comes about, the 125 motive of curiosity about ideas, the play of mind, is not accounted a social possibility. But subversion is.

[10] That is why full democracy has simply extended the no-politics-or-religion rule to any strong opinion. Yeats, moving in circles full of intellectuals and full of ideas, could yet long for the con-130 versation of a *society,* for gaiety of mind and the fantasy that prepares matured convictions, for the kind of agreement that comes with, and not instead of, the free play of Intellect. What he found and what we have is the political judgment of dissidence carried into the living room and using the threat of mild or harsh ostracism to prevent even 135 the shadow of conflict.

[11] In putting first the political, I do not mean to overlook other impeding emotions. Good conversation, like any game, calls for equals in strength. But in a social system where movement is easy and frequent, one meets mostly strangers, whose equality other than 140 legal and abstract has to be presumed. To safeguard that presumption, democratic manners prevent a jousting in which somebody might say that democratic society is without snobbery. But like our public opin-

ion, our accepted snobbery seldom ventures outside the tangible. It relies on differences that are not subject to dispute, such as disinfected wealth or descent from a famous historical event. Otherwise, 145 the assumption of social equality indispensable to our life is preserved by blinking or suppressing all signs of the contrary.

[12] This description may suggest that underneath its amiability the democratic group hides ugly sentiments. This is rarely true. Whatever his unconscious fear of Intellect, the democrat's conscious desire 150 is philanthropic; he wants love to prevail; he wants to add friends to friends and find them friends to one another, as in Euclid; he wants, above all, that everything and everybody should be agreeable, by which he means interchangeable, indistinguishable—like a prefabricated part—until the taste for human encounters is purified and up- 155 lifted from the social to the gregarious. The highest merit and pleasure is to love people, to want to be with people, to be "good with people."

[13] Only a churlish man could profess insensibility to so much warmth and such regal indifference to the marks, precisely, of differ- 160 ence. For the true-born democrat, origin, education, and intellect matter no more than clothes, speech, and deportment. He no longer sees them, or he feels remorse when the thought of them breaks through his proper manners to his conscious mind.

[For treatment of this selection, see p. 220.]

Is Literacy Passé?   WALTER J. ONG

[1] It may be that we have come to the end of the Gutenberg era. The electronic age may not yet have made printing obsolete, but it certainly has ended the monopoly-rule of published matter over our habits of thinking.

[2] Our "typographical culture" began about five hundred years 5 ago with the invention of the printing press, which enabled handwrit-

From *Saturday Review,* November 28, 1959. Reprinted by permission of the *Saturday Review.*

ten documents to be duplicated rapidly, thus facilitating the swift
diffusion of ideas; but more importantly, the press changed our sense
of what thinking itself is. To gauge the extent of that change we need
10 only reflect on the communications systems used by preliterate and
pre-typographical man.

[3] Preliterate man knew no history in our sense of the term. His
knowledge of the past was limited pretty much to what his parents
and grandparents or great-grandparents could tell him. He lived in
15 a voice-and-ear culture. His knowledge was stored in the mind, and
when verbalized was communicated primarily by the voice and by
other sounds. But sound, the ground of all verbal communication, is
time-bound and evanescent. It exists only while it is passing out of
existence. I cannot pronounce the last part of a word until the first
20 part no longer exists. The alphabet—which appeared quite late in
history, around 2000 B.C.—reduces the evanescence of sound in time
to relative permanence in space. Pictures also do this, in a way. They
enable us to recall an image or a concept, and thereby the word. But
the alphabet turns the picture process inside out and upside down. It
25 breaks the sound itself up into little spatial parts, which it reassembles
on a surface in countless configurations. The alphabet thus had a
revolutionary effect on our thinking processes.

[4] However, the tug of habit is a strong one: the oral-and-aural
tradition persisted long after the adoption and eventual spread of the
30 alphabet. When, a few decades before Christ, Marcus Tullius Cicero
wanted to bring Greek knowledge to the somewhat backward Romans
of his day, he did not read scrolls in order to master that knowledge,
but rather went to Greece to listen to the lecturers and orators of
that country. Significantly, Cicero used to speak his orations aloud,
35 then write them down as a kind of afterthought.

[5] With the dawn of the European Middle Ages, Western man
developed a "manuscript culture." Medieval scholars could not listen
to Rome's learned men as Cicero had "audited" those of Greece. So
they pored through handwritten manuscripts: medieval culture pro-
40 duced the bookworm. However, it also retained massive oral-aural
commitments. We know from Saint Augustine that men of his time
continued to read aloud even when they were reading to themselves.
Words were worth little unless they could be vocalized. In the medieval universities written exercises beyond the level of elementary in-
45 struction were absolutely unknown. Written texts abounded, but they
were used as take-off points for speeches, for lectures, or for "disputa-
tions," highly organized verbal tilts in which the students proved their

mastery of logic, physics, and other subjects. Yet despite the persistence of this oral-aural cast of mind, medieval culture was preeminently a manuscript culture, a fact which prepared the way for 50 printing and which perhaps made printing inevitable. For printing was and is a cheap way of producing what a manuscript culture wanted—something to read.

[6] After the invention of the printing press, man's whole way of thinking about his own intellectual processes changes subtly. The 55 "spatial parts" embodied in the alphabet are made even more maneuverable by the press's movable type, and are given greater permanence by its fonts. Thinking processes are now taken to be concerned with getting things into an order comparable with that observed in a printed book. Thought begins to have "content" just as books have 60 tables of contents—a concept quite foreign to medieval and ancient man, for whom truth was not commonly associated with some kind of containment or boxing process, but rather with communication or teaching ("doctrine").

[7] In our time a new drift, away from the "typographical" and 65 toward the "oral-and-aural" culture, toward the world of sound, has definitely set in. As human society, despite its swelling size, becomes more closely knit around the globe, sound asserts itself more and more, supplemented and augmented by such marvels as the telephone, TV, rapid transportation systems, and earth satellites which speak to 70 us in tiny, beep-beeping voices.

[8] As a corollary of this deep-rooted transformation, language itself is undergoing a profound overhauling. Grammar, which is based upon the written word, is giving way to linguistics, a discipline rooted in the spoken word, i.e., the word at first hand instead of at one 75 remove.

[9] In philosophical circles interest is veering away from logic to dialogue, from thinking conceived of as a private, silent affair, to thinking seen in its full social and public setting. There is a growing awareness that science itself at any moment is only arrested dialogue, 80 and that the difference between what we know and what men five hundred years ago knew, or between what we know and what men a hundred thousand years from now will know, can be charted not in terms of men's private thoughts but in terms of what they have said to one another. 85

[10] The new world will not forget the old. It never does. Printing is here to stay. But now, more than ever, it is only one part of a constellation of activities. Its monopoly is broken.

Much of the discussion of coherence in the whole theme is relevant to the paragraph. The ideas in a paragraph must be ordered so that their logical relations are immediately—or ultimately—clear to the reader; when necessary, transitional words or expressions, pronouns, or the device of repetition of key words should be used to point up relationships.

1. Explain how, in paragraph 1 of the Barzun selection, each of the following contributes to internal paragraph coherence:

    a. repetition of the word "conversation"
    b. "The word . . ." (sentence 2)
    c. ". . . its meaning . . . its nature" (sentence 2)
    d. "Yet . . ." (sentence 3)
    e. ". . . whether . . . or . . ." (sentence 3)
    f. ". . . more narrowly . . ." (sentence 3)
    g. "This is so because . . ." (sentence 4)
    h. ". . . these verbal relations" (sentence 5)
    i. ". . . therefore . . ." (sentence 6)
    j. ". . . solely . . ." (sentence 6)
    k. ". . . also . . ." (sentence 6)

2. Taking the selection paragraph by paragraph, indicate all words and phrases which similarly contribute to paragraph coherence.

3. Grammatically, what parts of speech and kinds of phrases have you found most frequently used for coherence? What does your answer to this question tell you about those parts of speech and kinds of phrases?

4. Do you find as many words and phrases used for coherence in the Ong selection as in the Barzun? Point out where, in each selection, the author has relied on one or another type of order to hold his paragraphs together. Which author, if either, relies more heavily on the use of order? What do your answers indicate about the subjects of the two selections? What, if anything, about the two writers?

5. In which piece are the paragraphs longer? Why? How is this consideration relevant to your answers to the questions in 4 above?

6. In which selection do you find more explicit words, phrases, sentences, or even paragraphs which link the paragraphs to one another? Again, account for your answer in terms of subject-matter. What is the over-all order of the Barzun selection? of the Ong?

7. Which piece is more difficult to understand? Why?

8. Compare the following pairs of paragraphs. Explain how, with each change made from the original, coherence was either improved or impaired.

    a. "The new world will not forget the old. It never does. Printing is here to stay. But now, more than ever, it is only one part of a constellation of activities. Its monopoly is broken."

b. The new world will not forget the old world. People never really forget their predecessors; and a new culture, while it brings with it many innovations, always borrows from old cultures. Printing, like many other elements of cultures older than our own, is here to stay. But now printing is one of many means of communication. No longer does it have a monopoly.

a. "Conversation being difficult, the reality of it has always been inferior to the ideal. We can nevertheless deduce almost as much from the ideal—or the lack of it—as from the audible reality. The reader will have noticed that I did not speak of sociable conversation as the *exchange,* but as the *sifting* of opinion. The 'exchange' view is a nearly correct description of modern practice: A delivers an opinion while B thinks of the one he will inject as soon as he decently can. It is an exchange in the same sense that we 'exchange' greetings: we offer a formula and are offered another, but generally go off with our own."

b. Conversation is difficult. The reality of it has always been inferior to the ideal. But we can deduce almost as much from the ideal as from the audible reality. I did not speak of sociable conversation as the exchange, but as the sifting of opinion. The former view is a nearly correct description of modern practice. *A* delivers an opinion while *B* thinks of another opinion which he will inject as soon as he can. This is the same sense in which we exchange greetings. We offer a formula and we are offered another formula, but each of us generally goes off with his own.

Alternate selections for the study of Coherence: Maxwell E. Perkins, "Letter from the Editor"; Tyrone Guthrie, "Do We Go to the Theatre for Illusion?"

Theme Assignment: The range of man's ability to communicate through language is impressive. The most abstruse, complex facts of nuclear fission can be exactly communicated, but a husband may find it impossible to communicate exactly to his wife his feelings about his job or his plans for the future. Failure to communicate has been blamed for family strife, divorces, community tensions, alienation of teenagers, and even international incidents. Literary masterpieces have been built on the problems of communication of man with his fellow man.

Select from your own life an incident or situation in which failure to communicate played a role. Were you, perhaps, unable to convince a teacher of your innocence in a cheating episode? Have you failed to communicate adequately with your parents about your vocational aims or your choice of friends or your political thinking? Have you lost a significant human relationship—with a potential husband or wife or lifelong friend—because of a breakdown in communications? Write a theme about the incident or situation (or relationship) in which you make clear the role of inadequate communication. Pay attention to paragraph coherence.

or

Barzun pokes gentle fun at the notion that "politics and religion should be excluded from general conversation." Write a theme in which you either attack or support this aphorism. Be specific in your arguments and "cement" them together well.

Adequacy

The Wonderful World of Culture Or: A Strictly Highbrow and Artistic Subject

RICHARD FRANKO GOLDMAN

[1] Some time ago I toyed with the idea of organizing a committee for the purpose of raising equestrian statues of American composers to form an avenue approaching Lincoln Center. While the encouragement I received was negligible, the idea recurs to me whenever I am forced to consider the consistently pedestrian nature of most pro- 5
nouncements on the arts circulated in these United States. The *Summa Theologica,* or monument to America's current concern with the arts, appeared in the spring of 1965 under the imposing and characteristic title, *The Performing Arts: Problems and Prospects,* with the subtitle, *Rockefeller Panel Report on the future of theatre,* 10
dance, music in America. This is, properly speaking, not a book; it is a publication: a model of the new style in Communications Arts that is destined to replace prose, and perhaps even exchange of ideas.

[2] Although the volume is called a report, its tone is that of a

Rreprinted from *The American Scholar,* Volume 35, Number 3, Summer, 1966. Copyright © 1966 by the United Chapters of Phi Beta Kappa. By permission of the publishers.

15 Manifesto. But some readers may look at it in other ways: as a
romance in the tradition of *Erewhon, Looking Backward, Brave New
World*, or even *1984;* as an unconventional horror story somewhat
deficient in suspense; as a contribution to the new folklore; or simply
as a lexicon of misuse of the English language. Perhaps it is a com-
20 bination of all of these. If, as has been said, the camel is a horse designed by a committee, there are grounds for suspecting that the
writing of committee reports is on occasion entrusted to the camel.

[3] One might begin with this possibility. "The performing arts"
is itself a vulgarism so established that no one, apparently, any longer
25 notices it. It is matched, in the language of this volume, by such delights as "the charitable dollar," "religious giving," and a variety of
catachreses bewildering in their ingenuity and inelegance. But when
writing of art and culture, or, more exactly, of "arts organizations"
and "cultural standards," a certain imprecision and even incoherence
30 are perhaps necessary. And perhaps the experts, "researchers," and
members of the Sanhedrin who are the joint begetters of this work do
in fact mean that the arts perform and that the dollar expresses emotion. When one considers, one sees that this is literally so: the arts,
in partnership with the artistic dollar, are expected to perform
35 miracles. It is the arts that will raise our "cultural standards" and that
must "enhance the nation's cultural life." We are not permitted to
conceive, in this mythology, that art *reflects* a culture or a way of
life, or that culture, while it may have roots and traditions and em-
bodiments, can hardly be said to have "standards." On the contrary:
40 it is plain that in this folklore, art and culture are special varieties of
consumer goods, foods that are "enriched," to be marketed in conventional ways, "with all the resources of advertising and public relations." The spectacular difference is that it is morally virtuous to sell
these goods, *because they are good for the consumer.* One merely
45 has to persuade more consumers that this is so.

[4] They are also good for the manufacturers and distributors. According to the *National Economic Review* published by the New
York *Times* on January 11, 1965, culture was a three billion dollar
business in 1964, and will be worth seven billion by 1970. The *Re-*
50 *view* notes that "Culture is the latest big business in the country . . .
Interest in culture, say researchers in the field [*sic!*], has become the
newest status symbol, and conspicuous esthetics may become the
norm, to the surprise of no one."

[5] And this, despite sanctimonious phrases about the beauty and
55 the efficacy of art and culture, is what the *Report* is about. Its es-

thetics are, at the mildest, as conspicuous as Lincoln Center. There is something touching in the *Report*'s assumptions that art is a cure for most of our ills, including idleness (which, in the *Report,* is of course called *leisure*), that art "reminds us of our better nature," and so on, but these positions seem, in context, a bit strained. When it is possible to write cheerfully about "the sale of arts services" (by "arts organizations"), one is assuming either that the reader has accepted the premise that he is a consumer, or that the reader has no idea what one is talking about. The procedure is dishonest in either case.

[6] As one would expect, the *Report* is concerned with "elemental matters" (elementary? fundamental?) such as "numbers of performing groups, types of facilities, character of services, and sources of financial support." It does admit that after all matters of "arts organization" are taken care of, "there must also be a sizable public, prepared through education . . ." and laments that it is impossible to determine "with statistical accuracy" whether such an audience exists today. That accuracy in these matters is never statistical is a concept foreign to the authors of nearly all reports; but no doubt we shall, eventually, as the folklore gains "increasing acceptance," be persuaded to accept as an Index of our Enhancement the accurate statistical reporting of such matters as the annual per capita consumption of Brahms in the United States, with breakdowns by sex, age, income, social status and locality. The exhortation that inevitably follows is that we must do everything in our power, statistically speaking, to increase our individual and collective Brahms-ratings.

[7] The *Report* is an almost flawless model of the twentieth century's most popular style. It is immensely *significant,* without ever being serious. Its most striking characteristic is its attempt to substitute for serious matters, such as art and culture, the factitious seriousness of "arts services," "arts organizations" and "cultural standards." The tone of the *Report* is earnest; but being earnest is not the same as being serious, any more than being nervous is the same as being sensitive. The significance of the *Report* resides precisely in this pretension of seriousness, in its confusion of the vocabularies of art and marketing, and in its substitution of statistical clichés and easy pieties for any real notions of the concerns of art. The *Report* is all the more important, or "significant," for these reasons. It defines for us the vocabulary of the art and culture trade, and lets us know, once and for all, the nature of the thinking that creates arts centers.

[8] For those whose dream it is to dwell in marble halls, Lincoln Center may well represent "a pioneering experiment." We are to have

arts centers, if the dream of the *Report* comes true, wherever the artistic dollar can put them. The *Report* handsomely concedes (p. 117) that when the arts centers are built, "of *equal importance* [italics mine] is the attention devoted to planning the artistic program for which the facilities will be used . . ." The horse—or the camel—is now lost somewhere behind the cart, but at least we know in which direction it has gone. The first televised production from the Los Angeles Music Center was a program featuring Dinah Shore, Bob Hope, Henry Mancini, a jazz organist, and a virtuoso of the *bossa nova,* a use of the facility that does show a certain kind of devoted attention. And Lincoln Center wishes to persuade us that an expensive arts center is needed to present plays by Arthur Miller and S. N. Behrman. This suggests that the artistic dollar, too, is subject to inflation.

[9] "Equal importance" finds its parallel in the *Report*'s doctrine of equal talent: "As talent is needed to create and perform a work of art, so equal talent—though of a different sort—is needed to create and govern the institutions that provide the settings for these arts." There are—or are there?—perhaps just a few concerned with the arts who will not accept this equation of the talent of a Beethoven with the talent of a Board member, however carefully auditioned the Board member may have been ("Board members should be as carefully screened as performers." p. 151).

[10] In 1872 Nietzsche wrote: "Never has there been so much loose talk about art, and so little respect for it." He was born too soon. Nevertheless, in *The Birth of Tragedy* he said almost everything that can be said about the nature and fate of "the performing arts" in our day. Yet even he did not foresee the assumption that culture can be purchased or imposed, or imagine the mentality that could state as a matter of course that "for an arts institution to reach stardom requires time." He did foresee, with considerable loathing, the mentality that relates the pursuit of art to the collection of statistics and that suggests that "the performing arts have perforce been laggard in sharing in the research revolution." Nietzsche, moreover, knew exactly what this meant, which the authors of the *Report* quite evidently do not. In their charmingly innocent view, what this means is that "arts organizations" must study "their long-range goals in the community," acquire pertinent information about "audience composition and tastes," and "explore systematically what the continuing scientific revolution . . . can mean for the technological improvement

of their artistic endeavors and for the strengthening of their economic sinews."

[11] The notion of culture as something to be measured and consumed is a commonplace of the new folklore. It is defensible as a recognition of fact, the moment one redefines culture, or restores it to its original meaning in biology: "The artificial development of microscopic organisms in prepared media." This is the definition that the *Report* seems to accept; it conceals a real animosity toward people, who are conceived as organisms to be manipulated or developed. Art is in this way to serve the purpose of giving people, individually and collectively, a status rather than a function, and an image rather than an identity.

[12] In a sentence remarkable for its grammatical slovenliness, art as the giver of image is delineated: "When the arts go abroad, as they are in increasing degree through cultural exchanges they can disclose the vital and creative aspects of the countries originating them." This fine flower of thought for export is perhaps designed to show that we have rejected English as a means of communication, and substituted culture, or aspects. There are guilt and fear as well as bad grammar here. And the same guilt and fear underlie the statement that "a thriving development of the arts is essential to a well and safely balanced society." One wonders about safety, and whether no one has ever told the authors of the *Report* that art can be dangerous. (But not "the arts.") And when one comes on the thought that "increased leisure also creates a social imperative for the development of the arts," one can begin to worry as well as wonder.

[13] On the other hand, there is reassurance in the *Report*'s explicit statements. "The arts can be a major source of strength for the business community . . . Their availability certainly encourages new firms to locate in a city and helps attract tourists and conventions. They constitute a growing market and provide expanding avenues for employment. There are, therefore, compelling reasons why, in the interests of his community and, indeed, in his own self-interest, a businessman and his firm should be concerned with the cultural and artistic life of his community."

[14] Has anyone heard this before?

Some of you may feel that it's out of place here to talk on a strictly highbrow and artistic subject, but I want to come out flatfooted and ask you boys to O.K. the proposition of a Symphony Orchestra for Zenith . . . Culture has become as necessary an adornment and advertisement for a city today as pavements and bank-clearances. It's Culture, in theaters and art-galleries and so on, that brings thousands of visitors to New York every year and, to be frank, for all our splendid attainments we haven't yet got the Culture of a New York or Chicago or Boston—or at least we don't get the credit for it. The thing to do then, as a live bunch of go-getters, is to *capitalize* Culture; to go right out and grab it.

Pictures and books are fine for those that have the time to study 'em, but they don't shoot out on the road and holler "This is what little old Zenith can put up in the way of Culture." That's precisely what a Symphony Orchestra does do . . . it goes right into Beantown and New York and Washington; it plays at the best theaters to the most cultured and moneyed people; it gives such class-advertising as a town can get in no other way; and the guy who is so short-sighted as to crab this orchestra proposition is passing up the chance to impress the glorious name of Zenith on some big New York millionaire that might—that might establish a branch factory here!

[15] The paragraphs above are from *Babbitt,* by Sinclair Lewis, published in 1922.[1] The research revolution has not greatly refined
175 thought or speech on strictly highbrow and artistic subjects. But it is no longer out of place to talk about them anywhere.

[16] To be sure, the *Report* does allude, on every fourth or fifth page, to Excellence, a quality that it finds admirable, and of which we should have as much as we can get. All of this concern for ex-
180 cellence would be considerably more convincing if the *Report* itself showed the slightest respect for the English language, or the slightest indication of concern with excellence in its use. The compilation and writing of the *Report* took two years, the labor of thirty members of the Panel, a "Special Studies Project Staff," forty-four "panel par-
185 ticipants," thirty-one "others contributing to the study," a number of experts who prepared papers, and, obviously, a good deal of money. In view of this, one might think that the Fund might have been able to afford a copy editor, if not a writer or two, instead of another two or three "researchers" whose labors over the allotted time pro-
190 duced the staggering information that orchestral musicians, dancers and actors are not overpaid, and that opera companies operate at a deficit. But the propriety of showing respect for art by showing respect for language obviously never occurred even to those members

[1] Copyright, 1922, by Harcourt, Brace & World, Inc.; copyright, 1950, by Sinclair Lewis. Reprinted by permission of Harcourt, Brace & World, Inc.

of the party who should know better. In the new folklore a "writer" is evidently anyone who owns a typewriter, just as "researcher" is anyone empowered by a committee to go about asking people what time it is.

[17] One wonders how the authors of this *Report* define excellence in art. Perhaps they think it is the same as "stardom." Matthew Arnold was a polite, well-educated man, who used words precisely, and who, despite his good manners, or perhaps because of them, was able, when writing of Culture, to use the words Philistine and Barbarian. We may need these words again, as we need a Matthew Arnold to remind us of what excellence really is, and where it dwells: "among high and steep rocks, . . . reached only by those who sweat blood to reach her." As an antidote to the Rockefeller's bathetic little manifesto on Culture and Organization, one might do worse than turn again to the literate decency of *Culture and Anarchy*.

[For treatment of this selection, see p. 242.]

✏ *The Case against Modern Architecture* LEWIS MUMFORD

[1] Three quarters of a century ago, the tides of modern architecture were rising, as the great technical resources that engineers like Telford, Paxton, and Brunel had introduced were applied, at last, to other forms of building. This was the period when Jenney, Sullivan, and their colleagues developed steel-frame construction and found a form for the skyscraper, when Eiffel produced his tower and Freyssinet his Hall of Machines, and when the new spirit that H. H. Richardson had brought to the design of traditional domestic buildings in stone and wood was spreading everywhere, from the houses of Ashbee, Voysey, and Parker in England to the far shores of California, where at the turn of the century Maybeck had begun work.

[2] For reasons that no one has successfully uncovered, this wave

© 1962 by Lewis Mumford. Reprinted from his volume, *The Highway and the City,* by permission of Harcourt, Brace & World, Inc.

spent itself during the decade before the First World War: except in the design of purely utilitarian structures, there was a return to the pseudo-historic and outwardly traditional, at least in the decorative facing of buildings: skyscrapers with Gothic pinnacles vied with those that were crowned with Greek temples of love; and the splendid train hall of the Grand Central Station, now effaced by a loud smear of advertisement, was betrayed earlier by its imitative Renaissance façade. When modern architecture came back in the twenties, first in France with Le Corbusier and Lurçat, and in Germany with Mendelsohn and Gropius, in Holland with Dudok, Wijdeveld, and Oud, it was forced to refight the battle that had already seemed won in 1890.

[3] Within the last thirty years, modern architecture has swept around the world. The victory of the modern movement over its traditional enemies has been so complete that special courses must now be offered, outside the usual architectural school curriculum, to provide architects with sufficient historic knowledge to maintain and restore ancient monuments preserved for their historic value. Yet many ominous signs have appeared, during the last fifteen years, that indicate that the victorious forces do not know how to make full use of the victory; that contradictions and conflicts have developed among various groups of architects sufficient already to have broken up the once united front of the C.I.A.M.; that, indeed, the differences that have come forth within the ranks of the modern architects are quite as serious as those that divided the pioneers of modern architecture from the traditionalists who sought to continue the old forms and the eclectics who sought to mask the new ones.

[4] The order and the consensus that modern architecture seemed ready to establish in the thirties are still far to seek: indeed, some of the most brilliant exponents, like the late Eero Saarinen, boasted a theory of form that denied the need for continuity and made of each separate project an essay in abstract design, without any affiliation to the work of other architects in our period or to the architect's own designs, before or after. As in the advertising copy of our period, the successful modern architects have been saying, in effect: 'And now! a new taste sensation.' Or, 'You, too, can be *years ahead* with the latest model.'

[5] This situation has given hope and comfort to minds that are so radically committed to past forms that they would solve the problems that modern architecture faces by merely erasing the history of the last century and going back to the classic shells of antiquity, particularly Roman antiquity. This is the last hope of Henry Reed; too

empty and vulnerable to merit more than a passing smile. But though Mr. Reed's remedies are absurd, the situation in modern architecture is in fact profoundly unsatisfactory: almost as chaotic and irrational as the political situation of the modern world, in which the heads of state solemnly threaten each other to solve their problems, if the other side does not yield, by mutilating the human race and wiping out civilization.

[6] The very fact that one can make such a comparison points to certain underlying errors about the nature of technical and social progress that crept into modern architecture almost from the moment that the conception of new forms, which reflected the needs and ideals of our period, became articulate in the writings of a few architectural critics and thinkers, like Adolf Loos and, much later, Le Corbusier. The moment has come to examine these conceptions and to reformulate the ideas and ideals that have, up to this moment, governed the development of the whole movement. We shall perhaps find, when we do so, a need for restoring some of the values that were too ruthlessly discarded in the development of modern form.

[7] Beneath the belief in modern architecture lay certain preconceptions about the nature of modern civilization; and these preconceptions have proved so inadequate that it is time to give them a thorough overhauling.

[8] Perhaps the most central of these beliefs was the belief in mechanical progress. Concealed within this notion was the assumption that human improvement would come about more rapidly, indeed almost automatically, through devoting all our energies to the expansion of scientific knowledge and to technological inventions; that traditional knowledge and experience, traditional forms and values, acted as a brake upon such expansion and invention, and that since the order embodied by the machine was the highest type of order, no brakes of any kind were desirable. Whereas all organic evolution is cumulative and purposeful, in that the past is still present in the future, and the future, as potentiality, is already present in the past, mechanical progress existed in a one-dimensional time, the present. Under the idea of mechanical progress only the present counted, and continual change was needed in order to prevent the present from becoming *passé,* and thus unfashionable. Progress was accordingly measured by novelty, constant change, and mechanical difference, not by continuity and human improvement.

[9] In every department, the nineteenth century ruthlessly swept

away old ideas, old traditions and institutions, and not least old build-
95 ings, confident that nothing would be lost that the machine could not
replace or improve. Have we forgotten that the central shrine of our
Independence and our Constitution, Independence Hall, was almost
sold off to the highest bidder in the early part of that century? But
this anti-traditionalism imposed a penalty upon modern architecture;
100 and that is, it was deprived by its own assumptions of either recog-
nizing its essential continuity with the past or of building upon its
own tradition. In wiping out the past, unfortunately, the cult of the
machine surreptitiously destroyed its own future—and left only an
under-dimensioned present, scheduled, like any speculative building
105 investment, for quick replacement.

[10] Beneath this belief in mechanical progress as an end in itself
was still another conviction: that one of the important functions of
architecture was to express its civilization. This conviction was a
sound one; and indeed, even without conviction, that condition
110 whether openly recognized or unconsciously fulfilled is unavoidable.
But those of us who insisted upon the value of this expression were
perhaps unprepared for what it would reveal about 'modern times.'
We used the word modern as a 'praise-word,' in Robert Frost's vocabulary; and we overlooked the possibility that modern technics,
115 which had given us instant communication, would also provide us
with instantaneous mass extermination: or the fact that while its
hospitals, medical services, and sanitary precautions would reduce
older forms of disease, technical progress would also pollute our food,
befoul the air with smog, and produce new tensions and new diseases
120 and new anxieties, as crippling as those that have been banished.
Modern psychology has introduced man to the depths of his own
nature, in all its immense variety and creative potentiality; but it has
also produced the bureaucratic personality, sterilized, regimented, over-
controlled, ultimately hostile to every other form of life than its
125 own: cut off from human resources and human roots.

[11] Since modern architecture has begun to express modern civilization, without the hypocrisy and concealment that the eclectic architects used to practice, it is not perhaps surprising that the unpleasant
features of our civilization should be as conspicuous as its finest and
130 most admirable achievements. We have been living in a fool's paradise, so far as we took for granted that mechanical progress would
solve all the problems of human existence, by introducing man into
the brave new, simplified, automatic world of the machine. If we look
at our buildings today, with open eyes, we shall find that even in

handling the great positive forces of our time, with admirable con- 135
structive facility, the greater number of them have neglected even the
scientific data they need for a good solution. There is hardly a single
great innovation in building this last thirty years—total air-condition-
ing, all-day fluorescent lighting, the all-glass wall—that pays any respect to either the meteorological, the biological, or the psychological 140
knowledge already available, for this knowledge calls for radical alterations in their present use. And still less do these innovations heed
human activities or personal desires.

[12] In so far as modern architecture has succeeded in expressing
modern life, it has done better in calling attention to its lapses, its 145
rigidities, its failures, than in bringing out, with the aid of the architect's creative imagination, its immense latent potentialities. The modern architect has yet to come to grips with the multi-dimensional
realities of the actual world. He has made himself at home with
mechanical processes, which favor rapid commercial exploitation, and 150
with anonymous repetitive bureaucratic forms, like the high-rise
apartment or office building, which lend themselves with mathematical simplicity to financial manipulation. But he has no philosophy
that does justice to organic functions or human purposes, and that
attempts to build a more comprehensive order in which the machine, 155
instead of dominating our life and demanding ever heavier sacrifices
in the present fashion, will become a supple instrument for humane
design, to be used, modified, or on occasion rejected at will.

[13] Despite the shallowness of the theory of mechanical progress,
the first erections of modern architecture, beginning with the Crystal 160
Palace in 1851, rested on a firm foundation: the perception that the
technology of the nineteenth century had immensely enriched the
vocabulary of modern form and facilitated modes of construction that
could hardly have been dreamed of in more ponderous materials,
while it made possible designs of a far more organic nature than the 165
heavy shells that constituted buildings in the past.

[14] In their pride over these new possibilities, the engineers who
turned these processes over to the architect naturally over-emphasized
this contribution; and when Louis Sullivan proclaimed that form followed function, his successors falsely put the emphasis on mechanical 170
form and mechanical function. Both are in fact essential to the constitution of modern architecture; but neither by itself—nor both together
—is sufficient. Frank Lloyd Wright understood this from the beginning, and insisted, quite properly, that he was something more than

175 a 'functionalist,' though in the last phase of his great career, as in the Johnson Laboratory and the Guggenheim Museum, he succumbed to the fascination of an elegant mechanical solution, treated as an end in itself.

[15] In the new beginning that dates from Le Corbusier's *Vers*
180 *une architecture,* the machine occupied a central place: its austerity, its economy, its geometric cleanness were proclaimed almost the sole virtues of the new architecture. Thus the kitchen became a laboratory, and the bathroom took on the qualities of a surgical operating room; while the other parts of the house, for a decade or so, achieved
185 excellence almost to the degree that they, too, were white, cleanable, empty of human content. This was in fact a useful period of cleansing and clarification. A few critics, notably Henry-Russell Hitchcock, recognized that this was the primitive state in the evolution of an historic style; and that, at a later date, certain elements, like orna-
190 ment, that had been discarded in this new effort at integrity, might return again—though in fact they had never been abandoned by Wright.

[16] Unfortunately, this interpretation of the new mechanical possibilities was in itself dominated by a superficial esthetic, which sought
195 to make the new buildings *look* as if they respected the machine, no matter what the materials or methods of construction; and it was this superficial esthetic, openly proclaiming its indifference to actual mechanical and biological functions or human purposes that was formally put forward, by Philip Johnson and his associate Hitchcock, as
200 The International Style, though it was Alfred Barr who coined the dubious name. From this, only a short step took the architect, with Mies van der Rohe to guide him, from the Machine to the Package. Mies van der Rohe used the facilities offered by steel and glass to create elegant monuments of nothingness. They had the dry style of
205 machine forms without the contents. His own chaste taste gave these hollow glass shells a crystalline purity of form: but they existed alone in the Platonic world of his imagination and had no relation to site, climate, insulation, function, or internal activity; indeed, they completely turned their backs upon these realities just as the rigidly
210 arranged chairs of his living rooms openly disregarded the necessary intimacies and informalities of conversation. This was the apotheosis of the compulsive, bureaucratic spirit. Its emptiness and hollowness were more expressive than van der Rohe's admirers realized.

[17] Here perhaps was the turning point in the development of
215 modern architecture. The principle of functionalism, stated even in

its crudest terms, was sound as far as it went; and if modern architecture was to develop further, that principle needed to be applied to every aspect of architecture. It was necessary to develop functional analysis to its limits, not merely embracing the physical elements of building, but the internal services; not merely the external structure, but the plan, and the relation of the building to its site; and the site itself to the rest of the urban or rural environment. And even this is only a beginning, because human purposes modify all these functional characteristics; so that the so-called open plan for the dwelling house turns out to be far from acceptable as a universal solution, once one takes account of the need for privacy, solitude, withdrawal, or of the differences between the extroverted, the introverted, and the integrated personality. As one adds biological and social functions, and personal desires and needs, to those of the purely physical requirements of structure, one must get, as a resultant design, a much more complex and subtle result, than if one centered attention upon only one set of conditions.

[18] How far modern architecture has withdrawn from the effort to achieve such organic richness one learns from recent architectural exhibitions, which have shown modern buildings as spatialized abstractions, in utter isolation. Some of the most famous architects of our time defiantly throw away their best opportunities: thus more than one new business building has been placed in the middle of a large country estate, with all the advantages of a lovely landscape, only to turn its back completely to its surroundings, defiling the approach with an acre of parking lot, whilst the building itself, air-conditioned and curtained in Venetian blinds, mocks its open site, its possible exposure to sunlight and fresh air, by turning inward upon a closed court. The result is the characterless package, which has become the main hallmark of fashionable architecture for the last decade.

[19] Is Le Corbusier's Unity House at Marseille an exception to this rule? Far from it. Its powerful concrete façade, with variations produced by the ill-conceived and almost abandoned market area, esthetically distinguishes it from the less expensive and less sculptural façades of similar buildings; but for all that, it is a mere package, because the plan of the individual apartments is cramped and tortured to fit the arbitrary allotment of space, in a fashion that is as archaic as that of a New York brownstone front that has been built over the back yard and is full of narrow, dark rooms, without exposure. The genius of Le Corbusier here consisted in making a mere package look like a real building; and the feebleness of current archi-

tectural criticism is recorded in the chorus of praise that this extravagant piece of stage decoration still calls forth.

[20] Meanwhile, the advance of technology has presented the
260 architect with a vast array of new metallic alloys and new plastics, with new structural materials like prestressed concrete, with new large-scale elements useful for modular designs, and with new mechanical devices that add to the total cost of the structure, as well as the upkeep. On the assumption that mechanical progress is itself
265 more important than human purposes, the architect has felt, it would seem, almost a moral obligation to use all these materials and methods, if only to maintain his status as a creative designer. In this respect, the architect finds himself in almost the same unfortunate position as the physician, overwhelmed by the enormous number of
270 new antibiotics and other drugs that are thrust on the market by the great pharmaceutical organizations, and often unable to follow through one remedy before a new one is thrust on him.

[21] Who would dare to single out the most notorious examples of the salesmanship that have often led the architect to make un-
275 fortunate choices? To make a detailed examination would in fact bring one close to legal libel. But what has happened with many new materials and forms has also taken place with a respectably ancient material, glass; and this will serve to bring out the underlying irrationality of much superficially modern design.

280 [22] Glass is plainly an indispensable part of the architect's equipment; but it has two great drawbacks. One is that it seriously lessens the ultra-violet rays, which kill bacteria and in contact with the skin supply Vitamin D to the body: hence a solid wall of glass is less desirable than openable windows that admit direct sunlight. The other
285 weakness of glass, when used as a wall, is the excessive admission of radiant heat in the warmer seasons and the excessive seepage of indoor heat in colder weather. In attempting to make glass do duty as both wall and window the modern architect has succeeded in fulfilling neither function satisfactorily. Instead, he has produced the
290 most flagrantly uneconomic and uncomfortable buildings of modern times, which can be inhabited only with the aid of the most expensive devices of heating and refrigeration: esthetically dull, technically absurd.

[23] The irrationality of this whole system of construction is visi-
295 ble today in every city from New York to San Francisco: glass-sheathed buildings without any contact with fresh air, sunlight, or

view, since at most times of the day glass sheathing is made endurable only through the use of Venetian blinds or their vertical modern equivalents over the whole façade. To make this form even more ridiculous, the window is often carried down to the floor: a device that on the lower stories not merely reveals the natural litter and trash on the floor itself but, in providing light that has no visual value below desk level, it also deprives the office of needed wall space that windows set above the level of a four-drawer filing case would permit. Frank Lloyd Wright, in his Larkin Building in Buffalo, long ago demonstrated the desirable relation of high window to usable outside wall in an office building.

[24] I am aware that the reaction against the all-glass façade has already begun, as in the design of the new John Hancock Life Insurance Building in San Francisco. But so far this reaction is a superficial one, since it merely returns to the traditional alternation of window and wall; and it has not yet gone on to explore a possibility that modern construction methods present: not merely the restoration of the openable window, but likewise the provision of an entirely new feature, a movable insulating wall-panel inside, which will slide open and shut to the full width of the window, in a fashion that will make unnecessary the once-daring, but now sadly obsolete, Venetian blinds. So much for the misuse of an older technical achievement.

[25] But the advances of technology, which have opened those breath-taking possibilities for new forms that Eric Mendelsohn so brilliantly anticipated in his imaginative sketches back in the twenties, have also revealed the possibility of two new architectural perversions. One of them is the utilization of sensational methods of construction merely to produce equally sensational forms, which have no purpose other than that of demonstrating the esthetic audacity of the designer. The external shell of the new opera house at Sydney reveals this order of design; so, for that matter, does the too-often-quoted Guggenheim Museum in New York, and even more Wright's new municipal building in Marin County; and all over the country today, one finds new churches whose very form of construction reveals nothing except a desire to compete on equal esthetic terms with the supermarket and the hot-dog emporium. This is not functional and purposeful creativity: it is the creativity of the kaleidoscope, so far the most successful of all inventions for imitating creativity by juggling mechanical forms.

[26] When a child is bored or an adult is ill, the esthetics of the

kaleidoscope is enchanting; and I do not underestimate its fascination. Nor would I deny that, related to our emergent needs, many new forms must and will appear in modern architecture, which will reveal meanings and values, intuitions about the nature of the cosmos or the condition of man, that are not present in any earlier architectural system. But creativity, in order to be assimilated, requires an underlying basis of order; and what is more, the most original form needs to be repeated, with modifications, if its full value is to be absorbed by the user and the spectator.

[27] The desire for architectural originality through a succession of kaleidoscopic changes, made possible by modern technological agents, when the inner purpose and contents are ruled out of the equation, inevitably degrades the creative process. Such technical facility, such esthetic audacity, poured forth on a great scale, promises only to enlarge the domain of chaos. Already the architectural magazines show projects, and even buildings, that look as if they were ingeniously cut out of paper and twisted together, shapes full of fantasy and capable of giving childish pleasure—provided they are not carried out in more solid constructions.

[28] One may explain this excessive virtuosity, with which modern architecture is now threatened, by two conditions. This is plainly, on one hand, a revolt against the excessive regimentation that has gone on in every part of our lives: that regimentation whose symbol is the vast repetitive inanity of the high-rise slab. And on the other hand, it is due to the fact that genuine creativity, which takes into account all the possibilities of structure, the nature of an institution's function and purposes, the values that the client draws from the community and in turn must give back to the community, is a slow process. Because such knowledge and such facility cannot be improvised in a few weeks, the creative architect must build from structure to structure on his own experience, and absorb that of other architects, past and present. It is far easier to create a sensational shell, with the constructive facilities now available, than to fulfill all the functions of architecture. An engineer of genius, like Nervi, has shown the way toward more solid achievement; but even he has succeeded best when the inner content of the building was as simple as tiers of spectators watching sport, or an exhibition or market hall whose contents could be adequately enclosed by a mere shell.

[29] But there is an alternative to kaleidoscopic creativity that would be equally disastrous to architecture and to the human spirit, though the threat comes from the opposite point of our machine

economy. Instead of an endless succession of superficial new forms, dazzling Christmas packages that have no relation to contents, we are threatened by another form of technologic facility, whose present favored form is the geodesic dome. Under this potential technical triumph, buildings as such would disappear, except perhaps as improvised rooms within a mechanically controlled environment, dedicated to producing uniform temperature, lighting, and ultimately, with the aid of drugs, surgery, and genetic intervention, uniform human beings.

[30] Whether above ground or below ground, this development would bring to an end, in a world of colorless uniformity, the long history of man's building: he would return to the cave from which he originally emerged, none the richer or wiser for his experience. I will not examine this particular possibility in detail, except to note that many minds are now busily engaged in preparing for this grand act of suicide. So committed indeed are many architects in our day to the automatism of the machine, that they fall under a compulsion to follow the process to its limit, even though that final stage is a colorless and dehumanized existence, just one breath more alive than the world that might emerge from a nuclear catastrophe.

[31] If modern architecture is not to continue its disintegration into a multitude of sects and mannerisms—international stylists, empiricists, brutalists, neo-romantics, and what not—it must rest on some principle of order; and that order must ally architecture to an equally coherent theory of human development. The notion of mechanical progress alone will not do, because it leaves out the one element that would give significance to this progress, man himself; or rather, because it makes the human personality a passive tool of the processes that should in fact serve it.

[32] Man himself is an organism whose existence is dependent upon his maintaining the delicate balance that exists between all the forces of nature, physical and organic, from sunlight and air and the soil, the bacteria, the molds, and growing plants right up to the complex interaction of thousands of species. Despite the great advances in technology, man controls only a small part of these processes: for neither destruction nor mechanical substitution is in fact a mode of control. From this complex biological inheritance man extracts and perfects those portions that serve his own purposes. Organic order is based on variety, complexity, and balance; and this order provides continuity through change, stability through adaptation, harmony

through finding a place for conflict, chance, and limited disorder, in
420 ever more complex transformations. This organic interdependence
was recognized and expressed in every historic culture, particularly
in its cosmic and religious conceptions, with their genuinely sacred
buildings, and though these buildings have outlived their technologies
they still speak to the human soul.

425 [33] Greenough's original analysis of form, on a basis of the biological and physiological nature of organisms, did justice to both
process and function, but overlooked their transformation through a
still higher and more complex category, that of human purpose. Man
is not just an actor and a fabricator: he is an interpreter and a trans-
430 former. On the higher levels of existence, form determines function,
no less than function form. At this point the continued development of
the whole man takes precedence over the continued development of
his instruments and his machines; and the only kind of order that
can ensure this is one that provides a many-sided environment
435 capable of sustaining the greatest variety of human interests and human purposes. An environment or a structure that has been reduced to the level of the machine, correct, undeviating, repetitious,
monotonous, is hostile to organic reality and to human purpose: even
when it performs, with a certain efficiency, a positive function, such
440 as providing shelter, it remains a negative symbol, or at best a neutral one.

[34] There are three sources for this larger order: nature is one,
the cumulative processes of history and historic culture are another,
and the human psyche is the third. To turn one's back upon these
445 sources, in the name of mechanical progress, for the sake of purely
quantitative production, mechanical efficiency, bureaucratic order, is
to sterilize both architecture and the life that it should sustain and
elevate. An age that worships the machine and seeks only those
goods that the machine provides, in ever larger amounts, at ever ris-
450 ing profits, actually has lost contact with reality; and in the next
moment or the next generation may translate its general denial of life
into one last savage gesture of nuclear extermination. Within the
context of organic order and human purpose, our whole technology
has still potentially a large part to play; but much of the riches of
455 modern technics will remain unusable until organic functions and
human purposes, rather than mechanical processes, dominate.

[35] An organic approach will handle, with equal dexterity, but
with greater freedom of choice, every kind of function: it will not
automatically reject daylight in favor of a facile mechanical substi-

tute, or fresh air, renovated by vegetation, for a purely mechanical system of modifying the air. But neither will it turn banks into frivolous glass-enclosed pleasure palaces, office-building entrances into cathedrals, or churches into airport terminals. On the contrary, purpose and function will provide an organic criterion of form at every stage of the design process; and in the end this will produce, not merely an esthetic variety and exuberance that are now almost unknown, but even mechanical economies that have been flouted by our compulsive overcommitment to the machine.

[36] There are two movements now visible that indicate a beginning in the right direction, which will lead, not away from functionalism, but toward a multi-functional approach to every architectural problem.

[37] One of these movements, visible in the architectural schools today, is the students' demand for architectural and town planning history. The desire behind this is not for forms to imitate, but for experience and feeling to assimilate, for spiritual nourishment beyond that which is offered by the immediate environment or a brief present moment. This is a healthy reaction against the notion that the experience of a single generation, or a single decade in a generation, is sufficient to provide the knowledge and insight man needs to create a human environment of sufficient richness and depth.

[38] The other movement became visible last summer in the meeting of the younger architects who have broken away from the Old Masters of the C.I.A.M. In their attempt to redefine the province of architecture today they expressed many differences with the generation of Le Corbusier and Gropius, as well as personal and characterological differences within their own ranks; but at the end they were united, in a large degree, on one final conclusion: that architecture was more than the art of building: it was rather the art of transforming man's entire habitat. This concept has already struck root in California, for the school of architecture at Berkeley has been reconstituted and renamed the School of Environmental Design.

[39] If human development does not become sterile and frustrated through an excessive effort to conquer nature without drawing upon all the resources of history and culture to rehumanize man, the architecture of the future will again become a true polytechnics, utilizing all the resources of technics, from the human hand to the latest automatic device. It will be closer in spirit and richness of form to the work of Frank Lloyd Wright and Bernard Maybeck than to the masters of the C.I.A.M.; and it will go beyond them, because

it will draw upon the richer human resources now worldwide in cultural scope, which are happily available for collective as well as individual expression.

There is no clear-cut answer to the question, "How long should a paragraph be?" or—to put the matter another way—"When is a paragraph adequately developed?" The writer's judgment must guide him in deciding just how many details or examples to supply, just how far to carry a comparison, or just how many methods of development to combine in dealing with a given topic. Sometimes the question answers itself: the main idea in a paragraph may lend itself to only one type of development and the development comes to its own natural conclusion. At other times, the writer must make decisions. An exceptionally long paragraph may be needed to do justice to a given topic, while another topic can best be handled in a short, crisp paragraph. The writer who is aware of the problem of adequacy—of making his paragraphs just the right length to serve their purpose—will usually solve the problem quite satisfactorily.

1. Taking into account the guiding purpose of the selection, explain and account for the tone of the title of the Goldman selection.

2. Point out all the means by which coherence is achieved in the first paragraph.

3. What is the topic sentence of paragraph 2? By what method is the paragraph developed? Is its development adequate? Explain.

4. Why does Goldman call the term "the performing arts" (paragraph 3) a vulgarism? Comment on the function and length of paragraph 3. What would have been gained or lost had the paragraph been shorter? If you had to shorten it, how would you do so?

5. How is coherence achieved between paragraphs 3 and 4? What is gained by the brevity of paragraph 4? Why does the author use [*sic!*] in the third sentence of the paragraph?

6. Note that paragraph 5 begins with the word "and." Is this poor writing? Why or why not? Identify and explain the figure of speech in the paragraph. What contribution does it make to tone? What are the topic sentence and method (or methods) of development of the paragraph?

7. Comment on the adequacy of development of paragraph 7.

8. Rewrite the material quoted in the first sentence of paragraph 12, eliminating the jargon and faulty grammar.

9. What is the relevance to the selection of the excerpt from *Babbitt* (paragraph 14)? Where and how adequately is that relevance made explicit? Comment on the question "Has anyone heard this before?" (paragraph 14).

10. Select five paragraphs from the Mumford selection and discuss their methods of development, adequacy of development, and length, taking into account the content and function of each paragraph.

11. What method of paragraph development is used most frequently in the Mumford selection? Do you feel that the author has used that method too frequently? If so, suggest alternative methods for at least three paragraphs. If not, justify his use of the method where you find it used.

Alternate selections for the study of Adequacy: Archibald Mac-Leish, "Of the Librarian's Profession"; Moses Hadas, "Climates of Criticism."

Exercise: Select one paragraph of the Mumford article and re-write it, using a different method or different methods of development. Be prepared to discuss which method you think more adequate, yours or Mumford's, and why.

Theme Assignment: Study with considerable care the statement in paragraph 11 of "The Wonderful World of Culture"—"Art is in this way to serve the purpose of giving people, individually and collectively, a status rather than a function, and an image rather than an identity." You will want to reread the passage in which this statement appears.

Select a television show which you think corrupts art in the way Goldman describes. Write a theme in which you apply Goldman's statement to that show, providing the validity of his statement. Or, if you prefer, show how a program on television does *not* corrupt art in this manner. Your paragraphs should show that you have learned to solve the problem of adequacy.

or

Write a theme applying Mumford's criticism of modern architecture to a building on your campus, in your hometown, or in a city near your campus or town. You may agree or disagree with Mumford, but justify your position in adequately developed paragraphs.

Variety

Should the Artist Come to the Campus? JAMES A. PERKINS

[1] John Quincy Adams was prophetic when he said we must learn the arts of war and independence so that our children can learn engineering and architecture so that their grandchildren may learn fine arts and painting. The arts involve more than a leisure-time
5 activity. We are interested in the arts because we have come to realize that they not only enrich but illuminate our lives. Without them we are doomed to the monotonous rationality of a computer. With them, we can hope that creative imagination will continue to suggest new insights and new ventures for mankind. If John Gardner is cor-
10 rect in suggesting that continuous renewal is the price of survival, then the arts must surely be part of our strategy for survival.

[2] Although the university has come to recognize art history and art criticism as both legitimate and necessary parts of the curriculum, the production of art and the performance of artistic work is not a
15 fully accepted part of liberal education. It can be said that art as part of liberal education is still essentially a spectator sport. Yet only a practicing professional artist can bring real understanding of art into the liberal curriculum. Only he can feed the aspirations of the

From *Saturday Review*, July 17, 1965, pp. 45–47. Reprinted by permission of the *Saturday Review* and the author.

244

amateur for professional standards. Only he can deal with the student who contemplates a professional career. And only he can infuse a campus with a desire for beauty, whether in its buildings, its art collections, or its music and theatrical programs. He is the cutting edge for future growth in any university's commitment to the arts. Out of this need he has arrived on the campus to take his marriage vows with the scholar, and it is this marriage that is the heart of the matter. It is the success of this marriage that will determine the future vitality of the arts in the university.

[3] The arts were widely introduced into the university around the turn of the century as an accepted part of liberal education. That emphasis was on the historical rather than the creative aspect. Students were brought into the presence of the arts by methods and techniques long accepted by the scholarly tradition. But once the arts had come into the curriculum as a proper subject for study, neither teachers nor students were long content with this platonic relationship. As often happens when a glamorous visitor comes to call, another kind of interest emerged—an interest in the subject itself, in art as art.

[4] It would be hard to exaggerate the importance of this development. It opened the door wide to the professional artist—at least it created the need for a teacher who had real training in his discipline. Now this development—the acceptance of the professional artist on campus—led logically to the next: the arrival of the student who wished to work with the professional artist as part of his regular course of studies, as full preparation for a professional career. At the same time similar forces were at work in the extra-curricular world. While the mandolin club of the Twenties was giving way to the orchestra, the senior theatrical farce was being replaced by the presentation of Greek tragedies, and the glee club was blossoming into the full-fledged chorus. The demands of extracurricular work in the arts supplemented the curricular demand for the professional artist as instructor, and together they provided the strongest possible internal motive for attracting the artist to the campus. Meanwhile, the artist was, if I may say so, not being over-employed or over-appreciated in the world outside the university.

[5] So the fact of the matter is that both parties to this marriage of artist and scholar badly needed each other. This is, therefore, no springtime romance, but a relation based upon the more durable foundations of mutual dependence. Some artists, to be sure, may

have been seduced by simple security and some universities motivated merely by consideration of prestige. But it is imperative that we realize that deeper and more permanent factors were present on both sides of this marriage, promising an interest that will increase with time. The artist is probably a permanent feature of the university landscape.

[6] If this is so, then we should recognize that the marriage does have problems. The parties do not always speak the same language. They frequently do not keep the same hours. The artist frequently feels that his new mate would rather play scholarly poker with his scholarly friends than work at the business of helping the artist become a part of his new community.

[7] And the adjustment is all the more difficult because some in the university and artistic worlds are by no means convinced that this alliance may not be disastrous for both parties. Some observers believe that as universities are now organized, the creative artist, both student and teacher, should stick to his garret if he would survive. At the same time, others are viewing this invasion of the scholarly citadel as a kind of Trojan horse of anti-intellectualism. Is it any wonder that the appropriate integration of the artist into the university community will take some doing? But, I repeat, he is there to stay, so we had better get to the task of understanding the adjustments that will be required.

[8] Let us speak first of the artist and then of the scholar. First off, the university is not the place for all artists—maybe not even for a majority of them. It will surely be easier on those with verbal skills, with reasonably catholic tastes, and for those who find it possible to concentrate in the midst of many potential distractions. It will also be more attractive to those whose concentration on their own artistic output does not preclude an interest in the work of others.

[9] If our university artist has these characteristics, the adjustment will surely be easier. But even so, problems will remain. He must learn to live with the amateur—the interested amateur, but the amateur. And this means learning to live with those who are not absorbed to the same degree with the artist's own professional enthusiasm for his own field. The artist frequently must be content with giving the interested amateur a glimpse, however brief, of the standards of performance of the full artist. He will have to curb an

instinct for dismissing the amateur as part of an offensive mass culture. Let him bear in mind that general taste cannot improve unless the interested amateurs are shown a better world.

[10] A more formidable difficulty is the heavy reliance of the scholarly world on the written word and the verbal tradition. Indeed, most universities have equated knowledge with the written word, saying in effect that human experience is recorded in books, professors write them, and students read them. The verbal tradition is powerful and pervasive and the artist who works in the nonverbal media of sound, color, shape, movement or voice inflection, will find that the university receiving sets are not always tuned to his wave length.

[11] And there is the very delicate but tricky matter of the different styles of the artistic and scholarly approach to reality. The scholar, particularly the scholar-scientist, is preoccupied with the universal not the particular, the general rule not the specific instance. In this mode he tries to erase the bias of his own individuality. Value judgments must be avoided at all costs as contributing to distortions of the truth.

[12] The artist does not try to remove his own personality from the creative process. On the contrary, he feels that it is his particular mission to reorder the data of his media to express an image of his own design. This image once projected onto canvas, or into clay, or a music score or the stage of a theater, has an objective reality for the artist as solid as the newest particle for the nuclear physicist, maybe even more solid. But the process involves the explicit stamp of his own personality on his work, be he Giotto, Nijinsky, or Pablo Picasso.

[13] In short, the artist tries to express a universal truth through the particular while the scholar will use the particular as only a means of illustrating the universal. This difference in style complicates communication between artist and scholar, makes it difficult to apply similar standards of judgments to their work. Without familiar standards of evaluation, the scholar cannot measure artistic performance and frequently concludes that a performance that cannot be evaluated does not belong in a university. The artist on the other hand is puzzled by the seeming depersonalization of the scholarly enterprise.

[14] He notes, however, with a faint sigh of relief, that many scholars have indeed left their own personal imprint. Aristotle and Descartes, Pasteur and Einstein, Herodotus and Winston Churchill have all left their individual styles as bookmarks in their works. The

difference is that such a discovery, frequently pleasing to the artist,
140 makes the scholar uneasy.

[15] The artist must adjust to these differences. To him harsh
judgments are more than reflections on the success of his work; they
bite into and reflect on the artist himself as an individual. He will
have to develop a tougher skin. But through all this he must retain
145 his own individuality, his own integrity. He must encourage amateurs
but not become one. He will have to acquire an understanding of
verbal systems of communication without losing his feeling for the
senses. And he will have to cling to his determination to show what
is in him even if it means exposing his soul. And it is possible that he
150 may even become a greater artist in the process.

[16] Turning to the other partner of the marriage, there are
warnings and adjustments that must be reported here, too. There are
universities and universities. The large private universities on the
Eastern seaboard were among the first to introduce the arts as liberal
155 studies. But it has been the state and land-grant institutions with diverse professional schools that have, with notable exceptions, pio-
neered with programs by and for the professional artist. Their tradition of response to social interest has been strong. And their
professional schools have accustomed them to practice as well as
160 theory. A university environment with these two traditions in its
blood stream will surely have an easier time absorbing the professional artist with his distinctive standards and techniques.

[17] To these universities the concentrated preoccupation of the
creative and performing artist will not seem so strange. They are
165 already accustomed to programs that bridge the gaps between the university and the world at large. All professional programs try to combine thought and action. All are driven by the necessity for concentration rather than diffusion, by the desire for specialized rather than
generalized education, and by a sense of preparing for a specific role
170 in society rather than merely an understanding of society. In one
sense, they are all preparing for specific careers and in this milieu the
artist will feel, at least relatively, at home. Perhaps all these professionals agree with a persistent parable that may have had its origins in Xenophon that reads: he who knows the theory but not the
175 practice does not know the whole theory.

[18] But if I have given the impression that I believe the public
university with strong and influential professional schools is already
adjusted and ready to receive the artist, let me correct that impres-

sion at once. I only meant to suggest that they are relatively more ready. Serious problems remain even for them.

[19] The scholar in even these universities must make an effort to understand the artist's different mode of thought and style of expression—just as I have suggested that the artist must try to understand the scholar. The scholar will have to learn to recognize the existence of different systems of communication. He will even have to realize that they are not inferior, only different. He will have to recognize the extent to which the artist has exposed his own psyche in his work and treat such work with the restraint of the surgeon who holds the beating human heart in his hand. He must recognize the need of the creative artist for isolation, for stretches of time for concentrated work, and for continuous association with fellow artists in his own field.

[20] But the scholar may also wish at the same time to reflect seriously on his own assumptions. He may wish to re-examine his instinctive reflex to the notion of value judgments. He may find that he has underemphasized the importance of the individual in the very substance of the scholarly enterprise.

[21] But over and beyond these adjustments required of the artist and scholar, a big decision must be made if, in the words of UCLA Chancellor Franklin Murphy, we are to "bring the creative arts into the university as a fully professional discipline, with the same prestige, the same opportunities, and the same vigor that we brought to medicine and the other appropriate professions."

[22] And this decision has not really been made. It has not been made because the scholar and artist still understand each other imperfectly. It has not been made because we have not really faced up to the costs of the special facilities that will be required. It has not been made because the universities have not yet seen the nature of the organizational arrangements that will be required. Or when they have seen them, they have not been bold enough to propose them and urge their adoption.

[23] When the decision is made, the university will get seriously to work on the administrative consequences. One line of organizational solution would be the establishment of a separate college of the creative arts. This solution would be based on the belief that the particular requirements of artistic creativity in all fields are so similar as to require a separate but coherent organization. However, if the interaction between the creative, historical, and analytic features of a particular media seems to be of overriding importance, then a close

220 integration with existing colleges of arts and fine arts would be in order.

[24] A separate college would have, of course, close working relations with established departments. Its admissions standards and testing techniques would be developed to identify artistic and creative 225 talent as well as intelligence. Perhaps, in time, it will not seem so strange to have college board scores on artistic as well as verbal and mathematical aptitudes. As a matter of fact, such tests are already in the process of development.

[25] Students in such a college would, of course, take their 230 fundamental work in the liberal arts in established colleges. But they would be permitted to follow rather hand-tailored programs that recognized their special requirements for uninterrupted time for work and practice.

[26] With either decision, special facilities would have to be pro- 235 vided along with special admissions arrangements. Practice rooms, demonstration rooms, and work rooms geared to the artistic requirement and artistic climate are an obvious must. But places to perform and exhibit and listen to high professional performance and see first-class art are equally necessary. It is hard to believe that a full-fledged 240 art program, for example, can flower without a first-class teaching museum.

[27] In addition, the presence of a repertory theater, a professional orchestra, and artists-in-residence would become a natural part of the artistic scene. And finally, such a college might wish to develop ap- 245 propriate relations with secondary schools in its area to devise programs for the talented youngster.

[28] But in making this big decision and working out both structure and theory to implement it, we may find we have raised an enormously important matter that could affect the whole of the uni- 250 versity. If art is only a particular form of creative activity, then in examining the circumstances of the artist, we may have to ask if the steps required to protect the creative artist may not have to be applied to other fields as well. The nasty thought intrudes that maybe the university has too quickly applied general rules to all its students 255 and faculty without proper consideration to that precious fraction whose creative genius requires very special handling.

[29] In short, are we really hospitable to creativity across the board? If we hesitate at all in answering this question, then we may thank our lucky stars that the creative artist has come along to make 260 us take a hard look at ourselves.

[30] Specifically, we should ask whether we really know where the creative talent exists on our campus. Can we distinguish between creativity and mere productivity? If we cannot, we had better find out how to do it.

[31] Do we feel that a professor is a professor and a student is a student? Do we adhere to rigid rules that might destroy or cripple really creative talent caught in our administrative gears? If so, we have some self-study on our hands.

[32] We all believe in the doctrine that every professor should teach. But teach whom and teach how? Should the really creative mind be forced to teach those who cannot understand him? Must we be more careful to match the capabilities of student with the particular characteristics and value of our professors?

[33] We know that periods of concentration are needed by the creative artist who would maintain his creativity. Can we be sure that the routines we have established for student and faculty may not be exquisitely but unconsciously calculated to weed out and suppress creativity rather than encourage it?

[34] It may be that we will find ourselves giving far more attention than we have to differentiating between those whose great forte is dealing with and stimulating the ideas of the student, and those whose contributions to society and others in the same field may well be a practically complete preoccupation with their own ideas. Both talents are an absolute requirement in any university department. To say that the creative wing must leave the campus, as has been suggested, is to remove from any field the diamond bit that makes it possible to cut through the rocks of both ignorance and tradition to the goals we seek.

[35] And so, I would say: Artist beware, but university prepare. Let the artist learn where his real talent lies and how it can be most effectively adjusted into a university environment and protected from what is inimical to its development. And at the same time, let the university recognize the need for the special treatment required for creative talent whether working in the field or the arts or in other fields.

[36] And, although the idea may be startling, it is by no means certain that in this process the artist on the campus may not make a greater contribution to the future of the university than the university can make to the future of the artist.

Variety among the paragraphs of an essay is obtained in several ways: most obvious is varying the lengths of the several paragraphs that make up the essay. The placing of a topic sentence at the beginning of one paragraph and at the end of another supplies variety, as does the occasional use of an implied topic sentence. In addition, the use of different methods of paragraph development with consequent differences in the structure of the paragraphs is a major source of variety.

1. In the first paragraph, is the second sentence or the third sentence the topic sentence or is the topic sentence implied? Justify your answer.

2. What function is served in paragraph 2 by the repetition of "Only he"? Are the last two sentences of the paragraph climactic or anticlimactic? Explain.

3. Compare the order of materials in paragraphs 1 and 2. Has Perkins used order to achieve variety between the paragraphs or similarity?

4. By what method or methods does Perkins develop paragraph 2? Explain why you think the paragraph is or is not unified.

5. Comment on the relative lengths of paragraphs 1, 2, and 3. Is paragraph 3 shorter only to achieve variety? Explain.

6. Indicate the means by which Perkins achieves coherence in paragraph 4. Does the last sentence violate the unity of the paragraph? Explain.

7. Comment on the relative lengths and the placement of the topic sentences in paragraphs 5 and 6.

8. By what means does Perkins effect a transition between paragraphs 6 and 7? What is the function of the last sentence of paragraph 7?

9. To what content are paragraphs 8, 9, and 10 devoted? How could these three paragraphs have been combined into one long one without violating paragraph unity? What would have been gained or lost had Perkins combined these three?

10. Similarly, paragraphs 11 and 12 could have been combined. Why do you think Perkins did not combine them?

11. By what method is paragraph 13 developed? Comment on the effectiveness of the method at this point in the essay.

12. Is achieving variety the only reason for the relative shortness of paragraph 18? Explain.

13. What similarities do you find in the structure of paragraphs 19 and 20? Is Perkins at fault here for not achieving greater variety? Explain.

14. Analyze several sets of related paragraphs from the remainder of the essay to show the means by which Perkins achieves variety.

Alternate selections for the study of Variety: Gilbert Highet, "The Gettysburg Address"; Meg Greenfield, "Editorial Disorder and Early Sorrow."

Theme Assignment: Write a theme in which you explain the place of the creative arts on your campus—in the curriculum and in the extracurricular program. You may have to consult your college bulletin and perhaps interview some members of the faculty and some upper-class students to get adequate information. You may wish to include an evaluation of the arts programs in the light of the Perkins essay. Your paragraphs should be adequately developed and varied.

Paragraphs in Combination

✐ The Camera Creative

JOHN MASON BROWN

[1] There was a person, his name is not known, who on an undated day of the highest excitement and importance, looked upon a block of marble and suddenly realized that in that cold stone the spirit and body of a man or woman existed, if only (this was the
5 tantalizing "if"), if only he could employ his chisel so as to set them free. In some such fashion stones long used for buildings were put to a new and unsuspected use, and sculpture began.

[2] Of course, it may have begun earlier with man's urge to represent life, or personify his deities, first expressing itself in a more
10 malleable substance such as clay or even in that designful whittling of wood called carving. But the marble guaranteed, or seemed to guarantee, permanence, and artists being human are not exempt from vanity. What people had lived in as homes or flocked to as temples and public edifices, they now started to inhabit in a novel and un-
15 dreamed-of fashion. They were not housed in stone; they were caught in it. Denied their flesh, when so portrayed they were not what they

From *Still Seeing Things* by John Mason Brown. New York: McGraw-Hill, Inc. Copyright 1950 by John Mason Brown. Reprinted by permission of the author.

once were. Yet their loss was a gain. They were not such men and women as they themselves had seen or as we see. They were such men and women as an artist had seen and wanted us to see. Although their motions were arrested, their bodies were alive with motion. That their hearts were of stone did not mean that they could not feel and express great emotion.

[3] All of us had thought that by now we knew what the camera could do. All of us were certain of our familiarity with its proved wonders. All of us were aware that, due to it, within our lifetimes another new medium, thrilling in its possibilities, had raced from the crudest of infancies to incredible technical maturity. With the advent, first of radio, then of television, we had come to regard the motion pictures as almost venerable. We were conscious that in them, as in a play, a novel, a poem, a painting, or a sculpture, things could be done and said as they could be nowhere else.

[4] Like many another, I had thought, until I saw the story of Michelangelo as told in *The Titan* (—Story of Michelangelo, an adaptation of the Curt Oertel film), that I knew what these things were. But this extraordinary film, the first of its kind ever to be shown in this country, has opened my eyes to a world of the camera hitherto unexplored and superb in its resources. *The Titan* is an old picture, as pictures go. Yet it is newer in its technique than the latest picture to be produced. It was made in 1938–40, chiefly in Florence and Rome, by the Swiss producer Curt Oertel. In its original form it lasted ninety-five minutes, whereas in the reassembled and re-edited American version, equipped as it is with a new script, an excellent score, and a fine running narrative finely spoken by Fredric March, it runs for only seventy minutes. During the war it is said to have been seized by the Germans, distributed proudly as a proof of Nazi culture, and was afterward discovered in France by the American Army.

[5] When seen by Robert J. Flaherty, one of the screen's true artists, it won his immediate interest. As a director responsible for welcome innovations in such sensitive and unhackneyed films as *Nanook of the North, Moana, Man of Aran,* and *Louisiana Story,* Mr. Flaherty was quick to appreciate the innovational virtues of *The Titan.* It was he who acquired its American rights. And it is he who, with Robert Snyder and Ralph Alswang, has brought together such a talented group of craftsmen as Richard Lyford, Norman Borisoff, and Alois Melichar, to direct and edit and supply the script and music for the picture as it is now shown in the United States.

[6] The novelties, the fascinations, and the excitements of *The Titan* are many and irresistible. Although in procedure no less than in purpose it is a documentary in a stricter sense than those pictures usually so described, it is like none of the documentaries to which we are accustomed. We have had documentaries which have dramatized geography and elevated the travelogue into the realm of art. We have had documentaries which, because of the eloquent use to which they have put newsreel clips, have presented us with history in the making. We have had documentaries which in their animated maps and diagrams have demonstrated the unrivaled role they can play as swift elucidators of complicated problems. We have seen them do their stirring part as propagandists, watched them breathlessly as they had recorded battle exploits or true sagas of adventure. We have grown increasingly grateful for the sense of truth their methods have created in fictional scenarios. Until *The Titan,* however, we had never sat before a documentary in which the chief concern was beauty and an artist's biography was told in terms of his art.

[7] The screen, of course, has offered us biographies galore—some good, some bad, some tasteful, and more tasteless. But all these previous re-creations of the past have depended upon living actors; actors dressed up and bewigged; actors pretending to be Pasteur, Queen Christina, Henry VIII, Madame Curie, Woodrow Wilson, Thomas A. Edison, Zola, or George M. Cohan. *The Titan* is different; wonderfully, stirringly different. It dispenses with flesh-and-blood players as completely as if it had taken to heart Duse's famous hyperbole: "To save the Theatre, the Theatre must be destroyed, the actors and actresses must all die of the plague. They poison the air, they make art impossible."

[8] In *The Titan,* although no one impersonates Michelangelo, Lorenzo, Savonarola, or Pope Julius II, each of these great Renaissance figures seems to be present. Their struggles, their hopes, their plots, their cruelties, and, above all, the works of art which they either created or commissioned are present, too. Florence, Bologna, and Rome in all their glory supply the settings. Portraits, prints, paintings, architectural details, and statues emerge as players. The dialogue is written not with a scenarist's pen but by Michelangelo's chisel and brush.

[9] The tragic tenderness of his first "Pietà," the vigor of his "David," the pagan abandon of his "Bacchus," the power of his "Moses," the agony of his "Slave," the richness of the Sistine ceiling, the brooding profundity of his "Dawn" and "Night," the soaring

greatness of the dome of St. Peter's, the fury of his "Last Judgment," and the final sorrow of his "Deposition"—all these speak both for themselves and for Michelangelo. Without seeing him we see what he was. With the aid of the narrative and especially due to the camera's chaperonage, we follow his life and sense the grandeur of his genius. The result is a masterpiece composed of masterpieces. In it a period writes its own history even as the art of an artist writes his biography. 100 ... 105

[10] All of us who have made our pilgrimages to admire Michelangelo's works may have felt that we were well acquainted with their marvels. But most of us would, I suspect, now have to confess we had never really *seen* them until we saw *The Titan*. As highlighted by Klieg lights, as surveyed through the camera's eye, as approached 110 from unexpected angles, or viewed in dramatic close-ups, they leap and lunge into a life even more amazing than that which we had prized as theirs.

[11] One can only hope that what *The Titan* does so magnificently for the work of one magnificent artist will be done again and again 115 with the same brilliance and integrity for other artists and their works.

Although we have been considering the paragraph as a unit and discussing its attributes and its method or methods of development, it would be virtually impossible to find a piece of writing which is composed exclusively of paragraphs developed according to some one method. Since the topic sentence of each paragraph grows ultimately out of the guiding purpose, it is the guiding purpose which governs the organization of individual paragraphs and the combinations of types of paragraphs. For example, in a piece on how to drive a car, the guiding purpose might well necessitate the use of one or more paragraphs of definition (What is "power steering," an "emergency brake," "automatic transmission"?); paragraphs developed according to the principle of accumulation of detail (What are the minimal tools which every car should have?); paragraphs of comparison or contrast (What constitutes parking that will satisfy the requirements of the road test and what does not?); plus paragraphs that fall outside any rigid pattern but are governed by a step-by-step explanation of the process of driving.

1. Though John Mason Brown in "The Camera Creative" is actually reviewing the motion picture *The Titan,* he devotes his first two paragraphs to sculpture. Precisely what is the relevance of these paragraphs to the rest of the selection? Why do you suppose he chose not to combine paragraphs 1 and 2 into a single paragraph?

2. What is the topic sentence of paragraph 2? By what method or methods is it developed?

3. Does Brown violate coherence by the abrupt introduction of the camera in paragraph 3? Does he use any transitional device to relate paragraph 3 to paragraphs 1 and 2? What is the topic sentence of paragraph 3?

4. How is the transition effected between paragraphs 3 and 4? What is the topic sentence of paragraph 4? By what method or methods is it developed?

5. Paragraphs 6 and 7 combine two methods of paragraph development. What are they? Comment on the adequacy with which each of the paragraphs is developed.

6. State the implied topic sentence of paragraph 8. Which sentence in paragraph 9 might have served as the topic sentence of both paragraphs 8 and 9? Had it been used in this way, where would it have been placed? Is it more effective placed where it is? Why or why not?

7. What is the topic sentence of paragraph 10? By what method or methods is it developed? What additional methods might have been used to develop it more adequately?

8. Is the brevity of paragraph 11 justifiable? Why or why not?

Alternate selections for the study of Paragraphs in Combination: Robert Benchley, "How I Create"; D. H. Lawrence, from "Making Pictures."

Theme Assignment: John Mason Brown says that marble (really a figure of speech for stone, hence for sculpture) represented permanence. Art itself is the expression of man's desire for permanence, for a kind of immortality. Having children represents another way of expressing the desire for permanence. And yet children themselves can be said to represent change; they are ever-changing, and they often desire change.

Write a theme in which you discuss permanence and change as you experience them and understand them in your own life. You may want to define each term, list examples of each, compare and contrast them. Consequently you will need to make use of a number of methods of paragraph development.

THE
SENTENCE

Types of
Sentences

✐ *The Censor of Plays*

JOSEPH CONRAD

[1] A couple of years ago I was moved to write a one-act play—
and I lived long enough to accomplish the task. We live and learn.
When the play was finished I was informed that it had to be licensed
for performance. Thus I learned of the existence of the Censor of
Plays. I may say without vanity that I am intelligent enough to have   5
been astonished by that piece of information: for facts must stand
in some relation to time and space, and I was aware of being in
England—in the twentieth-century England. The fact did not fit the
date and the place. That was my first thought. It was, in short, an
improper fact. I beg you to believe that I am writing in all seriousness   10
and am weighing my words scrupulously.

[2] Therefore I don't say inappropriate. I say improper—that is:
something to be ashamed of. And at first this impression was confirmed by the obscurity in which the figure embodying this after all
considerable fact had its being. The Censor of Plays! His name was   15
not in the mouths of all men. Far from it. He seemed stealthy and
remote. There was about that figure the scent of the far East, like the

peculiar atmosphere of a Mandarin's back yard, and the mustiness of the Middle Ages. . . .

20   [3] It was a disagreeable impression. But I reflected that probably the censorship of plays was an inactive monstrosity; not exactly a survival, since it seemed obviously at variance with the genius of the people, but an heirloom of past ages, a bizarre and imported curiosity preserved because of that weakness one has for one's old possessions
25 apart from any intrinsic value; one more object of exotic *virtù,* an Oriental *potiche,* a *magot chinois* conceived by a childish and extravagant imagination, but allowed to stand in stolid impotence in the twilight of the upper shelf.

    [4] Thus I quieted my uneasy mind. Its uneasiness had nothing
30 to do with the fate of my one-act play. The play was duly produced, and an exceptionally intelligent audience stared it coldly off the boards. It ceased to exist. It was a fair and open execution. But having survived the freezing atmosphere of that auditorium I continued to exist, laboring under no sense of wrong. I was not pleased, but I
35 was content. I was content to accept the verdict of a free and independent public, judging after its conscience the work of its free, independent and conscientious servant—the artist.

    [5] Only thus can the dignity of artistic servitude be preserved— not to speak of the bare existence of the artist and the self-respect of
40 the man. I shall say nothing of the self-respect of the public. To the self-respect of the public the present appeal against the censorship is being made and I join in it with all my heart.

    [6] For I have lived long enough to learn that the monstrous and outlandish figure, the *magot chinois* whom I believed to be but a
45 memorial of our forefathers' mental aberration, that grotesque *potiche,* works! The absurd and hollow creature of clay seems to be alive with a sort of (surely) unconscious life worthy of its traditions. It heaves its stomach, it rolls its eyes, it brandishes a monstrous arm: and with the censorship, like a Bravo of old Venice with a more
50 carnal weapon, stabs its victim from behind in the twilight of its upper shelf. Less picturesque than the Venetian in cloak and mask, less estimable, too, in this, that the assassin plied his moral trade at his own risk deriving no countenance from the powers of the Republic, it stands more malevolent, inasmuch that the Bravo striking in the
55 dusk killed but the body, whereas the grotesque thing nodding its mandarin head may in its absurd unconsciousness strike down at any time the spirit of an honest, of an artistic, perhaps of a sublime creation.

[7] This Chinese monstrosity, disguised in the trousers of the Western Barbarian and provided by the State with the immortal Mr. Stiggins's plug hat and umbrella, is with us. It is an office. An office of trust. And from time to time there is found an official to fill it. He is a public man. The least prominent of public men, the most unobtrusive, the most obscure if not the most modest.

[8] But however obscure, a public man may be told the truth if only once in his life. His office flourishes in the shade; not in the rustic shade beloved of the violet but in the muddled twilight of mind, where tyranny of every sort flourishes. Its holder need not have either brain or heart, no sight, no taste, no imagination, not even bowels of compassion. He needs not these things. He has power. He can kill thought, and incidentally truth, and incidentally beauty, providing they seek to live in a dramatic form. He can do it, without seeing, without understanding, without feeling anything; out of mere stupid suspicion, as an irresponsible Roman Caesar could kill a senator. He can do that and there is no one to say him nay. He may call his cook (Molière used to do that) from below and give her five acts to judge every morning as a matter of constant practice and still remain the unquestioned destroyer of men's honest work. He may have a glass too much. This accident has happened to persons of unimpeachable morality—to gentlemen. He may suffer from spells of imbecility like Clodius. He may . . . what might he not do! I tell you he is the Caesar of the dramatic world. There has been since the Roman Principate nothing in the way of irresponsible power to compare with the office of the Censor of Plays.

[9] Looked at in this way it has some grandeur, something colossal in the odious and the absurd. This figure in whose power it is to suppress an intellectual conception—to kill thought (a dream for a mad brain, my master!)—seems designed in a spirit of bitter comedy to bring out the greatness of a Philistine's conceit and his moral cowardice.

[10] But this is England in the twentieth century, and one wonders that there can be found a man courageous enough to occupy the post. It is a matter for meditation. Having given it a few minutes I come to the conclusion in the serenity of my heart and the peace of my conscience that he must be either an extreme megalomaniac or an utterly unconscious being.

[11] He must be unconscious. It is one of the qualifications for his magistracy. Other qualifications are equally easy. He must have done nothing, expressed nothing, imagined nothing. He must be obscure,

100 insignificant and mediocre—in thought, act, speech and sympathy.
He must know nothing of art, of life—and of himself. For if he did
he would not dare to be what he is. Like that much questioned and
mysterious bird, the phoenix, he sits amongst the cold ashes of his
predecessor upon the altar of morality, alone of his kind in the sight
105 of wondering generations.

[12] And I will end with a quotation reproducing not perhaps the
exact words but the true spirit of a lofty conscience.

[13] "Often when sitting down to write the notice of a play,
especially when I felt it antagonistic to my canons of art, to my tastes
110 or my convictions, I hesitated in the fear lest my conscientious blame
might check the development of a great talent, my sincere judgment
condemn a worthy mind. With the pen poised in my hand I hesitated,
whispering to myself 'What if I were perchance doing my part in
killing a masterpiece.' "

115 [14] Such were the lofty scruples of M. Jules Lemaître—dramatist
and dramatic critic, a great citizen and a high magistrate in the
Republic of Letters; a Censor of Plays exercising his august office
openly in the light of day, with the authority of a European reputation. But then M. Jules Lemaître is a man possessed of wisdom, of
120 great fame, of a fine conscience—not an obscure hollow Chinese
monstrosity ornamented with Mr. Stiggins's plug hat and cotton umbrella by its anxious grandmother—the State.

[15] Frankly, is it not time to knock the improper object off its
shelf? It has stood too long there. Hatched in Pekin (I should say)
125 by some Board of Respectable Rites, the little caravan monster has
come to us by way of Moscow—I suppose. It is outlandish. It is not
venerable. It does not belong here. Is it not time to knock it off its
dark shelf with some implement appropriate to its worth and status?
With an old broom handle for instance.

A piece of writing may be well organized and adequately para-
graphed, but if its sentences are not both grammatically correct and
rhetorically effective, the writing cannot be said to meet a reasonable
college standard. The ability to write grammatically correct sentences—sentences in which the subject agrees with the verb in number, sentences in which independent clauses are correctly connected,
sentences in which verbals are not used as though they were finite
verbs, and so on—is idealistically considered to be a minimum requirement for college entrance; realistically, college handbooks have

sections devoted to the problems of grammatical correctness of sentences.

But grammatically correct sentences are not enough to make good writing. The individual sentence should communicate clearly and efficiently. Words should not be wasted, for, as Alexander Pope says in his "Essay on Criticism,"

Words are like leaves; and where they most abound,
Much fruit of sense beneath is rarely found.

The relations among the parts of the idea expressed should be reflected in the structure of the sentence. The parts of the sentence should follow normal English order, and there should be variety in structure from sentence to sentence. In addition, sentence rhythms should be not only pleasing to the reader but also, when relevant, functional as well.

One of the advantages of English as a language for the communication of ideas of some complexity is the flexibility of its sentence structure. This very flexibility, however, presents the writer with the constant necessity of having to decide which of the several possible ways of saying something—of constructing a sentence—is best for his purposes. For example, each of the following sentences communicates essentially the same idea, but notice the considerable differences in structure and, consequently, in effect among them.

    a. The president of the college wanted to help the students and he wanted to please the faculty too and consequently he decided to appoint several highly trained student counselors who would guide students and in this way relieve faculty members of some of their heavy work programs.

    b. Wanting to give students good guidance and to reduce the work load of the faculty, the president of the college appointed several highly trained student counselors.

    c. Several highly trained student counselors were appointed by the president of the college to give students guidance and thus take the counseling burden off the overworked faculty.

    d. The overworked faculty was relieved of the burden of student counseling when the president of the college appointed several highly trained student counselors, much to the delight of the student body.

1. Which of the sentences communicates most efficiently? least efficiently? What are the specific differences in content among the sentences? In which sentence or sentences is the relation among the various parts of the idea communicated not explicitly clear? On what grounds would you decide which of the sentences is best?

For the purposes of rhetorical analysis of sentences, that is, the close study of the structure of sentences to understand their over-all effectiveness (or lack of effectiveness), it is helpful to know the following standard classification of sentences.

Simple: a sentence consisting of a single main clause:

a. The train left.
b. The book fell from the man's hands.
c. The duke and duchess loved and obeyed their king and queen.

Compound: a sentence consisting of two or more main clauses:

a. The woman walked, but the man ran.
b. There were two chairs and a table in the room; the walls and floor were entirely bare.
c. "Give me liberty, or give me death."

Complex: a sentence consisting of one main clause and one or more subordinate clauses:

a. When it rained, we stayed indoors.
b. Students sometimes fail examinations because they don't read the questions carefully enough.
c. After the war had ended but before the soldiers had returned from the combat areas, the heads of the warring countries became involved in the beginnings of the "cold war."

Compound-Complex: a sentence consisting of two or more main clauses and at least one subordinate clause:

a. When dinner was over, the adults settled into somnolent conversation and the children began to play in front of the house.
b. The clock struck; the man shuddered because this was the moment he had most feared.
c. Living on a secluded lake shore is rewarding; it gives a man time to take stock of himself when he is closest to nature.

Just as some ideas can be developed in a paragraph by one method rather than another, with the writer scarcely aware of having made a choice of method, so many sentences fall into one or another of the normal English patterns almost automatically. Yet a knowledge of the different types of sentences and an awareness of the differences in effect among them will aid the writer in understanding the effectiveness of prose he reads and in achieving greater effectiveness in his own writing; his very awareness of the potentialities of English sentences can increase his ability to achieve clarity and variety in his own sentences. A writer does not usually decide to write a simple sentence or a compound-complex sentence: he expresses himself in sentences which come naturally to him. In revising his writing, however, to make it clearer or more efficient or more effective, he may well decide to combine two simple sentences into a compound sentence, say, and subsequently to change the compound sentence into a complex sentence both because the content demands the subordination of one of the parts to another and because he may already have too many compound sentences in the paragraph.

2. Five of the nine sentences in the first paragraph of the Conrad selection are simple; identify them. Why do you suppose so skillful a writer as Conrad piled up so many simple sentences in his first paragraph? In other words, what effect is achieved through the simple sentences? How do you classify the remaining sentences in the paragraph?

3. Conrad uses two sentence fragments in the second paragraph; identify them. Is the use of each justifiable? Why or why not? On what criterion (or criteria) did you base your answer? What additional criteria might be used to justify the occasional use of a sentence fragment?

4. The second sentence of paragraph 3 is highly complicated; it provides a good opportunity for you to test your ability to work out the grammatical structure of a sentence and to classify it.

5. Six of the eight sentences in paragraph 4 are simple sentences. Study their length and grammatical structure: what conclusions can you come to concerning simple sentences, their length, and their simplicity or complexity structure? Classify the two remaining sentences in the paragraph and justify your classifications. Combine sentences 2 and 3 into one compound-complex sentence. Is effectiveness increased or decreased? Why? What is the simplest method of combining sentences 5 and 6 into one compound sentence? Why do you think Conrad chose not to make the combination? Does the proportionately large number of simple sentences in the paragraph result in monotony of style? Why or why not?

6. Classify the third sentence of paragraph 6. Without making any changes in word order, change the sentence into a simple sentence. Which sentence is more effective, yours or Conrad's? Why?

7. Paragraph 7 consists solely of simple sentences and sentence fragments. What effect or effects does Conrad achieve in the paragraph as a whole? To arrive at a precise answer, you might try rewriting the paragraph to eliminate the fragments.

8. Make sentences 4 and 5 of paragraph 8 into a compound sen-

tence in two different ways. Then make them into a complex sentence. Which of the versions (including Conrad's) is most effective? Why?

9. Compare the following rewriting of paragraph 10 with the original: precisely what is gained or lost by each of the changes made?

> But this is England in the twentieth century. One wonders that there can be found a man courageous enough to occupy the post. Since it is a matter for meditation, I have given it a few minutes of thought and I have come to the conclusion in the serenity of my heart and the peace of my conscience that he must be one of two things. He must be an extreme megalomaniac. Or he must be an utterly unconscious being.

10. Rewrite paragraph 11, making the following changes: make sentences 1 and 2 into a single complex sentence; make sentence 4 into three simple sentences; make sentences 5, 6, 7 into a single compound-complex sentence. Compare your version of the paragraph with Conrad's, taking into account each of the changes. Which is more effective and why?

11. Classify each of the sentences in paragraph 15. How can you justify the number of simple sentences? the fragment?

12. If you were allowed but one word to characterize Conrad's feelings about the Censor of Plays, what word would you use? what two words? What type of sentence appears most frequently in "The Censor of Plays"? Can you draw a tenable generalization about a writer's feelings about his subject matter and the type (or types) of sentence he is most likely to use? Explain. Support your position by referring to one or two other selections in this book in which you feel that a writer's feelings are or are not reflected in the types of sentences he uses.

Alternate selection for the study of Types of Sentences: Jacques Barzun, "The Decay of Conversation."

Theme Assignment: It is clear that Conrad felt strongly about what he considered the evil of censorship. His strong feeling contributed much to the effectiveness of his essay. Choose what you consider to be an evil in our society about which you feel strongly and write a theme in which you expose the evil. Presumably you will write your first version without thinking particularly of the various types of sentences you have been studying. Analyze each of your sentences to determine its type; wherever necessary, thoroughly revise your sentences to make them as efficient, clear, and effective as you can. Make a list of the types of sentences you used in your first version and in your revised version. Be prepared to submit both versions and lists to your instructor.

Variety of Structure

From *The Art of Fiction*

W. SOMERSET MAUGHAM

[1] Flaubert was aware that in setting out to write a book about commonplace people he ran the risk of writing a dull one. He desired to produce a work of art, and he felt that he could only surmount the difficulties presented by the sordid nature of his subject and the vulgarity of his characters by means of beauty of style. Now, I do 5 not know whether such a creature exists as the natural born stylist; certainly Flaubert was not; his early works, unpublished in his lifetime, are said to be verbose, turgid and rhetorical. It is generally stated that his letters show little sign that he had a feeling for the elegance and distinction of his native tongue. I don't think that is true. 10 They were, for the most part, written late at night, after a hard day's work, and sent to their recipients uncorrected. Words are misspelt, and the grammar is often faulty; they are slangy and sometimes vulgar; but there are in them brief descriptions of scenery so real, so rhythmical, that they would not have seemed out of place in 15 *Madame Bovary;* and there are passages, when he was moved to

fury, that are so incisive, so direct, that you feel no revision would have served to improve them. You hear the sound of his voice in the short, crisp sentences. But that was not the way in which Flaubert
20 wanted to write a book. He was prejudiced against the conversational style, and was blind to its advantages. He took for his models La Bruyère and Montesquieu. His aim was to write a prose that was logical, precise, swift and various, rhythmical, sonorous, musical as poetry, and yet preserving the qualities of prose. He was of opinion
25 that there were not two ways of saying a thing, but only one, and that the wording must fit the thought as the glove fits the hand. "When I find an assonance or a repetition in one of my phrases," he said, "I know that I am ensnared in something false." (As examples of assonance, the Oxford Dictionary gives man and hat, nation and
30 traitor, penitent and reticent.) Flaubert claimed that an assonance must be avoided, even if it took a week to manage it. He would not allow himself to use the same word twice on a page. That does not seem sensible: if it is the right word in each place, it is the right word to use, and a synonym or a periphrase can never be as apt. He was
35 careful not to allow the sense of rhythm which was natural to him, as it is to every writer, to obsess him (as George Moore in his later works was obsessed) and took pains to vary it. He exercised all his ingenuity to combine words and sounds to give an impression of speed or languor, lassitude or intensity; in short, of whatever state
40 he desired to express.

[2] When writing, Flaubert would sketch out roughly what he wished to say, and then work on what he had written, elaborating, cutting, rewriting, till he got the effect he wanted. That done, he would go out on his terrace and shout out the words he had written,
45 convinced that if they did not sound well, there must be something wrong with them. In that case, he would take them back and work over them again till he was satisfied. Théophile Gautier thought that Flaubert attached too great a value to the cadence and harmony with which he sought to enrich his prose; they were, according to him,
50 only evident when Flaubert in his booming voice read them aloud; but a phrase, he added, is made to read to oneself, not to be bellowed. Gautier was inclined to mock at Flaubert's fastidiousness: "You know," he said, "the poor chap suffers from a remorse that poisons his life. You don't know what the remorse is; it's to have put two
55 genitives together in *Madame Bovary,* one on the top of the other: *une couronne de fleurs d'oranger.* It tortures him, but however hard he tried, he found it impossible to avoid." It is fortunate for us that

by means of our English genitive we can escape this difficulty. We can say: "Where is the bag of the doctor's wife"; but in French you would have to say: "Where is the bag of the wife of the doctor?" It 60 must be confessed that it is not pretty.

[3] Louis Bouilhet would come to Croisset of a Sunday; Flaubert read to him what he had written during the week, and Bouilhet criticized. Flaubert stormed and argued, but Bouilhet held his ground, and in the end Flaubert accepted the emendations, the 65 elimination of superfluous incidents and irrelevant metaphors, the correction of false notes, which his friend insisted on. No wonder the novel proceeded at a snail's pace. In one of his letters Flaubert wrote: "The whole of Monday and Tuesday was taken up with the writing of two lines." This does not mean that he wrote only 70 two lines in two days, he may well have written a dozen pages; it means that with all his labour he only succeeded in writing two lines to his satisfaction. Flaubert found the strain of composition exhausting. Alphonse Daudet believed that this was attributable to the bromide that his malady obliged him to make constant use of. If 75 there is anything in this, it may account for the effort it evidently was to him to set down on paper in coherent order the huddle of ideas in his mind. We know how laborious a task he found it to write the well-known scene in *Madame Bovary* of the agricultural show. Emma and Rodolphe are seated at a window overlooking the *place*. 80 A representative of the *préfet* has come to deliver a speech. What Flaubert wanted to do he told in a letter to Louise Colet: "I have to situate together in the same conversation five or six people (who talk), several others (of whom one hears), the spot where this occurs, the feel of the place, while giving physical descriptions of people 85 and things, and to show in the midst of all a man and a woman who begin (by their common sympathies of taste) to feel a little attracted to one another." That does not seem a very difficult thing to do, and Flaubert has in fact done it extremely well, but, though it was only twenty-seven pages long, it took him two solid months. Balzac would 90 have written it in his own way no less well in the inside of a week. The great novelists, Balzac, Dickens and Tolstoy, had what we are accustomed to call inspiration. It is only in a scene here and there that you feel that Flaubert had it; for the rest he seems to have depended on sheer hard work, the advice and suggestions of Bouilhet, 95 and his own acuteness of observation. This is not to depreciate *Madame Bovary;* but it is strange that so great a work should have been produced, not as we feel *Le Père Goriot* or *David Copperfield* was

produced in the free flow of an exuberant fancy, but by almost pure
100 ratiocination.

[4] It is not unreasonable to ask oneself how near Flaubert came,
by taking the immense pains I have described, to achieve the perfect
style at which he aimed. Style is a matter of which a foreigner, even
though he knows a language pretty well, can be but an uncertain
105 judge: the finer points, the music, the subtlety, the aptness, the
rhythm, can hardly fail to escape him. He must accept the opinions
of the native born. For a generation after Flaubert's death, his style
was highly regarded in France; now it is less admired. The French
writers of to-day find in it a lack of spontaneity. He had, as I have
110 before mentioned, a horror of "this new maxim that one must write
as one speaks." And of course one must no more write as one speaks
than one must speak as one writes; but written language has life and
vitality only if it is firmly grounded on current speech. Flaubert was
a provincial, and in his prose was apt to use provincialisms which
115 offend the purists; I don't suppose that a foreigner, unless they
were pointed out to him, would be aware of them; nor would he notice the grammatical mistakes of which Flaubert, like nearly every
writer who ever wrote, was sometimes guilty. Few Englishmen, though
able to read French with ease and pleasure, could point out what is
120 grammatically wrong with the following phrase: "*Ni moi! reprit vive-
ment M. Homais, quoiqu'il lui faudra suivre les autres au risque de
passer pour un Jésuite;*" and fewer still could tell how to put it right.

[5] The French language tends to rhetoric, as the English to imagery (thereby marking a profound difference between the two
125 peoples), and the basis of Flaubert's style is rhetorical. He made
abundant, even excessive use of the triad. This is the sentence of
three members which are arranged, as a rule, either in an ascending
or a descending scale of importance. It is both an easy and a satisfying
way of achieving balance, and orators have taken full advantage of
130 it. Here is an example from Burke: "Their wishes ought to have great
weight with him; their opinion, high respect; their business, unre-
mitted attention." The danger of this sort of sentence, and one from
which Flaubert did not escape, is that when used too often it is
monotonous. Flaubert in one of his letters wrote: "I'm devoured
135 with similes as one is with lice, and I spend all my time crushing
them, my phrases swarm with them." Critics have observed that in
his letters the similes are spontaneous, whereas in *Madame Bovary*
they are too studied, too neatly balanced, to be natural. Here is a
good example: Charles Bovary's mother has come to pay Emma

and her husband a visit. "*Elle observait le bonheur de son fils, avec* [140] *un silence triste, comme quelqu'un de ruiné qui regarde, à travers les carreaux, des gens attablés dans son ancienne maison.*" This is admirably put, but the simile is in itself so striking that it distracts your attention from the mood it is supposed to illustrate; the object of a simile, however, is to add force and importance to a statement, [145] not to weaken it.

[6] The best French writers of to-day, so far as I have been able to discover, deliberately avoid rhetoric. They attempt to say what they have to say simply and naturally. They eschew the effective triad. They avoid similes, as though they were indeed the vermin [150] to which Flaubert likened them. That, I believe, is why they are apt to hold his style in small esteem, at least the style of *Madame Bovary,* for when he came to write *Bouvard et Pécuchet* he abandoned every form of ornament and decoration; and that is why they prefer the easy, flowing, animated and natural manner of his [155] letters to the laboured manner of his great novels. This is, of course, merely a matter of fashion, and justifies us in forming no judgment on the merits of Flaubert's style. A style may be stark, like Swift's, flowery, like Jeremy Taylor's, or grandiloquent, like Burke's: each is good, and whether you prefer one to another depends merely on [160] your individual taste.

Structures of sentences should make sense, but they are not inviolable. There is always more than one way to say something, usually more than one effective way. And sentences, though they stand alone grammatically, do not literally "stand alone." They appear, most frequently, in combination with other sentences, and they affect one another. Thus, no matter how "right" a simple sentence may be for expressing a particular thought, an unrelieved string of simple sentences is tiresome; each loses some of its effectiveness in combination with so many others like itself—just as an Easter bonnet, strikingly original at home, loses some of its effectiveness in the Easter parade if there are too many others just like it. On the other hand, a simple sentence is heightened in effectiveness if it appears in combination with sentences of more complicated structure. At the same time, the sentences of more complicated structure are more effective if they are well spaced or paced. Too many unrelieved sentences of any one structure call attention away from the thought to the structure itself; too many extremely involved sentences become heavy and cumbersome.

Variety can be achieved not only through the functional mingling of types of sentences but also by varying the order of the parts within the sentence. The most elementary order is subject, verb, object. But if sentence after sentence follows this sequence, the result is singsong, and this is not the only possible sequence of English sentences. (The old man cried, "Fire!" *or* "Fire!" cried the old man.) Note that since inversion affects emphasis it is a useful device for pointing up precise meaning and should be used for this purpose as well as to attain variety. It is also often desirable to defer the main clause and open with a dependent element, such as a phrase or dependent clause; to separate the main elements from one another by the inclusion of a dependent element; or to compound one or another of the major elements. A periodic sentence (in which the basic meaning is not complete until the end or near the end) may supply variety when introduced among several loose sentences (in which the basic meaning is made clear well before the end). Occasionally, where it can logically be introduced without sounding forced or false, an exclamation, question, or even command may help to break the monotony of repeated declarative sentences. But all of these methods of varying the sentence structure must be used judiciously; they must further the meaning, not merely embellish it.

1. In paragraph 5, Maugham says, "The French language tends to rhetoric, as the English to imagery (thereby marking a profound difference between the two peoples), and the basis of Flaubert's style is rhetorical." Judging from this selection, would you say that Maugham (an Englishman) describes his own style accurately? Use Maugham's sentence structure to corroborate your answer. (See page 391 for a discussion of imagery.)

2. Determine the type of every sentence in paragraph 1. What do your findings reveal about variety of sentence structure?

3. Select a passage from elsewhere in the selection (it need not be more than two or three sentences) which you think illustrates the effectiveness of varied sentence structures. Justify your selection.

4. State in your own words the guiding purpose of the selection. What idea or ideas has each paragraph contributed to that guiding purpose? Which sentences are irrelevant to it? Why do you suppose Maugham included them?

5. Comment on the structure and length of the following sentences as reflective of their meaning:

"You hear the sound of his voice in the short, crisp sentences." (paragraph 1)

" 'When I find an assonance or a repetition in one of my phrases . . . I know that I am ensnared in something false.' " (paragraph 1)

"This [the triad] is the sentence of three members which are arranged, as a rule, either in an ascending or a descending scale of importance." (paragraph 5)

"It must be confessed that it is not pretty." (paragraph 2)

"Flaubert was a provincial, and in his prose was apt to use provincialisms which offend the purists; I don't suppose that a foreigner, unless they were pointed out to him, would be aware of them; nor would he notice the grammatical mistakes of which Flaubert, like nearly every writer who ever wrote, was sometimes guilty." (paragraph 5)

"A style may be stark, like Swift's, flowery, like Jeremy Taylor's, or grandiloquent, like Burke's: each is good, and whether you prefer one to another depends merely on your individual taste." (paragraph 6)

6. Rewrite paragraph 5, using only simple sentences. Comment on the relative effectiveness of your paragraph and Maugham's.

7. Justify the order of parts of the first three sentences of paragraph 2. What would have been gained *and* lost had they been ordered differently?

8. Is the first sentence of paragraph 4 loose or periodic? What do you think guided Maugham's choice?

9. In what way or ways is the sentence structure of paragraph 6 like or unlike that of the paragraphs that precede it? Justify your answer, taking into account the meaning and purposes of the paragraphs.

Alternate selections for the study of Variety of Structure: Robert Allen Durr, from "The Last Days of H. L. Mencken"; George F. Kennan, "The Experience of Writing History"; Roger Fry, from "Culture and Snobbism."

In his speech of acceptance of the Nobel Prize for Literature, William Faulkner said, ". . . the young man or woman writing today has forgotten the problems of the human heart in conflict with itself which alone can make good writing because only that is worth writing about, worth the agony and the sweat." The human heart, today as always, is the arena of many conflicts: Should one strive to perfect a talent at the possible sacrifice of personal relations? Should a young person move away from home, go away to study or to live, or remain with or near his parents? Should one give up a love because someone else might be hurt by it? Is it possible to understand and, understanding, to relinquish a self-destructive habit or way of life? Should a student who has embarked upon a premedical course largely because his father is a doctor and who discovers that what he really wants to study is classical Greek change his major? These questions are not easily answered; perhaps some of them have no one right answer. But they involve emotional conflict and are fairly easily illustrated.

Write a theme on a "problem of the human heart in conflict with itself," one of these or another which this list may suggest to you. Be as specific as you can about the conflict; you will surely want to illustrate it by at least one example. (Your whole theme may be devoted to a single example.) You may or may not resolve the conflict, depending upon your own conviction. Be sure to make use of the principle of writing under consideration in this section—variety of sentence structure. And don't forget that you are *expected* to experience "agony and sweat."

or

Set yourself the writing assignment Flaubert set himself, as Maugham quotes and describes it in paragraph 3. You need not use as many subordinate characters as Flaubert used; two or three will do. If you like, you may read the passage in *Madame Bovary,* Chapter VIII. Remember that variety of sentence structure will help you to achieve the variety of effects called for.

or

Write a theme in which you describe Maugham's style in this selection and comment on his last sentence. You may compare and contrast his style with that of another of the writers included in this book, or you may limit yourself to an analysis and evaluation of Maugham's style. Remember that your instructor will be looking at your style!

Length

How I Create

ROBERT BENCHLEY

[1] In an article on How Authors Create, in which the writing methods of various masters of English prose like Conrad, Shaw, and Barrie are explained (with photographs of them in knickerbockers plaguing dogs and pushing against sun-dials), I discover that I have been doing the whole thing wrong all these years. The interviewer 5 in this case hasn't got around to asking me yet—doubtless because I have been up in my room with the door shut and not answering the bell—but I am going to take a chance anyway and tell him how I do my creative work and just how much comes from inspiration and how much from hashish and other perfumes. I may even loosen up and tell 10 him what my favorite hot-weather dishes are.

[2] When I am writing a novel I must actually live the lives of my characters. If, for instance, my hero is a gambler on the French Riviera, I make myself pack up and go to Cannes or Nice, willy-nilly, and there throw myself into the gay life of the gambling set until I 15 really feel that I *am* Paul De Lacroix, or Ed Whelan, or whatever my hero's name is. Of course this runs into money, and I am quite likely to have to change my ideas about my hero entirely and make him a bum on a tramp steamer working his way back to America, or

From *The Benchley Roundup* selected by Nathaniel Benchley. Copyright 1932 by Robert Benchley. Reprinted by permission of Harper & Row, Publishers.

20 a young college boy out of funds who lives by his wits until his friends at home send him a hundred and ten dollars.

[3] One of my heroes (Dick Markwell in "Love's How-do-you-do"), after starting out as a man-about-town in New York who "never showed his liquor" and was "an apparently indestructible ma-
25 chine devoted to pleasure," had to be changed into a patient in the Trembly Ward of a local institution, whose old friends didn't recognize him and furthermore didn't want to.

[4] But, as you doubtless remember, it was a corking yarn.

[5] This actually living the lives of my characters takes up quite a
30 lot of time and makes it a little difficult to write anything. It was not until I decided to tell stories about old men who just sit in their rooms and shell walnuts that I ever got around to doing any work. It doesn't make for very interesting novels, but at any rate the word-age is there and there is something to show the publishers for their
35 advance royalties. (Publishers are crotchety that way. They want copy, copy, copy all the time, just because they happen to have advanced a measly three hundred dollars a couple of years before. You would think that printing words on paper was their business.)

[6] And now you ask me how I do my work, how my inspiration
40 comes? I will tell you, Little Father. Draw up your chair and let me put my feet on it. Ah, that's better! Now you may go out and play!

[7] Very often I must wait weeks and weeks for what you call "inspiration." In the meantime I must sit with my quill pen poised in air over a sheet of foolscap, in case the divine spark should come like
45 a lightning bolt and knock me off my chair on to my head. (This has happened more than once.) While I am waiting I mull over in my mind what I am going to do with my characters.

[8] Shall I have Mildred marry Lester, or shall Lester marry Evelyn? ("Who is Evelyn?" I often say to myself, never having heard
50 of her before.) Should the French proletariat win the Revolution, or should Louis XVI come back suddenly and establish a Coalition Cabinet? Can I afford to let Etta clean up those dishes in the sink and get them biscuits baked, or would it be better to keep her there for another year, standing first on one foot and then on the other?

55 [9] You have no idea how many problems an author has to face during those feverish days when he is building a novel, and you have no idea how he solves them. Neither has he.

[10] Sometimes, while in the throes of creative work, I get out of bed in the morning, look at my writing desk piled high with old bills,
60 odd gloves, and empty ginger-ale bottles, and go right back to bed

again. The next thing I know it is night once more, and time for the Sand Man to come around. (We have a Sand Man who comes twice a day, which makes it very convenient. We give him five dollars at Christmas.)

[11] Even if I do get up and put on a part of my clothes—I do all my work in a Hawaiian straw skirt and a bow tie of some neutral shade—I often can think of nothing to do but pile the books which are on one end of my desk very neatly on the other end and then kick them one by one off on to the floor with my free foot.

[12] But all the while my brain is work, work, working, and my plot is taking shape. Sometimes it is the shape of a honeydew melon and sometimes a shape which I have never been quite able to figure out. It is a sort of amorphous thing with two heads but no face. When this shape presents itself, I get right back in bed again. I'm no fool.

[13] I find that, while working, a pipe is a great source of inspiration. A pipe can be placed diagonally across the keys of a typewriter so that they will not function, or it can be made to give out such a cloud of smoke that I cannot see the paper. Then, there is the process of lighting it. I can make lighting a pipe a ritual which has not been equaled for elaborateness since the five-day festival to the God of the Harvest. (See my book on Rituals: the Man.)

[14] In the first place, owing to twenty-six years of constant smoking without once calling in a plumber, the space left for tobacco in the bowl of my pipe is now the size of a medium body-pore. Once the match has been applied to the tobacco therein, the smoke is over. This necessitates refilling, relighting, and reknocking. The knocking out of a pipe can be made almost as important as the smoking of it, especially if there are nervous people in the room. A good, smart knock of a pipe against a tin wastebasket and you will have a neurasthenic out of his chair and into the window sash in no time.

[15] The matches, too, have their place in the construction of modern literature. With a pipe like mine, the supply of burnt matches in one day could be floated down the St. Lawrence River with two men jumping them. . . .

[16] When the novel is finished, it is shipped to the Cutting and Binding Room, where native girls roll it into large sheets and stamp on it with their bare feet. This accounts for the funny look of some of my novels. It is then taken back to the Drying Room, where it is rewritten by a boy whom I engage for the purpose, and sent to the publishers. It is then sent back to me.

[17] And so you see now how we creative artists work. It really

isn't like any other kind of work, for it must come from a great emotional upheaval in the soul of the writer himself; and if that emotional upheaval is not present, it must come from the works of any other
105 writers which happen to be handy and easily imitated.

There is nothing intrinsically good or bad about sentences of any particular length. Indeed, there are few rules about sentence length that stand up under scrutiny. The most valid rule seems to be "It depends. . . ." It depends on what you have to say; it depends on the purpose for which you are writing; it depends on your audience. The same writer may employ a preponderance of short sentences in one situation and of long ones in another. For example, no sentence in Faulkner's speech of acceptance of the Nobel Prize for Literature runs to more than about sixty-five words, whereas in many of Faulkner's novels occasional sentences run to well over two hundred words. Granted, these are extreme examples. And granted, too, that no piece of writing would be effective with all short or all long sentences. There must be some variety. But this does not mean padding or chopping apart thoughts that belong together. Nor does it follow that simple sentences are always short; and compound, complex, or compound-complex sentences always long. "I came, I saw, I conquered" contains three independent clauses, yet there are few shorter announcements in history.

What *can* be said is that sentences should not be pointlessly or needlessly long or short. There is obviously no point in "The red-headed man driving the old green Ford truck, battered from many trips and many accidents at home or on highways from one coast to another and up and down the seaboard from Canada to Mexico, grasped the broken steering wheel tightly in both his work-roughened but still youthful-looking hands and squinted into the lights of the oncoming car." Or in "The man had red hair. He was driving a Ford truck. It was old and green. It was battered from many trips. It had also been in many accidents. Some of these accidents took place at home. Others occurred on highways. The truck had been across the country many times. It had gone from Canada to Mexico, ..."

Appropriateness, then, is the best rule of thumb for sentence length— appropriateness to meaning, purpose, and audience. Some variety of course, is desirable.

1. Though one of Benchley's purposes in "How I Create" was to be amusing, he had also a serious purpose. What was it? How do you know? For what kind of audience do you suppose he was writing? On what evidence do you base your answer?

2. Compare the length and structure of the sentences in paragraph 1 with the length and structure of the sentences in paragraphs 5 and 12. What similarities and differences do you find? In terms of Benchley's purposes and tone, how do you account for what you find? Answer in detail.

3. Why did Benchley not make part of paragraph 3 the one short sentence of which paragraph 4 consists?

4. Precisely what effect does Benchley achieve by piling up the short sentences in paragraph 6?

5. What means does Benchley use to achieve variety in the structure of paragraph 8?

6. How can you justify the brevity of paragraph 9? What is gained by the juxtaposition of the long and the short sentence in this paragraph?

7. What effects are achieved through the variety in sentence length in paragraph 16?

8. Find a paragraph in the Benchley selection (other than those to which your attention has been directed by the questions above) in which you think variety in sentence length is particularly effective. To validate your judgment, rewrite the paragraph to alter sentence length and then show the superiority of Benchley's paragraph over your own.

Alternate selections for the study of Length: Harold Ross, "*The New Yorker* Prospectus"; Saul Bellow, "Cloister Culture."

Assignment: Bring to class the lead editorials from at least three of the following:

a. your college newspaper
b. a small local newspaper
c. a large metropolitan newspaper
d. a weekly news magazine
e. a weekly popular magazine
f. a monthly magazine

Study the length of sentences in each of the editorials and be prepared to comment in class on the relationships you find between sentence length and content, reading audience, point of view, tone, and over-all effectiveness.

or

Write separate sets of directions for reaching your home from the center of the nearest town or city for each of the following:

a. a kindergarten class
b. your grandfather, who lived in that town as a child and hasn't been back since
c. a travel folder
d. a sociologist on a field trip

Remember that your sentence lengths will vary from one set of directions to another as your audience and tone vary.

Parallelism

✐ The London Theatres

HENRY JAMES

[1] A person taking up his residence in a foreign city is apt, I think, to become something of a play-goer. In the first place he is usually more or less isolated, and in the absence of complex social ties the theatres help him to pass his evenings. But more than this, they offer him a good deal of interesting evidence upon the manners 5 and customs of the people among whom he has come to dwell. They testify to the civilization around him, and throw a great deal of light upon the ways of thinking, feeling, and behaving of the community. If this exotic spectator to whom I allude is a person of a really attentive observation, he may extract such evidence in very large quanti- 10 ties. It is furnished not by the stage alone, but by the *theatre* in a larger sense of the word: by the audience, the attendants, the arrangements, the very process of getting to the playhouse. The English stage of to-day, of which I more particularly speak, certainly holds the mirror as little as possible up to nature—to any nature, at least, 15 usually recognized in the British islands. Nine-tenths of the plays performed upon it are French originals, subjected to the mysterious process of "adaptation"; marred as French pieces and certainly not

mended as English; transplanted from the Gallic soil into a chill and
20 neutral region where they bloom hardly longer than a handful of cut
flowers stuck into moist sand. They cease to have any representative
value as regards French manners, and they acquire none as regards
English; they belong to an order of things which has not even the
merit of being "conventional" but in which barbarism, chaos, and
25 crudity hold undisputed sway. The English drama of the last century
deserved the praise, in default of any higher, of being "conventional";
for there was at least a certain method in its madness; it had its own
ideal, its own foolish logic and consistency. But he would be wise who
should be able to indicate the ideal, artistic and intellectual, of the
30 English drama of today. It is violently and hopelessly irresponsible.
When one says "English drama" one uses the term for convenience'
sake; one means simply the plays that are acted at the London
theatres and transferred thence to the American. They are neither
English nor a drama; they have not that minimum of ponderable
35 identity at which appreciation finds a starting-point. As the meta-
physicians say, they are simply not cognizable. And yet in spite of
all this, the writer of these lines has ventured to believe that the
London theatres are highly characteristic of English civilization. The
plays testify indirectly if not directly to the national manners, and
40 the whole system on which play-going is conducted completes the
impression which the pieces make upon the observer. One can imagine, indeed, nothing more characteristic than such a fact as that
a theatre-going people is hopelessly destitute of a drama.

[2] I ventured a month ago to record in these pages a few remi-
45 niscences of the Comédie Française; and I have a sort of feeling that
my readers may, in the light of my present undertaking, feel prompted
to accuse me of a certain levity. There is a want of delicacy, they may
say, in speaking of the first theatre in the world one day and of the
London stage the next. You must choose, and if you talk about one,
50 you forfeit the right to talk about the other. But I think there is something to be done in the way of talking about both, and at all events
there are few things it is not fair to talk about if one does so with a
serious desire to understand. Removing lately from Paris to the British metropolis, I received a great many impressions—a sort of un-
55 broken chain, in which the reflections passing through my fancy as I
tried the different orchestra-stalls were the concluding link. The
impressions of which I speak were impressions of outside things—the
thing with which in a great city one comes first into contact. I supposed that I had gathered them once for all in earlier years; but I

found that the edge of one's observation, unlike that of other tren- 60
chant instruments, grows again if one leaves it alone. Remain a long
time in any country, and you come to accept the manners and customs of that country as the standard of civilization—the normal type.
Other manners and customs, even if they spring from the same soil
from which you yourself have sprung, acquire by contrast an unrea- 65
sonable, a violent, but often a picturesque relief. To what one may
call a continentalized vision the aspect of English life seems strange
and entertaining; while an Anglicized perception finds, beyond the
narrow channel, even greater matter for wonderment.

[3] The writer of these lines brought with him, at the outset of a 70
dusky London winter, a continentalized, and perhaps more particularly a Parisianized, fancy. It was wonderful how many things that
I should have supposed familiar and commonplace seemed strikingly
salient and typical, and how I found, if not sermons in stones and
good in everything, at least examples in porter-pots and reflections in 75
coal-scuttles. In writing the other day of the Théâtre Français, I spoke
of M. Francisque Sarcey, the esteemed dramatic critic; of the serious
and deliberate way in which he goes to work—of the distance from
which he makes his approaches. During the first weeks I was in
London, especially when I had been to the play the night before, I 80
kept saying to myself that M. Francisque Sarcey ought to come over
and "do" the English theatres. There are of course excellent reasons
why he should not. In the first place, it is safe to assume that he
comprehends not a word of English; and in the second, it is obliga-
tory to believe that he would, in the vulgar phrase, not be able to 85
"stand" it. He would probably pronounce the English stage hopelessly and unmitigably bad and beneath criticism, and hasten back to
Delaunay and Sarah Bernhardt. But if we could suppose him to fight
it out, and give the case a hearing, what a solid dissertation we
should have upon it afterward at the bottom of the *Temps* news- 90
paper! How he would go into the causes of the badness, and trace
its connections with English civilization! How earnestly he would
expatiate and how minutely he would explain; how fervently he would
point the moral and entreat his fellow countrymen not to be as the
English are lest they should lapse into histrionic barbarism! 95

[4] I felt, to myself, during these days, in a small way, very much
like a Francisque Sarcey; I don't mean as to the gloominess of my
conclusions, but as to the diffusiveness of my method. A spectator
with his senses attuned to all those easy Parisian harmonies feels himself, in London, to be in a place in which the drama cannot, in the 100

nature of things, have a vigorous life. Before he has put his feet into
a theatre he is willing to bet his little all that the stage will turn out
to be weak. If he is challenged for the reasons of this precipitate
scepticism, he will perhaps be at a loss to give them; he will only
105 say, "Oh, I don't know, *cela se sent.* Everything I see is a reason. I
don't look out of the window, I don't ring the bell for some coals,
I don't go into an eating-house to dine, without seeing a reason."
And then he will begin to talk about the duskiness and oppressiveness
of London; about the ugliness of everything that one sees; about
110 beauty and grace being never attempted, or attempted here and there
only to be woefully missed; about the visible, palpable Protestantism;
about the want of expression in people's faces; about the plainness
and dreariness of everything that is public and the inaccessibility of
everything that is private; about the lower orders being too miserable
115 to know the theatre, and the upper classes too "respectable" to understand it.

[5] And here, if the audacious person we are conceiving is very
far gone, he will probably begin to talk about English "hypocrisy"
and prudery, and to say that these are the great reasons of the feeble-
120 ness of the stage. When he approaches the question of English
"hypocrisy" you may know that he is hopelessly Gallicized, or Ro-
manized, or Germanized, or something of that sort; and indeed his
state of mind at this point strikes me myself with a certain awe. I
don't venture to follow him, and I discreetly give up the attempt. But
125 up to this point I can see what he may have meant, in the midst of
his flippancy, and I remember how to my own imagination at first
everything seemed to hang together, and theatres to be what they
were because somehow the streets, and slopes, and hotels, and eating-
houses were what they were. I remember something I said to myself
130 after once witnessing a little drama of real life at a restaurant. The
restaurant in question is in Piccadilly, and I am trying to think under
which of the categories of our Gallicized observer it would come. The
remarkable façade, covered with gilded mosaics and lamps, is certainly a concession to the idea of beauty; though whether it is a
135 successful one is another question. Within it has, besides various
other resources, one of those peculiar refectories which are known in
England as grill-rooms, and which possess the picturesque feature of
a colossal gridiron, astride of a corresponding fire, on which your
chops and steaks are toasted before your eyes. A grill-room is a bad
140 place to dine, but it is a convenient place to lunch. It always contains

a number of tables, which accommodate not less than half-a-dozen persons; small tables of the proper dimensions for a *tête-à-tête* being, for inscrutable reasons, wholly absent from English eating-houses.

[6] The grill-room in question is decorated in that style of which the animus is to be agreeable to Mr. William Morris, though I suspect that in the present application of his charming principles he would find a good deal of base alloy. At any rate, the apartment contains a number of large medallions in blue pottery, pieced together, representing the heathen gods and goddesses, whose names are inscribed in crooked letters in an unexpected part of the picture. This is quite the thing that one would expect to find in one of those cloisters or pleasances, or "pleached gardens," in which Mr. Morris's Gothic heroines drag their embroidered petticoats up and down, as slow-pacedly as their poet sings. Only, in these pretty, dilettantish cloisters there would probably be no large tickets suspended alongside of the pictorial pottery, inscribed with the monstrous words, *Tripe! Suppers!* This is one of those queer eruptions of plainness and homeliness which one encounters at every turn in the midst of the massive luxury and general expensiveness of England—like the big, staring announcement, *Beds,* in the coffee-house windows, or *Well-aired Beds* painted on the side walls of taverns; or like a list of labels which I noticed the other day on a series of japanned boxes in a pastry-cook's shop. They seemed to me so characteristic that I made a note of them.

[7] The reason of my being in the pastry-cook's shop was my having contracted in Paris the harmless habit of resorting to one of these establishments at the luncheon hour, for the purpose of consuming a little *gateau.* Resuming this innocent practice on English soil, I found it attended with serious difficulties—the chief of which was that there were no *gateaux* to consume. An appreciative memory of those brightly mirrored little shops on the Paris boulevards, in which tender little tarts, in bewildering variety, are dispensed to you by a neat-waisted *patissière,* cast a dusky shadow over the big buns and "digestive biscuits" which adorn the counter of an English bakery. But it takes a good while to eat a bun, and while you stand there solemnly disintegrating your own, you may look about you in search of the characteristic. In Paris the pastry-cooks' shops are, as the French say, coquettish—as coquettish as the elegant simplicity of plate glass, discreet gilding, polished brass, and a demonstrative *dame de comptoir* can make them. In London they are not coquettish —witness the grim nomenclature alluded to above; it was distributed

over a series of green tin cases, ranged behind the counters: Tops
and bottoms—royal digestives—arrow-root—oat-cake—rice biscuit
—ratafias.

[8] I took my seat in the grill-room at a table at which three
185 gentlemen were sitting: two of them sleek British merchants, of a
familiar and highly respectable type, the other a merchant too presumably, but neither sleek nor British. He was evidently an American.
He was a good-looking fellow and a man of business, but I inferred
from the tentative, experimental, and even mistrustful manner with
190 which he addressed himself to the operation of lunching, and observed the idiosyncrasies of the grill-room, that he found himself for
the first time in England. His experiment, however, if experiment it
was, was highly successful; he made a copious lunch and departed.
He had not had time to reach the door when I perceived one of the
195 British merchants of whom I just now spoke beginning to knock the
table violently with his knife-handle, and to clamour, "Waiter, waiter!
Manager, manager!" The manager and the waiter hastened to respond, while I endeavoured to guess the motive of his agitation,
without connecting it with our late companion. As I then saw him
200 pointing eagerly to the latter, however, who was just getting out of
the door, I was seized with a mortifying apprehension that my innocent compatriot was a dissembler and a pickpocket, and that the
English gentleman, next whom he had been sitting, had missed his
watch or his purse. "He has taken one of these—one of these!" said
205 the British merchant. "I saw him put it into his pocket." And he held
up a bill of fare of the establishment, a printed card, bearing on its
back a coloured lithograph of the emblazoned façade that I have
mentioned. I was reassured; the poor American had pocketed this
light document with the innocent design of illustrating his day's ad-
210 ventures to a sympathetic wife awaiting his return in some musty
London lodging. But the manager and the waiter seemed to think
the case grave, and their informant continued to impress upon them
that he had caught the retiring visitor in the very act. They were at a
loss to decide upon a course of action; they thought the case was
215 bad, but they questioned whether it was bad enough to warrant them
in pursuing the criminal. While this weighty point was being discussed
the criminal escaped, little suspecting, I imagine, the perturbation
he had caused. But the British merchant continued to argue, speaking
in the name of outraged morality. "You know he oughtn't to have
220 done that—it was very wrong in him to do it. That mustn't be done,
you know, and you know I ought to tell you—it was my duty to tell

you—I couldn't *but* tell you. He oughtn't to have done it, you know. I thought I *must* tell you." It is not easy to point out definitely the connection between this little episode, for the triviality of which I apologize, and the present condition of the English stage; but—it ₂₂₅ may have been whimsical—I thought I perceived a connection. These people are too highly moral to be histrionic, I said; they have too stern a sense of duty.

One of the devices or variations which may be employed in constructing the sentence is parallelism. Since sentences are composed of various units—the word, the phrase, the clause—these units may be repeated much as a pattern is repeated in a fabric or a design repeated in the façade of a building. Coordinate units of thought, equal in importance and hence in weight, are expressed in parallel constructions.

These parallel constructions are alike in grammatical structure or syntax; they serve the same grammatical function in the sentence. They may be words (He was tall, dark, and handsome); phrases ("that government of the people, by the people, and for the people . . ."); adjective clauses ("Oh how great is thy goodness, which thou hast laid up for them that fear thee; which thou has wrought for them that trust in thee before the sons of men!"—*Psalms* 31:19); or adverbial clauses ("Hear the voice of my supplications, when I cry unto thee, when I lift up my hands toward thy holy oracle."—*Psalms* 28:2). Each of the parallel grammatical units derives from or modifies or is dependent in some way upon one element within the sentence. The words "tall," "dark," "handsome" all modify "He"; "of the people," "by the people," "for the people" all modify "government"; the clauses "which thou hast laid up for them that fear thee" and "which thou has wrought for them that trust in thee" modify "goodness"; "when I cry unto thee" and "when I lift up my hands toward thy holy oracle" modify "Hear."

The meaning of parallel structure is frequently extended to include similarly constructed independent clauses (The man walked slowly down the road; the dog limped along at his side) and even sentences (An auto, which travels on the ground, can create an illusion of speed. An airplane, which speeds through the air, can suggest utter motionlessness).

No device should ever be used solely as an end in itself, though in itself it may be pleasing. Parallelism is certainly pleasing: discovery of pattern and rediscovery of the familiar have delighted our senses since we learned "Pat-a-cake." But parallelism, like any other device, must also be, and it is, functional. It helps to delineate fine points of meaning; thus it is a device of coherence. It enables the reader to anticipate and then to follow the sense of the sentence; hence it is an aid to clarity. Just because it is patterned, it contributes to the cadences or rhythm of the sentence. And it is a device for avoiding wordiness. Compare, for example, these two units for succinctness:

a. The family huddled around the fireplace because it was the only warm place in the house. It was light there, too. Also, they were able to enjoy each other's company that way.
b. The family huddled around the fireplace for warmth, light, and companionship.

1. Henry James uses parallelism in paragraph 1 of "The London Theatres" to clarify his use of the word "theatre." In precisely what way or ways does parallelism perform this function?

2. James speaks, in paragraph 2, of his "impressions of outside things" on his "removal" from Paris to London. Point out at least three examples, throughout the selection, of the use of parallelism to convey to the reader these "impressions." For each example you select, explain what emotional as well as sensory "impression" is conveyed.

3. Explain how parallelism is used for humor in paragraph 3.

4. In paragraph 4, how does parallelism help James to characterize the Frenchman? to describe London and a certain attitude toward it? What is that attitude? By what method is paragraph 4 developed? How is parallelism helpful to that method of paragraph development?

5. Parallelism is useful, as we have seen, for humor. It may be employed to convey contrast; it is valuable for preciseness and compression. Describe its use to all four of these ends in paragraph 6.

6. Parallelism may be effectively used to develop examples or illustrations of a point, the piling up of detail. Show where and how this is done in paragraph 7. Is the device used for any other purpose in this paragraph? Explain.

7. Characterization, climax—the ascending order which distinguishes among similar objects or ideas—and contrast all appear in paragraph 8. Show how James uses parallelism to achieve all three.

8. In which paragraphs do you find the most parallelism? How do you account for your answer in terms of the topic sentences, implied or stated, of these paragraphs?

9. What is the guiding purpose of the selection? What is its overall method of organization? Explain your answer, being as specific as you can. Why is that method appropriate to the guiding purpose? In what way or ways do your answers to these questions account for the frequency with which James employs parallelism?

Alternate selection for the study of Parallelism: Rainer Maria Rilke, "The Raw Material of Poetry."

Theme Assignment:　　　Through his characterization of the British and American merchants in the grill-room, James manages to chide both the native Britishers and the souvenir-collecting traveler. Perhaps at no time are we more aware of ourselves as belonging to a particular locale than when we leave it. At home, we take certain, at least, of our habits for granted; away from home, we are suddenly made aware that we are "different" (though we are much more likely to think that the people we are visiting are the ones who are "different"). For example, away from our own part of the country we are suddenly aware of differences of speech, dress, attitudes of storekeepers, pace at which services are performed, and the like.

Recall some occasion in your own life when you were away from home (it need have been no farther than the next block where you spent a week-end with a friend). Write a theme in which you give an account of this event, or highlight it in some way by describing something which you saw, something which points up the "difference" you felt between the familiar and the unfamiliar. Be sure to avail yourself of the services of parallelism.

Balance

From *Of Studies*

SIR FRANCIS BACON

Studies serve for delight, for ornament, and for ability. Their chief use for delight is in privateness and retiring; for ornament, is in discourse; and for ability, is in the judgment and disposition of business. For expert men can execute and perhaps judge of particulars, one by one; but the general counsels, and the plots and marshaling of affairs, come best from those that are learned. To spend too much time in studies is sloth; to use them too much for ornament is affectation; to make judgment wholly by their rules is the humor of a scholar. They perfect nature, and are perfected by experience; for natural abilities are like natural plants, that need proyning by study; and studies themselves do give forth directions too much at large, except they be bounded in by experience. Crafty men contemn studies; simple men admire them; and wise men use them: for they teach not their own use; but that is a wisdom without them and above them, won by observation. Read not to contradict and confute; nor to believe and take for granted; nor to find talk and discourse; but to weigh and consider. Some books are to be tasted, others to be swallowed, and some few to be chewed and digested: that is, some books are to be read only in parts; others to be read, but not curiously; and some few to be read wholly, and with diligence and attention. Some books also may be read by deputy, and extracts made of them by others;

but that would be only in the less important arguments, and the meaner sort of books; else distilled books are like common distilled waters, flashy things. Reading maketh a full man; conference a ready man; and writing an exact man. And therefore, if a man write little, he had need have a great memory; if he confer little, he had need have a present wit; and if he read little, he had need have much cunning, to seem to know that he doth not. Histories make men wise; poets witty; the mathematics subtile; natural philosophy deep; moral grave; logic and rhetoric able to contend. *Abeunt studia in mores.* Nay, there is no stond or impediment in the wit, but may be wrought out by fit studies, like as diseases of the body may have appropriate exercises. Bowling is good for the stone and reins; shooting for the lungs and breast; gentle walking for the stomach; riding for the head; and the like. So if a man's wit be wandering, let him study the mathematics; for a demonstration, if his wit be called away never so little, he must begin again: if his wit be not apt to distinguish or find differences, let him study the schoolmen; for they are *cymini sectores:* if he be not apt to beat over matters, and to call one thing to prove and illustrate another, let him study the lawyers' cases: so every defect of the mind may have a special receipt.

One of the dictionary definitions of balance is "harmonious arrangement or adjustment, especially in the arts of design." The most elemental concept of balance is based on an equal distribution of weight or color or mass: in a well-decorated room, chairs and couches are arranged so that the weightier and larger pieces are distributed fairly equally through the room. An extremely large or heavy piece of furniture is balanced by several smaller pieces across the room. In automobiles, the longer hoods made necessary by large engines are balanced by large rear fins. Balance plays a part, then, not only in the arts (in symphonic music, the balance maintained among the various sections of the orchestra is partly responsible for the listener's pleasure; in sculpture and painting, much of the esthetic pleasure is derived from the subtle balancing of part against part) but also in many of the facets of everyday life—from a balanced diet to a balanced checkbook.

Balance is no less important in English prose—particularly in sentences. It is achieved essentially by constructing a sentence so that two or more of its parts are grammatically equivalent or coordinate: two independent clauses of approximately the same length and structure connected by a semicolon or a coordinating conjunction make a balanced sentence:

The students protested vigorously, but the faculty seemed unconcerned.

Similarly, balance can be achieved by playing one subordinate clause off against another:

The man who takes seriously his responsibilities as a voter is the citizen who helps most to make democracy work.

Words, phrases, and even sentences can be made parts of a balanced structure. Parallelism is, of course, a major means of achieving balance.

Though balanced structure is being presented here as an asset to the writer, it should not be used too frequently; overuse of balanced structure results in stilted, pompous, artificial writing. When content demands its use, it should be used, but not otherwise. The crispness and fluidity of modern prose compared with the heaviness and formality of earlier English prose stem in part from limiting the use of balanced sentence structure. Balanced structure is rather like food: enough of it, when needed, is good; too much of it is unpleasant.

1. What is the guiding purpose of the Bacon selection? Does your wording of the guiding purpose suggest that a number of balanced sentences would be appropriate? If not, reword your formulation so that it does.

2. How many balanced sentences do you find in the selection? Analyze each to show the sentence elements that are in balance and to show where parallelism is used to achieve balance. Has Bacon overdone the use of balance in the selection? If you think so, rewrite one or more of the sentences—effectively—to reduce the amount of balance in the paragraph.

3. In the context of the essay, which sentence in each of the following pairs is more effective? Justify your answer.

a. (1) "To spend too much time in studies is sloth; to use them too much for ornament is affectation; to make judgment wholly by their rules is the humor of a scholar."

(2) It is sheer laziness to spend too much time in studies. Although using them as a means of showing off is nothing but affectation, only the scholar is guided wholly by book-learning.

b. (1) "Some books are to be tasted, others to be swallowed, and some few to be chewed and digested; that is, some books are to be read only in parts; others to be read, but not curiously; and some few to be read wholly, and with diligence and attention."

(2) We read different books differently—that is, in different amounts and with differing care.

c. (1) "Read not to contradict and confute; nor to believe and take for granted; nor to find talk and discourse; but to weigh and consider."

(2) Read not to contradict, believe, nor find talk; but to consider.

4. Taking into account not only the balanced sentence but sentence rhythms and variety of structure as well, characterize Bacon's prose style in some detail.

5. Select one balanced sentence in the paragraph and show how Bacon achieves variety within it.

Alternate selections for the study of Balance: Catherine Drinker Bowen, "Harold Ober: Literary Agent"; Moses Hadas, "Climates of Criticism."

Assignment: Find at least five examples of balanced sentences in your current reading in newspapers and periodicals. Copy or cut out and bring to class the paragraph in which each sentence appears, and be prepared to comment on the effectiveness (or lack of it) achieved through the balance.

Subordination

Notre-Dame de Chartres

WALTER PATER

[1] Like a ship forever asail in the distance, thought the child, everywhere the great church of Chartres was visible, with the passing light or shadow upon its grey, weather-beaten surfaces. The people of La Beauce were proud, and would talk often of its rich store of
5 sacred furniture. The busy fancy of Gaston, multiplying this chance hearsay, had set the whole interior in array—a dim, spacious, fragrant place, afloat with golden lights. Lit up over the autumn fields at evening, the distant spires suggested the splendour within, with so strong an imaginative effect, that he seemed scarcely to know whether
10 it was through the mental or bodily eye that he beheld. When he came thither at last, like many another well-born youth, to join the episcopal household as a kind of half-clerical page, he found (as happens in the actual testing of our ideals) at once more and less than he had supposed; and his earlier vision was a thing he could
15 never precisely recover, or disentangle from the supervening reality. What he *saw,* certainly, was greater far in mere physical proportion, and incommensurable at first by anything he knew,—the volume of the wrought detail, the mass of the component members, the bigness of the actual stones of the masonry, contrary to the usual Gothic
20 manner, and as if in reminiscence of those old Druidic piles amid which the Virgin of Chartres had been adored, long before the birth of Christ, by a mystic race, possessed of some prophetic sense of the

grace in store for her. Through repeated dangers good fortune has saved that unrivalled treasure of stained glass; and then, as now, the word "awful," so often applied to Gothic aisles, was for once really 25 applicable. You enter, looking perhaps for a few minutes' cool shelter from the summer noonday; and the placid sunshine of La Beauce seems to have been transformed in a moment into imperious, angry fire.

[2] It was not in summer, however, that Gaston first set foot there; 30 he saw the beautiful city for the first time as if sheathed austerely in repellent armour. In his most genial subsequent impressions of the place, there was always a lingering trace of that famous frost through which he made his way, wary of petrifying contact against things without, to the great western portal, on Candelmas morning. The 35 sad, patient images by the doorways of the crowded church seemed suffering now chiefly from the cold. It was almost like a funeral—the penitential violet, the wandering taperlight of this half-lenten feast of Purification. His new companions, at the head and in the rear of the long procession, forced every one, even the Lord Bishop himself, to 40 move apace, bustling along, crossbearer and acolyte, in their odd little copes, out of the bitter air, which made the jolly life Gaston now entered on, around the great fire of their hall in the episcopal palace, seem all the more winsome.

[3] Notre-Dame de Chartres! It was a world to explore, as if one 45 explored the entire Middle Age; it was also one unending, elaborate, religious function—a life, or a continuous drama, to take one's part in. Dependent on its structural completeness, on its wealth of well-preserved ornament, on its unity in variety, perhaps on some undefinable operation of genius, beyond, but concurrently with, all 50 these, the church of Chartres has still the gift of a unique power of impressing. In comparison, the other famous churches of France, at Amiens for instance, at Rheims or Beauvais, may seem but formal, and to a large extent reproducible, effects of mere architectural rule on a gigantic scale. 55

[For treatment of this selection, see pp. 302–303.]

✐From *The Ivory Tower*

E. M. FORSTER

[1] The phrase "The Ivory Tower" was first used, in the literary sense, by Sainte-Beuve, when he was examining the work of his friend and contemporary Alfred de Vigny. De Vigny had led an active life, but he was aloof and fastidious, rather disdainful, prone to mysticism,
5 and when he took to writing he tended to withdraw from the hurry, noisiness, muddle, and littleness of the world, and contemplate action from the heights like a god, or from within a fortress where he remained unscathed. To hit off this tendency, Sainte-Beuve borrowed from religion the phrase *la tour d'ivoire,* the tower where the poet
10 retreats *avant midi,* before the heat and the weariness of the battle have developed. The phrase had been used for centuries as a symbol of the Virgin Mary, and it occurs in the Song of Solomon, but Sainte-Beuve first applied it to literature.

[2] It has come in again lately in a derogatory sense as a synonym
15 for "escapism." "Escapism," like most words ending in -*ism,* is abusive, and prejudges the issue it professes to. define. There is much to be said for escaping from the world, when it is the world of 1938, so that, if we are to discuss the problem dispassionately, "The Ivory Tower" in Sainte-Beuve's sense seems the better title. It is noncom-
20 mittal. Is there such a thing as an Ivory Tower? And if there is, shall we fortify it and make it stronger, or shall we try to pull it down? To put the problem in other words: Can books be an escape from life, and if they can be, ought they to be? Do writers (all or some) escape from life when they write? Do readers (all or some) escape when
25 they read? And when we speak of "life" here, what meaning do we attach to that much belabored word? The subject strays into philosophy and politics, but its main line is literary: the proper function of books.

[3] Let us start with a generalization upon human nature.

30 [4] Man is an animal, but a queer one. He possesses the herd

From *The Atlantic Monthly,* January 1939. Reprinted by permission of The Atlantic Monthly.

instinct, so that he readily forms tribes, gangs, nations. But, unlike other gregarious animals, he has the instinct for solitude as well. Consequently he is always contradicting himself in his conduct and getting into muddles—one of which we are examining now. He wants to be alone even when he is feeling fit. That is one of the differences be- 35 tween a man and a chicken. A chicken wants to be alone only when it is feeling poorly. When a hen withdraws herself from her female companions and even from her gentleman friend and walks about in solitude with a glassy eye, making sad little noises, you know she is probably ill. The other hens think so too, and give her a peck in 40 passing, to show how different they are feeling themselves.

[5] But a man who goes about alone is probably not ill, but trying to enter his Ivory Tower. He needs the Ivory Tower just as much as he needs the human chicken-run, the city. Both are part of his heritage—solitude and multitude. He is the gregarious animal who wants 45 to be alone even when he feels well, and his glassy eye and sad little noises are often symptoms of something important. He may be getting a clearer view of the world, or thinking out a social problem, or developing his spirit, or creating a poem. He may be bored with the life around him, which is regrettable, and, worse still, he may be afraid 50 of it. But, whatever his motive, he has an incurable desire to be alone. The instinct may not be as old as his gregarious instinct, but it goes back to the beginning of civilization, and has a particular bearing on the development of literature, philosophy, and art. As far back as history stretches, we can see men trying to retire into their 55 Ivory Towers and there to resist or to modify the instincts which they possess as members of the herd.

[6] If we look back nearly two thousand years, at the country which was recently Czechoslovakia, we shall see there a general conducting military operations. The general is thoroughly competent, but 60 when he has a spare moment he takes out his pen and begins to write philosophy. His name is Marcus Aurelius. He had, and knew he had, an Ivory Tower. It was to him the more important side of his heritage; the public side, when he worked with the herd and was regarded as their emperor, meant nothing to him. 65

[7] If we look back four hundred years we can see a tough, unscrupulous politician, who loves bits of Italy, his country, and is merciless in his methods of serving them. He is also a practical farmer, who runs his own estate, so when the evening comes he is covered in mud in both senses of the word. Then he washes himself, 70 puts on a nice suit of clothes, has candles of the best-quality wax lit

in fine candlesticks of silver, and sits down to read about the heroes and the virtues of antiquity. His name is Machiavelli. Machiavelli too had an Ivory Tower, though it was to him the less important side of
75 his heritage: he needed to retire into it after getting the better of his fellow men.

[8] A third example. Sixty years ago there lived a great revolutionary, who did more than anyone else to put his fellow men against the existing structure of society. All his life was devoted to this—he
80 worked for the herd and through the herd. And yet he could not stop himself from occasionally writing a poem, a lyric poem. He had no illusions about the merits of his poems, yet he says: "The best of them made me see what Poetry is—an unattainable fairy palace, at the sight of which my own creations fell to dust." The name of this
85 yearning writer is Karl Marx. To Marx the Ivory Tower was not at all important, and he will be surprised at being assigned one. He would dismiss it as a regrettable bourgeois weakness, and his followers have developed some important arguments against it. But he illustrates my point—that it is part of the human heritage, that it pops
90 up in the most unlikely landscapes, and that to deny its existence is false psychology.

[9] A fourth example is Milton. Milton understands our problem, and his life illustrates it perfectly. He began in seclusion: he was a scholar and a Cambridge intellectual who knew himself to be a poet,
95 and deliberately planned his aesthetic career. *Il Penseroso* is a manifesto of that early faith; it invokes the delightful sadness which exists in the globe of its own shade, and is untainted either by regrets or by fears, and it looks forward—at the age of twenty-five—to an old age which will attain "to something like prophetic strain." Wisdom is to
100 come to the poet through seclusion, and in the Ivory Tower itself:—

> Or let my lamp, at midnight hour,
> Be seen in some high lonely tower,
> Where I may oft outwatch the Bear,
> With thrice great Hermes, or unsphere
> The spirit of Plato . . .

There young John is to be happy and wise, and his descents into human activity, when he makes them, are no more than visits to a country dance; the muddles and the cruelties of daily life never entangle him, nor its poverty, nor disease.

> These pleasures, Melancholy, give,
> And I with thee will choose to live.

[10] That is the Milton of the first period, and then—while he is finishing off his education in Italy (a necessary step, for *Il Penseroso* is bad Italian)—the civil wars start, and his plans have to be scrapped. He is obliged to take sides, as intellectuals all over the world are doing today; he has to come down from his tower and take service under the Commonwealth, and "write with his left hand" for nearly twenty years. One would have expected that to be the end of him, but he has a third phase which makes him very valuable as a specimen: he returns to the Tower and writes *Paradise Lost* and *Samson* in it. His side has lost, but the seventeenth century, unlike the twentieth, did not kill intellectuals who fought on the losing side, and Milton is allowed to work out his poetic plan. We know how the plan was carried out, and how once more—aided this time by his blindness—he detached himself from the world. But Melancholy—what has become of her in the interval? She is no longer the bringer of pleasures, but one of the Furies, the sister of Fear and Remorse; she presides over the lazar house and the punishment of dissolute days:—

> . . . In fine,
> Just or unjust alike seem miserable,
> For oft alike both come to evil end.

[11] That is the "prophetic strain" which he promised himself when he was twenty-five, and it's a terrible sort of tower to be shut up in, brass for ivory; still it does recall the architecture of his youth, and so is significant for us. It suggests that there are some types who naturally prefer solitude to multitude, and revert to it if they can. In many cases the man is worn out by the business of daily life before he can get back, but the normal tendency is to get back.

If parallelism applies to the structuring and positioning of equal sentence units, subordination applies to the structuring and positioning of unequal units. Not all elements within the sentence are of equal importance. The backbone of the sentence consists of the subject and predicate; the noun (or noun substitute) and the verb; the person, place, or thing and the action it performs. The elements, then, which are subordinate must stand in some meaningful relation to the subject and predicate (or subjects and predicates). Most often this relation is descriptive or explanatory; the subordinate element may be adjectival, modifying a noun or noun substitute, or it may be adverbial, modifying a verb, adjective, or adverb. A "thing" may be modified in kind, color, size, shape, quality. An action may be modified in cause, effect, time, place, purpose, or method. The elements in a sentence which stand in any of these relations to the main clause or to the major sentence elements are said to be subordinate. They may be single words, phrases, or clauses.

Why subordinate one idea to another? Part of the answer to this question might be put as another question: are not some ideas more important than others? Since they surely are, the writer gains in precision by being able to use the tool of subordination. He is able to emphasize (and de-emphasize), to vary the rhythms of his prose, to chisel the deep lines and etch the fine ones. The main point (or points) which the sentence is making should be put in the main clause or clauses, subsidiary points in subordinate units. The rule can most easily be understood by seeing what happens when this logical weighing is overturned and a minor point grammatically outweighs the major one:

a. When the plane crashed, killing twenty-two people, much valuable property was destroyed.

b. As the first rocket carrying a man to the moon took off, many people crowded around the entrance to the restricted area.

There is another method by which the writer can control and communicate relative weights within the sentence. It has been pointed out that words must be experienced in time (or, if you think of the printed page, in space). Any block of writing, then, has its strategic spots. This is true for the whole piece of writing; the beginning and ending have certain potentialities which the middle usually does not have. It is true for the paragraph; the topic sentence most often appears at either the beginning or the end. These same places (or times) are strategic points in the sentence. The midportion of the sentence is normally a position of de-emphasis or subordination; the beginning is stronger than the middle but not so strong as the end.

1. Give as many reasons as you can to justify which unit in each of the following groups you prefer:

a. (1) "Like a ship forever asail in the distance, thought the child, everywhere the great church of Chartres was visible, with the passing light or shadow upon its grey, weather-beaten surfaces."

(2) The child thought about the cathedral of Chartres. It was like a ship which was forever asail in the distance. It was visible everywhere, and the passing light or shadow always showed on its surfaces, which were grey and weather-beaten

b. (1) "The people of La Beauce were proud, and would talk often of its rich store of sacred furniture."

   (2) The proud people of La Beauce would talk often of its rich store of sacred furniture.

c. (1) "The busy fancy of Gaston, multiplying this chance hearsay, had set the whole interior in array—a dim, spacious, fragrant place, afloat with golden lights."

   (2) The fancy of Gaston was busy. It multiplied this chance hearsay and set the whole interior in array. In his fancy the interior was a dim place. It was afloat with golden lights, spacious, and fragrant.

d. (1) "When he came thither at last, like many another well-born youth, to join the episcopal household as a kind of clerical half-page, he found (as happens in the actual testing of our ideals) at once more and less than he had supposed; and his earlier vision was a thing he could never precisely recover or disentangle from the supervening reality."

   (2) He came thither at last, like many another well-born youth, to join the episcopal household as a kind of clerical half-page, finding (This happens in the actual testing of our ideas.) at once more and less than he had supposed, his earlier vision being a thing he could never precisely recover or disentangle from the supervening reality.

e. (1) "The phrase 'The Ivory Tower' was first used, in the literary sense, by Sainte-Beuve, when he was examining the work of his friend and contemporary Alfred de Vigny."

   (2) Sainte-Beuve was examining the work of his friend and contemporary Alfred de Vigny when he first used the phrase "The Ivory Tower" in the literary sense.

f. (1) " 'Escapism,' like most words ending in *-ism,* is abusive, and prejudges the issue it professes to define."

   (2) "Escapism" is like most words ending in *-ism,* abusive, prejudging the issues they profess to define.

g. (1) "The subject strays into philosophy and politics, but its main line is literary: the proper function of books."

   (2) Although its main line is literary—the proper function of books—the subject strays into philosophy and politics.

h. (1) "Man is an animal, but a queer one."

   (2) Man is a queer animal.

2. Illustrate as many varieties of sentence structure as you can find in the Pater selection. What does the sentence structure tell you about the selection? about Walter Pater?

3. What is the method of development of paragraph 4 of the Forster piece? Explain the relevance of the paragraph to the selection.

4. Justify the order "tribes, gangs, nations," in paragraph 4 by Forster.

5. Parallelism, balance, and subordination have been used throughout paragraph 5 of the Forster selection. Rewrite the paragraph in at least two ways, using as many sentences as you need. Be prepared to point out the differences in meaning among the versions.

6. Identify and justify another outstanding method of paragraph development used throughout the Forster selection.

Alternate selections for the study of Subordination: Maxwell E Perkins, "Letter from the Editor"; Thomas Bailey Aldrich, "Writers and Talkers."

Assignment: Following are two sets of lists of nouns and verbs which might be related to one another. Write up to a dozen sentences in one or more paragraphs using as many words (in their appropriate forms) from either set of paired lists as you can. Remember that some of these nouns and verbs, in whatever form or structure you use them, will and should be more important than others.

	I		II
A	B	A	B
a campus	to arrive	a newspaper	to see
an auditorium	to see	a headline	to hear
a band	to dress	a television set	to ring
flowers	to hear	a picture	to call
a platform	to march	a telephone call	to drive
a rostrum	to sing	a car	to sit
a microphone	to cry	a friend	to shout
a flag	to run	a chair	to cry
a banner	to speak	a voice	to dream
mortar boards	to lose	silence	to scream
gowns	to leave	a wife	to believe
a child	to forget	children	to fly
a speaker	to take	a police car	to go
parents	to go	a dream	to wreck
tears	to remember	a dog	to take
a smile	to realize	an ambulance	to get
a diploma	to play	a doctor	to kill
a camera	to wish	a week end	
a professor		an airplane	
rain		a gun	
an umbrella			
a car			

Rhythm

The Patron and the Crocus

VIRGINIA WOOLF

[1] Young men and women beginning to write are generally given the plausible but utterly impracticable advice to write what they have to write as shortly as possible, as clearly as possible, and without other thought in their minds except to say exactly what is in them. Nobody ever adds on these occasions the one thing needful: "And be 5 sure you choose your patron wisely," though that is the gist of the whole matter. For a book is always written for somebody to read, and, since the patron is not merely the paymaster, but also in a very subtle and insidious way the instigator and inspirer of what is written, it is of the utmost importance that he should be a desirable man. 10

[2] But who, then, is the desirable man—the patron who will cajole the best out of the writer's brain and bring to birth the most varied and vigorous progeny of which he is capable? Different ages have answered the question differently. The Elizabethans, to speak roughly, chose the aristocracy to write for and the playhouse public. 15 The eighteenth-century patron was a combination of coffee-house wit and Grub Street book-seller. In the nineteenth century the great

writers wrote for the half-crown magazines and the leisured classes.
And looking back and applauding the splendid results of these differ-
20 ent alliances, it all seems enviably simple, and plain as a pikestaff
compared with our own predicament—for whom should we write?
For the present supply of patrons is of unexampled and bewildering
variety. There is the daily Press, the weekly Press, the monthly
Press; the English public and the American public; the best-seller
25 public and the worst-seller public; the high-brow public and the red-
blood public; all now organised self-conscious entities capable through
their various mouthpieces of making their needs known and their
approval or displeasure felt. Thus the writer who has been moved by
the sight of the first crocus in Kensington Gardens has, before he sets
30 pen to paper, to choose from a crowd of competitors the particular
patron who suits him best. It is futile to say, "Dismiss them all
think only of your crocus," because writing is a method of communication; and the crocus is an imperfect crocus until it has been shared
The first man or the last may write for himself alone, but he is an
35 exception and an unenviable one at that, and the gulls are welcome
to his works if the gulls can read them.

[3] Granted, then, that every writer has some public or other at
the end of his pen, the high-minded will say that it should be a sub-
missive public, accepting obediently whatever he likes to give it
40 Plausible as the theory sounds, great risks are attached to it. For in
that case the writer remains conscious of his public, yet is superior
to it—an uncomfortable and unfortunate combination, as the work
of Samuel Butler, George Meredith, and Henry James may be taken to
prove. Each despised the public; each desired a public; each failed
45 to attain a public; and each wreaked his failure upon the public by a
succession, gradually increasing in intensity, of angularities, obscuri-
ties, and affectations which no writer whose patron was his equal and
friend would have thought it necessary to inflict. Their crocuses in
consequence are tortured plants, beautiful and bright, but with some-
50 thing wry-necked about them, malformed, shrivelled on the one side
overblown on the other. A touch of the sun would have done them
world of good. Shall we then rush to the opposite extreme and accept
(if in fancy alone) the flattering proposals which the editors of the
Times and the Daily News may be supposed to make us—"Twenty
55 pounds down for your crocus in precisely fifteen hundred words
which shall blossom upon every breakfast table from John o' Groats
to the Land's End before nine o'clock tomorrow morning with the
writer's name attached"?

[4] But will one crocus be enough, and must it not be a very brilliant yellow to shine so far, to cost so much, and to have one's name attached to it? The Press is undoubtedly a great multiplier of crocuses. But if we look at some of these plants, we shall find that they are only very distantly related to the original little yellow or purple flower which pokes up through the grass in Kensington Gardens about this time of year. The newspaper crocus is amazing but still a very different plant. It fills precisely the space allotted to it. It radiates a golden glow. It is genial, affable, warmhearted. It is beautifully finished, too, for let nobody think that the art of "our dramatic critic" of the *Times* or of Mr. Lynd of the *Daily News* is an easy one. It is no despicable feat to start a million brains running at nine o'clock in the morning, to give two million eyes something bright and brisk and amusing to look at. But the night comes and these flowers fade. So little bits of glass lose their lustre if you take them out of the sea; great prima donnas howl like hyenas if you shut them up in telephone boxes; and the most brilliant of articles when removed from its element is dust and sand and the husks of straw. Journalism embalmed in a book is unreadable.

[5] The patron we want, then, is one who will help us to preserve our flowers from decay. But as his qualities change from age to age, and it needs considerable integrity and conviction not to be dazzled by the pretensions or bamboozled by the persuasions of the competing crowd, this business of patron-finding is one of the tests and trials of authorship. To know whom to write for is to know how to write. Some of the modern patron's qualities are, however, fairly plain. The writer will require at this moment, it is obvious, a patron with the book-reading habit rather than the play-going habit. Nowadays, too, he must be instructed in the literature of other times and races. But there are other qualities which our special weaknesses and tendencies demand in him. There is the question of indecency, for instance, which plagues us and puzzles us much more than it did the Elizabethans. The twentieth-century patron must be immune from shock. He must distinguish infallibly between the little clod of manure which sticks to the crocus of necessity, and that which is plastered to it out of bravado. He must be a judge, too, of those social influences which inevitably play so large a part in modern literature, and able to say which matures and fortifies, which inhibits and makes sterile. Further, there is emotion for him to pronounce on, and in no department can he do more useful work than in bracing a writer against sentimental-

ity on the one hand and a craven fear of expressing his feeling on
100 the other. It is worse, he will say, and perhaps more common, to be
afraid of feeling than to feel too much. He will add, perhaps, something about language, and point out how many words Shakespeare
used and how much grammar Shakespeare violated, while we, though
we keep our fingers so demurely to the black notes on the piano,
105 have not appreciably improved upon *Antony and Cleopatra*. And if
you can forget your sex altogether, he will say, so much the better; a
writer has none. But all this is by the way—elementary and dispu-
table. The patron's prime quality is something different, only to be
expressed perhaps by the use of that convenient word which cloaks
110 so much—atmosphere. It is necessary that the patron should shed
and envelop the crocus in an atmosphere which makes it appear a
plant of the very highest importance, so that to misrepresent it is
the one outrage not to be forgiven this side of the grave. He must
make us feel that a single crocus, if it be a real crocus, is enough
115 for him; that he does not want to be lectured, elevated, instructed, or
improved; that he is sorry that he bullied Carlyle into vociferation,
Tennyson into idyllics, and Ruskin into insanity; that he is now
ready to efface himself or assert himself as his writers require; that
he is bound to them by a more than maternal tie; that they are twins
120 indeed, one dying if the other dies, one flourishing if the other flourishes; that the fate of literature depends upon their happy alliance—
all of which proves, as we began by saying, that the choice of a
patron is of the highest importance. But how to choose rightly? How
to write well? Those are the questions.

Rhythm is so major an element of poetry that the student-writer
may not have realized that rhythm plays a role in good prose too.
Repetition is the essence of rhythm: in painting, the repetition of a
pattern or color or line produces visual rhythm; in music, the repetition of a pattern of beats produces rhythm; in poetry, the repetition
of a pattern of stressed and unstressed sounds produces rhythm. In
prose, rhythm is produced by the repetition—always with some variation possible—of patterns of stressed and unstressed words. Prose
rhythms are subtle and frequently so varied that a certain amount of
training and practice is needed before a reader can respond fully to
the best rhythmical prose.

In metered poetry, the rhythmical unit is the foot, consisting of one
stressed sound and one or more unstressed sounds arranged in any
one of several possible patterns; in prose, however, the rhythmical unit

ranges from the various parts of a sentence (words, phrases, clauses) to the whole sentence itself. For example, in the following sentences, the rhythmical units are indicated by slashes:

> The boy,/with a bedraggled looking dog behind him,/ ran to the corner,/peered into the car,/ and then ran off again.
>
> Higher education is considered a necessity today/ not only for the man who wants a professional career/ but also for the woman who wants to be a wife and mother.
>
> The idea was loathsome./ The man who proposed it/ was even more loathsome.

Reading a sentence aloud to communicate its meaning will normally enable the reader to sense the rhythmical units of which it is composed.

An infinite variety of effects—of different movements—can be achieved through the varying lengths of rhythmical units and their relations within and between sentences. Several short units placed together in a sentence can result in choppy or staccato or clogged movement:

> The gymnasium,/ completed only recently,/ towered embarrass-ingly,/ most faculty members thought,/ over the small, dilapidated buildings/ in which were taught/ the humanities,/ the social sciences,/ and the natural sciences.

Larger units strategically placed—and perhaps varied with one or two smaller units—can result in smooth, flowing movement:

> For century after century after century,/ thinking man has exerted the best efforts of his mind and imagination/ to penetrate the mysteries of the natural world about him.

It must be pointed out here that no pat generalizations of any validity can be made about the best number of rhythmical units per sentence or the best relations among units or the best length of units. The only meaningful criteria to use in evaluating prose rhythms (or sentence movements) are the propriety of the movement to the content and the pleasure (or lack of it) felt by the reader as he reads. Sentences expressing smooth, flowing action or movement should move smoothly and flowingly; sentences expressing ideas rather than action or movement should move easily, without the clogging effect of several short units following one after another. Awareness of sentence movements and the ability to analyze them in the student's own writing as well as in the writing of prose masters will sharpen sensitivity and help in the achievement of rhythmically pleasing prose. But there is more to sentence movement than the recognition of rhythmical units. Any normal English sentence when read aloud (or even silently, for that matter) has certain words which the content demands giving more stress to than to others. Using the symbol ´ to indicate a stressed word (understanding that not all stressed words are equally stressed) and the symbol ˘ to indicate an unstressed word, we may show the normal reading of a sentence as follows:

    a. Lóoking aroŭnd tŏ seĕ whĕre thĕ bóat hăd bĕen tíed,/ thĕ húnter wăs hórrified tŏ fínd/ thăt he hăd bĕen lĕft alóne ŏn thĕ ísland.

This is a typical English sentence in its larger number of unstressed than stressed words and in the repetition—with variation—in the third unit of the basic rhythmical pattern of the first unit. The repetition is not so pronounced, however, that it makes the sentence singsong or "versified."

    b. The úp-grading/ ŏf stóck íssues/ by thĕ Bóard mĕmbers/ fóoled búyers,/ séllers,/ ănd brókers tóo.

Sentence *b* has a movement quite different from that of sentence *a*: it has a larger percentage of stressed words (9 of 15 compared with 8 of 25 in *a*), and a stressed word follows a stressed word several times, whereas in sentence *a* every stressed word is separated from every other stressed word by at least one unstressed word. In addition, sentence *a*, with 25 words, has only 3 rhythmical units; *b*, with 15 words, has 6 rhythmical units. In over-all effect, sentence *a* moves with a certain rapidity which echoes its meaning; *b* has a clogged, somewhat staccato movement, a rather unpleasant movement.

    In analyzing prose rhythms or sentence movement, it is always necessary to take into account not only the number, length, and interrelations of rhythmical units, but also the patterns of stressed and unstressed words for whatever effects they may create. Piling stressed word on stressed word may result in heavy, emphatic delivery or in slow, clogged movement; a large number of unstressed words separating stressed words usually results in light, rapid movement.

    Closely related to prose rhythms are the sound patterns of sentences. Continuant consonants—consonants whose sounds can be drawn out when spoken aloud (*l, m, n, r,* for example)—aid in producing smoothness of movement; stop consonants (*b, d, k, p, t,* for example) help produce a staccato movement. The most skillful prose writer manages his sentences so that sound and movement are as appropriate as possible to his content.

1. In paragraph 2, sentences 3, 4, and 5 constitute a series. Indicate by means of the symbols ´ (a stressed word) and ˘ (an unstressed word) how you would read aloud the sentences to communicate their meaning. What similarities do you find in the rhythmical patterns of the three sentences? Do these similarities serve a function or are they merely fortuitous? Explain in detail.

2. What characterizes the structure of sentence 8 in paragraph 2? By marking the scansion, show how the structure of the sentence has created a strong rhythmical pattern. What contribution does this pattern make to the idea the sentence communicates? What would have been gained or lost had Virginia Woolf placed the list of the various processes and publics at the end rather than at the beginning of the sentence? Explain.

3. In which sentence of paragraph 3 is structure most effectively used for the creation of a rhythmical pattern? Describe the structure. At what point in the sentence does the rhythmical pattern change? In terms of the content of the sentence, what is the effect of the change?

4. In paragraph 4, several consecutive sentences employ essentially the same construction, thus establishing a rhythmical pattern. Identify the sentences; mark the scansion of each sentence and show the means by which variation is achieved within the rhythmical pattern.

5. Analyze the last three sentences of paragraph 4 to show what rhythm contributes to each of the sentences individually and to the three in combination.

6. Balanced sentence structure and parallelism are used in several places in paragraph 5, creating once again strong rhythmical patterns. Do you think that Virginia Woolf has overused the technique of creating rhythms through a particular type of sentence structure? Why or why not?

7. For what "patron" do you think Virginia Woolf is writing? Do her rhythms help you to identify the "patron"? Explain.

Alternate selections for the study of Rhythm: Rainer Maria Rilke, "The Raw Material of Poetry"; Walter Pater, "Notre-Dame de Chartres"; Thomas Wolfe, from "A Letter to Mabel Wolfe Wheaton."

Assignment: For each of the following, write a single sentence of some length in which the rhythm is as appropriate to the content as you can make it:

   a. Describe the approach of a violent thunder storm.
   b. Bring to life a description of a small-town, patriotic parade.
   c. Show how irritating a woman vacuuming a rug can be.
   d. Re-create the sensation of plunging into cold water.

e. Recapture the excitement of the final minutes of an Alfred Hitchcock movie.

f. Communicate the "white hot indignation" of a person unjustly accused of a crime.

g. Defend your family's honor against a scurrilous attack.

h. Describe an outdoor panoramic scene you know well.

i. What does the kitchen sound like before your family Thanksgiving dinner?

j. How do you recognize hunger when you experience it?

DICTION

Succinctness

How to Read a Newspaper

CARL SANDBURG

[1] The newspaper goes everywhere. Like rain it falls on the just and the unjust. Like history it begins and ends anywhere and leaves much to be expected. The more terrible its headlines, the more welcome it is and the more copies go to anxious readers.

[2] In schools and colleges there should be class discussions of the question "What is the best way to read a newspaper?" so that the young might learn there are many different ways.

[3] How to read the classics of literature has long been taught in the schools and universities. How to know good books from bad, how to use books for laughter and entertainment or spiritual light or practical help, of this there has been much teaching.

[4] But the great universal classic of the common people's reading —the newspaper—has been neglected.

[5] Some ten years ago I was asked if I would care to conduct a university course and meet a class once a week on any subject I chose. I answered I wouldn't be able to find the time, but if I could the subject would be "How to Read a Newspaper."

[6] Now I have before me a textbook published by Scott, Fores-

From *Home Front Memo,* copyright 1943, by Carl Sandburg. Reprinted by permission of Harcourt, Brace & World, Inc.

man and Company of Chicago, written by Edgar Dale of Ohio State
20 University, and the title *How to Read a Newspaper*.

[7] I would like to see this book go far. It should be handled in
bookstores for the general public. It deserves a place in all public
libraries. And there should be talk about it, up, down, and across.

[8] What is news? Who says what is news and what isn't? Where
25 do local reporters get the news they write? How do foreign corre-
spondents get the news they cable, wireless, or telephone across the
oceans? How can you guide yourself on what to believe or not believe
in the headlines and news accounts?

[9] Those are live questions to every serious newspaper reader
30 who reads hoping to learn something about the immense events of
history in the making, now.

[10] Between the reader and the news are several strategic points.
At each of these the news can get slanted, angled, even mangled or
deleted and lost. Before reaching the reader's eyes the news has been
35 handled by the reporter on the spot, by the censor, by the home-
office editors, by the headline-writer, and each of these, deleting
the censor, somewhat directly responsible to the owner or publisher
who originates and shapes what is termed "the policy" of the paper.

[11] Then there is the time element. Mistakes creep in because
40 time waits for no man and the trucks wait in the alley to rush today's
paper out today.

[12] Class exercise: Find a news story you think strictly factual
and well written. Find another news story you think distorted, explain
why you think it distorted, and tell how you would write it better.
45 [13] Bring in examples of perfect headlines indicating what the
reader may expect. Bring in examples of misleading headlines where
the headline writer was either careless and well meaning or inten-
tionally was editorializing in line with the policy of the paper. Pick a
lead paragraph you feel lacks color and see whether you can brighten
50 it in rewriting.

[14] Will Irwin, biographer of Herbert Hoover and a newsman
many of us respect, once wrote: "More than twenty years ago I sat at
luncheon with a group of American publishers, talking shop. Conversation turned to the decline of the editorial as a social and
55 political force. 'My front page is my editorial,' said one of the
company. 'The headlines are mine,' said another."

[15] In Dale's book we are given cases of the misleading headline
that has its purpose. We could paraphrase "I care not who makes the
laws of a nation if I may write its songs" to "I care not who writes

the news story if I may shape the headline that gives it the slant I 60
want."

[16] The human oddities, the endless marvels of fun and preposterous pomposity, these too are in Dale's book. A country weekly in
Iowa once told its readers: "We were the first in the state to announce, on the 11th instance, the news of the destruction in Des 65
Moines, by fire, of the mammoth paint establishment of Jenkins &
Bros. We are now the first to inform our readers that the report was
absolutely without foundation."

[17] We are asked to scrutinize news stories with ten questions,
the last two: "Has prejudice entered into the writing or editing of the 70
news dispatch? Is the reporter likely to have such a deep personal
interest in some possible outcome of a question that he cannot, even
though he tries, write accurately about it?"

[18] Then there is the quote from that war horse of the Toledo
Blade, Grove Patterson: "I am less disturbed about freedom of the 75
press in the United States than I am with the disposition of too
many newspaper editors not to do anything with the freedom that is
theirs."

[19] Anyhow and ennyhoo, I would submit, news services and
newspapers now are a grand improvement on one and two genera- 80
tions ago. Those who know how to read, inquire, and think get more
information and entertainment for their pennies and nickels than they
did in the days of Horace Greeley, James Gordon Bennett, and
Abraham Lincoln who would not have been President if Greeley or
Bennett had had the say-so.   85

[For treatment of this selection, see pp. 321–322.]

✍The New Yorker *Prospectus*

HAROLD ROSS

ANNOUNCING A NEW WEEKLY MAGAZINE

[1] The New Yorker will be a reflection in word and picture of metropolitan life. It will be human. Its general tenor will be one of gaiety, wit and satire, but it will be more than a jester. It will not be what is commonly called radical or highbrow. It will be what is
5 commonly called sophisticated, in that it will assume a reasonable degree of enlightenment on the part of its readers. It will hate bunk.

[2] As compared to the newspaper, The New Yorker will be interpretative rather than stenographic. It will print facts that it will have to go behind the scenes to get, but it will not deal in scandal
10 for the sake of scandal nor sensation for the sake of sensation. Its integrity will be above suspicion. It hopes to be so entertaining and informative as to be a necessity for the person who knows his way about or wants to.

[3] The New Yorker will devote several pages a week to the
15 covering of contemporary events and people of interest. This will be done by writers capable of appreciating the elements of a situation and, in setting them down, of indicating their importance and significance. The New Yorker will present the truth and the whole truth without fear and without favor, but will not be iconoclastic.

20 [4] Amusements and the arts will be thoroughly covered by departments which will present, in addition to criticism, the personality, the anecdote, the color and chat of the various subdivisions of this sphere. The New Yorker's conscientious guide will list each week all current amusement offerings worth-while—theatres, motion pic-
25 tures, musical events, art exhibitions, sport and miscellaneous entertainment—providing an ever-ready answer to the prevalent query,

The original prospectus for *The New Yorker* as reprinted in *The Vicious Circle* by Margaret Case Harriman (Rinehart, 1951). Reprinted with the permission of The New Yorker Magazine, Inc.

"What shall we do with this evening?" Through The New Yorker's Mr. Van Bibber III, readers will be kept apprised of what is going on in the public and semi-public smart gathering places—the clubs, hotels, cafes, supper clubs, cabarets and other resorts. 30

[5] Judgment will be passed upon new books of consequence, and The New Yorker will carry a list of the season's books which it considers worth reading.

[6] There will be a page of editorial paragraphs, commenting on the week's events in a manner not too serious. 35

[7] There will be a personal mention column—a jotting down in the small-town newspaper style of the comings, goings, and doings in the village of New York. This will contain some josh and some news value.

[8] The New Yorker will carry each week several pages of prose 40 and verse, short and long, humorous, satirical and miscellaneous.

[9] The New Yorker expects to be distinguished for its illustrations, which will include caricatures, sketches, cartoons and humorous and satirical drawings in keeping with its purpose.

[10] The New Yorker will be the magazine which is not edited 45 for the old lady in Dubuque. It will not be concerned with what she is thinking about. This is not meant in disrespect, but The New Yorker is a magazine avowedly published for a metropolitan audience and thereby will escape an influence which hampers most national publications. It expects a considerable national circulation, 50 but this will come from persons who have a metropolitan interest.

The New Yorker will appear early in February.
The price will be: Five dollars a year
Fifteen cents a copy

ADVISORY EDITORS

Ralph Barton	George S. Kaufman
Heywood Broun	Alice Duer Miller
Marc Connelly	Dorothy Parker
Edna Ferber	Laurence Stallings
Rea Irvin	Alexander Woollcott

H. W. Ross, Editor

One of the major characteristics of poetry is compression—the saying of much in few words, each word carrying a maximum burden of meaning. The Japanese *Haiku,* five of which are reprinted below, from *Japanese Haiku,* with the permission of the Peter Pauper Press, Mt. Vernon, New York, beautifully illustrates compression through economy of diction, or succinctness, as it is often called—an asset in prose as well as in poetry.

I
Since there is no rice . . .
    Let us arrange these
    Flowers
For a lovely bowl

II
I raised my knife to it
    Then walked on
    Empty-handed on . . .
Proud rose of Sharon

III
Reciting scriptures . . .
    I find a strange
    Wondrous blue
In morning-glories

IV
In the city park
    Contemplating
    Cherry-trees . . .
Strangers are like friends

V
Dead my old fine hopes
    And dry my dreaming
    But oh . . .
Iris, blue each spring!

1. In *Haiku* I, there is communicated in the first line (including the three dots) one of the stark and tragic realities of life in seventeenth-century Japan—famine as a result of rice-crop failure; the remaining three lines show not only resignation to the famine, but the positive response to beauty—here, ironically, the beauty of nature which has failed to supply the foodstuff necessary to maintain life. This statement of the content, tone, and feelings shows how much is communicated through the fourteen words.

Taking into account not only the explicit words but also the turn in thought and feeling indicated by the sets of dots, summarize in your own words the essentials of all that is communicated through the *Haiku* II through V. Make a word count of each *Haiku* and of each of your summaries; what conclusions can you draw about professional writers of *Haiku?*

2. Study each *Haiku* to see whether it has any verbiage—any word or words that can be removed without destroying meaning. Be prepared to justify the deletion of any words you decide can be deleted. Can you substitute a single word for any combinations of words in any of the *Haiku* without destroying meaning or decreasing effectiveness? If so, where?

3. In the edition from which the *Haiku* were reprinted here, the second line has been split in two, a result of certain typographical considerations. In its purest form, the *Haiku* contains three lines, the first and third having five syllables each and the second, seven syllables. Write a *Haiku* on any one of the following or a subject of your own choosing:

a. a sudden change in weather
b. a disappointed hope
c. a disabled car
d. a tough steak
e. a tattered coat

Apply the tests indicated in 2 above to your own *Haiku*. If the tests show that your *Haiku* needs revision, revise it as many times as necessary to have it "pass" the tests; preserve the various versions for comparative analysis.

4. Find five sentences in which Sandburg uses parallelism to achieve succinctness; by reconstructing each of the sentences, show how much more wordy it would have been without the parallelism.

5. Select five of Sandburg's longest sentences. Rewrite each one, attempting to increase succinctness. With how many did you succeed? Are your sentences better—in any way—than Sandburg's? Why or why not?

6. Find an example in the Sandburg selection of a simple sentence,

a compound sentence, a complex sentence, and a compound-complex sentence. Do you find significantly greater succinctness in any one of the types of sentences compared with the others? What generalization, if any, can you make about the relation between types of sentences and succinctness? between length and succinctness?

7. Though succinctness is an important criterion by which to evaluate sentences, it is by no means the only one. What are some others? Compare the sentences in each of the following pairs, weighing gains or losses in succinctness against other criteria to determine which sentence (or group of sentences) of each pair is better. Make clear your criteria.

a. (1) "Its general tenor will be one of gaiety, wit and satire, but it will be more than a jester."
   (2) Though its general tenor will be gay, witty, and satiric, it will be more than a jester.

b. (1) "It will not be what is commonly called radical or highbrow. It will be what is commonly called sophisticated, in that it will assume a reasonable degree of enlightenment on the part of its readers."
   (2) It will not be radical or highbrow but, rather, sophisticated; it will assume enlightened readers.

c. (1) "The New Yorker will devote several pages a week to the covering of contemporary events and people of interest. This will be done by writers capable of appreciating the elements of a situation and, in setting them down, of indicating their importance and significance."
   (2) *The New Yorker* will devote several pages a week to contemporary events and people of interest, covered by writers who, appreciative of the elements of a situation, will indicate their importance and significance.

d. (1) "There will be a page of editorial paragraphs, commenting on the week's events in a manner not too serious."
   (2) A page of editorial paragraphs will comment—not too seriously—on the week's events.

8. What is the tone of Harold Ross' prospectus for *The New Yorker?* Just what does sentence length contribute to establishing the tone?

9. How well do you think *The New Yorker* has lived up to the prospectus? Document your answer with specific references to at least one issue of the magazine.

Alternate selections for the study of Succinctness: Sir Francis Bacon, from "Of Studies," Robert Frost, "Education by Poetry."

Theme Assignment: In a sense, the title "How to Read a News-paper" promises more than Sandburg delivers. His perspective is that of a writer, not a reader; consequently, he tells us more about how a newspaper is written than about how it is read. Different people do read newspapers differently from one another; the same people read different newspapers differently.

Write a theme in which you explain how you or someone you know well reads one or more newspapers. Your explanation should tell us something about the reader (his profession, primary interests, politics, personality, education) and about the newspaper (its caliber, editorial policies, general level of readership, circulation). This is a broad topic; its coverage will require skillful use of compression or succinctness.

or

Choose a magazine which you read regularly and know well. In approximately the same wordage as used by Harold Ross, write a "prospectus" which, though as succinct as you can make it, will also be inviting to potential subscribers.

Cliché
and Jargon

From *Babbitt* SINCLAIR LEWIS

[1] As Babbitt marched into his private room, a coop with semi-partition of oak and frosted glass, at the back of the office, he reflected how hard it was to find employees who had his own faith that he was going to make sales.

. . . .

5 [2] As he looked from his own cage into the main room Babbitt mourned, "McGoun's a good stenog., smart's a whip, but Stan Graff and all those bums—" The zest of the spring morning was in the stale office air.

[3] Normally he admired the office, with a pleased surprise that 10 he should have created this sure lovely thing; normally he was stimulated by the clean newness of it and the air of bustle; but today it seemed flat—the tiled floor, like a bathroom, the ocher-colored metal ceiling, the faded maps on the hard plasterwalls, the chairs of varnished pale oak, the desks and filing-cabinets of steel painted in 15 olive drab. It was a vault, a steel chapel where loafing and laughter were raw sin.

[4] He hadn't even any satisfaction in the new water-cooler! And it was the very best of water-coolers, up-to-date, scientific, and right-thinking. It had cost a great deal of money (in itself a virtue). It possessed a nonconducting fiber ice-container, a porcelain water-jar 20 (guaranteed hygienic), a dripless nonclogging sanitary faucet, and machine-painted decorations in two tones of gold. He looked down the relentless stretch of tiled floor at the water-cooler, and assured himself that no tenant of the Reeves Building had a more expensive one, but he could not recapture the feeling of social superiority it had 25 given him. He astoundingly grunted, "I'd like to beat it off to the woods right now. And loaf all day. And go to Gunch's again tonight, and play poker, and cuss as much as I feel like, and drink a hundred and nine-thousand bottles of beer."

[5] He sighed; he read through his mail; he shouted "Msgoun," 30 which meant "Miss McGoun"; and began to dictate.

[6] This was his own version of his first letter:

[7] "Omar Gribble, send it to his office, Miss McGoun, yours of twentieth to hand and in reply would say look here, Gribble, I'm awfully afraid if we go on shilly-shallying like this we'll just naturally 35 lose the Allen sale, I had Allen up on carpet day before yesterday and got right down to cases and think I can assure you—uh, uh, no, change that: all my experience indicates he is all right, means to do business, looked into his financial record which is fine—that sentence seems to be a little balled up, Miss McGoun; make a couple sentences 40 out of it if you have to, period, new paragraph.

[8] "He is perfectly willing to pro rate the special assessment and strikes me, am dead sure there will be no difficulty in getting him to pay for title insurance, so now for heaven's sake let's get busy—no, make that: so now let's go to it and get down—no, that's enough— 45 you can tie those sentences up a little better when you type 'em, Miss McGoun—your sincerely, etcetera."

[9] This is the version of his letter which he received, typed, from Miss McGoun that afternoon:

BABBITT-THOMPSON REALTY CO.
Homes for Folks
Reeves Bldg., Oberlin Avenue & 3d St., N.E.
Zenith

Omar Gribble, Esq.,
576 North American Building,
Zenith

Dear Mr. Gribble:

50   [10] Your letter of the twentieth to hand. I must say I'm awfully afraid that if we go on shilly-shallying like this we'll just naturally lose the Allen sale. I had Allen up on the carpet day before yesterday, and got right down to cases. All my experience indicates that he means to do business. I have also looked into his financial record, 55 which is fine.

   [11] He is perfectly willing to pro rate the special assessment and there will be no difficulty in getting him to pay for title insurance.

   [12] *So Let's go!*

Yours sincerely,

   [13] As he read and signed it, in his correct flowing business-col-
60 lege hand, Babbitt reflected, "Now that's a good, strong letter, and clear's a bell. Now what the—I never told McGoun to make a third paragraph there! Wish she'd quit trying to improve on my dictation! But what I can't understand is: why can't Stan Graff or Chet Laylock write a letter like that? With punch! With a kick!"

65   [14] The most important thing he dictated that morning was the fortnightly form-letter, to be mimeographed and sent out to a thousand "prospects." It was diligently imitative of the best literary models of the day; of heart-to-heart-talk advertisements, "sales-pulling" letters, discourses on the "development of Will-power," and
70 hand-shaking house-organs, as richly poured forth by the new school of Poets of Business. He had painfully written out a first draft, and he intoned it now like a poet delicate and distrait:

SAY, OLD MAN!

   [15] I just want to know can I do you a whaleuva favor? Honest! No kidding! I know you're interested in getting a house, not merely

a place where you hang up the old bonnet but a love-nest for the 75
wife and kiddies—and maybe for the flivver out beyant (be sure
and spell that b-e-y-a-n-t, Miss McGoun) the spud garden. Say, did
you ever stop to think that we're here to save you trouble? That's
how we make a living—folks don't pay us for our lovely beauty!
Now take a look: 80
   [16] Sit right down at the handsome carved mahogany escritoire
and shoot us in a line telling us just what you want, and if we can
find it we'll come hopping down your lane with the good tidings,
and if we can't, we won't bother you. To save your time, just fill out
the blank enclosed. On request will also send blank regarding store 85
properties in Floral Heights, Silver Grove, Linton, Bellevue, and all
East Side residential districts.

Yours for service,

P.S.—Just a hint of some plums we can pick for you—some genuine
bargains that came in to-day:

   [17] SILVER GROVE.—Cute four-room California bungalow, 90
a.m.i., garage, dandy shade tree, swell neighborhood, handy car line.
$3,700, $780 down and balance liberal, Babbitt-Thompson terms,
cheaper than rent.
   [18] DORCHESTER.—A corker! Artistic two-family house. all
oak trim, parquet floors, lovely gas log, big porches, colonial, 95
HEATED ALL-WEATHER GARAGE, a bargain at $11,250.
   [19] Dictation over, with its need of sitting and thinking instead
of bustling around and making a noise and really doing something,
Babbitt sat creakily back in his revolving deskchair and beamed on
Miss McGoun. He was conscious of her as a girl, of black bobbed 100
hair against demure cheeks. A longing which was indistinguishable
from loneliness enfeebled him. While she waited, tapping a long, precise pencil-point on the desk-tablet, he half identified her with the
fairy girl of his dreams. He imagined their eyes meeting with terrifying recognition; imagined touching her lips with frightened reverence 105
and—She was chirping, "Any more, Mist' Babbitt?" He grunted,
"That winds it up, I guess," and turned heavily away.

[For treatment of this selection, see p. 334.]

✐ *Jargon*   BROOKS ATKINSON

[1] Forecasting the weather for the next day, the man said that we should expect "shower activity." "Rain shower activity," in fact, as distinguished from showers of meteors. If he had warned us to be prepared for "showers" he would have been one of us—lineal de-
5 scendants of the natural man. By adding the formal word "activity" he moved up into the graver category of scientist or technologist—learned, disinterested and abstract. He indicated that he had no personal interest in showers, though, the Lord knows, we needed them. On the contrary, he was impersonally giving us the facts after he had
10 processed the weather map. All he had done really was to contact the United States Weather Bureau.

[2] He was also illustrating a current tendency to remove English prose from the arena of human beings and pass it through the laboratory, where knowledge can be sterilized. As for instance, news
15 is "structured" in the mass media. (All plurals like "media" and "stadia" should be dumped into the "crematoria.") Since the masses who consume the media are the proletariat, which meekly responds to the appropriate stimuli, commercial products nowadays receive gratifying "public acceptance." That is, the public buys them for hard
20 cash or on the lay-away plan after the advertising panjandri have implemented a scientifically planned program. "Syndrome" is another imposing word that probably ought to be dropped in here somewhere.

[3] No writer wants to be a square, especially in public. The social
25 sciences and technologies have taught him that human beings are statistics, outer-directed toward status symbols. They can be intrigued into believing almost anything. Science and technology can (and I quote) amass, disaggregate and restructure any information that is available. In these circumstances, a writer would be a fool to
30 write as though human beings have minds of their own and say what they think. The jargon of science and technology spares him the embarrassment of committing himself to a belief in men and women.

From *Tuesdays and Fridays* by Brooks Atkinson. (New York: Random House, Inc., 1963.) Reprinted by permission of the publisher.

[4] Several weeks ago this column remarked that *Daedalus,* the journal of the American Academy of Arts and Sciences, contains some of the densest prose of the generation. The remark was not uni- 35 versally admired. But perhaps we can finalize the argument by reference to "Some Mechanisms of Sociocultural Evolution" by Julian H. Steward and Demitri B. Shimkin in the summer issue. They never call a spade a spade. They never use one word when ten will do.

[5] For example: "Our treatment of culture and its evolution 40 rests upon nine heuristic concepts which constitute a mixture of hypothetical postulates and real but tentative observations."

[6] "Culture summates the body of adaptive, cognitive and expressive behavior and its consequences."

[7] There is more where that came from. 45

[8] When the social scientists talk among themselves (conducting a "dialogue," as even nonscientists love to remark) they require abstract terms that are precise, that are understood by other scientists and that convey information without contaminating it with opinion. Granted. But it is difficult to believe that prose like the excerpts 50 quoted above is anything except a pedantic affectation, conveying a grain of information in a ton of words. Information does not have to be conveyed that way, as other articles in the current *Daedalus* indicate.

[9] The Anglo-Saxon survivals in the modern English language 55 are vivid and clear because they are derived from human experience. They deal with realities frankly. "Tip" is a healthier word than "remuneration" because it tells the truth bluntly. The fatuous intrusion of scientific and technological terms in current prose recalls with gratitude a terse remark that Pogo made last spring: "Albert, you is 60 took leave of your brain bone."

[For treatment of this selection, see pp. 332–335.]

✑ Enemies of Jargon

BROOKS ATKINSON

[1] Thanks to the resourcefulness of readers, the discussion of woolly prose can be continued, fortified with some ironic examples. Joseph G. Shea of New York submits Quiller-Couch's dehydrated version of a Hamlet soliloquy: "To be, or the contrary? Whether the
5 former or the latter be preferable, would seem to admit of some difference of opinion."

[2] Winthrop Parkhurst of Staten Island has clipped from *Product Engineering* a modern rendering of: "And God said: Let there be light, and there was light." According to a mischievous writer in
10 *Product Engineering,* an educated technologist would express the same thought as follows: "In response to a verbal stimulus for luminosity, initiated by the Master Control, a complete spectrum of visible radiation occurred."

[3] Dr. William B. Bean of the University of Iowa quotes Lionel
15 Trilling's learned gloss on a simple statement that "They fell in love and married." Professor Trilling thinks a full professor would phrase it more profoundly: "Their libidinal impulses being reciprocal, they activated their individual erotic drives and integrated them within the same frame of reference."

20 [4] Dr. Eric G. DeFlon of Chadron, Nebraska, is holding his head over ponderous statements he discovered in *The Lonely Crowd,* by David Reisman, Nathan Glazer and Reuel Denney. Dr. DeFlon says he "clubbed" himself into reading, among other examples of jargon: "Thus, all human beings are inner-directed in the sense that,
25 brought up as they are by people older than themselves, they have acquired and internalized some permanent orientations from them."

[5] In a droll article entitled "Tower of Babel 1961," contributed to the July issue of *Archives of Internal Medicine,* Dr. Bean tries his hand at composing a conference report on a scheme for improving
30 the intellectual content of students. Dr. Bean thinks one sentence

From *Tuesdays and Fridays* by Brooks Atkinson. (New York: Random House, Inc., 1963.) Reprinted by permission of the publisher.

would be greatly admired if it were written as follows: "The curriculum diagnosticians and guidance coordinators work on the very
frontier of experimentation where they contrive to see that at all
levels every participant can profit ability-wise from an overall, en-
riched-type, meaningful, on-going program."   35

[6] If you seldom see these barbarisms or circumlocutions in the
New York *Times,* it is because an anonymous grammarian tyrannizes
over the staff in a curt sheet called "Winners and Sinners." Just now
it is celebrating, if that is not too joyous a word, ten years of scaring
the living daylights out of the writers and editors of the *Times.* By 40
reading this newspaper closely, the editor of W & S, as it dubs itself,
finds plenty of stuff over which to wince—well, to wince over.

[7] A headline that declares "Elm Beetle Infestation Ravishing
Thousands of Trees in Greenwich" offends his sense of propriety.
"Keep your mind on your work, buster," he growls. "The word you 45
want is 'ravaging.' " The W & S editor can hardly believe headlines
like these: "Harriet Burns a Fiancée" and "Gladys Glad Jewels
Stolen." Flouting error, he flaunts erudition in every issue. Amid the
richness of a fine prose sentence that has euphony and elevation, he
swoops down on an example of litotes, and applies the stiletto rear- 50
wards. He is probably the only man who knows the exact meaning
of "shambles."

[8] Although "Winners and Sinners" is anonymous, it is the lonely
enterprise of Theodore M. Bernstein, assistant managing editor of the
Times. He sits in an orderly office in the southeast corner of the 55
newsroom where, as he phrases it, he "second guesses" prose written
under pressure. His bristling guide to blunders has a circulation of
sixteen hundred among employes of the *Times,* and among thirty-six
hundred outside moochers who are trying to improve their minds.
Three years ago, using material from W & S, Mr. Bernstein wrote a 60
grammar, *Watch Your Language.* About thirty-five thousand copies
have been sold. (Never say "It has sold thirty-five thousand copies,"
which is English the Queen wouldn't like.)

[9] Being impartial, equitable, just, fair, merciful, magnanimous
and charitable, W & S compliments about as many *Times* writers as 65
it eviscerates. About half of Mr. Bernstein's clients are winners. But
it is the sinners who give his sheet its astringent flavor. After he is
through with them, they cultivate the kind of writing up with which
Mr. Bernstein will put in silence.

The inexperienced speaker, called upon to "say a few words," notoriously becomes tongue-tied. Sometimes the inexperienced writer becomes "pen-tied"; more often, unfortunately, he does not. He not only writes too much but also thinks he has to "Write," with a capital W. Suppose he wants to say that it is raining hard. He will probably write one of two things: either "It is raining cats and dogs" or "The precipitation is profuse." Both are bad, for somewhat different reasons. "It is raining cats and dogs" is a cliché; "The precipitation is profuse" is jargon.

A cliché is an expression which was once fresh but has become exhausted from overuse. There is nothing intrinsically wrong with it; it is neither ungrammatical nor inexact. But it has been said so often that it no longer evokes any vivid image in the reader's mind; a writer uses it out of laziness or misunderstanding.

Students often ask how they can recognize clichés. Isn't *any* expression a cliché, they ask, because everything has been said before? Any expression can become a cliché if it is used too often, but expressions which already have been used too often are fairly easy to identify. If you hear half of an expression, and can supply the other half, it's a cliché. So, given these two lists:

as warm as _____
as free as _____
as comfortable as _____
as jumpy as _____
as sly as _____
as wise as _____
as pretty as _____
an old shoe
a picture
an owl
toast
a fox
a bird
a cat

you have no difficulty pairing them off. But not all clichés are comparisons. The following lists are equally easy to match:

sing for _____
pay _____
the straight _____
chip off _____
the sum _____

the old block
and substance
your supper
the piper
and narrow

All these expressions have their origin in human observation. They often derive from nature and were once concrete and imaginative. But now, when you read "as jumpy as a cat," for example, you don't picture a cat and think how apt the comparison is. Your mind simply clicks off the meaning "jumpy," and the writer might as well not have bothered with the rest. It is the writer's job to think up a new way of saying "jumpy" (jumpy as a jockey or a bingo player or a contestant in a spelling bee) or to say it straight. The word alone is stronger and clearer if it doesn't have to carry dead wood.

Jargon has two meanings. It may mean specialized shop- or trade-talk of a particular group. Thus "audiovisual aids," "upward mobility," "ability to relate to his peers in a social situation," "hard sell," "Man, that's way out," "He hit the sack at twenty-three hundred," "The patient is spiking 104° in the afternoons" are all examples of the jargon of various groups. In general, this kind of writing should be avoided when the writer addresses any but the members of his own group. At best, it is the mark of the newcomer trying on his still-squeaky boots; at worst, it is pretentious and ill-mannered. Again it should be emphasized that this type of jargon is perfectly acceptable when members of a particular group or profession are communicating with one another.

The other, more important meaning of the word "jargon" was explained by Sir Arthur Quiller-Couch in his *On the Art of Writing*. He calls jargon clumsy, roundabout, vague, "woolly," affected, "elegant" writing. The writer of jargon uses such meaningless, unnecessary phrases as "in connection with," "with regard to," "according as to whether." He never hits a point head-on, but prefers to walk all around it; instead of writing "no," Quiller-Couch says, he writes "The answer to the question is in the negative"; instead of writing "It is raining," he writes "The precipitation is profuse." He is in love with the sound of his own words, particularly if they are long. He dotes on "vague, woolly, abstract" nouns such as "case, instance, quality, thing, factor, character, condition, state." He is afraid to repeat himself and so uses what Quiller-Couch calls "the trick of Elegant Variation." So, he says, if the writer is talking of Byron, he cannot call him Byron twice on the same page, but uses instead affected variations: "that great but unequal poet," or "the meteoric darling of society." As an amusing example of honesty, of brevity, of concreteness, he cites " 'The hand that rocked the cradle has kicked the bucket.' "

1. Sinclair Lewis' real-estate salesman Babbitt is the personification of jargon and the cliché, both in his thoughts and in his business transactions. Find at least five examples of clichés and three of jargon in the excerpt from the novel presented here. Does Miss McGoun, in her editing of Babbitt's correspondence, remove these evils from his writing? Upon what evidence do you base your answer?

2. From the brief portrait of Babbitt, how do you explain his linguistic habits?

3. How do you explain the fact that paragraphs 3 and 4 of the selection from *Babbitt* are not "vague, woolly, abstract"? What do you learn about Babbitt from these paragraphs? about Lewis?

4. Suppose that you, instead of Miss McGoun, were asked to "tie up those sentences a little better." Rewrite one of Babbitt's letters, removing all clichés and jargon from it. Compare your letter with the original. What has been gained or lost in the process of rewriting?

5. Which of the two types of jargon is "rain shower activity" in paragraph 1 of the Atkinson essay, "Jargon"?

6. In paragraph 2, what examples of Jargon does Atkinson use in his own writing? For what purpose?

7. In paragraph 3, Atkinson says, "(and I quote)" but he does not use quotation marks. Just what is he quoting? Why does he not use quotation marks? Comment on "outer-directed toward status symbols."

8. What jargon does Atkinson use in paragraph 4?

9. Explain why you prefer the normal English equivalents of the jargon statements in paragraphs 1, 2, and 3 of the essay "Enemies of Jargon."

10. Put into straightforward English the content of the two sentences quoted from the article in *Daedalus* and the jargon sentences quoted in paragraphs 4 and 5 of the essay "Enemies of Jargon."

11. Comment on the last sentence of "Enemies of Jargon."

12. How does Atkinson account for the prevalence of jargon in today's writing?

13. From your own reading find three examples of jargon. (Textbooks and "learned journals" are often all too rich sources of it.) Rewrite the passages you find in straightforward prose.

Alternate selection for the study of Cliché and Jargon: Richard Franko Goldman, "The Wonderful World of Culture Or: A Strictly Highbrow and Artistic Subject."

Assignment: Write a brief description of your own home, making it appealing to a prospective tenant but avoiding clichés, jargon, and logical fallacies.

Theme Assignment: Write a theme in which you try to convince a particular group that an action it is about to take is wrong. For example:

a farmers' grange is planning to petition against a school tax;

a hospital workers' union is planning to go out on strike;

a group of refugees is planning a demonstration against a foreign diplomat visiting this country on official business;

a group of teen-agers is planning to exclude a newcomer from its organization;

a faculty committee is planning to abolish fraternities and sororities the following semester;

a Congressional committee is considering a proposal to extend compulsory military training to women;

a state highway commission is considering granting permission for billboards to be posted along the state turnpike.

Remember that—especially because you are addressing a specialized group—any insincerity on your part will be easily detected. Since you are trying to convince the opposition of your way of thinking, you must be direct and forceful. Your worst enemies will be clichés and jargon.

Concreteness

✍From *A Book about Myself*

THEODORE DREISER

[1] During the year 1890 I had been formulating my first dim notion as to what it was I wanted to do in life. For two years and more I had been reading Eugene Field's "Sharps and Flats," a column he wrote daily for the Chicago *Daily News,* and through this, the
5 various phases of life which he suggested in a humorous though at times romantic way, I was beginning to suspect, vaguely at first, that I wanted to write, possibly something like that. Nothing else that I had so far read—novels, plays, poems, histories—gave me quite the same feeling for constructive thought as did the matter of his daily
10 notes, poems, and aphorisms, which were on Chicago principally, whereas nearly all others dealt with foreign scenes and people.

[2] But this comment on local life here and now, these trenchant bits on local street scenes, institutions, characters, functions, all moved me as nothing hitherto had. To me Chicago at this time
15 seethed with a peculiarly human or realistic atmosphere. It is given to some cities, as to some lands, to suggest romance, and to me Chicago did that hourly. It sang, I thought, and in spite of what I deemed my various troubles—small enough as I now see them—I was singing

with it. These seemingly drear neighborhoods through which I walked each day, doing collecting for an easy-payment furniture company, 20 these ponderous regions of large homes where new-wealthy packers and manufacturers dwelt, these curiously foreign neighborhoods of almost all nationalities; and, lastly, that great downtown area, surrounded on two sides by the river, on the east by the lake, and on the south by railroad yards and stations, the whole set with these new tall 25 buildings, the wonder of the western world, fascinated me. Chicago was so young, so blithe, so new, I thought. Florence in its best days must have been something like this to young Florentines, or Venice to the young Venetians.

[3] Here was a city which had no traditions but was making them, 30 and this was the very thing that every one seemed to understand and rejoice in. Chicago was like no other city in the world, so said they all. Chicago would outstrip every other American city, New York included, and become the first of all American, if not European or world, cities. . . . This dream many hundreds of thousands of its 35 citizens held dear. Chicago would be first in wealth, first in beauty, first in art achievement. A great World's Fair was even then being planned that would bring people from all over the world. The Auditorium, the new Great Northern Hotel, the amazing (for its day) Masonic Temple twenty-two stories high, a score of public institu- 40 tions, depots, theaters and the like, were being constructed. It is something wonderful to witness a world metropolis springing up under one's very eyes, and this is what was happening here before me.

[4] Nosing about the city in an inquiring way and dreaming half-formed dreams of one and another thing I would like to do, it finally 45 came to me, dimly, like a bean that strains at its enveloping shell, that I would like to write of these things. It would be interesting, so I thought, to describe a place like Goose Island in the Chicago River, a mucky and neglected realm then covered with shanties made of up-turned boats sawed in two, and yet which seemed to me the height 50 of the picturesque; also a building like the Auditorium of the Masonic Temple, that vast wall of masonry twenty-two stories high and at that time actually the largest building in the world; or a seething pit like that of the Board of Trade, which I had once visited and which astonished and fascinated me as much as anything ever had. That 55 roaring, yelling, screaming whirlpool of life! And then the lake, with its pure white sails and its blue water; the Chicago River, with its black, oily water, its tall grain elevators and black coal pockets; the great railroad yards, covering miles and miles of space with their cars.

60 [5] How wonderful it all was! As I walked from place to place
collecting I began betimes to improvise rhythmic, vaguely formulated
word-pictures or rhapsodies anent these same and many other things
—free verse, I suppose we should call it now—which concerned
everything and nothing but somehow expressed the seething poetry
65 of my soul and this thing to me. Indeed I was crazy with life, a little
demented or frenzied with romance and hope. I wanted to sing, to
dance, to eat, to love. My word-dreams and maunderings concerned
my day, my age, poverty, hope, beauty, which I mouthed to myself,
chanting aloud at times. Sometimes, because on a number of occa-
70 sions I had heard the Reverend Frank W. Gunsaulus and his like
spout rocket-like sputterings on the subjects of life and religion, I
would orate, pleading great causes as I went. I imagined myself a
great orator with thousands of people before me, my gestures and
enunciation and thought perfect, poetic, and all my hearers moved to
75 tears or demonstrations of wild delight.

[6] After a time I ventured to commit some of these things to
paper, scarcely knowing what they were, and in a fever for self-
advancement I bundled them up and sent them to Eugene Field. In
his column and elsewhere I had read about geniuses being occasion-
80 ally discovered by some chance composition or work noted by one in
authority. I waited for a time, with great interest but no vast depres-
sion, to see what my fate would be. But no word came and in time
I realized that they must have been very bad and had been dropped
into the nearest waste basket. But this did not give me pause nor
85 grieve me. I seethed to express myself. I bubbled. I dreamed. And I
had a singing feeling, now that I had done this much, that some day I
should really write and be very famous into the bargain.

[For treatment of this selection, see pp. 342–343.]

A Visit with the Brownings

NATHANIEL HAWTHORNE

[1] *Florence, June 9th [1858]*—Mamma, Miss Shepard, and I went last evening, at eight o'clock, to see the Brownings: and after some search and inquiry, we found the Casa Guidi, which is a palace in a street not very far from our own. It being dusk, I could not see the exterior, which, if I remember, Browning has celebrated in song; at 5 all events, he has called one of his poems the "Casa Guidi Windows." The street is a narrow one, but on entering the house, we found a spacious staircase, and ample accommodations of vestibule and hall; the latter opening on a balcony, where we could hear the chanting of priests in a church close by. Browning told us that this was the first 10 church where an oratorio had ever been performed. He came into the ante-room to greet us; as did his little boy, Robert, whom they nickname Penny for fondness. This latter cognomen is a diminutive of Appennini, which was bestowed upon him at his first advent into the world, because he was so very small; there being a statue in Florence 15 nicknamed Appennini, because it is so huge. I never saw such a boy as this before; so slender, fragile, and spritelike, not as if he were actually in ill-health, but as if he had little or nothing to do with human flesh and blood. His face is very pretty and most intelligent, and exceedingly like his mother's, whose constitutional lack of stamina 20 I suppose he inherits. He is nine years old, and seems at once less childlike and less manly than would befit that age. I should not quite like to be the father of such a boy, and should fear to stake so much interest and affection on him as he cannot fail to inspire. I wonder what is to become of him—whether he will ever grow to be a 25 man—whether it is desirable that he should. His parents ought to turn their whole attention to making him gross and earthly, and giving him a thicker scabbard to sheathe his spirit in. He was born in Florence, and prides himself on being a Florentine, and is indeed as un-English a production as if he were native in another planet. 30

From the text of the *Italian Notebooks* established by Norman Holmes Pearson and reprinted with his permission.

[2] Mrs. Browning met us at the door of the drawing-room and greeted us most kindly; a pale little woman, scarcely embodied at all; at any rate, only substantial enough to put forth her slender fingers to be grasped, and to speak with a shrill, yet sweet, tenuity
35 of voice. Really, I do not see how Mr. Browning can suppose that he has an earthly wife, any more than an earthly child; both are of the elfin breed, and will flit away from him some day, when he least thinks of it. She is a good and kind fairy, however, and sweetly disposed towards the human race, although only remotely akin to it. It
40 is wonderful to see how small she is; how diminutive, and peaked, as it were, her face, without being ugly; how pale her cheek; how bright and dark her eyes. There is not such another figure in this world; and her black ringlets cluster down into her neck and make her face look the whiter for their sable profusion. I could not form any judg-
45 ment about her age; it may range anywhere within the limits of human life, or elfin-life. When I met her in London, at Mr. Milnes's breakfast-table, she did not impress me so strangely; for the morning light is more prosaic than the dim illumination of their great, tapestried drawing-room; and besides, sitting next to her, she did not then
50 have occasion to raise her voice in speaking, and I was not sensible what a slender pipe she has. It is as if a grasshopper should speak. It is marvellous to me how so extraordinary, so acute, so sensitive a creature, can impress us as she does, with a certainty of her benevolence. It seems to me there were a million chances to one that she
55 would have been a miracle of acidity and bitterness.

[3] We were not the only guests. Mr. and Mrs. Eckers, Americans, recently from the East, and on intimate terms with the Brownings, arrived after us; also, Miss Fanny Haworth, an English literary lady, whom I have met several times in Liverpool; and lastly came the
60 white head and palmer-like beard of Mr. [William Cullen] Bryant, with his daughter. Mr. Browning was very efficient in keeping up conversation with everybody, and seemed to be in all parts of the room and in every group at the same moment; a most vivid and quick-thoughted person, logical and common-sensible, as I presume poets
65 generally are, in their daily talk. Mr. Bryant, as usual, was homely and plain of manner, with an old-fashioned dignity, nevertheless, and a remarkable deference and gentleness of tone, in addressing Mrs. Browning. I doubt, however, whether he has any high appreciation either of her poetry or her husband's; and it is my impression that
70 they care as little about his.

[4] We had some tea and some strawberries, and passed a pleasant

evening. There was no very noteworthy conversation; the most interesting topic being that disagreeable, and now wearisome one, of spiritual communications, as regards which Mrs. Browning is a believer, and her husband an infidel. Bryant appeared not to have made 75 up his mind on the matter, but told a story of a successful communication between Cooper, the novelist, and his sister, who had been dead fifty years. Browning and his wife had both been present at a spiritual session held by Mr. Hume, and had seen and felt the unearthly hands; one of which had placed a laurel wreath on Mrs. 80 Browning's head. Browning, however, avowed his belief that these aforesaid hands were affixed to the feet of Mr. Hume, who lay extended in his chair, with his legs stretching far under the table. The marvellousness of the fact, as I have read of it, and heard it from other eye-witnesses, melted strangely away, in his rude, hearty 85 grip, and at the sharp touch of his logic; while his wife, ever and anon, put in a little shrill and gentle word of expostulation. I am rather surprised that Browning's conversation should be so clear, and so much to the purpose of the moment; since his poetry can seldom proceed far without running into the high grass of latent meanings 90 and obscure allusions.

[5] Mrs. Browning's health does not permit late hours; so we began to take leave at about ten o'clock. I heard her ask Mr. Bryant if he did not mean to re-visit Europe, and heard him answer, not uncheerfully, taking hold of his white hair, "It is getting rather too late 95 in the evening now." If any old age can be cheerful, I should think his might be; so good a man, so cool, so calm—so bright, too, we may say—his life has been like the days that end in pleasant sunsets. He has a great loss, however—or what ought to be a great loss—soon to be encountered in the death of his wife, who, I think, can hardly live 100 to reach America. He is not eminently an affectionate man. I take him to be one who cannot get closely home to his sorrow, nor feel it so sensibly as he gladly would; and in consequence of that deficiency, the world lacks substance to him. It is partly the result, perhaps, of his not having sufficiently cultivated his animal and emotional 105 nature; his poetry shows it, and his personal intercourse—though kindly—does not stir one's blood in the least.

[6] Little Penny, during the evening, sometimes helped the guests to cake and strawberries; joined in the conversation when he had anything to say, or sat down upon a couch to enjoy his own medita- 110 tions. He has long curling hair, and has not yet emerged from his

frock and drawers. It is funny to think of putting him into breeches. His likeness to his mother is strange to behold.

One of the most important ingredients that distinguish good writing from pedestrian writing, a work of art from a second-rate attempt, an *A* paper from a *B,* is concreteness. For it is not enough to be accurate; it is not even enough to have something to say—essential as both are to communication. The rule is easy enough to state: be specific. Never be satisfied with the abstract: *be specific.* Narrow down until you can narrow down no further. (Would you rather go on a blind date with "a girl" or with "a blue-eyed blond who won a beauty contest at Lake Champlain last summer"? with "a guy" or with "the six-foot-two life guard with the red Impala convertible"?) Never say "dress" when you mean "red wool jersey sheath"; "soldier" when you mean "top sergeant" or "rookie" or "company commander"; "animal" when you mean "tiger" or "deer" or "jaguar" or "puppy" or "skunk." Never say "go" when you mean "run," "drive at sixty miles an hour," "toddle," "skip," or "push your way through the crowd."

1. Formulate the guiding purpose of the Dreiser selection. If your formulation is correct, you should be aware that Dreiser faced the problem of making a somewhat abstract idea and set of feelings specific and concrete enough so that the reader would be convinced of his sincerity. What is the abstract idea? In a sentence or two, describe the set of feelings. Select one of Dreiser's sentences which deals with the set of feelings and compare it with your sentence (or sentences). Which is more concrete, more effective, more convincing? By the end of the selection, are you convinced of Dreiser's sincerity? Why or why not?

2. Dreiser gives us some idea of Eugene Field's newspaper column in the following terms:

"a column he wrote daily for the Chicago *Daily News*"
"the various phases of life which he suggested in a humorous though at times romantic way"
"his daily notes, poems, and aphorisms, which were of Chicago principally"
"this comment on local life here and now"
"these trenchant bits on local street scenes, institutions, characters, functions"

Which are most abstract? Which most specific and concrete? Is there any significance to the order Dreiser established for these terms? Explain. Show how you can make even the most concrete of Dreiser's terms still more specific and concrete. What does the fact that you can do this suggest about the meaning of the word "concrete"?

3. What is the topic sentence of the second paragraph? Does it express an essentially abstract or concrete idea? By what method (or methods) is it developed? Does its development increase its concreteness? Explain.

4. What abstract idea in paragraph 3 is made concrete through Dreiser's mention of "A great World's Fair," "The Auditorium," "the new Great Northern Hotel," "the . . . Masonic Temple"?

5. What does Dreiser achieve through the simile, "like a bean that strains at its enveloping shell," in the first sentence of paragraph 4? How appropriate is the simile in its context? Supply an entirely different simile which you think would serve Dreiser's purpose as well as his own simile.

6. What part of speech (noun? verb? adjective? adverb?) contributes most to the concreteness which Dreiser achieves in paragraph 4? Does the evidence on which your answer depends justify a generalization on the relation between concreteness and one or another of the parts of speech? Explain.

7. In his description of his feelings in paragraph 5, Dreiser uses words and phrases that range from the vague and abstract to the specific and concrete. Make a list of these words and phrases, arranged from most vague and abstract to most specific and concrete.

8. What is the relevance of "the Reverend Frank W. Gunsaulus and his like" to the central point of paragraph 5? How does Dreiser in only three words make the Reverend Gunsaulus come to life?

9. What impression do you get of Penny in the first paragraph of the Hawthorne selection? What comparisons—either expressed or implied—does Hawthorne use to convey the impression? What additional information might Hawthorne have given to make the impression even more concrete and vivid?

10. What quality or characteristic of Mrs. Browning does Hawthorne emphasize in paragraph 2? List all the means Hawthorne uses to make the quality or characteristic concrete and specific for the reader. Why do you suppose Hawthorne felt "there were a million chances to one that she [Mrs. Browning] would have been a miracle of acidity and bitterness"?

11. Indicate the means by which Hawthorne points up the contrast between Mr. Browning and Mr. Bryant in paragraph 3.

12. What additional impression do you get of Browning in paragraph 4? In which sentence is the impression made most concrete? Justify your answer.

13. How does Hawthorne make convincing in paragraph 5 his idea that Bryant's old age "can be cheerful"? What is your total impression of Bryant? On what do you base it?

14. How can you justify Hawthorne's returning to Penny in his last paragraph?

Alternate selections for the study of Concreteness: Aldous Huxley, from "Words and Behavior"; Virgil Barker, "Pieter Bruegel the Elder."

Theme Assignment: The following words were spoken by Thomas Jefferson as part of his first inaugural address:

> About to enter, fellow citizens, on the exercise of duties which comprehend everything dear and valuable to you, it is proper you should understand what I deem the essential principles of our government, and consequently those which ought to shape its administration. I shall compress them within the narrowest compass they will bear, stating the general principle, but not all its limitations. Equal and exact justice to all men, of whatever state or persuasion, religious or political; peace, commerce, and honest friendship with all nations, entangling alliances with none; the support of the State governments in all their rights, as the most competent administrations for our domestic concerns, and the surest bulwarks against anti-republican tendencies; the preservation of the general government in its whole constitutional vigor, as the sheet-anchor of our peace at home and safety abroad; a jealous care of the right of election by the people; a mild and safe correction of abuses which are lopped by the sword of revolution, where peaceable remedies are unprovided; absolute acquiescence in the decisions of the majority, the vital principle of republics, from which is no appeal but to force, the vital principle and immediate parent of despotism; a well-disciplined militia, our best reliance in peace and for the first moments of war, till regulars may relieve them; the supremacy of the civil over the military authority; economy in the public expense, that labor may be lightly burdened; the honest payment of our debts, and sacred preservation of the public faith; encouragement of agriculture, and of commerce as its handmaid; the diffusion of information and arraignment of all abuses at the bar of the public reason; freedom of religion, freedom of the press, and freedom of person, under the protection of the Habeas Corpus; and trial by juries impartially selected.

Jefferson said that he was simply stating "the general principle, but not all its limitations." Select one of his principles and write a theme defining, illustrating, or discussing it in as concrete terms as possible.

Active
Verbs

Popular Fallacies: That the Worst Puns Are the Best

CHARLES LAMB

[1] If by worst be only meant the most far-fetched and startling, we agree to it. A pun is not bound by the laws which limit nicer wit. It is a pistol let off at the ear; not a feather to tickle the intellect. It is an antic which does not stand upon manners, but comes bounding into the presence, and does not show the less comic for being dragged in some times by the head and shoulders. What though it limp a little, or prove defective in one leg—all the better. A pun may easily be too curious and artificial. Who has not at one time or other been at a party of professors (himself perhaps an old offender in that line), where, after ringing a round of the most ingenious conceits, every man contributing his shot, and some there the most expert shooters of the day; after making a poor *word* run the gauntlet till it is ready to drop; after hunting and winding it through all the possible ambages of similar sounds; after squeezing, and hauling, and tugging at it, till the very milk of it will not yield a drop further, —suddenly some obscure, unthought-of fellow in a corner, who was never 'prentice to the trade, whom the company for very pity passed

over, as we do by a known poor man when a money-subscription is
going round, no one calling upon him for his quota—has all at once
20 come out with something so whimsical, yet so pertinent; so brazen
in its pretensions, yet so impossible to be denied; so exquisitely good,
and so deplorably bad, at the same time,—that it has proved a Robin
Hood's shot; any thing ulterior to that is despaired of; and the party
breaks up, unanimously voting it to be the very worst (that is, best)
25 pun of the evening. This species of wit is the better for not being
perfect in all its parts. What it gains in completeness, it loses in
naturalness. The more exactly it satisfies the critical, the less hold it
has upon some other faculties. The puns which are most entertaining
are those which will least bear an analysis. Of this kind is the follow-
30 ing, recorded with a sort of stigma, in one of Swift's Miscellanies.

[2] An Oxford scholar, meeting a porter who was carrying a hare
through the streets, accosted him with this extraordinary question:
"Prithee, friend, is that thy own hare, or a wig?"

[3] There is no excusing this, and no resisting it. A man might
35 blur ten sides of paper in attempting a defence of it against a critic
who should be laughter-proof. The quibble in itself is not considerable. It is only a new turn given, by a little false pronunciation, to a
very common, though not very courteous inquiry. Put by one gentleman to another at a dinner-party, it would have been vapid; to the
40 mistress of the house, it would have shown much less wit than rude-
ness. We must take in the totality of time, place, and person; the pert
look of the inquiring scholar, the desponding looks of the puzzled
porter; the one stopping at leisure, the other hurrying on with his
burthen; the innocent though rather abrupt tendency of the first
45 member of the question, with the utter and inextricable irrelevancy
of the second; the place—a public street, not favourable to frivolous
investigations; the affrontive quality of the primitive inquiry (the
common question) invidiously transferred to the derivative (the new
turn given to it) in the implied satire; namely, that few of that tribe
50 are expected to eat of the good things which they carry, they being
in most countries considered rather as the temporary trustees than
owners of such dainties,—which the fellow was beginning to understand; but then the *wig* again comes in, and he can make nothing
of it: all put together constitute a picture: Hogarth could have made
55 it intelligible on canvas.

[4] Yet nine out of ten critics will pronounce this a very bad pun,
because of the defectiveness in the concluding member, which is its
very beauty, and constitutes the surprise. The same persons shall cry

up for admirable the cold quibble from Virgil about the broken
Cremona; because it is made out in all its parts, and leaves nothing 60
to the imagination. We venture to call it cold; because of thousands
who have admired it, it would be difficult to find one who has heartily
chuckled at it. As appealing to the judgment merely (setting the
risible faculty aside), we must pronounce it a monument of curious
felicity. But as some stories are said to be too good to be true, it may 65
with equal truth be asserted of this bi-verbal allusion, that it is too
good to be natural. One cannot help suspecting that the incident was
invented to fit the line. It would have been better had it been less
perfect. Like some Virgilian hemistichs, it has suffered by filling up.
The *nimium Vicina* was enough in conscience; the *Cremonae* after- 70
wards loads it. It is in fact a double pun; and we have always observed that a superfoetation in this sort of wit is dangerous. When a
man has said a good thing, it is seldom politic to follow it up. We do
not care to be cheated a second time; or, perhaps, the mind of man
(with reverence be it spoken) is not capacious enough to lodge two 75
puns at a time. The impression, to be forcible, must be simultaneous
and undivided.

Standard grammars point out that the function of verbs is to make
an assertion or to communicate action or state of being. The verb is
the very heart of most English sentences; except where the verb may
be clearly implied in context, as in dialogue, a "sentence" without a
verb fails to communicate. So important a part of speech deserves the
attention of every writer.

Beyond one or two generalizations, however, little of value can be
said in the abstract about the most effective use of verbs. The generalizations are, first, to use verbs in the active voice rather than the
passive whenever possible and, second, to use the most vivid and
appropriate verb to communicate action rather than vaguely suggesting action.

"He kicked the ball" (active voice) is a crisp sentence.

"The ball was kicked by him" (passive voice) emphasizes the ball
rather than the man and reverses the normal forward movement of
English sentences.

"He went over the fence" is far less effective than "He clambered
over the fence" because the action is left vague and general.

English as a language is rich in verbs, and care in the selection of
just the right verb will do much to improve writing.

1. List ten particularly effective verbs (or verbals) in the first paragraph of the Lamb selection. Why are they as effective as you think

they are? List at least two synonyms for each of the ten; are any of your synonyms more effective than Lamb's verbs? Why or why not?

    2. Comment on the use of the verb "blur" in the second sentence of paragraph 3; of "pronounce" in the first sentence of paragraph 4; of "cry up" in the second sentence of paragraph 4.

    3. In paragraphs 3 and 4, are verbs or nouns and adjectives more important in achieving vividness? Rewrite parts of both paragraphs, changing as many verbs and nouns and adjectives as necessary to increase vividness.

    4. Comment on the use and effectiveness of parallelism in paragraph 3.

    5. Identify the type of sentence 6, paragraph 3. Rewrite the sentence in at least two ways, using as many sentences as you think desirable. What has been gained or lost in each rewrite?

    6. Account for the distribution of vivid and vague verbs throughout the selection. Does your answer indicate that one part is more effective than another? Why or why not? If you feel one part is more effective than another, rewrite that part of the selection which you feel needs more active and vivid verbs and comment on the results you obtain.

Alternate selection for the study of Active Verbs: D. H. Lawrence from "Making Pictures."

    Assignment: Substitute five alternatives for each of the verbs in the following sentences; arrange each set of your alternatives in ascending order of effectiveness:

    1. The car went over the embankment.
    2. She moved away from him.
    3. The president walked to the microphone.
    4. The crowd reacted favorably to the performance.
    5. We all want peace.
    6. The medicine hurt his head.
    7. The dreamer got up and went into the next room.
    8. The bride came down the aisle.
    9. As the child went into the street, his mother called him.
    10. The minister spoke with great feeling about his deepest convictions.
    11. An unfeeling parent retards the development of a child's talent.
    12. The group stepped off the elevator, thankful that the dangerous ride was over.
    13. The man looked at his wife as he passed through the room.
    14. The refrigerator went on; the electric clock ran; the radio played.
    15. The fire burned.

Levels of Diction

✐ Watson Was a Woman

REX STOUT

GASOGENE: TANTALUS: Buttons: Irregulars:

[1] You will forgive me for refusing to join your commemorative toast, "The Second Mrs. Watson," when you learn it was a matter of conscience. I could not bring myself to connive at the perpetuation of a hoax. Not only was there never a second Mrs. Watson; there 5 was not even a first Mrs. Watson. Furthermore, there was no Doctor Watson.

[2] Please keep your chairs.

[3] Like all true disciples, I have always recurrently dipped into the Sacred Writings (called by the vulgar the Sherlock Holmes 10 stories) for refreshment; but not long ago I reread them from beginning to end, and I was struck by a singular fact that reminded me of the dog in the night. The singular fact about the dog in the night, as we all know, was that it didn't bark; and the singular fact about Holmes in the night is that he is never seen going to bed. The writer of 15 the tales, the Watson person, describes over and over again, in detail, all the other minutiae of that famous household—suppers, breakfasts, arrangement of furniture, rainy evenings at home—but not once are

From *Saturday Review*, March 1, 1941.

we shown either Holmes or Watson going to bed. I wondered, why
20 not? Why such unnatural and obdurate restraint, nay, concealment,
regarding one of the pleasantest episodes of the daily routine?
[4] I got suspicious.

[5] The uglier possibilities that occurred to me, as that Holmes
had false teeth or that Watson wore a toupee, I rejected as prepos-
25 terous. They were much too obvious, and shall I say unsinister. But
the game was afoot, and I sought the trail, in the only field available
to me, the Sacred Writings themselves. And right at the very start,
on page 9 of "A Study in Scarlet," I found this:

> . . . It was rare for him to be up after ten at night, and he had invari-
> ably breakfasted and gone out before I rose in the morning.

[6] I was indescribably shocked. How had so patent a clue escaped
30 so many millions of readers through the years? That was, that only
could be, a woman speaking of a man. Read it over. The true authentic speech of a wife telling of her husband's—but wait. I was not
indulging in idle speculation, but seeking evidence to establish a
fact. It was unquestionably a woman speaking of a man, yes, but
35 whether a wife of a husband, or a mistress of a lover . . . I admit I
blushed. I blushed for Sherlock Holmes, and I closed the book. But
the fire of curiosity was raging in me, and soon I opened again to
the same page, and there in the second paragraph I saw:

> The reader may set me down as a hopeless busybody, when I con-
> fess how much this man stimulated my curiosity, and how often I
> endeavored to break through the reticence which he showed on all that
> concerned himself.

[7] You bet she did. She would. Poor Holmes! She doesn't even
40 bother to employ one of the stock euphemisms, such as, "I wanted to
understand him better," or, "I wanted to share things with him." She
proclaims it with brutal directness, "I endeavored to break through
the reticence." I shuddered, and for the first time in my life felt that
Sherlock Holmes was not a god, but human—human by his suffer-
45 ing. Also, from that one page I regarded the question of the Watson
person's sex as settled for good. Indubitably she was a female, but
wife or mistress? I went on. Two pages later I found:

> . . . his powers upon the violin . . . at my request he has played me
> some of Mendelssohn's *Lieder* . . ."

[8] Imagine a man asking another man to play him some of Mendelssohn's *Lieder* on a violin!

[9] And on the next page:

. . . I rose somewhat earlier than usual, and found that Sherlock Holmes had not yet finished his breakfast . . . my place had not been laid nor my coffee prepared. With . . . petulance . . . I rang the bell and gave a curt intimation that I was ready. Then I picked up a magazine from the table and attempted to while away the time with it, while my companion munched silently at his toast.

[10] That is a terrible picture, and you know and I know how bitterly realistic it is. Change the diction, and it is practically a love story by Ring Lardner. That Sherlock Holmes, like other men, had breakfasts like that is a hard pill for a true disciple to swallow, but we must face the facts. The chief thing to note of this excerpt is that it not only reinforces the conviction that Watson was a lady—that is to say, a woman—but also it bolsters our hope that Holmes did not through all those years live in sin. A man does not munch silently at his toast when breakfasting with his mistress; or, if he does, it won't be long until he gets a new one. But Holmes stuck to her—or she to him—for over a quarter of a century. Here are a few quotations from the later years:

. . . Sherlock Holmes was standing smiling at me. . . . I rose to my feet, stared at him for some seconds in utter amazement, and then it appears that I must have fainted. . . ."
—*The Adventure of the Empty House,* page 4.
I believe that I am one of the most long-suffering of mortals.
—*The Tragedy of Birlstone,* page 1.
The relations between us in those latter days were peculiar. He was a man of habits, narrow and concentrated habits, and I had become one of them. As an institution I was like the violin, the shag tobacco, the old black pipe, the index books, and others perhaps less excusable.
—*The Adventure of the Creeping Man,* page 1.

[11] And we have been expected to believe that a man wrote those things! The frank and unconcerned admission that she fainted at sight of Holmes after an absence! "I am one of the most long-suffering of mortals"—the oldest uxorial cliché in the world; Aeschylus used it; no doubt cavemen gnashed their teeth at it! And the familiar pathetic plaint, "As an institution I was like the old black pipe!"

[12] Yes, uxorial, for surely she was wife. And the old black pipe
itself provides us with a clincher on that point. This comes from page
16 of "The Hound of the Baskervilles":

> . . . did not return to Baker Street until evening. It was nearly nine
> o'clock when I found myself in the sitting room once more.
> My first impression as I opened the door was that a fire had broken
> out, for the room was so filled with smoke that the light of the lamp
> upon the table was blurred by it. As I entered, however, my fears
> were set at rest, for it was the acrid fumes of strong coarse tobacco
> which took me by the throat and set me coughing. Through the haze
> I had a vague vision of Holmes in his dressing gown coiled up in an
> armchair with his black clay pipe between his lips. Several rolls of
> paper lay around him.
> "Caught cold, Watson?" said he.
> "No, it's this poisonous atmosphere."
> "I suppose it *is* pretty thick, now that you mention it."
> "Thick! It is intolerable!"
> "Open the window, then!"

[13] I say husband and wife. Could anyone alive doubt it after
reading that painful banal scene? Is there any need to pile on the
evidence?

[14] For the last-ditch skeptic there is more evidence, much more.
The efforts to break Holmes of the cocaine habit, mentioned in
various places in the Sacred Writings, display a typical reformist wife
in action, especially the final gloating over her success. A more complicated, but no less conclusive, piece of evidence is the strange, the
astounding recital of Holmes's famous disappearance, in "The Final
Problem," and the reasons given therefor in a later tale, "The Adventure of the Empty House." It is incredible that this monstrous
deception was not long ago exposed.

[15] Holmes and Watson had together wandered up the valley of
the Rhone, branched off at Leuk, made their way over the Gemmi
Pass, and gone on, by way of Interlaken, to Meiringen. Near that
village, as they were walking along a narrow trail high above a tremendous abyss, Watson was maneuvered back to the hotel by a fake
message. Learning that the message was fake, she (he) flew back to
their trail, and found that Holmes was gone. No Holmes. All that was
left of him was a polite and regretful note of farewell, there on a rock
with his cigarette case for a paperweight, saying that Professor Moriarty had arrived and was about to push him into the abyss.

[16] That in itself was rather corny. But go on to "The Adventure

of the Empty House." Three years have passed. Sherlock Holmes has 95
suddenly and unexpectedly reappeared in London, causing the
Watson person to collapse in a faint. His explanation of his long
absence is fantastic. He says that he had grappled with Professor
Moriarty on the narrow trail and tossed him into the chasm; that,
in order to deal at better advantage with the dangerous Sebastian 100
Moran, he had decided to make it appear that he too had toppled
over the cliff; that, so as to leave no returning footprints on the
narrow trail, he had attempted to scale the upper cliff, and, while he
was doing so, Sebastian Moran himself had appeared up above and
thrown rocks at him; that by herculean efforts he had eluded Moran 105
and escaped over the mountains; that for three years he had wandered around Persia and Tibet and France, communicating with no
one but his brother Mycroft, so that Sebastian Moran would think
he was dead. *Though by his own account Moran knew, must have
known, that he had got away!* 110

[17] That is what Watson says that Holmes told her (him). It is
simply gibberish, below the level even of a village half-wit. It is impossible to suppose that Sherlock Holmes ever dreamed of imposing
on any sane person with an explanation like that; it is impossible to
believe that he would insult his own intelligence by offering such an 115
explanation even to an idiot. I deny that he ever did. I believe that all
he said, after Watson recovered from the faint, was this: "My dear,
I am willing to try it again," for he was a courteous man. And it was
Watson who, attempting to cook up an explanation, made such a
terrible hash of it. 120

[18] Then who was this person whose nom de plume was "Doctor
Watson"? Where did she come from? What was she like? What was
her name before she snared Holmes?

[19] Let us see what we can do about the name, by methods that
Holmes himself might have used. It was Watson who wrote the im- 125
mortal tales, therefore if she left a record of her name anywhere it
must have been in the tales themselves. But what we are looking for
is not her characteristics or the facts of her life, but her *name,* that
is to say, her *title;* so obviously the place to look is in the *titles* of the
tales. 130

[20] There are sixty of the tales all told. The first step is to set
them down in chronological order, and number them from 1 to 60.
Now, which shall we take first? Evidently the reason why Watson was
at such pains to conceal her name in the clutter of titles was to

135 *mystify* us, so the number to start with should be the most *mystical* number, namely seven. And to make it doubly sure, we shall make it seven times seven, which is 49. Very well. The 49th tale is "The Adventure of the Illustrious Client." We of course discard the first four words, "The Adventure of the," which are repeated in most of the
140 titles. Result: "ILLUSTRIOUS CLIENT."

[21] The next most significant thing about Watson is her (his) constant effort to convince us that those things happen exactly as she (he) tells them; that they are on the *square*. Good. The first square of an integer is the integer 4. We take the title of the 4th tale and get
145 "REDHEADED LEAGUE."

[22] We proceed to elimination. Of all the factors that contribute to an ordinary man's success, which one did Holmes invariably exclude, or eliminate? Luck. In crap-shooting, what are the lucky numbers? Seven and eleven. But we have already used 7, which elimi-
150 nates it, so there is nothing left but 11. The 11th tale is about the "ENGINEER'S THUMB."

[23] Next, what was Holmes's age at the time he moved to Baker Street? Twenty-seven. The 27th tale is the adventure of the "NORWOOD BUILDER." And what was Watson's age? Twenty-six. The
155 26th tale is the adventure of the "EMPTY HOUSE." But there is no need to belabor the obvious. Just as it is a simple matter to decipher the code of the Dancing Men when Holmes has once put you on the right track, so can you, for yourself, make the additional required selections now that I have explained the method. And you will in-
160 evitably get what I got:

> *Illustrious Client*
> *Red-headed League*
> *Engineer's Thumb*
> *Norwood Builder*
> *Empty House*
>
> *Wisteria Lodge*
> *Abbey Grange*
> *Twisted Lip*
> *Study in Scarlet*
> *Orange Pips*
> *Noble Bachelor*

[24] And, acrostically simple, the initial letters read down, the carefully hidden secret is ours. Her name was Irene Watson.

[25] But not so fast. Is there any way of checking that? Of dis-

covering her name by any other method, say *a priori?* We can try
and see. A woman wrote the stories about Sherlock Holmes, that has   165
been demonstrated; and that woman was his wife. Does there appear,
anywhere in the stories, a woman whom Holmes fell for? Whom he
really cottoned to? Indeed there does. "A Scandal in Bohemia" opens
like this:

> To Sherlock Holmes she is always *the woman.* . . . In his eyes she
> eclipses and predominates the whole of her sex.

[26] And what was the name of *the* woman? Irene!   170
[27] But, you say, not Irene Watson, but Irene Adler. Certainly.
Watson's whole purpose, from beginning to end, was to confuse and
bewilder us regarding her identity. So note that name well. Adler.
What is an adler, or, as it is commonly spelled, addler? An addler is
one who, or that which, addles. Befuddles. Confuses. I admit I ad-   175
mire that stroke; it is worthy of Holmes himself. In the very act of
deceiving and confusing us, she has the audacity to employ a name
that brazenly announces her purpose!

[28] An amusing corroborative detail about this Irene of "Scandal
in Bohemia"—*the* woman to Holmes according to the narrator of the   180
tales—is that Holmes was present at her wedding at the Church of
St. Monica in the Edgeware Road. It is related that he was there as a
witness, but that is pure poppycock. Holmes himself says, "I was
half-dragged up to the altar, and before I knew where I was I found
myself mumbling responses. . . ." Those are not the words of an   185
indifferent witness, but of a reluctant, ensnared, bulldozed man—in
short, a bridegroom. And in all the 1323 pages of the Sacred Writings, that is the only wedding we ever see—the only one, so far as we
are told, that Holmes ever graced with his presence.

[29] All this is very sketchy. I admit it. I am now collecting ma-   190
terial for a fuller treatment of the subject, a complete demonstration
of the evidence and the inevitable conclusion. It will fill two volumes,
the second of which will consist of certain speculations regarding
various concrete results of that long-continued and—I fear, alas—
none-too-happy union. For instance, what of the parentage of Lord   195
Peter Wimsey, who was born, I believe, around the turn of the century—about the time of the publication of "The Adventure of the
Second Stain"? That will bear looking into.

There are various levels of diction in English. Appropriateness is a major criterion in the choice of a level of diction for a given kind of communication. Without attempting to make a highly formal and rigid classification of the levels of diction, it is nevertheless useful to draw a few distinguishing lines among the various levels.

The most formal English is used in such writings as learned articles, on scholarly subjects addressed to scholars, philosophical treatises, documents of historical import (*The Constitution of the United States,* for example), reports and minutes of parliamentary bodies. Somewhat less formal English—though still formal—is used in such writings as good newspaper editorials, articles in periodicals addressed to an educated and cultivated audience (*Harper's, Atlantic Monthly, Saturday Review,* for example), formal correspondence between educated people, college students' term papers, and most expository themes. Informal English is appropriate for social correspondence, the casual conversation of educated people, certain kinds of personal (or informal) essays.

The lines distinguishing these levels, one from another, are not hard and fast. Many words are quite correct and appropriate on all levels; the place of some words has changed with time, and the place of other words will change with time. What was once a slang or objectionable word may now be a standard word, and what is now a highly formal word or expression may become appropriate for informal usage.

Appropriateness of diction depends on whether the communication is written or spoken, on the speaker or writer, on the reader or listener, and on the circumstances under which the communication takes place. Spoken English is usually less formal than the most formal English, but sometimes it may be just as formal—a sermon, for example, or even at times a university commencement address or the citations read aloud to recipients of honorary degrees. For a college professor to order groceries over a telephone as though he were lecturing on archaeology would obviously be inappropriate; for the grocery clerk to address the professor as he would his bowling club intimates would be just as inappropriate. The college student who writes, "The collation served after the jam session was super" or "The iniquities of the Nazis were pretty hard to take" is guilty of mixing levels of diction, one or another of which is inappropriate.

Provincialisms and dialects, technical or trade vocabularies, and slang form additional levels of diction. Except in fiction in which characters are made to speak as they would in a particular part of the country or with a particular foreign-language background, there is normally no place for provincialisms and dialects in written communication of any formality. Technical or trade vocabularies (the golfer's "birdie," "eagle," and "divot"; the horse racer's "win," "place," and "show"; the college student's "flunk," "crib," and "cut"; the newspaper man's "lead," "head," and "cut") have a place only in the communication—usually informal—among members of the group or trade for which the vocabulary came into being. For a golfer to avoid golf terms or for a reporter to avoid newspaper terms would be just as inappropriate as for a student to write in tennis or baseball terms about agrarian reforms in nineteenth-century England.

Slang is defined in part by the *American College Dictionary* as "language . . . regarded as below the standard of cultivated speech." Slang is never admitted into the most formal writing and only rarely into less formal writing. There are two chief objections to slang: it is usually ineffective, vague, unimaginative (the dance was swell; the food was lousy), and it frequently is in vogue for only a short time; when the vogue dies, communication is impaired. Occasionally a slang expression is effective, however, and it may have a long enough life to become quite respectable. The use of a particularly effective slang expression in informal or semiformal writing just because it is effective and lends variety is not objectionable; but it must be remembered that a little slang goes a long way.

Slang should not be confused with colloquialisms—the style, diction, and usage of informal communication. And the diction most characteristic of colloquial speech should not be mixed with the diction peculiar to more formal written communication. The *American College Dictionary*, in pointing out that there is nothing "bad" about colloquial English, says that "it is merely a familiar style used in speaking rather than in writing."

It is obviously impossible to draw up exhaustive lists of words appropriate to various types of written communication that will guide you into using appropriate diction. Reading various types of writing; analyzing the diction of occasional pieces of writing; listening to and conversing with people of various occupations, professions, and levels of society; remaining constantly aware of the necessity for propriety of diction in your own writing; and consulting a dictionary to find out whether a given word is slang or a colloquialism or a provincialism, say, will do much to help you avoid serious errors in diction.

1. Formulate the guiding purpose of Stout's essay and characterize as exactly as you can the audience for which you think Stout was writing. Precisely how do you characterize the tone of the essay?

2. Find at least ten places in the essay in which Stout juxtaposes formal English with informal, colloquial, or even slangy English. Comment on the appropriateness of each juxtaposition, indicating the effect or effects achieved by each. Take into account your answers to question 1.

3. Rewrite five of Stout's formal sentences in less formal English.
4. Rewrite five of Stout's informal sentences in more formal English.
5. Of what logical fallacies is Stout guilty? Make specific references to the essay.
6. From the selections in this book, choose three which seem to you to represent a variety of levels of diction. How do you account for the level of diction of each of the three? In any of the pieces you have selected, do you find more than one level of diction used? If so, is the mixing of levels functional? Explain.

Alternate selections for the study of Levels of Diction: Max Shulman, "Love Is a Fallacy"; Robert Benchley, "How I Create"; Meg Greenfield, "Editorial Disorder and Early Sorrow."

Theme Assignment: Everyday situations demand different kinds of manners and different levels of diction—including, often enough, "technical or trade vocabularies" and even slang. A conversation with a garage mechanic about fixing your car will sound quite different from the instructions you may give to a barber or beauty shop operator about cutting your hair. Though you may at all times be polite, your manner of ordering in a diner will (and should) be quite different from your manner of ordering in an exclusive and expensive restaurant. Your behavior and levels of diction will be quite different when you are in a funeral home and a sports arena, a college classroom and a student lounge, a bank and a butcher shop.

Write a richly illustrated theme on differences in manners and levels of diction in various everyday situations; you need not, of course, limit yourself to the situations in the preceding paragraph. This is your opportunity to use some of the techniques of narration—particularly dialogue—to develop an expository idea.

or

Imagine yourself, for the purposes of this assignment, a devotee of Sherlock Holmes. Write a theme in which—using the "evidence" presented by Stout and any additional evidence that you may wish to garner from the Sherlock Holmes stories—you refute Stout's central thesis. If you so choose, you may use logical fallacies, but yours should be as subtle and palatable as Stout's. You will have to decide what level or levels of diction will best serve your purpose.

Connotation and Denotation

✐ From *Life with Picasso*

FRANÇOISE GILOT and CARLTON LAKE

[1] I met Pablo Picasso in May 1943, during the German Occupation of France. I was twenty-one and I felt already that painting was my whole life. At that time I had as house-guest an old school friend named Geneviève, who had come up from her home near Montpellier, in the south of France, to spend a month with me. With 5 her and the actor Alain Cuny, I went to have dinner one Wednesday at a small restaurant then much frequented by painters and writers. It was called *Le Catalan* and was in the Rue des Grands-Augustins on the Left Bank, not far from Notre Dame.

[2] When we got there that evening and were seated, I saw Picasso 10 for the first time. He was at the next table with a group of friends: a man, whom I didn't recognize, and two women. One of the women I knew to be Marie-Laure, Vicomtesse de Noailles, the owner of an important collection of paintings, who is now something of a painter herself. At that time, though, she had not yet taken up painting—at 15 least publicly—but she had written a poetic little book called *The*

Tower of Babel. She had a long, narrow, somewhat decadent-looking face framed by an ornate coiffure that reminded me of Rigaud's portrait of Louis XIV in the Louvre.

20 [3] The other woman, Alain Cuny whispered to me, was Dora Maar, a Yugoslav photographer and painter who, as everyone knew, had been Picasso's companion since 1936. Even without his help I would have had no trouble identifying her, because I knew Picasso's work well enough to see that this was the woman who was shown in the
25 *Portrait of Dora Maar* in its many forms and variants. She had a beautiful oval face but a heavy jaw, which is a characteristic trait of almost all the portraits Picasso has made of her. Her hair was black and pulled back in a severe, starkly dramatic coiffure. I noticed her intense bronze-green eyes, and her slender hands with their long,
30 tapering fingers. The most remarkable thing about her was her extraordinary immobility. She talked little, made no gestures at all, and there was something in her bearing that was more than dignity—a certain rigidity. There is a French expression that is very apt: she carried herself like the holy sacrament.
35 [4] I was a little surprised at Picasso's appearance. My impression of what he ought to look like had been founded on the photograph by Man Ray in the special Picasso number that the art review *Cahiers d'Art* had published in 1936: dark hair, bright flashing eyes, very squarely built, rugged—a handsome animal. Now, his graying
40 hair and absent look—either distracted or bored—gave him a withdrawn, Oriental appearance that reminded me of the statue of the Egyptian scribe in the Louvre. There was nothing sculptural or fixed in his manner of moving, however: he gesticulated, he twisted and turned, he got up, he moved rapidly back and forth.
45 [5] As the meal went on I noticed Picasso watching us, and from time to time acting a bit for our benefit. It was evident that he recognized Cuny, and he made remarks that we were obviously supposed to overhear. Whenever he said something particularly amusing, he smiled at us rather than just at his dinner companions. Fi-
50 nally, he got up and came over to our table. He brought with him a bowl of cherries and offered some to all of us, in his strong Spanish accent, calling them *cerisses,* with a soft, double-*s* sound.
  [6] Geneviève was a very beautiful girl, of French Catalan ancestry but a Grecian type, with a nose that was a direct prolongation
55 of her forehead. It was a head, Picasso later told me, that he felt he had already painted in his work of the Ingresque or Roman pe-

riod. She often accentuated that Grecian quality, as she did that evening, by wearing a flowing, pleated dress.

[7] "Well, Cuny," Picasso said. "Are you going to introduce me to your friends?" Cuny introduced us and then said, "Françoise is 60 the intelligent one." Pointing to Geneviève, he said, "She's the beautiful one. Isn't she just like an Attic marble?"

[8] Picasso shrugged. "You talk like an actor," he said. "How would you characterize the intelligent one?"

[9] That evening I was wearing a green turban that covered much 65 of my brow and cheeks. Geneviève answered his question.

[10] "Françoise is a Florentine virgin," she said.

[11] "But not the usual kind," Cuny added. "A secularized virgin." Everybody laughed.

[12] "All the more interesting if she's not the ordinary kind," 70 Picasso said. "But what do they do, your two refugees from the history of art?"

[13] "We're painters," Geneviève answered.

[14] Picasso burst out laughing. "That's the funniest thing I've heard all day. Girls who look like that can't be painters." I told him 75 that Geneviève was only on holiday in Paris and that she was a pupil of Maillol in Banyuls and that although I wasn't anybody's pupil, I was very much a painter. In fact, I said, we were having a joint exhibition of paintings and drawings right at the moment in a gallery in the Rue Boissy d'Anglas, behind the Place de la Concorde. 80

[15] Picasso looked down at us in mock-surprise. "Well . . . I'm a painter, too," he said. "You must come to my studio and see some of *my* paintings."

[16] "When?" I asked him.

[17] "Tomorrow. The next day. When you want to." 85

[18] Geneviève and I compared notes. We told him we'd come not tomorrow, not the next day, but perhaps the first of the next week. Picasso bowed. "As you wish," he said. He shook hands all around, picked up his bowl of cherries, and went back to his table.

[19] We were still at table when Picasso and his friends left. It 90 was a cool evening and he put on a heavy mackinaw and a beret. Dora Maar was wearing a fur coat with square shoulders and shoes of a type many girls wore during the Occupation, when leather, along with so many other things, was scarce. They had thick wooden soles and high heels. With those high heels, the padded shoulders, and her 95 hieratic carriage, she seemed a majestic Amazon, towering a full head over the man in the hip-length mackinaw and the *béret basque*.

[20] The following Monday morning, about eleven o'clock, Geneviève and I climbed a dark, narrow, winding staircase hidden away
in a corner of the cobblestone courtyard at 7 Rue des Grands-
Augustins and knocked on the door of Picasso's apartment. After a
short wait it was opened about three or four inches, to reveal the
long, thin nose of his secretary, Jaime Sabartés. We had never seen
him before but we knew who he was. We had seen reproductions
of drawings Picasso had made of him, and Cuny had told us that
Sabartés would be the one to receive us. He looked at us suspiciously
and asked, "Do you have an appointment?" I said we did. He let
us in. He looked anxious as he peered out from behind his thick-
lensed glasses.

[21] We entered an anteroom where there were many birds—
turtledoves and a number of exotic species in wicker cages—and
plants. The plants were not pretty; they were the spiky green ones
you see frequently in copper pots in a concierge's *loge*. Here they
were arranged more appealingly, though, and in front of the high
open window they made a rather pleasing effect. I had seen one of
those plants a month before in a recent portrait of Dora Maar that
was hung, in spite of the Nazi ban on Picasso's work, in an out-of-
the-way alcove of the Louise Leiris gallery in the Rue d'Astorg. It
was a magnificent portrait, in pink and gray. In the background of
the picture there was a framework of panels like the panes of the
large antique window I now saw, a cage of birds, and one of those
spiky plants.

[22] We followed Sabartés into a second room which was very
long. I saw several old Louis XIII sofas and chairs, and spread out
on them, guitars, mandolins, and other musical instruments which, I
supposed, Picasso must have used in his painting during the Cubist
period. He later told me that he had bought them after he painted
the pictures, not before, and kept them there now as a remembrance
of his Cubist days. The room had noble proportions but everything
was at sixes and sevens. The long table that stretched out before us
and two long carpenter's tables, one after the other, against the right-
hand wall, were covered with an accumulation of books, magazines,
newspapers, photographs, hats, and miscellaneous clutter. Resting on
one of these tables was a rough piece of amethyst crystal, about the
size of a human head, in the center of which was a small, totally
enclosed cavity filled with what appeared to be water. On a shelf
underneath the table I saw several men's suits folded up and three
or four pairs of old shoes.

[23] As we walked past the long table in the center of the room, I noticed that Sabartés moved out around a dull brownish object lying on the floor near the door that led into the next room. When I came closer to it I saw that it was a sculpture of a skull cast in bronze. 140

[24] The next room was a studio almost entirely filled with sculptures. I saw *The Man with the Sheep,* now cast in bronze and standing in the square at Vallauris, but at that time simply in plaster. 145 There were a number of large heads of women that Picasso had done at Boisgeloup in 1932. There was a wild disorder of bicycle handlebars, rolls of canvas, a fifteenth-century Spanish polychromed wooden Christ, and a weird and spindly sculpture of a woman holding an apple in one hand and what looked like a hot-water bottle in 150 the other arm.

[25] The most striking thing, though, was a glowing canvas by Matisse, a still life of 1912, with a bowl of oranges on a pink tablecloth against a light ultramarine and bright pink background. I remember also a Vuillard, a Douanier Rousseau, and a Modigliani; but 155 in that shadowy studio, the glow of color of the Matisse shone among the sculptures. I couldn't resist saying, "Oh, what a beautiful Matisse!" Sabartés turned and said austerely, "Here there is only Picasso."

[26] By another little winding staircase, on the far side of the 160 room, we climbed to the second floor of Picasso's apartments. Upstairs the ceiling was much lower. We passed into a large studio. On the other side of the room I saw Picasso, surrounded by six or eight people. He was dressed in an old pair of trousers that hung loosely from his hips, and a blue-striped sailor's jersey. When he saw us, 165 his face lighted up in a pleasant smile. He left the group and came over to us. Sabartés muttered something about our having an appointment and then went downstairs.

[27] "Would you like me to show you around?" Picasso asked. We said we would indeed. We hoped he would show us some of his 170 paintings but we didn't dare ask. He took us back downstairs into the sculpture studio.

[28] "Before I came here," he said, "this lower floor was used as a workshop by a weaver, and the upper floor was an actor's studio—Jean-Louis Barrault's. It was here, in this room, that I painted *Guer-* 175 *nica."* He settled back on one of the Louis XIII tables in front of a pair of windows that looked out onto an interior courtyard. "Other than that, though, I hardly ever work in this room. I did *L'Homme au Mouton* here," he said, pointing to the large plaster sculpture of

180 the man holding the sheep in his arms, "but I do my painting upstairs and I generally work on my sculpture in another studio I have
a little way up the street.

[29] "That covered spiral stairway you walked up to get here," he
said, "is the one the young painter in Balzac's *Le Chef-d'Oeuvre*
185 *Inconnu* climbed when he came to see old Pourbus, the friend of
Poussin who painted pictures nobody understood. Oh, the whole
place is full of historical and literary ghosts. Well, let's get back
upstairs," he said. He slid off the table and we followed him up the
winding staircase. He took us through the big studio, around the
190 group of people, none of whom looked up at us as we passed through,
and into a small room in the far corner.

[30] "This is where I do my engraving," he said. "And look here."
He walked over to a sink and turned on a faucet. After a while the
water became steamy. "Isn't it marvelous," he said. "In spite of the
195 war, I have hot water. In fact," he added, "you could come here
and have a hot bath any time you liked." Hot water wasn't really
the thing that interested us most, in spite of its scarcity at that time.
Looking over at Geneviève I thought, Oh, if he'll only stop going
on about the hot water and show us some pictures! Instead, he gave
200 us a short course in how to make resin. I was just at the point of
deciding we'd probably have to leave without seeing any paintings
and never get back there again when finally he took us out into the
large studio and began to show us some. I remember one was a
cock, very colorful and powerful in its features, crowing lustily. Then
205 there was another one, of the same period but very severe, all in
black and white.

[31] About one o'clock the group around us broke up and everyone started to leave. The thing that struck me as most curious that
first day was the fact that the studio seemed the temple of a kind
210 of Picasso religion, and all the people who were there appeared to
be completely immersed in that religion—all except the one to whom
it was addressed. He seemed to be taking it all for granted but not
attaching any importance to it, as if he were trying to show us that
he didn't have any desire to be the central figure of a cult.

215 [32] As we turned to go, Picasso said, "If you want to come back
again, by all means come. But if you do come, don't come like pil-
grims to Mecca. Come because you like me, because you find my
company interesting and because you want to have a simple, direct
relationship with me. If you only want to see my paintings, you'd
220 do just as well to go to a museum."

[33] I didn't take that remark too seriously. In the first place, there were almost no paintings of his to be seen in any of the Paris museums at that time. Then, too, since he was on the Nazi list of proscribed painters, no private gallery was able to show his work openly or in quantity. And looking at another painter's work in a 225 book of reproductions is no satisfaction for a painter. So if anyone wanted to see more of his work—as I did—there was almost nowhere to go but 7 Rue des Grands-Augustins.

[34] A few days after that first visit I dropped in at the gallery where Geneviève and I were having our exhibition. The woman who 230 ran it told me excitedly that a little earlier a short man with piercing dark eyes, wearing a blue-and-white-striped sailor's jersey, had come in. She had realized, after the first shock, that he was Picasso. He had studied the paintings intently and then walked out without saying anything, she told me. When I got home I told Geneviève about his 235 visit. I said he had probably gone to see how bad our paintings were and prove to himself the truth of what he had said when he met us at *Le Catalan:* "Girls who look like that can't be painters."

[35] Geneviève took a more idealistic view of it. "I think it's a nice human touch," she said. "It shows he takes a real interest in 240 young artists' work."

[36] I wasn't convinced. At best it was curiosity, I felt. "He just wanted to see what we had inside—if anything."

[37] "Oh, you're so cynical," she said. "He seemed to me very kind, open-minded, and simple." 245

[38] I told her I thought he perhaps wanted to appear simple but I had looked into those eyes of his and seen something quite different. It hadn't frightened me, though. In fact it made me want to go back. I temporized for about another week and then, one morning, with Geneviève in tow, returned to the Rue des Grands-Augustins. It 250 was Sabartés, of course, who opened the door for us again, his head sticking outside like a little sand fox. This time he admitted us without comment.

[39] Remembering, from our first visit, the very pleasant entrance with its many plants and exotic birds in wicker cages lighted by the 255 high window, we had decided to add a little color to the greenery and so we arrived carrying a pot of cineraria. When Picasso saw us he laughed.

[40] "Nobody brings flowers to an old gent," he said. Then he noticed that my dress was the same color as the blossoms, or vice 260 versa. "You think of everything; I can see that," he said. I pushed

Geneviève in front of me. "Here's beauty, followed by intelligence," I reminded him.

[41] He looked us over carefully, then said, "That remains to be
265 seen. What I see now are simply two different styles: archaic Greece and Jean Goujon."

[42] On our first visit he had shown us only a few pictures. This time he made up for it. He piled them up almost like a scaffolding. There was a painting on the easel; he stuck another on top of that;
270 one on each side; piled others on top of those, until it seemed like a highly skilled balancing act of the human-pyramid kind. As I found out later, he used to arrange them that way almost every day. They always held together by some kind of miracle, but as soon as anyone else touched them they came tumbling down. That morning there
275 were cocks; a buffet of *Le Catalan* with cherries against a background of brown, black, and white; small still lifes, some with lemon and many with glasses, a cup, and a coffeepot, or with fruit against a checked tablecloth. He seemed to be playing with colors as he sorted them out and tossed them up onto the scaffolding. There was a large
280 nude, a three-quarter rear view that one saw at the same time front view, in earth tones, very close to the palette of the Cubist period. There were also scenes of the Vert Galant, that little tip of the Ile de la Cité near the Pont-Neuf, with trees on which each branch was made out of separate spots of paint, much in the manner of van
285 Gogh. There were several mothers with enormous children whose heads reached the very top of the canvas, somewhat in the spirit of the Catalan primitives.

[43] Many of the paintings he showed us that morning had a culinary basis—skinned rabbits or pigeons with peas—a kind of re-
290 flection of the hard time most people were having in getting food. There were others with a sausage stuck, almost, like a *papier collé,* onto an otherwise carefully composed background; also, some portraits of women wearing hats topped with forks or fishes and other kinds of food. Finally he showed us a group of portraits of Dora Maar,
295 very tortured in form, which he had painted over the past two years. They are among the finest paintings he has ever done, I believe. Generally on an off-white background, these figures seemed symbolic of human tragedy, rather than the simple deformation of a female face that they might appear on a superficial level.

300 [44] Suddenly he decided he had shown us enough. He walked away from his pyramid. "I saw your exhibition," he said, looking at me. I didn't have the courage to ask him what he thought of it, so

I just looked surprised. "You're very gifted for drawing," he went
on. "I think you should keep on working—hard—every day. I'll be
curious to see how your work develops. I hope you'll show me other   305
things from time to time." Then he added, to Geneviève, "I think
you've found the right teacher in Maillol. One good Catalan deserves
another."

[45] After that, little else he said that morning registered very
deeply with me. I left the Rue des Grands-Augustins feeling very   310
buoyant, impatient to get back to my studio and go to work.

[For treatment of this selection, see pp. 382–383.]

☞ James Thurber and the Art
of Fantasy   CHARLES S. HOLMES

[1] James Thurber is the outstanding American humorist of the
twentieth century. It would be hard to find anywhere an image of
modern life at once more perceptive, more amusing, and more unsettling than we are given in his work. Literary recognition is sometimes rather grudgingly accorded the humorous writer, but Thurber's   5
importance as an interpreter of the American scene was recognized
early, and it is a safe guess that his life and work will receive increasing attention from critics and historians of American culture as
time goes on. The best of his work is already, in Charles Brady's
phrase, part of "the living folklore of the present": Walter Mitty is   10
a more significant culture figure to twentieth-century Americans than
Rip Van Winkle, and in the predicaments pictured in Thurber's tales
and drawings, we recognize ourselves.

[2] He wrote chiefly about the conflicts and frustrations of everyday life. He once defined his special area as "the pathways between   15
office and home," "the little perils of routine living," and particularly
"that part of the familiar which is humiliating, distressing, and even
tragic." But it was one of the special marks of his genius that he
always managed to suggest the universal in the commonplace. His

From *The Yale Review*, Autumn 1965. Copyright © by the Yale University
Press and used with their permission.

20 central concern is the predicament of man in a baffling and alien world. Cut off from the simpler, stabler order of the past, modern man lives a precarious existence. He is trapped in a world of machines and gadgets which challenge his competence and threaten his sanity, a world of large organizations and mass-mindedness which
25 threaten his individuality, and—most painfully—a world of aggressive women who threaten his masculine identity. Maladjusted and apprehensive, the Thurber man suffers from a "twitchiness at once cosmic and mundane," and his life is a series of "confusions . . . panics . . . blunderings and gropings." It is around this image of
30 modern man as comic victim, non-hero, outsider, that the themes of Thurber's earlier work develop.

[3] But Thurber's later work, reflecting his growing concern for the quality of life in America in the era of the Cold War and "the dark age of McCarthy," pictures man as less the victim of a too-
35 complex society, and more a creature given over to folly and self-destruction. The major theme of his later pieces is cultural breakdown, the progressive vulgarization and dehumanization of modern life. The humor is still there, wild and inventive, but it is often in the service of anger ("which has become one of the necessary vir-
40 tues") and the didactic impulse.

[4] Like all genuine artists, Thurber looks at life in a highly original way. What he sees is a curious blend of reality and fantasy. He was a journalist by profession, and he placed a high value on the accurate observation of the real: the best comedy, he maintained,
45 should represent "the recognizable American Scene." On the other hand, he was unusually responsive to the world of dream and fantasy, and it is no coincidence that he was a lifelong admirer of Lewis Carroll, the great master of purposeful nonsense. What he said of his friend John McNulty, that "his world bordered on Oz and Wonder-
50 land," is even more true of Thurber himself. Fantasy is the distinguishing quality of his imagination, which at its best transmutes the familiar into the strange and the real into the sur-real.

[5] Nowhere is this more obvious than in his famous drawings, which haunt the imagination because they are pure dream-stuff. Their
55 queer, childlike simplification of the look of things sets them at a long remove from reality, and their subject matter is most characteristically the material of the unconscious—neurosis, dream-image, hallucination. Two of his most famous, "All Right, Have It Your Way —You Heard a Seal Bark," and "That's My First Wife Up There, and
60 This is the *Present* Mrs. Harris," for example, project a dream-like

intrusion of the macabre and the fantastic into the commonplace. Thurber himself refused to explain his more enigmatic drawings, describing them as "accidental" and "more or less unconscious."

[6] The strong bias of Thurber's imagination toward fantasy is equally evident in his fables. The fable form, in which truth is refracted through the glass of fantasy, was particularly congenial to him, and the Aesopian *Fables for Our Time* and *Further Fables for Our Time* and the longer fairy tale narratives like "The Last Clock" are among the best things he ever wrote. Taken as a group, the fables are probably Thurber's most representative body of writing; and certain individual pieces stand out with particular authority as quintessential expressions of his themes and values. "The Unicorn in the Garden," for example, could well serve as an introduction to Thurber's work as a whole. It tells the tale of man who looks out one morning to see a unicorn in his garden, eating roses. Happy at the sight, he tells his wife, who says only, " 'The unicorn is a mythical beast,' " and turns her back on him. When he returns with the news that the unicorn has eaten a lily, his wife looks at him coldly and says, " 'You are a booby, and I am going to have you put in the boobyhatch.' " When her husband leaves the house, she has "a gloat in her eye," and she telephones the police and a psychiatrist, telling them to bring a straitjacket. The police and the psychiatrist arrive, and when she tells them that her husband has seen a unicorn, they seize her and put her in the straitjacket. They ask the husband if he told his wife that he saw a unicorn. He says, " 'Of course not. The unicorn is a mythical beast.' " They take the wife away to an institution, and the husband lives happily ever after. Here, the battle of the sexes is presented as a part of the larger conflict between fantasy and reality; and—significantly—the fantasy-principle (male, loving, peaceable) triumphs over the reality-principle (female, cold, hostile).

[7] This conflict between the world of fantasy and the world of reality (and the worlds of husband and wife) is the theme of Thurber's most famous story, "The Secret Life of Walter Mitty." Inadequate to the demands of the real world, Walter Mitty finds both refuge and strength in fantasy and daydream. His wife bullies him, the parking lot attendent sneers at his awkward efforts to park the car, he cannot remember the shopping list. But in his secret world of fantasy, derived largely from bad movies, he triumphs over the humiliating forces of the actual. Driving his wife to town, he is Commander Walter Mitty, taking the SN 202 through the worst storm

in twenty years of Navy flying; passing the hospital, he is the celebrated surgeon, Dr. Walter Mitty, coolly taking over at a critical
operation when two colleagues lose their nerve; reading a magazine
105 in the hotel lobby, he is Captain Walter Mitty of the RFC, casually
tossing off a brandy before undertaking a suicidal mission (" 'It's
forty kilometers through hell, sir,' said the sergeant. . . . 'After all,'
he said softly, 'What isn't?' "). Mitty's daydreams are the veriest
claptrap, and their triteness serves to underline the pathos as well as
110 the comedy of his situation, but at the same time they are a source
of strength, the means by which he makes his life significant. The
issue is not as clear-cut here as in "The Unicorn in the Garden,"
because Mitty is so obviously, by the standards of the world, a pathetic and inadequate figure; but as the closing image of the story
115 suggests, he is in a deeper sense triumphant, and thus the point of
the two tales is essentially the same:

> "To hell with the handkerchief," said Walter Mitty scornfully. He took
> one last drag on his cigarette and snapped it away. Then, with that
> faint, fleeting smile playing about his lips, he faced the firing squad;
> erect and motionless, proud and disdainful, Walter Mitty the Unde-
> feated, inscrutable to the last.

[8] Fantasy is at the center of Thurber's work as a whole. It is
not only the esthetic hallmark of his drawings and his prose, but it
is also a principle, a standard of value, a quality of experience richer
120 than that offered by everyday life. In "The Admiral at the Wheel,"
Thurber describes the wonderfully strange world revealed to him
when he broke his eyeglasses: "I saw a cat roll across the street in
a small striped barrel, I saw bridges rise lazily into the air, like
balloons." He contrasts this with the world of things-as-they-are:
125 "With perfect vision, one is inextricably trapped in the workaday
world, a prisoner of reality, as lost in the commonplace America of
1937 as Alexander Selkirk was lost on his lonely island."

[9] The fantasy principle is, in fact, the keystone of a set of
closely related values which, until his later years, Thurber habitually
130 champions in opposition to the dominant values of contemporary
society. In a world committed to logic, organization, conformity, and
efficiency, Thurber stands for fantasy, spontaneity, idiosyncrasy, and
confusion. "Confusion" is a bad word in the world's dictionary, but
it is an honorific in Thurber's lexicon. It represents the forces of the
135 irrational and the unpredictable which are always upsetting the world

of convention, order, and system. Hence Thurber's fondness for situations involving eccentric behavior, elaborate practical jokes, breakdowns of communication, and the disruption of bureaucratic machinery. The challenge to order and system by fantasy and confusion is the theme of "Destructive Forces in Life," an essay which exposes 140 the basic fallacy of the popular psychology books which tell us how to dominate life through Masterful Adjustment. The central anecdote tells the story of how a prankster named Bert Scursey, who "enjoyed fantasy as much as reality, probably even more," completely destroys the neatly ordered world of Harry Conner, a devotee of Masterful 145 Adjustment. Scursey, an accomplished mimic, calls the Conner apartment, and without having planned to, finds himself impersonating Edith, a colored woman in search of work. Within a short time he has set in motion a series of wild misunderstandings which ends up with the too-confident Conner at cross-purposes with himself, his 150 wife, and the whole of New York City. The point of this cautionary little tale is clear: Scursey represents the unpredictable, the principle of fantasy and confusion which the worshipers of logic and efficiency ignore at their peril.

[10] The whole of *My Life and Hard Times,* Thurber's wonderful 155 account of his youthful days in Columbus, Ohio, is a celebration of oddity, eccentricity, chaos, and confusion. The titles of the separate pieces are indicative: "The Night the Bed Fell," "The Day the Dam Broke," "The Night the Ghost Got In," "More Alarms at Night," and so on. All of these episodes show the disruption of the 160 orderly pattern of everyday life by the idiosyncratic, the bizarre, the irrational.

[11] "The Night the Bed Fell" deals with chaos in the domestic circle: Father's unwonted decision to sleep in the attic, Mother's certainty that the attic bed would collapse, cousin Briggs Beall's neu- 165 rotic fear that he was likely to cease breathing at any time during the night and hence needed a bottle of spirits of camphor at his bedside, and the sudden collapse of the youthful Thurber's bed during the night set off a chain reaction reminiscent of the scenes of comic anarchy in G. W. Harris' Sut Lovingood tales, or in Faulkner's 170 "Spotted Horses." In "University Days" the theme is the disruptive impact of the atypical Thurber (the principle of Individual Difference) on the university system (the principle of Mass Production). Thurber's inability to see through a microscope in the botany lab is a challenge to the basic assumptions of science and higher education 175 that the professor is unprepared to meet:

"We'll try it," the professor said to me grimly, "with every adjustment of the microscope known to man. As God is my witness, I'll arrange this glass so that you see cells through it or I'll give up teaching. . . .' He cut off abruptly for he was beginning to quiver all over, like Lionel Barrymore, and he genuinely wished to hold on to his temper his scenes with me had taken a great deal out of him.

[12] The characters who populate the world of Thurber's youth are a notable collection of originals and eccentrics. There is Grand-father, the Civil War veteran, who was never quite sure whether he
180 was living in 1864 or 1910, and whose efforts to drive the electric automobile exhibit the family incompetence with machines and gadg-ets in its purest form; there is the maternal grandmother, who was convinced that electricity was dripping out of empty light sockets; there is Aunt Sarah Shoaf, who went to bed every night fearing that
185 a burglar was going to get in and blow chloroform under her door with a tube, and so piled all her valuables outside, with a note read-ing "This is all I have. Please take it and do not use your chloro-form, as this is all I have"; there is Aunt Wilma Hudson, whose reluctance to part with the smallest sum of money "could lift a sim-
190 ple dollar transaction into a dim and mystic realm of confusion all her own"; and there was Thurber's mother, who raised the practical joke to the level of art—on one notable occasion, during a lecture by a popular faith healer, she had herself taken down the aisle in a wheelchair, and at the climactic moment, leaped from the chair cry-
195 ing that she could walk again. The lecturer shouted, "Hallelujah, sister!" and a man at the back said, "Hey, that's my wheelchair!" The mild insanities and picturesque obsessions of these people are not only diverting to Thurber in his role of observer of the human comedy, but they also represent a particular kind of value to him—
200 in an age increasingly given over to standardization of character and behavior, they stand for the spontaneous, the idiosyncratic, the fan-tasy principle.

[13] One of Thurber's major subjects is the use and abuse of lan-guage, and here, too, his treatment of the real leads out toward the
205 sur-real. Because as a writer he valued language as a necessary prin-ciple of order, and as an instrument of precision and beauty in its own right, he was acutely aware of its possibilities for muddle, chaos, and confusion. The precarious nature of language, where the thinnest line separates sense from nonsense, is one of his central concerns,

and in "Such a Phrase as Drifts Through Dreams" he plays gloomily 210
with the possibilities for chaos inherent in the change of a single
letter in a word: " 'A stitch in time saves none . . . There's no business like shoe business . . . Don, give up the ship.' " The likelihood
that people will misunderstand more often than they will understand
each other is the theme of one of the grim little parables in *Further* 215
Fables for Our Time, "The Weaver and the Worm." The weaver,
admiring the silkworm spinning its cocoon, asks, " 'Where do you
get that stuff?' " The silkworm answers, " 'Do you want to make
something out of it?' " Both think they have been insulted. "We live,
man and worm, in a time when almost everything can mean almost 220
anything, for this is the age of gobbledygook, doubletalk, and gudda."

[14] Thurber took language seriously, because he saw it as an
instrument of order, clarity, and good sense, but at the same time
he was fascinated by its capacity to create an Alice-in-Wonderland
world where ordinary rational communication is transcended, and the 225
real gives way to the sur-real. In the sounds of words and in the
chains of association set in motion by unexpected combinations of
familiar words, he found a special avenue to the world of fantasy.
Lewis Carroll is the presiding genius here, as he is in so much of
Thurber's work. His classic nonsense poem "The Jabberwock" is a 230
kind of imaginative touchstone for Thurber, the definitive creation of
a fantasy-world through language. A relatively early piece, "What
Do You Mean It *Was* Brillig?," explores the comic possibilities of
the nonsense associations set off by the distortions of ordinary English words in speech. To talk with Della, the colored cook, is to 235
enter a strange and mysterious world. She has a brother who "works
into an incinerator where they burn the refuge," and a sister who
"got tuberculosis from her teeth, and it went all through her symptom." Her cryptic announcement that " 'They are here with the
reeves,' " sends Thurber to the dictionary. 240

"Are they here with strings of onions?" I asked. Della said they were
not. "Are they here with enclosures or pens for cattle, poultry, or pigs;
sheepfolds?" Della said no sir. "Are they here with administrative
officers?" From a little nearer the door Della said no again. "Then
they've got to be here," I said, "with some females of the common
European sandpiper. . . ." "They are here with the reeves for the
windas," said Della with brave stubbornness. Then, of course, I understood what they were there with; they were there with the Christmas
wreaths for the windows.

Thurber sums up these exchanges with Della as "the most satisfying flight from actuality I have ever known."

[15] One of Thurber's most original experiments with language is the series of drawings with captions titled "A New Natural History."
245 It is essentially an exploration of the comic possibilities of word-association, in which the interplay between the caption, representing conventional denotative meaning, and the picture, representing the surprising meanings suggested by the sound of the words, constitutes a highly sophisticated form of punning. Thus, "The Dungeon" (per-
250 haps suggesting "Gudgeon"? is pictured as a fish feeding in some reeds. "The Femur (left) and the Metatarsal" are visualized as a small fox-like creature ("Lemur"?) and a scaly, prehistoric-looking one (some sort of "saurus"?). More fanciful conceptions, where the gap between picture and label is even wider, are the scene in which
255 two improbable creatures looking out of the high grass are described as "A Scone (left) and a Crumpet, peering out of the Tiffin," and the face-to-face confrontation of two animals labeled "A Trochee (left) encountering a Spondee." In these strange conjunctions of word and picture, Thurber is—like Joyce—remaking language, al-
260 lowing the pressure of subconscious association to force new meanings onto familiar words and phrases, and, in effect, transforming the real into the sur-real.

[16] Thurber's sight began to fail in the late 1940's (during the last ten years of his life he was almost totally blind), and as he be-
265 came progressively isolated from the world of the eye, his imagination grew more and more responsive to verbal experience. The sound of words, the meaning of words, words as the medium through which we know reality become a major subject in his work after 1950. His comic method undergoes a significant change: whereas his earlier
270 work depends chiefly on character and anecdote, his later pieces make their points through conversational repartee, intricate puns, elaborately garbled quotations, anagrams, and other kinds of complicated verbal games. The word-game piece, a bravura display of dictionary learning, wit and verbal acrobatics, becomes one of Thur-
275 ber's most characteristic forms. The setting is usually a half-drunken conversation late at night, where the inhibitions of logic and custom have been melted away, or the lonely hours waiting for sleep, during which the insomniac's mind plays fast and loose with whatever it contemplates.

280 [17] The prototype of these word-game pieces is "Do You Want to Make Something Out of It?," a lively exercise in word-making

which shows Thurber's linguistic originality and inventiveness at their best. The first part of the essay describes a highly sophisticated spelling game in which the players are required to start in the middle of a word and spell backwards and forwards. Asked to spell some-   285
thing with *sgra,* Thurber exhausts the possibilities sactioned by the dictionary with *disgrace, grosgrain, cross-grained,* and *misgraff,* and then, leaving the realm of the actual behind, he begins to invent, of-fering a list of what he calls "bedwords," make-believe *sgra* words which have come to him in the small hours of the night. All of them   290
are combinations of familiar everyday words into fanciful com-pounds, and Thurber presents them in mock-dictionary style:

BLESSGRAVY. A minister or cleric; the head of a family; one who says grace. Not to be confused with praisegravy, one who extolls a woman's cooking, especially the cooking of a friend's wife; a gay fellow, a flirt, a seducer. *Colloq.,* a breakvow, a shrugholy.
FUSSGRAPE. 1. One who diets or toys with his food, a light eater, a person without appetite, a scornmuffin, a shuncabbage. 2. A man, usually American, who boasts of his knowledge of wines, a smugbottle.

And there are such other expressive coinages as *Kissgranny, Puss-grapple, Cussgravy, Bassgrave,* and *Hossgrace.* All of these comic compounds show Thurber's interest in remaking language, playing   295
with the relationship between sound and meaning, pushing back the limits of the familiar, and transforming the terrain into something strange and new.
[18] In "Here Come the Tigers" two tipsy friends descend upon Thurber late at night announcing that they have discovered a new   300
dimension of meaning in the old word-game of anagrams. The key to the game is in the haunting quatrain:

> There are lips in pistol
> And mist in times
> Cats in crystal
> And mice in chimes.

Developing the theme that there are animals hidden in a wide variety of common words, the guests identify the wolf in "flower," the gan-der in "danger," and the frog in "forget." Moving on, they discover a   305
startling constellation of entities in the single word "crystal": salt, slat, cyst, and cart, as well as star, cry, and satyr. At the end, Thur-ber is tossing restlessly in bed, hunting for the tiger in three six-

letter words. The game of anagrams (or complicated versions of it) becomes an obsessive activity in Thurber's later work. There is a kind of desperation in the restless energy with which he takes words apart, spells them backwards, and rearranges them into new patterns, as though he were looking for the key to reality in the structure of a word. The anatomy of the word "music" in "Conversation Piece: Connecticut" is a case in point:

> The word is icsum and mucsi. . . . It is also musci and scumi. If you say 'sicum!' your dog starts barking at nothing, and if you say 'sucim,' the pigs in the barnyard start squealing and grunting. 'Muics' is the cat's miaow. Say 'miscu' and your fingers are fungers, say 'umski' and the Russians are upon you. As for mucis—my God, are you ready for another drink already?

Here, as in most of Thurber's explorations of the hidden world of language, the effect is to transform the familiar into the strange, to move from the everyday into the world of fantasy. The sheer abundance, brilliance, and virtuosity of Thurber's verbal antics is dizzying, and after reading two or three of these word-game pieces in succession, one feels lost in a strange country where everything always seems to be turning into something else.

[19] Thurber's later work is darker in tone, harsher in judgment, and more penetrating in moral wisdom than the work of his early middle years. (One has only to compare such representative collections as *The Thurber Carnival* [1945] and *Lanterns and Lances* [1960] to see the differences.) He saw the postwar world as a time of intellectual and moral confusion. "I think there's been a fall-out of powdered fruitcake—everyone's going nuts," he remarked in an interview. Yet the vein of fantasy and the antic humor run as strongly as ever through his work. The comedy of these later years is a wild, dark comedy, often playing on the brink of hysteria, and in its bizarre anecdotes and extravagant verbal effects suggesting a world collapsing into chaos.

[20] The most characteristic form of this later period is the conversation piece, an invention of Thurber's own in which all sorts of fantastic variations are played upon a central theme. The setting is usually a party or other convivial occasion, and the talkers are expansive and uninhibited, creating out of the play of wild generalization, false example, garbled quotation, and outrageous pun a strange and dream-like world.

[21] "Midnight at Tim's Place" is typical of the surreal quality of many of these later pieces. The line between reality and fantasy blurs and shifts as the conversationalists assume false names, get off complex and subtle puns, and engage one another in contests of fanciful invention. The man across the table pretends to take Thurber for Bing Crosby. "How are you, Bing?" he asks. "*Non sum qualis eram sub regno bony Sinatra,*" replies Thurber, mixing ancient and modern cultures in an impressive display of linguistic virtuosity. The central anecdote, an unsettling parody of modern man's search for guidance and reassurance, deals with the experience of the man across the table when, on the edge of a nervous breakdown, he went to see his old philosophy professor, "the greatest symbol of security in my life." The professor, who specialized in such inspiring mottoes as "You can keep a stiff upper lip and smile too!" seemed totally unchanged after twenty years as he sat in his study, except that he was wearing two hats. "They were both gray felt hats, one on top of the other. The terrifying thing was that he didn't say anything about them. He just sat there with two hats on, trying to cheer me up." At the close of the sketch the worlds of fantasy and reality collide. Moved by the story of the mad professor, Thurber leaves the party wearing two hats, and hails a cab. The driver looks at him and says, "Not in this cab, Jack."

[22] "The Waters of the Moon" is perhaps the most brilliant and elaborately worked of the conversation pieces. The scene is a literary cocktail party, an appropriate setting for extravagant conversational encounters, parody, hoax, and esoteric literary allusion. In the swirl of pretentious intellectual party talk ("I had broken away from an undulant discussion of kinetic dimensionalism and was having a relaxed moment with a slender woman . . . who described herself as a chaoticist. . . .") Thurber encounters an intense, self-important editor who is obviously determined to trap him into a discussion of "the male American writer who peters out in his fifties." Moving expansively into his subject, the editor says that he would like to see the subject considered "from the viewpoints of marriage, extra-marital relations, the educational system, home environment, the failure of religion, the tyranny of money, and the rich breeding ground of decomposition . . . to be found in syphilophobia, prostatitis, early baldness, peptic ulcer, edentulous cases, true and hysterical impotence, and spreading of the metatarsals."

[23] Thurber then embarks upon an elaborate hoax, playing a series of deliberately absurd variations on the editor's theme. There

is the case of "poor old Greg Selby," for example, whose first wife
claimed to have discovered that "his last book, 'Filiring Gee,' was his
385 next-to-last book, 'Saint Tomany's Rain,' written backward"; or the
strange case of Greg's second wife, the author of the successful mystery novel, "Pussy Wants a Coroner." After her marriage, her books
began to take on "a curiously Gothic tone," and she explained to her
publishers that she was "trying to write for the understanding of in-
390 tellectuals a thousand years ago." The editor (the reality-principle,
although somewhat befuddled by drink) is suspicious, but Thurber
(the fantasy-principle) presses on more and more recklessly, pitting
his creative powers as a hoaxer against the common-sense resistance
of the editor. The climax of the hoax, the sad case of Douglas Bryce,
395 whose career ended in "the Lawrence Stone incident," depends upon
an elaborately subtle series of references to Browning's poem, "Let
Twenty Pass." When the editor recognizes the line which is the clue
to the joke ("Let twenty pass and stone the twenty-first") he retires
with alcoholic dignity. "I happen to be familiar with Browning," he
400 says, and the game is over.

[24] The most striking formal characteristic of the conversation
pieces is the ceaseless play of pun, twisted quotation, and literary allusion, in which familiar patterns of sound and meaning are constantly shifting and changing. There are the concise, classic puns
405 which are woven into the very texture of Thurber's prose—"We battle for the word while the very Oedipus of reason crumbles beneath
us," and so on. Thurber's most elaborate and original puns, however,
depend upon famous quotations and titles, or familiar adages. Most
often the quotations are garbled or twisted to fit an incongruous
410 situation, and the effectiveness of the device depends upon the unexpected and ludicrous significance given to a familiar line or saying.
In "Get Thee to a Monastery," Thurber and the pedantic Dr. Bach
conclude an involved discussion of the fate of Shakespeare in the
woman-dominated theater of today: "The rest is silex," intones Dr.
415 Bach as he goes off to make himself a cup of coffee; "Good night,
sweet Prince," says Thurber, picking up the cue from *Hamlet,* "and
flights of angels sing thee to thy rest." Here, the effect is that of
burlesque. The famous lines from Shakespeare are twisted out of
shape and made to bear an incongruous meaning. In Bergsonian
420 terms what takes place is a sudden transposition of key, from a
higher to a lower level of discourse. In a more subtle variation of the
method, the quotation is given intact, but a preposterous meaning is
assigned it, as in "The Danger in the House," where Thurber de-

scribes a curious dream about a woman in a long white dress who
appears to be holding some sort of mechanism in her right hand, and   425
Dr. Prell, the heavy-footed Freudian psychologist, asks whether the
mechanism might not have *been* her hand, quoting T. S. Eliot's famous lines in evidence:

> When lovely woman stoops to folly
> And finds herself again alone,
> She combs her hair with automatic hand
> And puts a record on the gramophone

[25] Titles of well-known books, songs, and plays undergo the
same sort of antic transformation: the anxieties of the Cold War   430
bring on dreams in which familiar titles become strange and unsettling—*Alias in Wonderland, Traitor-Island, Look Homeward,
Agent,* and so on. Television's tendency to make the classics into
Westerns raises some distressing possibilities—*Trelawney of the Wells
Fargo . . . She Shoots to Conquer . . . The Sheriff Misses Tan-*   435
queray. The obsession of the modern theater with neurotic and morbid themes suggests such revisions of popular titles as *Abie's Irish
Neurosis* and *Oklahomasexual.*

[26] The puns, quotations, and literary allusions of these later
pieces are not isolated jokes or simply decorative flourishes, but   440
a central part of Thurber's literary method. His mind was a storehouse of quotations from the standard authors, particularly Shakespeare and the nineteenth-century writers. A rough count of the literary references in his work puts Henry James, his favorite author, in
first place, followed by Lewis Carroll, Shakespeare, Tennyson,   445
Browning, Longfellow, Henley, Wordsworth, Shelley, Poe, and Lan-
dor. (There are scattered references to such twentieth-century figures
as Joyce, T. S. Eliot, Fitzgerald, and Hemingway.) Authors, titles,
and familiar quotations were an important part of Thurber's imagination, and so, when he wished to make a point, comic or other-   450
wise, it is entirely natural that he would set it in the context of
famous literary treatments of the subject.

[27] If one were to look for the quintessence of Thurber's later
world-view, it would most likely be found in one of the apocalyptic fables—"The Human Being and the Dinosaur," for example,   455
or "The Shore and the Sea." The best and most typical of these, in
its blend of comic fantasy and cosmic pessimism, is "The Last
Clock" (1959), a tale about an ogre who becomes a compulsive

eater of clocks, and the total inability of the intellectual elite of the
460 community to cope with the problem. The story is full of such fresh
comic details as the effect of a heavy diet of clock oil on the ogre's
speech: " 'Wuld wuzzle?' the ogre wanted to know. He hiccupped, and
something went *spong!*" The dominant theme of the fable is the fate
of a culture which worships specialization; the underlying theme is
465 the inexorable running-out of time. When the ogre's wife calls a doctor to treat her husband's strange malady, the doctor says, "This case
is clearly not in my area," and recommends a clockman. The clockman appears, but turns out to be a clogman, a specialist in clogged
drains: "I get mice out of pipes, and bugs out of tubes, and moles
470 out of tiles, and there my area ends." A general practitioner comes,
but announces that he treats only generals. The wife next calls upon
"an old inspirationalist," representing the moral and spiritual wisdom of the community, but his inspirationalism has become "a
jumble of mumble," and all he can offer is "The final experience
475 should not be mummum." Soon the ogre eats up all but one of the
clocks in the town, and in accordance with the dream-like logic exhibited by all the representatives of official culture in the story, it is
classified as a collector's item, and put in a museum. Life comes to
a standstill.
480   [28] The close of the fable presents a comic and frightening image of the ultimate meaning of our civilization. Before long the town
is buried under the sands of a nearby desert. More than a thousand
years later, when explorers from another planet are digging at the
site, they find a clock (whose function they do not recognize) and
485 the papers of the old inspirationalist, which include fragments of
poetry summing up the wisdom of the culture for which he was the
spokesman. The last words he had put down were

> We can make our lives sublime,
> And, departing, leave behind us,
> Mummum in the sands of time.

The world of "The Last Clock" is the world reduced to non-mean-
ing, chaos, the absurd. What more grotesque epitaph for our civiliza-
490 tion could be imagined than a garbled fragment of a second-rate
nineteenth-century poem celebrating optimism and moral uplift? This
final sequence is remarkably similar to the closing moment of
Ionesco's play *The Chairs,* in which the Orator, who is to put into
magnificent words the significance of the life of the old man and his

wife, can only utter unintelligible grunts. Although it will not do to claim Thurber for the cult of the Absurd in modern literature (Thurber having formed his view of life independently and long before the Absurd became a literary movement), the world of his later work is nonetheless close to the world as we find it in Ionesco—the apocalyptic vision, the fascination with the breakdown of communication as the primary symptom of a cosmic sickness, and the comic virtuosity are present in both.

[29] But such parallels should not be pushed too far. The sense of modern life as too bizarre and outrageous to be presented as anything other than a grotesque comedy is, in fact, a striking characteristic of much postwar writing, and Thurber's brilliant expression of this sense is not a matter of literary fashion, but an independent response to a common cultural and philosophical situation. In any case, the world of Thurber is larger than that of Ionesco. The dark fantasies and the melancholy strain in his work are balanced by a basic sanity and a positive relish of the whole human scene. The essential quality of Thurber's imagination is the tension between a strong sense of fact (throughout his life he considered himself primarily a journalist) and a strong bias toward fantasy. In his earlier career he searched out and celebrated disorder, illogic, and confusion, feeling that these qualities were desirable counterbalances in a society over-committed to logic and organization. Later, as history changed the world he knew, and as illogic and disorder on an international scale threatened to engulf mankind, he began to champion those things which hold a society together, and his fantasies and his brilliant images of disorder became warnings and distress-signals rather than signs of revelry.

[30] But he never lost his compensating faith in the saving power of humor and intelligence. "Let us not forget the uses of laughter or store them away in the attic," he wrote in "The Duchess and the Bugs." Comedy, humor, and laughter he saw as essential to the health of any society, because they demolish humbug and reveal the truth. The title of his last collection, *Lanterns and Lances* (1960), with its suggestion of attack and illumination, defines the role he thought comedy should play; and his basic faith in comedy, in intelligence, and in life is finely expressed in the advice he gives to the reader in the Foreword of that volume: "In this light, let's not look back in anger, or forward in fear, but around in awareness."

Dictionary definitions often list synonyms, other words which have the same meaning as the word being defined. Yet it is never possible to use these words interchangeably. For example, under the word "habitation," one dictionary lists "dwelling, residence, domicile, home" as synonyms. But you will never see a sampler embroidered "Domicile, sweet domicile." And you will never read "The young heiress took up habitation at the mansion." You expect a lease to say that "the premises are to be occupied as a private dwelling"; you do not expect it to say that "the place is to be lived in as a home."

Words do not mean only what they "mean" literally (denotative meaning); they carry with them an aura of surrounding meaning—suggestive, emotional overtones of meaning which come to mind when you hear or see them (connotative meaning).

These connotative meanings vary to some extent from person to person: "bread" can never mean the same thing to someone who has been a war prisoner that it means to a baker or a farmer. Time and history may alter the connotative meanings of a word—"bomb," for example. Some words have more connotative meanings than others. Think of the differences between a marketing list and a menu: in making up a marketing list, you might include "rolls" and "crabmeat"; these might appear on a menu as the mouth-watering item: "King Crab on Toasted Bun." Although "jasmine" is defined as "any of a genus of shrubs of the olive family," you would never open a book by your favorite mystery writer and read "The air was heavy with the smell of a shrub of the olive family." And, finally, the context of a word may give it connotative meaning. "Hat" may seem a bland enough word, yet its connotative meaning varies considerably (while its denotative meaning remains the same) in these sentences:

His *hat* was in the ring.
She put on her *hat* and marched out the door.
All that was visible on the surface of the lake was a *hat*.
She must have that *hat* and no other one.

1. In the selection by Gilot and Lake, several people are described. Which person is made most vivid to you by the description? How is this accomplished? List the words rich in connotative meaning used in the selection which contribute to the impression that person has made upon you. List the connotations, in context, of each of the words you select.

2. The authors use the word "coiffure" in paragraphs 2 and 3. List the connotative meanings which the word takes on from each of the two contexts. Is it more appropriate in one context than in the other? Explain. What would have been gained or lost had the word "hair-do" been used instead of "coiffure"?

3. What connotations does the Louvre have for you? the Left Bank? Notre Dame? Mecca?

4. With what do you associate "mackinaw" (paragraph 19)? Are your usual associations with the word evoked here? If not, what connotative meaning or meanings does the word have here? Similarly analyze the connotative meanings of the term "thick-lensed glasses" in and out of context (paragraph 20).

5. What do the following connote (a) in the context of the selection and (b) to you, out of context:

turtledoves
exotic species
wicker cages
spiky green plants
copper pots
a high open window
several old Louis XIII sofas and chairs
guitars
mandolins
two long carpenter's tables
an accumulation of books, magazines, newspapers, photographs, hats, and miscellaneous clutter
a rough piece of amethyst crystal

6. Use each of the words or phrases in question 5 in a sentence which gives it connotations different from those it has in context. If some of these words and phrases carry the same connotations for you both in and out of context, then use them in a sentence which again illustrates these connotations.

7. What do you expect to be the relationship between Picasso and Françoise? What in the selection gives rise to your expectation?

8. The Holmes selection, although of course it was not written to do so, offers an interesting contrast between the largely denotative use of words (Holmes') and highly connotative diction (Thurber's). Based on the guiding purpose of the selection as you understand it, discuss the difference in diction: how is each appropriate? how does Thurber's diction reflect his humor, as Holmes describes it? what exceptions to this generalization do you find?

Exercise: Write a paragraph summarizing your answers to question 8.

Theme Assignment: Expand your paragraph answer to question 8 into a theme. Remember that you are analyzing two styles, each appropriate to its own purpose, and that you will want to make clear each of those styles and its particular purpose. You may quote as extensively as you like from Holmes and use his quotations of Thurber as they seem apt. Your diction should reflect your own purpose.

or

Places have particular meanings for people as a result of things that have happened to them there, or perhaps merely as a result of reading about them.

Write a theme describing a place, giving it a special significance. This place may be the town or city in which you grew up, the resort where you spent your childhood vacations, the home of a friend or relative, a town in which you were once stranded (or lost), the place you always dream of seeing, or a place made famous by your favorite author. Make generous use of connotative meanings and connotative words to convey your impression to the reader.

Imagery

From *The Magic Maker: E. E. Cummings*

CHARLES NORMAN

[1] Patchin Place is a *cul-de-sac* of three-story brick houses in Greenwich Village. It has an iron gate at one end, a wooden fence and lamp-post at the other. The sidewalks are narrow; two may walk abreast if one is ready to step down. Between the sidewalks and brick walls thrust eight or nine ailanthus trees with curving trunks, 5 giving the street a dappled shade in summer and afterwards strewing its pavement with seed-pods and wrinkled leaves. The houses are all painted alike. In them have lived a number of writers and artists, and the street is—or was before radio and TV—a quiet residential enclave with an old New York look. Across Tenth Street, on which 10 Patchin Place abuts, stands Jefferson Market Court, no longer a court and no longer a market, and its Gothic tower clock no longer dependable.

[2] Daily from a house on the left-hand side of Patchin Place a man emerges, bound for Washington Square. A weathered hat rides 15 high on a head seeking to soar from squared shoulders loosely draped

in an old jacket, from the left pocket of which protrudes the top of a black notebook. The face under the hat takes daylight as though it and the light and air are friends. It is a face without guile. Hazel
20 eyes, which now seem abstracted—slight acquaintances complain of not being recognized on the street—can in the closer proximity of a room pierce disconcertingly or brim with laughter or mischief like a child's. The nose is strong, the mouth full and sensual, the chin arrogant. The ears are large and seemingly tense with listening; they
25 belong to a born eavesdropper of human speech or a dissolving sliver of bird-song. On rainy days the slim figure of this man strides buoyantly under an ancient black umbrella held aloft like a balloonman's bouquet of balloons. He has beautiful hands.

[3] Turning left on Tenth Street, and headed for Sixth Avenue—
30 now sans Elevated and officially "the Avenue of the Americas"—he passes the florist shop on the corner where he and the proprietor, Mr. S. Psomas, have often bowed to each other among the blossoms; for flowers are a necessity to him, and he thinks his friends—and sometimes strangers who have been charming or kind—should have
35 them, too. Diagonally across Sixth Avenue from the florist shop stands the stationery emporium of Mr. A. Schwartz, another friend. Now as he proceeds southward on the avenue, a number of pedestrians who are Village residents have become aware of his progress; some turn to watch, others name him to ignorant companions, hav-
40 ing seen him plain. He is Edward Estlin Cummings, poet and painter; or, as he has described himself, "an author of pictures, a draughtsman of words."

[For treatment of this selection, see pp. 391–392.]

From *Making Pictures*

D. H. LAWRENCE

[1] One has to eat one's own words. I remember I used to assert, perhaps I even wrote it: Everything that can possibly be painted has been painted, every brush-stroke that can possibly be laid on canvas has been laid on. The visual arts are at a dead end. Then suddenly, at the age of forty, I begin painting myself and am fascinated. 5

[2] Still, going through the Paris picture shops this year of grace, and seeing the Dufrys and Chiricos, etc., and the Japanese Ito with his wish-wash nudes with pearl-button eyes, the same weariness comes over one. They are all so would-be, they make such efforts. They at least have nothing to paint. In the midst of them a graceful 10
Fricsz flower-piece, or a blotting-paper Laurençin seems a masterpiece. At least here is a bit of *natural* expression in paint. Trivial enough, when compared to the big painters, but still, as far as they go, real.

[3] What about myself, then! What am I doing, bursting into 15
paint? I am a writer, I ought to stick to ink. I have found my medium of expression; why, at the age of forty, should I suddenly want to try another?

[4] Things happen, and we have no choice. If Maria Huxley hadn't come rolling up to our house near Florence with four rather 20
large canvases, one of which she had busted, and presented them to me because they had been abandoned in her house, I might never have started in on a real picture in my life. But those nice stretched canvases were too tempting. We had been painting doors and window-frames in the house, so there was a little stock of oil, turps and 25
colour in powder, such as one buys from an Italian drogheria. There were several brushes for house-painting. There was a canvas on which the unknown owner had made a start—mud-grey, with the beginnings of a red-haired man. It was a grimy and ugly begin-

30 ning, and the young man who had made it had wisely gone no
further. He certainly had had no inner compulsion: nothing in him,
as far as paint was concerned, or if there was anything in him, it had
stayed in, and only a bit of the mud-grey "group" had come out.

[5] So far the sheer fun of covering a surface and obliterating that
35 mud-grey, I sat on the floor with the canvas propped against a chair
—and with my house-paint brushes and colours in little casseroles,
I disappeared into that canvas. It is to me the most exciting moment—when you have a blank canvas and a big brush full of wet
colour, and you plunge. It is just like diving in a pond—then you
40 start frantically to swim. So far as I am concerned, it is like swimming in a baffling current and being rather frightened and very
thrilled, gasping and striking out for all you're worth. The knowing
eye watches sharp as a needle; but the picture comes clean out of instinct, intuition and sheer physical action. Once the instinct and in-
45 tuition gets into the brush-tip, the picture *happens,* if it is to be a
picture at all.

[6] At least, so my first picture happened. . . . In a couple of
hours there it all was, man, woman, child, blue shirt, red shawl, pale
room—all in the rough, but, as far as I am concerned, a picture. The
50 struggling comes later. But the picture itself comes in the first rush,
or not at all. It is only when the picture has come into being that one
can struggle and make it *grow* to completion.

[7] Ours is an excessively conscious age. We *know* so much, we
feel so little. I have lived enough among painters and around studios
55 to have had all the theories—and how contradictory they are—
rammed down my throat. A man has to have a gizzard like an ostrich
to digest all the brass-tacks and wire nails of modern art theories.
Perhaps all the theories, the utterly indigestible theories, like nails in
an ostrich's gizzard, do indeed help to grind small and make di-
60 gestible all the emotional and esthetic pabulum that lies in an artist's soul. But they can serve no other purpose. Not even corrective.
The modern theories of art make real pictures impossible. You can
get these expositions, critical ventures in paint, and fantastic nega-
tions. And the bit of fantasy that may lie in the negation—as in the
65 Dufry or a Chirico—is just the bit that has escaped theory and perhaps saves the picture. Theorise, theorise all you like—but when you
start to paint, shut your theoretic eyes and go for it with instinct and
intuition.

[8] Myself, I have always loved pictures, the pictorial art. I never
70 went to an art school, I have had only one real lesson in painting in

all my life. But of course I was thoroughly drilled in "drawing," the solid-geometry sort, and the plaster-cast sort, and the pin-wire sort. I think the solid-geometry sort, with all the elementary laws of perspective, was valuable. But the pin-wire sort and the plaster-cast light-and-shade sort was harmful. Plaster-casts and pin-wire outlines 75 were always so repulsive to me, I quite early decided I "couldn't draw." I couldn't draw, so I could never do anything on my own. When I did paint jugs of flowers or bread and potatoes, or cottages in a lane, copying from Nature, the result wasn't very thrilling. Nature was more or less of a plaster-cast to me—those plaster-cast heads 80 of Minerva or figures of Dying Gladiators which so unnerved me as a youth. The "object," be it what it might, was always slightly repulsive to me once I sat down in front of it, to paint it. So, of course, I decided I couldn't really paint. Perhaps I can't. But I verily believe I can make pictures, which is to me all that matters in this respect. The 85 art of painting consists in making pictures—and so many artists accomplish canvases without coming within miles of painting a picture.

[9] I learnt to paint from copying other pictures—usually reproductions, sometimes even photographs. When I was a boy, how I 90 concentrated over it! Copying some perfectly worthless scene reproduction in some magazine. I worked with almost dry water-colour, stroke by stroke, covering half a square-inch at a time, each square-inch perfect and completed, proceeding in a kind of mosaic advance, with no idea at all of laying on a broad wash. Hours and hours of 95 intense concentration, inch by inch progress, in a method entirely wrong—and yet those copies of mine managed, when they were finished, to have a certain something that delighted me: a certain glow of life, which was beauty to me. A picture lives with the life you put into it. If you put no *life* into it—no thrill, no concentration 100 of delight or exaltation of visual discovery—then the picture is dead, like so many canvases, no matter how much thorough and scientific work is put into it. Even if you only copy a purely banal reproduction of an old bridge, some sort of keen, delighted awareness of the old bridge or of its atmosphere, or the image it has kindled inside you, 105 can go over on to the paper and give a certain touch of life to a banal conception.

[10] It needs a certain purity of spirit to be an artist, of any sort. The motto which should be written over every School of Art is: "Blessed are the pure in spirit, for theirs is the kingdom of heaven." 110 But by "pure in spirit" we mean pure in spirit. An artist may be a

profligate and, from the social point of view, a scoundrel. But if he
can paint a nude woman, or a couple of apples, so that they are a
living image, then he was pure in spirit, and, for the time being, his
115 was the kingdom of heaven. This is the beginning of all art, visual or
literary or musical: be pure in spirit. . . .

[11] One may see the divine in natural objects; I saw it today, in
the frail, lovely little camellia flowers on long stems, here on the bushy
and splendid flower-stalls of the Ramblas in Barcelona. They were
120 different from the usual fat camellias, more like gardenias, poised
delicately, and I saw them like a vision. So now, I could paint them.
But if I had bought a handful, and started in to paint them "from
nature," then I should have lost them. By staring at them I should
have lost them. I have learnt by experience. It is personal experience
125 only. Some men can only get a vision by staring themselves blind, as
it were: like Cézanne; but staring kills my vision. That's why I could
never "draw" at school. One was supposed to draw what one
stared at.

[12] The only thing one can look into, stare into, and see only
130 vision, is the vision itself: the visionary image. That is why I am glad
I never had any training but the self-imposed training of copying
other men's pictures.

. . . .

[13] I must have made many copies in my day, and got endless
joy out of them.
135 [14] Then suddenly, by having a blank canvas, I discovered I
could make a picture myself. That is the point, to make a picture on
a blank canvas. And I was forty before I had the real courage to
try. Then it became an orgy, making pictures.

[15] I have learnt now not to work from objects, not to have
140 models, not to have a technique. Sometimes, for a water-colour, I
have worked direct from a model. But it always spoils the *picture*.
I can only use a model when the picture is already made; then I can
look at the model to get some detail which the vision failed me with,
or to modify something which I *feel* is unsatisfactory and I don't
145 know why. Then a model may give a suggestion. But at the beginning, a model only spoils the picture. The picture must all come out
of the artist's inside, awareness of forms and figures. We can call it
memory, but it is more than memory. It is the image as it lives in the
consciousness, alive like a vision, but unknown. I believe many peo-
150 ple have in their consciousness, living images that would give them

the greatest joy to bring out. But they don't know how to go about it. And teaching only hinders them.

[16] To me, a picture has delight in it, or it isn't a picture. The saddest pictures of Piero della Francesca or Sodoma or Goya, have still that indescribable delight that goes with the real picture. Modern 155 critics talk a lot about ugliness, but I never saw a real picture that seemed to me ugly. The theme may be ugly, there may be a terrifying, distressing, almost repulsive quality, as in El Greco. Yet it is all, in some strange way, swept up in the delight of a picture. No artist, even the gloomiest, ever painted a picture without the curious 160 delight in image-making.

Communication is essentially sharing, mutual participation or exchange. Before it can take place at all, there must be some community of experience between the sender and the recipient. All people, no matter how much they differ in surroundings, in history, in personality, in beliefs, discovered and continue to experience the world around them through their senses. They all see, hear, touch, taste, and smell the world. Therefore one extremely effective means of verbal communication is to evoke or create imagined sense impressions. These sense impressions are images; images in general are referred to as imagery.

Imagery may result from a simple reference to an impression of one or another of the senses: "a white sail made blue by the blue of the lake"; it may use one sense to evoke another: "Her call spiralled in the wind"; it may employ onomatopoeia—sound which echoes meaning: "drops of rain slipping softly, softly from the needles of the pines"; it is most often created by or combined with a figure of speech —with a simile, for example: "The old crone's hair was as greasy as a cold dish rag" or with personification: "The smell of the bacon came up the stairs and pulled the covers off me." But *any* sense impression is an image.

1. Charles Norman, in this excerpt from the beginning of his book about E. E. Cummings, makes the poet begin to be real for the reader largely through the use of images. Make a list of the images Norman uses in paragraphs 1 and 2. What order do you find in these images? Using the same images in a new order of your own, rewrite the two paragraphs. Which pair of paragraphs do you prefer? Why?

2. What is "a dissolving sliver of birdsong"? Why is this phrase more effective in context than "a dissolving birdsong"? than "a sliver of birdsong"? than "birdsong"?

3. What devices are used in the sentence: "On rainy days the slim

figure of this man strides buoyantly under an ancient black umbrella
held aloft like a balloonman's bouquet of balloons"? How does each
device you have named contribute to the effectiveness of the sentence?
4. Why does Norman not use imagery to describe the florist shop,
Mr. Psomas, the stationery emporium, or Mr. Schwartz in paragraph
3? What would have been gained or lost had he done so?
5. In his title, Norman refers to Cummings as "The Magic Maker."
Is this an image? Explain. In this passage, has Norman effectively
made Cummings a "magic maker"? Identify all the devices you have
studied which contribute to this effect.
6. Find a tactile image (image of touch) in the Lawrence selection;
another image combined with or derived from a figure of speech; a
visual image; an image or images used for purposes of comparison.
7. How do you account for the fact that there are relatively few
images in the selection? Rewrite one of the paragraphs, adding as
many images as you think desirable, and compare the effectiveness of
your paragraph with Lawrence's.
8. "One may see the divine in natural objects; I saw it today, in the
frail, lovely little camellia flowers on long stems . . ." Lawrence says.
Using whatever type or types of images (visual, auditory, gustatory,
olfactory, tactile, thermal) seem appropriate, write three sentences in
which you, too, attempt to experience and describe "the divine in
natural objects."
9. In your own words, state the theory of esthetic creativity which
Lawrence is propounding. Compare Lawrence's theory with Mencken's.
In what ways are they the same? In what ways do they differ?

Alternate selections for the study of Imagery: Rainer Maria
Rilke, "The Raw Material of Poetry"; Theodore Dreiser, from *A Book
about Myself;* James Agee, "Comedy's Greatest Era."

Theme Assignment: Recall as vividly as you can the most unpleasant traveling experience you have ever had. You may define
"traveling" broadly enough to include in addition to auto travel, flying, and boating such other travel as might be done on foot, on skates,
on skis, or even on water skis. Re-create the experience in a theme,
using as many types of imagery as are relevant to make the unpleasantness convincing to your reader.

or

Write a theme about one of the following places or activities; make
use of as many sense impressions as possible:

a hospital emergency room
a large department store
a New Year's Eve celebration
a public (or private) swimming pool
a manufacturing plant
a religious ceremony

Figurative Language

Comedy's Greatest Era

JAMES AGEE

[1] In the language of screen comedians four of the main grades of laugh are the titter, the yowl, the bellylaugh and the boffo. The titter is just a titter. The yowl is a runaway titter. Anyone who has ever had the pleasure knows all about a bellylaugh. The boffo is the
5 laugh that kills. An ideally good gag, perfectly constructed and played, would bring the victim up this ladder of laughs by cruelly controlled degrees to the top rung, and would then proceed to wobble, shake, wave and brandish the ladder until he groaned for mercy. Then, after the shortest possible time out for recuperation, he would
10 feel the first wicked tickling of the comedian's whip once more and start up a new ladder.

[2] The reader can get a fair enough idea of the current state of screen comedy by asking himself how long it has been since he has had that treatment. The best of comedies these days hand out plenty
15 of titters and once in a while it is possible to achieve a yowl without

overstraining. Even those who have never seen anything better must occasionally have the feeling, as they watch the current run or, rather, trickle of screen comedy, that they are having to make a little cause for laughter go an awfully long way. And anyone who has watched screen comedy over the past ten or fifteen years is bound 20 to realize that it has quietly but steadily deteriorated. As for those happy atavists who remember silent comedy in its heyday and the bellylaughs and boffos that went with it, they have something close to an absolute standard by which to measure the deterioration.

[3] When a modern comedian gets hit on the head, for example, 25 the most he is apt to do is look sleepy. When a silent comedian got hit on the head he seldom let it go so flatly. He realized a broad license, and a ruthless discipline within that license. It was his business to be as funny as possible physically, without the help or hindrance of words. So he gave us a figure of speech, or rather of 30 vision, for loss of consciousness. In other words he gave us a poem, a kind of poem, moreover, that everybody understands. The least he might do was to straighten up stiff as a plank and fall over backward with such skill that his whole length seemed to slap the floor at the same instant. Or he might make a cadenza of it—look vague, smile 35 like an angel, roll up his eyes, lace his fingers, thrust his hands palms downward as far as they would go, hunch his shoulders, rise on tiptoe, prance ecstatically in narrowing circles until, with tallow knees, he sank down the vortex of his dizziness to the floor, and there signified nirvana by kicking his heels twice, like a swimming frog. 40

[4] Startled by a cop, this same comedian might grab his hatbrim with both hands and yank it down over his ears, jump high in the air, come to earth in a split violent enough to telescope his spine, spring thence into a coattail-flattening sprint and dwindle at rocket speed to the size of a gnat along the grand, forlorn perspective of 45 some lazy back boulevard.

[5] Those are fine clichés from the language of silent comedy in its infancy. The man who could handle them properly combined several of the more difficult accomplishments of the acrobat, the dancer, the clown and the mime. Some very gifted comedians, unforgettably 50 Ben Turpin, had an immense vocabulary of these clichés and were in part so lovable because they were deep conservative classicists and never tried to break away from them. The still more gifted men, of course, simplified and invented, finding out new and much deeper uses for the idiom. They learned to show emotion through it, and 55 comic psychology, more eloquently than most language has ever

managed to, and they discovered beauties of comic motion which are hopelessly beyond reach of words.

[6] It is hard to find a theater these days where a comedy is play- ing; in the days of the silents it was equally hard to find a theater which was not showing one. The laughs today are pitifully few, far between, shallow, quiet and short. They almost never build, as they used to, into something combining the jabbering frequency of a ma- chine gun with the delirious momentum of a roller coaster. Saddest of all, there are few comedians now below middle age and there are none who seem to learn much from picture to picture, or to try any- thing new.

[7] To put it unkindly, the only thing wrong with screen comedy today is that it takes place on a screen which talks. Because it talks, the only comedians who ever mastered the screen cannot work, for they cannot combine their comic style with talk. Because there is a screen, talking comedians are trapped into a continual exhibition of their inadequacy as screen comedians on a surface as big as the side of a barn.

[8] At the moment, as for many years past, the chances to see silent comedy are rare. There is a smattering of it on television—too often treated as something quaintly archaic, to be laughed at, not with. Some two hundred comedies—long and short—can be rented for home projection. And a lucky minority has access to the comedies in the collection of New York's Museum of Modern Art, which is still incomplete but which is probably the best in the world. In the near future, however, something of this lost art will return to regular theaters. A thick straw in the wind is the big business now being done by a series of revivals of W. C. Fields's memorable movies, a kind of comedy more akin to the old silent variety than anything which is being made today. Mack Sennett now is preparing a sort of pot-pourri variety show called *Down Memory Lane* made up out of his old movies, featuring people like Fields and Bing Crosby when they were movie beginners, but in- cluding also interludes from silents. Harold Lloyd has re-released *Movie Crazy,* a talkie, and plans to revive four of his best silent comedies (*Grandma's Boy, Safety Last, Speedy* and *The Freshman*). Buster Keaton hopes to remake at feature length, with a minimum of dialogue, two of the funniest short comedies ever made, one about a porous homemade boat and one about a prefabricated house. . . .

[9] Mack Sennett made two kinds of comedy: parody laced with slapstick, and plain slapstick. The parodies were the unceremonious burial of a century of hamming, including the new hamming in serious

movies, and nobody who has missed Ben Turpin in *A Small Town Idol,* or kidding Erich von Stroheim in *Three Foolish Weeks* or as *The Shriek of Araby,* can imagine how rough parody can get and still remain subtle and roaringly funny. The plain slapstick, at its best, was even better: a profusion of hearty young women in disconcerting bathing suits, frisking around with a gaggle of insanely incompetent policemen and of equally certifiable male civilians sporting museum-piece mustaches. All these people zipped and caromed about the pristine world of the screen as jazzily as a convention of water bugs. Words can hardly suggest how energetically they collided and bounced apart, meeting in full gallop around the corner of a house; how hard and how often they fell on their backsides; or with what fantastically adroit clumsiness they got themselves fouled up in folding ladders, garden hoses, tethered animals and each other's headlong cross-purposes. The gestures were ferociously emphatic; not a line or motion of the body was wasted or inarticulate. The reader may remember how splendidly upright wandlike old Ben Turpin could stand for a Renunciation Scene, with his lampshade mustache twittering and his sparrowy chest stuck out and his head flung back like Paderewski assaulting a climax and the long babyish black hair trying to look lionlike, while his Adam's apple, an orange in a Christmas stocking, pumped with noble emotion. Or huge Mack Swain, who looked like a hairy mushroom, rolling his eyes in a manner patented by French Romantics and gasping in some dubious ecstasy. Or Louise Fazenda, the perennial farmer's daughter and the perfect low-comedy housemaid, primping her spit curl; and how her hair tightened a good-looking face into the incarnation of rampant gullibility. Or snouty James Finlayson, gleefully foreclosing a mortgage, with his look of eternally tasting a spoiled pickle. Or Chester Conklin, a myopic and inebriated little walrus stumbling around in outsize pants. Or Fatty Arbuckle, with his cold eye and his loose, serene smile, his silky manipulation of his bulk and his satanic marksmanship with pies (he was ambidextrous and could simultaneously blind two people in opposite directions).

[10] The intimate tastes and secret hopes of these poor ineligible dunces were ruthlessly exposed whenever a hot stove, an electric fan or a bulldog took a dislike to their outer garments: agonizingly elaborate drawers, worked up on some lonely evening out of some Godforsaken lace curtain; or men's underpants with big round black spots on them. The Sennett sets—delirious wallpaper, megalomaniacally scrolled iron beds, Grand Rapids *in extremis*—outdid even the underwear. It was their business, after all, to kid the squalid bragga-

docio which infested the domestic interiors of the period, and that
140 was almost beyond parody. These comedies told their stories to the
unaided eye, and by every means possible they screamed to it. That
is one reason for the India-ink silhouettes of the cops, and for con-
victs and prison bars and their shadows in hard sunlight, and for
barefooted husbands, in tigerish pajamas, reacting like dervishes to
145 stepped-on tacks.

[11] The early silent comedians never strove for or consciously
thought of anything which could be called artistic "form," but they
achieved it. For Sennett's rival, Hal Roach, Leo McCarey once devoted almost the whole of a Laurel and Hardy two-reeler to pie-
150 throwing. The first pies were thrown thoughtfully, almost philosophi-
cally. Then innocent bystanders began to get caught into the vortex.
At full pitch it was Armageddon. But everything was calculated so
nicely that until late in the picture, when havoc took over, every pie
made its special kind of point and piled on its special kind of laugh.

155 [12] Sennett's comedies were just a shade faster and fizzier than
life. According to legend (and according to Sennett) he discovered
the speed tempo proper to screen comedy when a green cameraman,
trying to save money, cranked too slow.[1] Realizing the tremendous
drumlike power of mere motion to exhilarate, he gave inanimate ob-
160 jects a mischievous life of their own, broke every law of nature the
tricked camera would serve him for and made the screen dance like
a witches' Sabbath. The thing one is surest of all to remember is how
toward the end of nearly every Sennett comedy, a chase (usually
called the "rally") built up such a majestic trajectory of pure anarchic
165 motion that bathing girls, cops, comics, dogs, cats, babies, automobiles, locomotives, innocent bystanders, sometimes what seemed
like a whole city, an entire civilization, were hauled along head over
heels in the wake of that energy like dry leaves following an express
train.

170 [13] "Nice" people, who shunned all movies in the early days,
condemned the Sennett comedies as vlugar and naive. But millions of
less pretentious people loved their sincerity and sweetness, their wild-
animal innocence and glorious vitality. They could not put these feelings into words, but they flocked to the silents. The reader who gets

---

[1] Silent comedy was shot at 12 and 16 frames per second and was speeded up
by being shown at 16 frames per second, the usual rate of theater projectors
at that time. Theater projectors today run at 24, which makes modern film
taken at the same speed seem smooth and natural. But it makes silent movies
fast and jerky.

back deep enough into that world will probably even remember the 175
theater: the barefaced honky-tonk and the waltzes by Waldteufel,
slammed out on a mechanical piano; the searing redolence of peanuts
and demirep perfumery, tobacco and feet and sweat; the laughter of
unrespectable people having a hell of a fine time, laughter as violent
and steady and deafening as standing under a waterfall. 180

[14] Sennett wheedled his first financing out of a couple of ex-
bookies to whom he was already in debt. He took his comics out of
music halls, burlesque, vaudeville, circuses and limbo, and through
them he tapped in on that great pipeline of horsing and miming which
runs back unbroken through the fairs of the Middle Ages at least to 185
ancient Greece. He added all that he himself had learned about the
large and spurious gesture, the late decadence of the Grand Manner,
as a stage-struck boy in East Berlin, Connecticut, and as a frustrated
opera singer and actor. The only thing he claims to have invented is
the pie in the face, and he insists, "Anyone who tells you he has 190
discovered something new is a fool or a liar or both."

[15] The silent-comedy studio was about the best training school
the movies had ever known, and the Sennett studio was about as free
and easy and as fecund of talent as they came. All the major comedians we will mention worked there, at least briefly. So did some of 195
the major stars of the twenties and since—notably Gloria Swanson,
Phyllis Haver, Wallace Beery, Marie Dressler and Carole Lombard.
Directors Frank Capra, Leo McCarey and George Stevens also got
their start in silent comedy; much that remains most flexible, spontaneous and visually alive in sound movies can be traced, through 200
them and others, to this silent apprenticeship. Everybody did pretty
much as he pleased on the Sennett lot, and everybody's ideas were
welcome. Sennett posted no rules, and the only thing he strictly for-
bade was liquor. A Sennett story conference was a most informal
affair. During the early years, at least, only the most important 205
scenario might be jotted on the back of an envelope. Mainly Sennett's
men thrashed out a few primary ideas and carried them in their heads,
sure the better stuff would turn up while they were shooting, in the
heat of physical action. This put quite a load on the prop man; he
had to have the most improbable apparatus on hand—bombs, trick 210
telephones, what not—to implement whatever idea might suddenly
turn up. All kinds of things did—and were recklessly used. Once a
low-comedy auto got out of control and killed the cameraman, but
he was not visible in the shot, which was thrilling and undamaged;
the audience never knew the difference. 215

[16] Sennett used to hire a "wild man" to sit in on his gag conferences, whose whole job was to think up "wildies." Usually he was an all but brainless, speechless man, scarcely able to communicate his idea; but he had a totally uninhibited imagination. He might say
220 nothing for an hour; then he'd mutter "You take . . ." and all the relatively rational others would shut up and wait. "You take this cloud . . ." he would get out, sketching vague shapes in the air. Often he could get no further; but thanks to some kind of thought-transference saner men would take this cloud and make something of it. The
225 wild man seems in fact to have functioned as the group's subconscious mind, the source of all creative energy. His ideas were so weird and amorphous that Sennett can no longer remember a one of them, or even how it turned out after rational processing. But a fair equivalent might be one of the best comic sequences in a Laurel and Hardy
230 picture. It is simple enough—simple and real, in fact, as a nightmare. Laurel and Hardy are trying to move a piano across a narrow suspension bridge. The bridge is slung over a sickening chasm, between a couple of Alps. Midway they meet a gorilla.

[17] Had he done nothing else, Sennett would be remembered for
235 giving a start to three of the four comedians who now began to apply their sharp individual talents to this newborn language. The one whom he did not train (he was on the lot briefly but Sennett barely remembers seeing him around) wore glasses, smiled a great deal and looked like the sort of eager young man who might have quit divinity
240 school to hustle brushes. That was Harold Lloyd. The others were grotesque and poetic in their screen characters in degrees which appear to be impossible when the magic of silence is broken. One, who never smiled, carried a face as still and sad as a daguerreotype through some of the most preposterously ingenious and visually
245 satisfying physical comedy ever invented. That was Buster Keaton. One looked like an elderly baby and, at times, a baby dope fiend; he could do more with less than any other comedian. That was Harry Langdon. One looked like Charlie Chaplin, and he was the first man to give the silent language a soul.

250 [18] When Charlie Chaplin started to work for Sennett he had chiefly to reckon with Ford Sterling, the reigning comedian. Their first picture together amounted to a duel before the assembled professionals. Sterling, by no means untalented, was a big man with a florid Teutonic style which, under this special pressure, he turned on
255 full blast. Chaplin defeated him within a few minutes with a wink of the mustache, a hitch of the trousers, a quirk of the little finger.

[19] With *Tillie's Punctured Romance,* in 1914, he became a major star. Soon after, he left Sennett when Sennett refused to start a landslide among the other comedians by meeting the raise Chaplin demanded. Sennett is understandably wry about it in retrospect, but he still says, "I was right at the time." Of Chaplin he says simply, "Oh, well, he's just the greatest artist that ever lived." None of Chaplin's former rivals rate him much lower than that; they speak of him no more jealously than they might of God. We will try here only to suggest the essence of his supremacy. Of all comedians he worked most deeply and most shrewdly within a realization of what a human being is, and is up against. The Tramp is as centrally representative of humanity, as many-sided and as mysterious, as Hamlet, and it seems unlikely that any dancer or actor can ever have excelled him in eloquence, variety or poignancy of motion. As for pure motion, even if he had never gone on to make his magnificent feature-length comedies, Chaplin would have made his period in movies a great one singlehanded even if he had made nothing except *The Cure,* or *One A.M.* In the latter, barring one immobile taxi driver, Chaplin plays alone, as a drunk trying to get upstairs and into bed. It is a sort of inspired elaboration on a soft-shoe dance, involving an angry stuffed wildcat, small rugs on slippery floors, a Lazy Susan table, exquisite footwork on a flight of stairs, a contretemps with a huge, ferocious pendulum and the funniest and most perverse Murphy bed in movie history—and, always made physically lucid, the delicately weird mental processes of a man ethereally sozzled.

[20] Before Chaplin came to pictures people were content with a couple of gags per comedy; he got some kind of laugh every second. The minute he began to work he set standards—and continually forced them higher. Anyone who saw Chaplin eating a boiled shoe like brook trout in *The Gold Rush,* or embarrassed by a swallowed whistle in *City Lights,* has seen perfection. Most of the time, however, Chaplin got his laughter less from the gags, or from milking them in any ordinary sense, than through his genius for what may be called *inflection*—the perfect, changeful shading of his physical and emotional attitudes toward the gag.

[21] A painful and frequent error among tyros is breaking the comic line with a too-big laugh, then a letdown; or with a laugh which is out of key or irrelevant. The masters could ornament the main line beautifully; they never addled it. In *A Night Out* Chaplin, passed out, is hauled along the sidewalk by the scruff of his coat by staggering Ben Turpin. His toes trail; he is a supine as a sled. Turpin

himself is so drunk he can hardly drag him. Chaplin comes quietly
to, realizes how well he is being served by his struggling pal, and
300 with a royally delicate gesture plucks and savors a flower.

[22] The finest pantomime, the deepest emotion, the richest and
most poignant poetry were in Chaplin's work. He could probably
pantomime Bryce's *The American Commonwealth* without ever blur-
ring a syllable and make it paralyzingly funny into the bargain. At
305 the end of *City Lights* the blind girl who has regained her sight,
thanks to the Tramp, sees him for the first time. She has imagined
and anticipated him as princely, to say the least; and it has never
seriously occurred to him that he is inadequate. She recognizes who
he must be by his shy, confident, shining joy as he comes silently to-
310 ward her. And he recognizes himself, for the first time, through the
terrible changes in her face. The camera just exchanges a few quiet
close-ups of the emotions which shift and intensify in each face. It is
enough to shrivel the heart to see, and it is the greatest piece of acting and the highest moment in movies.

Like rhythm and imagery, figurative language might be thought to
be the province of poetry rather than prose. But it does have its place
in prose: it can make the difference between dull, lifeless prose and
sparkling, imaginative prose; between prose that only partially communicates and prose that communicates exactly, efficiently, and effectively.

Figurative language uses words in senses other than the literal; yet
the words convey precise meaning. In the sentence, "The car shot up
the road," "shot" cannot be understood literally, but any reader knows
what the sentence means. Similarly, "He walks like an elephant" cannot be understood literally; a man cannot actually walk like an elephant, but his lumbering gait can suggest an elephant's walk.

Simile and metaphor are the two most frequently used figures of
speech. A simile expresses a comparison between two unlike things
which have one or more points in common: "He ate like a pig"; "The
house was like a barn"; "The party was as noisy as a circus on opening night." A metaphor, by speaking of one thing in terms of another
or by identifying one thing with another, implies a comparison between two unlike things which have one or more points in common:
"The little boy clawed at his food"; "The store had mountains of fruit
on one counter"; "He planted the knockout blow in the midsection."

Other frequently used figures in everyday speech as well as in more
formal writing are metonymy, "the use of the name of one thing for
that of another to which it has some logical relation, as 'scepter' for

'sovereignty,' or 'the bottle' for 'strong drink' " (*American College Dictionary*); synecdoche—a special form of metonymy—"by which a part is put for the whole or the whole for a part, the special for the general or the general for the special, as in 'a fleet of ten *sail*' (for *ships*), or 'a *Croesus*' (for a *rich man*)" (*American College Dictionary*); personification, in which human qualities and characteristics are attributed to inanimate objects, as "This old car eats up gas by the gallon"; hyperbole, in which gross or fanciful exaggeration is used, as "I'd fly to the moon just to see him laugh"; and litotes, which achieves understatement through the negation of the opposite of what is meant, as "The president of the United States is a man of no little importance."

Writing in which figures of speech are appropriately used can be effective for a number of reasons. Often, as Frost pointed out in his essay (see p. 45), the incomprehensible is made comprehensible only by comparison. When comparison is the basis of the figure (simile and metaphor particularly), the writer has the opportunity of achieving compression, since he speaks of one thing in terms of another— "two for the price of one." In addition, figurative language—by its very definition—uses words in new and sometimes startling ways; the reader can be surprised or even shocked into heightened awareness of rich meaning. Finally, good figurative language is the product of the creative imagination: the reader can get something of the same pleasure from figurative language as he gets from a painting or a piece of sculpture.

1. The first ten paragraphs of the Agee selection contain over 30 figures of speech; the tenth paragraph alone contains at least 15. Obviously, the large number is unusual. However, it is not inappropriate to Agee's purpose. Identify the passage within these paragraphs which justifies the inclusion of so many figures of speech. Having located that passage, put into your own words Agee's guiding purpose as you understand it.

2. What contribution to establishing the tone of the selection is made by the use of figures of speech in paragraph 1?

3. Justify the profusion of figures in paragraph 10, taking into consideration the meaning (what is the topic sentence?) and function of the paragraph.

4. Discuss in some detail the figure (or figures) in the sentence "All these people zipped and caromed about the pristine world of the screen as jazzily as a convention of water bugs" (paragraph 10). Include in your discussion the kind of figure (or kinds of figures); the effectiveness, propriety, and function of the figure (or figures).

5. Comment on the use of verbs in the selection. Identify at least

five verbs which are themselves figures of speech and analyze the figures contained in them.

6. Make as long a list as you can of connotative words or phrases which Agee uses.

7. Select ten figures of speech in the selection which you find particularly effective. Identify each and explain why you find it effective. Which one do you think is most effective? Why?

8. This selection first appeared as part of an article in *Life* magazine (on September 3, 1949). It elicited enthusiastic response, particularly from young people, who, in all probability, had not seen many silent films (surely none when they originally appeared). Using yourself as a guinea pig, explain why you think the article holds so much appeal for people who have limited experience with its subject-matter.

Alternate selections for the study of Figurative Language: Edward J. Steichen, from "The Living Joy of Pictures"; Walter Pater, "Notre-Dame de Chartres."

Assignment: Metaphors which have been in long and frequent use can lose their power to evoke comparison; such metaphors are called dead metaphors (a special kind of cliché). Following are some examples:

>the table leg
>the neck of a bottle
>the heart of the matter
>the leaves of a book
>to hammer a point home

a. Add five dead metaphors from everyday speech to the list above.

b. Create a fresh metaphor to describe each of the following:

>a sailboat on a windy day
>a car skidding on ice
>fear at an unexpected sound
>a blizzard
>a teacher without chalk
>a birch tree

c. Find in your daily reading, or create, an effective example of metonymy, synecdoche, litotes, and hyperbole; be prepared to account for the effectiveness of each.

Tone

Personal Animosity

GEORGE BERNARD SHAW

[1] Somebody has sent me a cutting from which I gather that a proposal to form a critics' club has reached the very elementary stage of being discussed in the papers in August. Now clearly a critic should not belong to a club at all. He should not know anybody: his hand should be against every man, and every man's hand against his. Artists insatiable by the richest and most frequent doses of praise; entrepreneurs greedy for advertisement; people without reputations who want to beg or buy them ready made; the rivals of the praised; the friends, relatives, partisans, and patrons of the damned: all these have their grudge against the unlucky Minos in the stalls, who is himself criticized in the most absurd fashion.

[2] People have pointed out evidences of personal feeling in my notices as if they were accusing me of a misdemeanor, not knowing that a criticism written without personal feeling is not worth reading. It is the capacity for making good or bad art a personal matter that makes a man a critic. The artist who accounts for my disparagement by alleging personal animosity on my part is quite right: when people do less than their best, and do that less at once badly and self-com-

From *Shaw on Music,* a selection from the music criticism of Bernard Shaw edited by Eric Bentley and published by Doubleday & Co., Inc. Reprinted by permission of the Society of Authors.

placently, I hate them, loathe them, detest them, long to tear them
20 limb from limb and strew them in gobbets about the stage or platform. (At the Opera, the temptation to go out and ask one of the
sentinels for the loan of his Martini, with a round or two of ammuni-
tion, that I might rid the earth of an incompetent conductor or a conceited and careless artist, has come upon me so strongly that I have
25 been withheld only by my fear that, being no marksman, I might hit
the wrong person and incur the guilt of slaying a meritorious singer.)

[3] In the same way, really fine artists inspire me with the warmest
personal regard, which I gratify in writing my notices without the
smallest reference to such monstrous conceits as justice, impartiality,
30 and the rest of the ideals. When my critical mood is at its height,
personal feeling is not the word: it is passion: the passion for artistic
perfection—for the noblest beauty of sound, sight, and action—that
rages in me. Let all young artists look to it, and pay no heed to the
idiots who declare that criticism should be free from personal feeling.
35 The true critic, I repeat, is the man who becomes your personal
enemy on the sole provocation of a bad performance, and will only
be appeased by good performances. Now this, though well for art and
for the people, means that the critics are, from the social or clubable
point of view, veritable fiends. They can only fit themselves for other
40 people's clubs by allowing themselves to be corrupted by kindly feelings foreign to the purpose of art, unless, indeed, they join Philistine
clubs, wherein neither the library nor the social economy of the place
will suit their nocturnal, predatory habits. If they must have a club,
let them have a pandemonium of their own, furnished with all the
45 engines of literary vivisection. But its first and most sacred rule must
be the exclusion of the criticized, except for those few stalwarts who
regularly and publicly turn upon and criticize their critics. (No critics'
club would have any right to the name unless it included—but the
printer warns me that I have reached the limit of my allotted space.)

[For treatment of this selection, see pp. 413–414.]

How to Tell a Major Poet
from a Minor Poet   E. B. WHITE

[1] Among the thousands of letters which I received two years ago from people thanking me for my article "How to Drive the New Ford" were several containing the request that I "tell them how to distinguish a major poet from a minor poet." It is for these people that I have prepared the following article, knowing that only through 5 one's ability to distinguish a major poet from a minor poet may one hope to improve one's appreciation of, or contempt for, poetry itself.

[2] Take the first ten poets that come into your head—the list might run something like this: Robert Frost, Arthur Guiterman, Edgar Lee Masters, Dorothy Parker, Douglas Fairbanks, Jr., Stephen 10 Vincent Benét, Edwin Arlington Robinson, Lorraine Fay, Berton Braley, Edna St. Vincent Millay. Can you tell, quickly and easily, which are major and which minor? Or suppose you were a hostess and a poet were to arrive unexpectedly at your party—could you introduce him properly: "This is Mr. Lutbeck, the major poet," or 15 "This is Mr. Schenk, the minor poet"? More likely you would have to say merely: "This is Mr. Masefield, the poet"—an embarrassing situation for both poet and hostess alike.

[3] All poetry falls into two classes: serious verse and light verse. Serious verse is verse written by a major poet; light verse is verse 20 written by a minor poet. To distinguish the one from the other, one must have a sensitive ear and a lively imagination. Broadly speaking, a major poet may be told from a minor poet in two ways: (1) by the character of the verse, (2) by the character of the poet. (Note: it is not always advisable to go into the character of the poet.) 25

[4] As to the verse itself, let me state a few elementary rules. Any poem starting with "And when" is a serious poem written by a major poet. To illustrate—here are the first two lines of a serious poem easily distinguished by the "And when":

And when, in earth's forgotten moment, I
Unbound the cord to which the soul was bound . . .

30   [5] Any poem, on the other hand, ending with "And how" comes
under the head of light verse, written by a minor poet. Following are
the *last* two lines of a "light" poem, instantly identifiable by the
terminal phrase:

> Placing his lips against her brow
> He kissed her eyelids shut. And how.

All poems of the latter type are what I call "light by degrees"—that
35   is, they bear evidences of having once been serious, but the last line
has been altered. The above couplet, for example, was unquestionably
part of a serious poem which the poet wrote in 1916 while at Dart-
mouth, and originally ended:

> Placing his lips against her brow
> He kissed her eyelids shut enow.

It took fourteen years of knocking around the world before he saw
40   how the last line could be revised to make the poem suitable for
publication.
        [6] While the subject-matter of a poem does not always enable
the reader to classify it, he can often pick up a strong clue. Suppose,
for instance, you were to run across a poem beginning:

> When I went down to the corner grocer
> He asked would I like a bottle of Welch's grape juice
> And I said, "No, Sir."

45   You will know that it is a minor poem because it deals with a trade-
marked product. If the poem continues in this vein:

> "Then how would you like a package of Jello,
> A can of Del Monte peaches, some Grape Nuts,
> And a box of Rinso—
> Or don't you thin' so?"

you may be reasonably sure not only that the verse is "light" verse
but that the poet has established some good contacts and is getting
along nicely.

[7] And now we come to the use of the word "rue" as a noun. All poems containing the word "rue" as a noun are serious. This word, rhyming as it does with "you," "true," "parvenu," "emu," "cock-a-doodle-doo," and thousands of other words, and occupying as it does a distinguished place among nouns whose meaning is just a shade unclear to most people—this word, I say, is the sort without which a major poet could not struggle along. It is the hallmark of serious verse. No minor poet dares use it, because his very minority carries with it the obligation to be a little more explicit. There are times when he would like to use "rue," as, for instance, when he is composing a poem in the A. E. Housman manner:

> When drums were heard in Pelham,
> The soldier's eyes were blue,
> But I came back through Scarsdale,
> And oh the . . .

[8] Here the poet would like to get in the word "rue" because it has the right sound, but he doesn't dare.

[9] So much for the character of the verse. Here are a few general rules about the poets themselves. All poets who, when reading from their own works, experience a choked feeling, are major. For that matter, all poets who read from their own works are major, whether they choke or not. All women poets, dead or alive, who smoke cigars are major. All poets who have sold a sonnet for one hundred and twenty-five dollars to a magazine with a paid circulation of four hundred thousand are major. A sonnet is composed of fourteen lines; thus the payment in this case is eight dollars and ninety-three cents a line, which constitutes a poet's majority. (It also indicates that the editor has probably been swept off his feet.)

[10] All poets whose work appears in "The Conning Tower" of the *World* are minor, because the *World* is printed on uncoated stock —which is offensive to major poets. All poets named Edna St. Vincent Millay are major.

[11] All poets who submit their manuscripts through an agent are major. These manuscripts are instantly recognized as serious verse. They come enclosed in a manila folder accompanied by a letter from the agent: "Dear Mr. ———: Here is a new group of Miss McGroin's poems, called 'Seven Poems.' We think they are the most important she has done yet, and hope you will like them as much as we do." Such letters make it a comparatively simple matter for an

85 editor to distinguish between serious and light verse, because of the
word "important."

[12] Incidentally, letters from poets who submit their work directly
to a publication without the help of an agent are less indicative but
are longer. Usually they are intimate, breezy affairs, that begin by
90 referring to some previously rejected poem that the editor has forgotten about. They begin: "Dear Mr. ———: Thanks so much for
your friendly note. I have read over 'Invulnerable' and I think I see
your point, although in line 8 the word 'hernia' is, I insist, the only
word to quite express the mood. At any rate, here are two new offer-
95 ings. 'Thrush-Bound' and 'The Hill,' both of which are rather timely.
I suppose you know that Vivien and I have rented the most amusing
wee house near the outskirts of Sharon—it used to be a well-house
and the well still takes up most of the living-room. We are as poor
as church mice but Vivien says, etc., etc."
100 [13] A poet who, in a roomful of people, is noticeably keeping at
a little distance and "seeing into" things is a major poet. This poet
commonly writes in unrhymed six-foot and seven-foot verse, beginning something like this:

When, once, finding myself alone in a gathering of people,
105 I stood, a little apart, and through the endless confusion of voices. . . .

This is a major poem and you needn't give it a second thought.

[14] There are many more ways of telling a major poet from a
minor poet, but I think I have covered the principal ones. The truth
is, it is fairly easy to tell the two types apart; it is only when one sets
110 about trying to decide whether what they write is any good or not
that the thing really becomes complicated.

[For treatment of this selection, see p. 414.]

✐From *A Letter to Mabel Wolfe Wheaton*

THOMAS WOLFE

[1] You, at least, know what I have in my heart: to create before I die something that is as honest, grand and beautiful as I can make it. If anyone thinks my first book is ugly and filthy, and can see no beauty or good in it, I am sorry; but I shall go on with my next as well as I can, and try to make it as good as I can. One man in 5 Asheville wrote in to Scribners saying that the rumor was Wolfe had said he had wanted to cut certain parts of the book, but that Scribners had insisted they be left in so that the book would make a lot of money. To think that any damned fool couldn't see that this book was not written for money—that if I'd wanted money I'd have 10 written something one third as long, full of the soothing syrup most of them want. We are all pleased here with the success the book has had—with the wonderful reviews, and also with the sale—but nobody is going to get rich off the book: there are hundreds of hack writers who make far more than I will make, and if money is my object, I 15 could make far more out of advertising or something else than I can ever make out of writing.

[2] Doesn't it mean anything to people at home to know that honest and intelligent critics all over the country have thought my book a fine and moving one? Surely there are people there who are 20 fair and generous enough to see that I am trying to be an artist, and that I am not a sensational hack. Does anyone seriously think that a man is going to sweat blood, lose flesh, go cold and dirty, work all night, and live in a sweatshop garret for almost two years as I did, if his sole purpose is to say something mean about Smith and Jones 25 and Brown? Listen, Mabel: what my book says in the first paragraph and what it continues to say on every page to the end is that men are

strangers, that they are lonely and forsaken, that they are in exile on this earth, that they are born, live, and die alone. I began to write that book in London: it is as true of people in London and Idaho as of people in Asheville. You say that women in clubs have called you up and lectured you or sympathized with you. Very well, let them. You are bigger than any of them and they cannot hurt you. I suppose the sympathy was because you had a brother like me. Very well. That's all right, too. Apparently you can rob banks, be a crooked lawyer, swill corn whiskey, commit adultery with your neighbor's wife—and be considered a fine, lovable, misunderstood fellow; but if you try to make something true and beautiful you are "viciously insane" and your "big overgrown body" ought to be dragged through the streets by a lynching mob. These phrases are from one of the letters sent to me.

[3] Well, they can not hurt us. I do not believe one fine person, worthy of being a friend, would ever turn either on you or me because I have written a book—and anyone who would is probably not worth knowing.

[4] I am a young man, just beginning his life's work. The sad thing about this whole thing is not that people have misunderstood my first book, but that they do not know at all what I am like or what my vision of life is. A great deal of water has gone under the bridge since I left Asheville ten years ago, but I had always hoped that when I brought my first work before the world, I would find sympathy and understanding among my old friends there. Now I feel as if I had been exiled; that they no longer know the person I have become, and that they will not recognize me in the work I shall do in the future. I say this is the sad thing about it all. It is like death. I know now that people do not die once but many times, and that life of which they were once a part, and which they thought they could never lose, dies too, becomes a ghost, is lost forever. There is nothing to be done about this. We can only love those who are lost, and grieve for their spirits. If, then, I am dead to people who once knew me and cared for me, there is nothing more to say or do—I must go on into a new world and a new life, with love and sorrow for what I have lost. If you like, remember the kid in the cherry tree, or the long-legged schoolboy, or the kid at college—I shall always remember you all with love and loyalty. . . .

"Tone" is one of those words whose meaning is perfectly clear until you try to explain it. We speak of one violin as having a better "tone" than another, and we know what we mean without thinking in technical or even semitechnical terms. We speak of "tones" of color— the "tones" of Van Gogh's yellows, for example—without consciously referring to pigment. We say that an animal responds to the "tone" of his trainer's voice; we are all familiar with the parental admonition, "Don't take that tone with me!"

The animal trainer can express, and the animal respond to, praise, anger, a specific command, even fear in the presence of danger—a feeling, a mood, a spirit. So, too, the child whose parent has warned him about his "tone" has been expressing, perhaps, defiance or resentment or fretful unwillingness to assume responsibility—also a feeling, a mood, a spirit.

The written word communicates tone just as surely as does a musical instrument or a color on canvas or an animal trainer's or a disobedient child's voice. The feeling, mood, or spirit of the writer is conveyed through every device he employs: organization; beginning and ending; paragraphing; sentence length and structure; sentence rhythms; word order; levels of diction; and choice of images, figures of speech, nouns, and verbs. And yet it is something more than the sum of all these parts; it is an elusive but not illusory flavor cooked in as if by magic.

Sometimes an author will write in fury, and the straightforward presentation of facts will imply his mood; sometimes he will say the opposite of what he means (irony) to point up the ridiculousness of a given attitude or state of affairs. His tone may be gentler, though his intention may still be to point up one or another human foible. His tone may be grim, gay, resigned, distraught, despairing, elated, triumphant, defiant, exalted, nostalgic, admiring, respectful, cold, affectionate, or as many other possible variations as there are emotions or situations to produce emotions.

Unless there is reason for a change, the writer should strive for unity of tone, rooting out of his writing all violations of unity. For example, he should not say, "Every man, woman, and child must be prepared to make great sacrifices in this hour of our country's need, by golly." You would not expect final examination instructions to read: "Students are herewith informed that any written matter will be taken as *prima facie* evidence that they are bad little boys and girls who aren't going to behave themselves." Similarly, in your own writing, you should avoid hopping from tone to tone, as for example: "It is my intention to show that juvenile delinquency almost always occurs in areas where people are squashed together like sardines."

1. How would you characterize the tone Shaw uses? Is he angry?

amused? serious? flippant? How do you know? What contribution does the ending make to his tone?

2. What are the connotations of each of the elements in the series in sentence 4, paragraph 1 of the Shaw selection? How do these connotations contribute to the tone? Does the use of parallelism in sentence 4 add anything to the communication of tone? Explain.

3. What one word best typifies the tone of the following passage from the Shaw selection: "when people do less than their best, and do that less at once badly and self-complacently, I hate them, loathe them, detest them, long to tear them limb from limb and strew them in gobbets about the stage or platform"? In what way or ways would the tone be changed if the passage had read "when people do less than their best, and do that less at once badly and self-complacently, I hate them"? In what way or ways would the sense of the sentence be changed if the words "and self-complacently" were omitted?

4. Why does Shaw call "justice, impartiality and the rest of the ideals" "monstrous conceits"? How does your answer corroborate what you already know about Shaw?

5. What do the words "idiots," "fiends," and "pandemonium," in paragraph 3, contribute to the tone?

6. What is the guiding purpose of the White essay? What part does *tone* play in your statement of that guiding purpose? If it does not play a considerable part, rephrase your statement to include it.

7. What is the over-all method of development of the White selection? In what way or ways is this method of development made to contribute to the tone?

8. What does distinguishing a major poet from a minor poet have to do with " 'How to Drive the New Ford' "? Justify the juxtaposition in terms of tone.

9. Where else in the selection is relevance or irrelevance made to contribute to the tone?

10. Explain what contributions to the tone are made by the beginning and ending of the White essay.

11. Find five examples of fallacies in logic in "How to Distinguish a Major Poet from a Minor Poet." What are they doing there?

12. Where and how does E. B. White make names contribute to his tone?

13. What contribution to the tone does sentence structure make in the following:

"You will know that it is a minor poem because it deals with a trade-marked product."

"For that matter, all poets who read from their own works are major, whether they choke or not."

14. In his letter to his sister, Thomas Wolfe says that "The sad thing . . . is . . . that they [people] do not know at all what I am like or what my vision of life is." Using this letter as your only sample of his writing, what do you know about what Wolfe was like and what his vision of life was? Try to account, in your answer, for the parts played by as many of the components of writing as you can— organization of the whole, the paragraph, the sentence, and the word. Your answer should take particularly into account the contribution made by tone to your understanding of the man and his vision of life.

Alternate selections for the study of Tone: Joseph Conrad, "The Censor of Plays"; Charles Lamb, "Popular Fallacies: That the Worst Puns are the Best"; John Ciardi, "Angel-Fluffs, Savages, and Dispensable Adults"; Brooks Atkinson, "Jargon" and "Enemies of Jargon."

Theme Assignment: Taking Shaw at his word, that a critic must and should be partisan and express his personal feelings, write a criticism or review of a book you have read, about which you have strong feelings. They may be negative or positive—or any shade in between, but they must be strong. And they must be strongly expressed. Call upon every device now at your command to help you.

Index of Authors and Titles